'Dr De Tommaso takes us on a meticulously documented journey from Nuremberg to the ILC's Draft Articles on Crimes against Humanity. Beyond this fascinating historical perspective, she ventures into new territory by looking at what incorporating corporate liability in the Rome Statute would look like, what provisions would need to be amended, and how. This insightful book pushes the boundaries of both business and human rights and international criminal law and invites reflection on the role of judicial institutions in addressing corporate atrocity crimes'.

Associate Professor Nadia Bernaz,
Wageningen University & Research,
Wageningen

'An outstanding contribution to scholarship in the field: *Corporate Liability and International Criminal Law* is impressive in terms of the author's attention to detail and the depth and range of research conducted. It will serve as an important point of reference for the future development of both law and policy'.

Dr Anthony Cullen, *Associate Professor,*
Middlesex University, London

'Alessandra De Tommaso has written a must-read analysis for those interested in the lasting challenges that stand in the way of corporate accountability. The rigorous research supporting the book focuses on international criminal law, but it provides invaluable lessons applicable to any legal field'.

Professor Elvira Domínguez-Redondo,
Kingston University, London

Corporate Liability and International Criminal Law

This book investigates whether corporate criminal liability should be incorporated within the scope of international criminal law. The work provides unique insight into the evolution of the debate on the international criminal liability of corporations to facilitate future discussion on the possibility of including corporations within the scope of international criminal law. It combines a detailed examination of Nuremberg and Rome with the examination of previously overlooked initiatives such as the Draft Code of Offences against Peace and Security of Mankind and the 1951 and 1953 Committees on International Criminal Jurisdiction. This analysis is also complemented by a review of significant post-1998 international and domestic developments around corporate criminal liability. In addition, it offers suggestions for the development of an amendment to hold corporations accountable under the Statute of the International Criminal Court.

This book contributes to the existing literature on the topic of corporate liability which attracts significant attention from scholars in the fields of Law, Business, and Political Science. It will be useful to professionals in the academic and diplomatic fields, researchers, legal advisors, and business leaders. It will also be of interest to anyone who wants to understand the debate on holding businesses accountable under international criminal law.

Alessandra De Tommaso is Lecturer in Law at Middlesex University, UK. She teaches Business and Human Rights, EU Law, and Evidence. Her research interests are in the areas of International Criminal Law and Business and Human Rights. She is a qualified lawyer in Italy.

Corporate Liability and International Criminal Law

Alessandra De Tommaso

Routledge
Taylor & Francis Group
LONDON AND NEW YORK

First published 2024
by Routledge
4 Park Square, Milton Park, Abingdon, Oxon OX14 4RN

and by Routledge
605 Third Avenue, New York, NY 10158

Routledge is an imprint of the Taylor & Francis Group, an informa business

British Library Cataloguing-in-Publication Data
A catalogue record for this book is available from the British Library

ISBN: 978-1-032-48741-0 (hbk)
ISBN: 978-1-032-48742-7 (pbk)
ISBN: 978-1-003-39053-4 (ebk)

DOI: 10.4324/9781003390534

Typeset in Galliard
by Deanta Global Publishing Services, Chennai

Contents

Foreword *x*
Acknowledgements *xiii*

Introduction **1**

1 Corporate Criminal Liability and the Nuremberg Experience **8**
1.1 Introduction 8
1.2 Criminal Organisations at Trial: The Nuremberg Experience 10
1.2.1 The Origin of the Prosecution's Case against Organisations 12
1.2.2 The London Charter 14
1.2.3 The Nuremberg Trial and Judgment 15
1.2.4 Crimes of Membership v Corporate Criminal Liability 19
1.3 Post-World War II Trials: The Industrialist Cases 23
1.3.1 Business Complicity in International Crimes: From the Failure of the Krupp Case at Nuremberg to the US Industrialist Trials 24
1.3.2 The Preparatory Phase of the U.S. Industrialist Cases: Pomerantz's Memorandum 27
1.3.3 The Industrialist Cases 31
1.4 Extra-Judicial Sanctioning of Farben 39
1.5 Conclusion 41
References 43

2 The Question of Corporations in the Aftermath of the Nuremberg Trials **47**
2.1 Introduction 47
2.2 The 1948 Convention on the Prevention and Punishment of the Crime of Genocide 48
2.3 The ILC Draft Code of Offences against Peace and Security of Mankind: An Early Debate on the Criminal Liability of Legal Entities 54

2.4 The Liability of Legal Persons in the Early Stage of the Debate on an International Criminal Court: The Role of the 1951 and 1953 Committees on International Criminal Jurisdiction 58
2.4.1 The 1951 Committee on International Criminal Jurisdiction 60
2.4.2 The 1953 Committee on International Criminal Jurisdiction 63
2.5 Conclusion 67
References 68

3 The Adoption of the Rome Statute: Corporate Criminal Liability's Swan Song? 72
3.1 Introduction 72
3.2 Resuming the Drafting of the Statute of the ICC: The ILC's Work (1982-1994) 73
3.3 The Establishment of the Ad Hoc Tribunals for the Former Yugoslavia and Rwanda 78
3.4 The Negotiation of the Statute of the ICC (1995-1998) 81
3.4.1 From the 1995 Ad Hoc Committee to the 1996 Preparatory Committee 82
3.4.2 The French Proposal on Corporate Criminal Liability: Origin and Early Debate 84
3.5 The 1998 Rome Conference for an International Criminal Court 89
3.5.1 The Final Working Paper on the Liability of Juridical Persons: The Last Stage of the Debate 94
3.6 Conclusion 100
References 101

4 Corporate Criminal Liability after Rome: International Developments in the Aftermath of the Adoption of the ICC Statute 107
4.1 Introduction 107
4.2 The Special Tribunal for Lebanon's Jurisdiction over Legal Persons: An Analysis of the 2014 Contempt Cases 109
4.2.1 The First Contempt Decision: Judge Baragwanath's View on Corporate Criminal Liability 110
4.2.2 Challenging Corporate Criminal Liability: The Point of View of Judge Lettieri 116
4.2.3 The Decision of the Appeals Panel in the New TV S.A.L. Case 121
4.3 Corporate Criminal Liability within the Statute of the (Proposed) African Court of Justice and Human Rights 128

4.3.1 Article 46C and the Principle of Attribution: An Organisational Approach to Corporate Criminal Liability 131
4.3.2 Sentencing System 138
4.4 The ILC's Draft Articles on Crimes against Humanity 140
4.4.1 The 2016 Debate on the Liability of Legal Persons 142
4.4.2 The Drafting Committee's Draft Paragraph on the Liability of Legal Persons 149
4.4.3 States' Comments on the Draft Provision on the Liability of Legal Persons 152
4.5 Conclusion 157
References 158

5 National Developments and the Comparative Law Argument in the Debate on Corporate Criminal Liability **166**
5.1 Introduction 166
5.2 The Comparative Law Argument 167
5.2.1 Limitations of the Comparative Law Argument 171
5.3 A Step Further: Corporate Criminal Liability as a General Principle of Law 178
5.3.1 General Principles of Law: Practical Implications 179
5.4 Conclusion 185
References 186

6 Translating Corporate Criminal Liability into the International Criminal Justice System: Amending the ICC Statute **191**
6.1 Introduction 191
6.2 The Applicability of the Rome Statute to Corporations: Some Considerations on the Mode of Attribution 192
6.3 Corporate Criminal Liability Arising from a Lack of Due Supervision 200
6.4 Reverse Onus, the Presumption of Innocence and Corporate Defendants 205
6.5 Corporations and Procedural Guarantees 213
6.5.1 Representation and the Right to Be Present at Trial: Article 63 ICC St. 215
6.6 A Sentencing System for Corporate Defendants 221
6.7 Conclusion 228
References 229

Conclusions **235**

Index *243*

Foreword

William Schabas

In one of their most enduring and oft-cited pronouncements, the judges at Nuremberg said that international crimes were committed by men, not abstract entities. Taken out of context, this might be misunderstood. The judges were answering the pleas of the defendants who claimed they were no more than vehicles for the will of the governments of which they were a part. They certainly did not mean to suggest that 'abstract entities' were excluded from the reach of international criminal justice. Indeed, the International Military Tribunal devoted considerable attention to the role of criminal organisations in the Nazi atrocities, as its Charter directed. But the focus was on corporate bodies with a political or military purpose rather than those that were, ostensibly at least, commercial in scope.

That 'business' could engage criminal responsibility was certainly on the agenda in these early days of international criminal justice. Although the British were initially unenthusiastic about international criminal trials, they were in no doubt about the need for accountability. Churchill's preference was for the summary execution of senior Nazis. Lists were prepared that included representatives of the business enterprises that had contributed to Nazi atrocities. When bureaucrats in the Foreign Office removed them from the list, Clement Atlee, the Deputy Prime Minister, protested. 'I think it is wrong that the big businessmen of Germany who financed Hitler should escape', he wrote in a memorandum for the War Cabinet. 'The group of men in the heavy industries sought to use the Nazis for their own nefarious ends. Some should be executed as an example to others. All should be deprived of their property'.[1]

German business interests were of course addressed in the post-war prosecutions. The Krupps evaded the International Military Tribunal but they were dealt with by the subsequent proceedings of the United States military tribunals in the Nuremberg courtroom. Alessandra De Tommaso's study assesses these efforts. She gives special attention to the I.G. Farben trial, described by

1 Treatment of Major Enemy War Criminals, Memorandum by the Deputy Prime Minister and Lord President of the Council, 26 June 1944, CAB/66/51, W.P. (44) 345.

the American prosecutor, Telford Taylor, as 'the biggest and most complicated of the industrialist cases'.

The early international criminal law treaties, namely the Genocide Convention of 1948 and the Apartheid Convention of 1973, did not contemplate the prosecution of business corporations, at least not explicitly. Arguably, the references to 'persons' in the Genocide Convention could be interpreted expansively to include them. But in 1993, when he was drafting the draft statute of the International Criminal Tribunal for the former Yugoslavia, the United Nations Secretary-General concluded that the 'ordinary meaning' of 'persons responsible for serious violations of international humanitarian law' must mean 'natural persons to the exclusion of juridical persons'. Perhaps this shows that the issue was being discussed. It was certainly part of the agenda when the Rome Statute of the International Criminal Court was being negotiated. But in the end, there was not enough momentum in favour of a French proposal to provide explicitly for the prosecution of 'legal persons', a notion in civil law that encompasses corporate entities. It is a sore point that returns again and again in discussions about how to fine-tune the Rome Statute.

That corporate bodies, as well as individuals and States, may be responsible for serious international crimes can hardly be understood as a new phenomenon. The atrocities perpetrated as part of colonialism, including slavery and the slave trade, are increasingly recognised as crimes against humanity. This is despite the fact that crimes against humanity were only first defined in positive international law in 1945, in the Charter of the International Military Tribunal. Recall the British East India Company, initially chartered by Elizabeth I in 1600 as the Governor and Company of Merchants of London Trading into the East-Indies. It ruled huge swathes of South Asia for many decades. The Company was deeply engaged in the slave trade, continuing with the practice for many years after it had been formally condemned by the British Government. It was also condemned for widespread torture in India. The Company promoted opium addiction in China.

Similar commercial enterprises, chartered by Portugal and the Netherlands, and later by Belgium, France, and the other colonial powers, were the engines of colonialism. Most of them drifted in and out of bankruptcy, as businesses tend to do. Nevertheless, even when the corporations falter, they may be propped up by the governments to which they owe their existence. When they fail, the wealth they have generated tends to stick to the fingers of their shareholders. Today, when we admire the glorious buildings, monuments, and chateaux of Europe's prosperous cities, its ancient universities and its glorious museums, we should remember that these are largely the dividends of the plunder perpetrated by historic business corporations. The contribution that the crimes of these corporate enterprises made to the present-day wealth of the Global North is immense.

Then, as now, business corporations are protected by governments. The creation of such bodies remains an act of State, the result of sophisticated legislation. Often the real owners are concealed through a tangled web of holding companies and similar entities crafted by the prosperous global law firms that advise them. Many of the profits are insulated from the taxation that ordinary people accept as a fact of life. Remnants of colonialism, like the British overseas territories and crown dependencies, provide these tax shelters.

Many challenges confront efforts to unleash the potential of international criminal accountability to deal with some of the worst abuses attributable to business corporations. Alessandra De Tommaso's rich and detailed study provides an essential contribution. It soberly and realistically addresses the difficulties that arise, including the apparent resistance of judicial bodies like the United States Supreme Court. At the same time, she provides creative guidelines to advance the project of criminal liability of corporations. This book is a precious resource for those who campaign to reform the law.

In the century or so since international criminal justice has emerged, it has managed to prosecute a rather tiny cohort of those who are most responsible for what the preamble of the Rome Statute labels as the 'most serious crimes of concern to the international community as a whole'. Only occasionally were the culprits associated with business activities. There was some excitement in the early days of the International Criminal Court when its first Prosecutor, Luis Moreno Ocampo, suggested he was interested in this dimension. He may have given the matter some thought, but he never delivered on the promise. And yet, when we take a peek behind the corporate veil we find that business and its DNA, profit and greed, continue to drive war and atrocity, just as these forces did centuries ago when the Global North sought to drain the Global South of its wealth. The obstacles to genuine accountability, and to the identification of the forces that are ultimately responsible for such unimaginable atrocities, must not be underestimated.

William Schabas
London

Acknowledgements

My gratitude goes to Professor William A. Schabas, for constantly challenging my knowledge and for encouraging me to do my best. His guidance and advice carried me through all the stages of writing this thesis. And I would like to thank Dr Anthony Cullen for always helping me keep perspective on where my research fits into the bigger picture. I would also like to express my gratitude to Dr Cathal Doyle for his insights on the subject matter and for his support in developing this thesis.

To the friends I made along the way, Michelle Coleman, Caleb Wheeler, Stefano Marinelli, Paul Brewster, Andrew Paterson, David Stephens, and Elena Borsacchi – thank you for your continued friendship, skype chats, laughs, and cups of tea along the way.

To my wonderful colleagues and friends, Alex Patrick and Lucas Taylor, thank you for your friendship and unwavering support and for listening with genuine (or feigned) interest when I described what I was working on.

To Jennifer, thank you for believing in me and for helping me overcome all my doubts. Talking to you about my ideas is what kept me sane and allowed me to persevere in this journey.

This journey would have not been possible if not for the love and support of my parents. They have always encouraged me to pursue my passion for international law, even when to do so I had to move to another country. Thank you for being there every time I need you.

Introduction

Recent years have seen an escalation in the number of allegations against corporations for their involvement in international crimes and serious violations of human rights.[1] Reports by the UN Panel of Experts on the Illegal Exploitation of Natural Resources and Other Forms of Wealth of the Democratic Republic of the Congo have highlighted the contribution made by several private companies in the ongoing conflict in the Democratic Republic of Congo.[2] Similar allegations have been made against companies operating in Angola,[3] South Sudan,[4] Sierra Leone,[5] Colombia,[6] and Syria.[7] The issue of corporate involve-

1 See, e.g., International Commission of Jurists, 'Corporate Complicity and Legal Accountability, Vol. I, Report of the International Commission of Jurists Expert Legal Panel on Corporate Complicity in International Crimes' (ICJ, 2008) https://www.icj.org/wp-content/uploads/2012/06/Vol.1-Corporate-legal-accountability-thematic-report-2008.pdf Accessed 26 March 2023.

2 UNSC S/2001/357, 12 April 2001. On corporate involvement in gross human rights abuses in DRC see also *Anvil Mining Ltd. v. Canadian Association Against Impunity* (CAAI) [2012] C.A. 117 (Can. Que.).

3 Philippe le Billon, 'Angola's Political Economy of War: The Role of Oil and Diamonds' (2001) 100 African Affairs 55.

4 European Coalition on Oil in Sudan (ECOS), 'UNPAID DEBT The Legacy of Lundin, Petronas and OMV in Sudan, 1997–2003' (ECOS, June 2010) https://www.ecosonline.org/reports/2010/UNPAID_DEBT_fullreportweb.pdf Accessed 26 March 2023. See also *Presbyterian Church v. Talisman Energy*, 582 F.3d 244 (2d Cir. 2009).

5 *Kadie Kalma & Others v. African Minerals Limited, African Mineral (SL) Limited and Tonkolili Iron Ore (SL) Limited* [2020] EWCA Civ 144.

6 International Human Rights Clinic, Colectivo de Abogados José Alvear Restrepo and International Federation for Human Rights, 'The Contribution of Chiquita Corporate Officials to Crimes against Humanity in Colombia: Article 15 Communication to the International Criminal Court' (FIDH, 18 May 2017) https://www.fidh.org/IMG/pdf/rapport_chiquita.pdf Accessed 26 March 2023. Caleb H Wheeler, 'Re-Examining Corporate Liability at the International Criminal Court through the Lens of the Article 15 Communication against Chiquita Brands International' (2018) 19(1) Melbourne Journal of International Law 369. See also *Does 1 Through 976, et al. v. Chiquita Brands International, Inc., et al.*, No. 19-13926 (11th Cir. 2022).

7 Madeline Young, 'LaFarge's Case Cemented: Holding Corporations Liable for Crimes Against Humanity' (2021) 36 Emory International Law Review Recent Developments 1, Center for

DOI: 10.4324/9781003390534-1

ment in international crimes, however, is not a new phenomenon. Already in World War II, the German industrial sector played a central role in the Nazi's war effort.[8] As evidence of corporate wrongdoing is growing,[9] it is time for a re-assessment of the role that international criminal law can play in addressing corporate involvement in international crimes.

To advance this argument, this book reassesses the historical dimension of the debate surrounding the international criminal liability of corporations to propose a more cohesive narrative of the way in which corporate criminal liability has been addressed in international criminal law. The existing literature on the topic often adopts a narrow approach to advance or contest the international criminal liability of corporations.[10] The focus of the analysis so far conducted on corporations and international criminal law has mostly centred on two Grotian Moments: the Nuremberg trials, on one side, and the adoption of the Rome Statute, on the other.[11] Little to no attention has been paid

Justice and Accountability, 'Corporate Complicity in ISIL Crimes against Humanity. Lafarge French Prosecution' (CJA, n.d.) https://cja.org/what-we-do/litigation/corporate-complicity-in-isil-crimes-against-humanity/ Accessed 26 March 2023.

8 Control Council Law No. 9, 'Providing for the Seizure of Property Owned by I.G. Farbenindustrie and the Control Thereof' (30 November 1945), reprinted in Enactments and Approved Papers of the Control Council and Coordinating Committee, 225, Military Government of Germany, Control of I.G. Farben, Special Report of Military Governor U.S. Zone (1 October 1945), 1. See also Leora Yedida Bilsky, *The Holocaust, Corporations, and the Law: Unfinished Business* (The University of Michigan Press 2017), Wim Huisman, Susanne Karstedt, Annika van Baar, 'The Involvement of Corporations in Atrocity Crimes' in Barbora Holá et al (eds), *The Oxford Handbook of Atrocity Crimes* (OUP 2022), Annika van Baar, 'Corporate involvement in the Holocaust and other Nazi crimes' in Judith van Erp et al. (eds), *The Routledge Handbook of White-Collar and Corporate Crime in Europe* (Routledge 2015).

9 See, e.g., International Commission of Jurists (n 1).

10 See, e.g., Joanna Kyriakakis, *Corporations, Accountability and International Criminal Law. Industry and Atrocity* (Edward Elgar 2021), Grietje Baars, *The Corporation, Law, and Capitalism: A Radical Perspective on the Role of Law in the Global Political Economy* (Haymarket Books 2020), Leora Bilsky, *The Holocaust, Corporations, and the Law. Unfinished Business* (University of Michigan Press 2017), Desislava Stoitchkova, *Towards Corporate Liability in International Criminal Law* (Intersentia 2010), Larissa van den Herik, 'Corporations as Future Subject of the International Criminal Court: An Exploration of the Counterarguments and Consequences' in Carsten Stahn and Larissa van den Herik (eds), *Future Perspectives on International Criminal Justice* (T.M.C. Asser Press 2010), Andrew Clapham, 'The Question of Jurisdiction under International Criminal Law over Legal Persons: Lessons from the Rome Conference on an International Criminal Court' in Menno T. Kamminga and Saman Zia-Zarifi (eds), *Liability of Multinational Corporations under International Law* (Kluwer Law International 2000), Florian Jeßberger, 'Corporate Involvement in Slavery and Criminal Responsibility under International Law' (2016) Journal of International Criminal Justice 327, James G Stewart, 'The Turn to Corporate Criminal Liability for International Crimes: Transcending the Alien Tort Statute' (2014) 47 New York University Journal of International Law and Politics 121, Ronald C Slye, 'Corporations, Veils, and International Criminal Liability' (2008) 33 Brooklyn Journal of International Law 955.

11 On the definition of Grotian moment see Michael P Scharf, 'The Grotian Moment Concept' (2011) 19 ILSA Quarterly 16, Boutros Boutros-Ghali, 'A Grotian Moment' (1994) 18(5)

to other developments occurring either in the years between Nuremberg and Rome or after the adoption of the Statute of the International Criminal Court.

While this mainstream narrative has undoubtedly shed relevant insights into the way in which corporate criminal liability was addressed in Nuremberg and Rome, it however has the effect of distorting the way in which the international criminal liability of corporations is currently debated as it confines the discussion to two distinct historical moments. This book argues that, to propel future discussion, it is essential to reconstruct the narrative surrounding corporate criminal liability under international criminal law to offer a more cohesive account of the way in which corporate criminal liability has been addressed beyond Nuremberg and Rome.

Consequently, this book combines a detailed investigation of the history of Nuremberg and Rome with the examination of previously overlooked initiatives, such as the drafting of a Code of Offences against Peace and Security of Mankind and the 1951 and 1953 Committees on International Criminal Jurisdiction. Post-Rome international and domestic developments around corporate criminal liability are also evaluated to highlight the ongoing relevance of the issue under consideration. This narrative offers solid foundations to the argument in favour of the inclusion of corporations within the framework of the international criminal justice system, and specifically within the Statute of the International Criminal Court. By looking at the way in which corporate criminal liability has been addressed since the early 1940s, it demonstrates that the question of an international criminal liability of corporations has continually been brought to the attention of those tasked with promoting the development of international criminal law. Far from being settled, the question of corporate criminal liability under international criminal law necessitates further attention.

The argument proceeds as follows. Chapter 1 starts by considering the early intersections between international criminal law and corporate criminal liability to evaluate the extent to which this latter concept was addressed in the aftermath of World War II. In particular, the chapter sheds light on the implication of Nuremberg and the post-World War II trials on the development of an international criminal liability of corporations. It first considers the position of groups and organisations during the trial conducted by the International Military Tribunal of Nuremberg in accordance with Articles 9 and 10 of the London Charter. The focus of the analysis then shifts to subsequent trials conducted by the US Military Tribunals pursuant to Control Council Law No.

Fordham International Law Journal 1609. An attempt to look beyond these two moments has been made in Michael J Kelly, *Prosecuting Corporations for Genocide* (OUP 2016) and Clapham (n 11).

10. Particular attention is paid to the *I.G. Farben* case[12] due to its significance in the debate on an international criminal liability of corporations.

The historical analysis continues in Chapter 2, which follows the evolution of the debate on corporate criminal liability under international criminal law from the late 1940s to the early 1950s. The chapter considers to what extent efforts were made to include legal persons within the domain of international criminal law in the years after Nuremberg. The chapter focuses on three initiatives promoted by the United Nations: the drafting of the Genocide Convention, the work of the International Law Commission on the Draft Code of Offences against Peace and Security of Mankind, and the work of the 1951 and 1953 Committees on International Criminal Jurisdiction. By looking at these often-overlooked initiatives, the chapter builds a bridge between Nuremberg and Rome to fill a gap in the existing literature on the international criminal liability of corporations.

Chapter 3 focuses on the drafting history of the Statute of the International Criminal Court. The negotiation of the Rome Statute necessarily occupies a central place in the debate on corporate criminal liability under international criminal law. The chapter looks at the attempts made by the French delegation to support the inclusion of legal persons within the Statute of the International Criminal Court. The chapter analyses the drafting history of the French proposal (from 1995 to 1998) to identify the approach suggested to impute international criminal liability to legal persons. It discusses the challenges that the proposal faced during the negotiation of the Rome Statute and the factors that ultimately led to its withdrawal. The examination highlights the complexity of the debate on international corporate criminal liability and offers insights into the views expressed by delegations on the opportunity of extending the Court's jurisdiction beyond natural persons.

While the withdrawal of the French proposal has been interpreted as the swan song of corporate criminal liability for international crimes,[13] it is incorrect to assume that Rome signalled the end of the discussion on the subject matter. Chapter 4 considers developments occurring after the Rome Conference to highlight the ongoing nature of the debate on international corporate criminal liability.

The chapter is structured in three parts. Firstly, it analyses the decision of the Special Tribunal for Lebanon to indict two Lebanese corporations (New TV S.A.L. and Akhbar Beirut S.A.L) for contempt of court. It examines the positions adopted by the Tribunal in the preliminary stage of the proceedings to recognise or reject its jurisdiction over legal persons. The chapter then looks

12 United States Military Tribunal at Nuremberg, *The United States of America vs. Carl Krauch et al., 'The I.G. Farben Case'*, Case No. 6, in *Trials of War Criminals Before the Nuremberg Military Tribunals Under Control Council Law No. 10* ("Green Series") (Washington 1952) Vol. VIII.

13 *Kiobel v. Royal Dutch Petroleum Co.*, 621 F.3d 111, at 117 (2d Cir. 2010), *Jesner v. Arab Bank, PLC*, 138 S. Ct. 1386, at 1400-1 (2018).

at the 2014 Malabo Protocol, which amended the statute of the (proposed) African Court of Justice and Human Rights to expand its jurisdiction over international and transnational crimes to offences perpetrated by corporations. It examines in detail Article 46C to offer insights into the merits and shortcomings of a model proposed in the Protocol. Lastly, the chapter considers the draft Articles on Crimes against Humanity. Specifically, the analysis focuses on draft Article 6(8) which mandates State Parties to provide for the liability of legal entities for their involvement in the crimes listed in the proposed convention.

Shifting the focus from the international level to the domestic level, Chapter 5 examines the way in which national developments have been seen as evidence of a change in states' attitudes towards corporate criminal liability. It has been argued that such a change of attitude may provide solid ground for the transposition of corporate criminal liability at the international level. The argument has merit as it challenges one of the main points made against the inclusion of corporations within the Statute of the International Criminal Court: the lack of general recognition of corporate criminal liability at the domestic level. The chapter analyses the relevance of what can be defined as the comparative law argument and assesses its value and intrinsic limitations.

Building on the analysis conducted in Chapters 1 to 5, Chapter 6 offers suggestions for the development of an appropriate international model to hold corporations criminally accountable for their involvement in international crimes. The chapter adopts the Statute of the International Criminal Court as a point of reference for discussion. Specific attention is paid to the model of attribution of international criminal liability to legal persons, to the applicability of fundamental procedural rights to corporate defendants, and to the question of sanctioning.

Overall, this book demonstrates how the question of corporate criminal liability under international criminal law is far from settled and necessitates further attention. In today's globalised world, where corporations are more and more present in conflict scenarios and in countries with poor human rights records, this question cannot be ignored. To further its fight against impunity, the international criminal justice system must evolve to recognise corporations as potential subjects of international criminal liability.

References

Primary Sources

UN Documents

UN Secretary-General, Letter dated 12 April 2001 from the Secretary-General to the President of the Security Council, UNSC S/2001/357, 12 April 2001

International Cases

United States Military Tribunal at Nuremberg, *The United States of America vs. Carl Krauch et al., 'The I.G. Farben Case'*, Case No. 6, in *Trials of War Criminals Before the Nuremberg Military Tribunals Under Control Council Law No. 10* ("Green Series") (Washington 1952) Vol. VIII

Domestic Cases

Anvil Mining Ltd. v. Canadian Association Against Impunity (CAAI) [2012] C.A. 117 (Can. Que.)
Presbyterian Church v. Talisman Energy, 582 F.3d 244 (2d Cir. 2009)
Kadie Kalma & Others v. African Minerals Limited, African Mineral (SL) Limited and Tonkolili Iron Ore (SL) Limited [2020] EWCA Civ 144
Kiobel v. Royal Dutch Petroleum Co., 621 F.3d 111 (2d Cir. 2010)
Jesner v. Arab Bank, PLC, 138 S. Ct. 1386 (2018)
Does 1 Through 976, et al. v. Chiquita Brands International, Inc., et al., No. 19-13926 (11th Cir. 2022)

Miscellaneous

Control Council Law No. 9, 'Providing for the Seizure of Property Owned by I.G. Farbenindustrie and the Control Thereof' (30 November 1945), reprinted in Enactments and Approved Papers of the Control Council and Coordinating Committee, 225, Military Government of Germany, Control of I.G. Farben, Special Report of Military Governor U.S. Zone (1 October 1945).

Secondary Sources

Books

Baars G, *The Corporation, Law, and Capitalism: A Radical Perspective on the Role of Law in the Global Political Economy* (Haymarket Books 2020)
Bilsky L Y, *The Holocaust, Corporations, and the Law: Unfinished Business* (The University of Michigan Press 2017)
Kelly M J, *Prosecuting Corporations for Genocide* (OUP 2016)
Kyriakakis J, *Corporations, Accountability and International Criminal Law. Industry and Atrocity* (Edward Elgar 2021)
Stoitchkova D, *Towards Corporate Liability in International Criminal Law* (Intersentia 2010)

Contribution to Edited Books

Clapham A, 'The Question of Jurisdiction under International Criminal Law over Legal Persons: Lessons from the Rome Conference on an International Criminal Court' in Menno T Kamminga and Saman Zia-Zarifi (eds), *Liability of Multinational Corporations under International Law* (Kluwer Law International 2000)
Huisman W, Karstedt S, and van Baar A, 'The Involvement of Corporations in Atrocity Crimes' in B Holá et al (eds), *The Oxford Handbook of Atrocity Crimes* (OUP 2022)
van Baar A, 'Corporate Involvement in the Holocaust and Other Nazi Crimes' in Judith van Erp et al. (eds), *The Routledge Handbook of White-Collar and Corporate Crime in Europe* (Routledge 2015)

van den Herik L, 'Corporations as Future Subject of the International Criminal Court: An Exploration of the Counterarguments and Consequences' in Carsten Stahn and Larissa van den Herik (eds), *Future Perspectives on International Criminal Justice* (T.M.C. Asser Press 2010)

Journal Articles

Boutros-Ghali B, 'A Grotian Moment' (1994) 18(5) Fordham International Law Journal 1609

Jeßberger F, 'Corporate Involvement in Slavery and Criminal Responsibility under International Law' (2016) Journal of International Criminal Justice 327

Philippe le Billon, 'Angola's Political Economy of War: The Role of Oil and Diamonds' (2001) 100 African Affairs 55

Scharf M P, 'The Grotian Moment Concept' (2011) 19 ILSA Quarterly 16

Slye R C, 'Corporations, Veils, and International Criminal Liability' (2008) 33 Brooklyn Journal of International Law 955

Stewart J G, 'The Turn to Corporate Criminal Liability for International Crimes: Transcending the Alien Tort Statute' (2014) 47 New York University Journal of International Law and Politics 121

Wheeler C H, 'Re-Examining Corporate Liability at the International Criminal Court through the Lens of the Article 15 Communication against Chiquita Brands International' (2018) 19(1) Melbourne Journal of International Law 369

Young M, 'LaFarge's Case Cemented: Holding Corporations Liable for Crimes Against Humanity' (2021) 36 Emory International Law Review Recent Developments 1

Miscellaneous

Center for Justice and Accountability, 'Corporate Complicity in ISIL Crimes Against Humanity. Lafarge French Prosecution' (CJA, n.d.) https://cja.org/what-we-do/litigation/corporate-complicity-in-isil-crimes-against-humanity/ Accessed 26 March 2023

European Coalition on Oil in Sudan (ECOS), 'UNPAID DEBT The Legacy of Lundin, Petronas and OMV in Sudan, 1997–2003' (ECOS, June 2010) https://www.ecosonline.org/reports/2010/UNPAID_DEBT_fullreportweb.pdf Accessed 26 March 2023

International Commission of Jurists, 'Corporate Complicity and Legal Accountability, Vol. I, Report of the International Commission of Jurists Expert Legal Panel on Corporate Complicity in International Crimes' (ICJ, 2008) https://www.icj.org/wp-content/uploads/2012/06/Vol.1-Corporate-legal-accountability-thematic-report-2008.pdf Accessed 26 March 2023

International Human Rights Clinic, Colectivo de Abogados José Alvear Restrepo and International Federation for Human Rights, 'The Contribution of Chiquita Corporate Officials to Crimes Against Humanity in Colombia: Article 15 Communication to the International Criminal Court' (FIDH, 18 May 2017) https://www.fidh.org/IMG/pdf/rapport_chiquita.pdf Accessed 26 March 2023

1 Corporate Criminal Liability and the Nuremberg Experience

1.1 Introduction

In recent years, different readings of Nuremberg and the post-World War II trials have been suggested to either advance or contest the liability of corporations under international criminal law.[1] This divide is particularly evident in the case law on corporate liability under the Alien Tort Statute in the United States.[2] On the one side, it has been argued that Nuremberg and the Allies' programme for occupied Germany laid the foundation for the recognition of corporate liability under international law.[3] This argument draws a parallel between the concept of 'criminal organisation', developed under Article 9 of the London Charter,[4] and the modern concept of corporate criminal liability to establish the precedential value of the Nuremberg experience. In this sense, it is said that the indictment of six groups and organisations at Nuremberg, and the subsequent declaration of criminality of three of those

1 Joanna Kyriakakis, *Corporations, Accountability and International Criminal Law. Industry and Atrocity* (Edward Elgar 2021), Desislava Stoitchkova, *Towards Corporate Liability in International Criminal Law* (Intersentia 2010), Andrew Clapham, 'The Question of Jurisdiction under International Criminal Law over Legal Persons: Lessons from the Rome Conference on an International Criminal Court' in Menno T Kamminga and Saman Zia-Zarifi (eds), *Liability of Multinational Corporations under International Law* (Kluwer Law International 2000). Contrary, *see* Florian Jeßberger, 'Corporate Involvement in Slavery and Criminal Responsibility under International Law' (2016) Journal of International Criminal Justice 327; Larissa van den Herik, 'Corporations as Future Subject of the International Criminal Court: An Exploration of the Counterarguments and Consequences' in Carsten Stahn and Larissa van den Herik (eds), *Future Perspectives on International Criminal Justice*, (T.M.C. Asser Press 2010) 350.

2 28 U.S. Code § 1350.

3 *Kiobel v. Royal Dutch Petroleum Co.*, 621 F.3d 111, at 149-188 (2d Cir. 2010) (Leval J, concurring). *Jesner v. Arab Bank, PLC*, 138 S. Ct. 1386, at 1419 et ss. (2018), (Sotomayor J. dissenting).

4 United Nations, *Agreement by the Government of the United Kingdom of Great Britain and Northern Ireland, the Government of the United States of America, the Provisional Government of the French Republic and the Government of the Union of Soviet Socialist Republics for the prosecution and punishment of the major war criminals of the European Axis ('London Agreement')*, 8 August 1945, 82 U.N.T.S. 279, Article 9.

DOI: 10.4324/9781003390534-2

entities, 'supports the ultimate conclusion that corporations – another type of juridical entity – can violate international law and be punished for doing so'.[5] The argument also looks at the subsequent trials against German industrialists and at the extra-judicial strategies implemented by the Allies against several German companies to further evidence the value of Nuremberg in the context of the debate on corporate liability under international criminal law.[6]

Against this interpretation stands the position of those who see Nuremberg as the triumph of individual criminal liability against all other forms of accountability, and thus contest its relevance for the development of a norm on corporate liability for international crimes.[7] This latter opinion has been embraced ***obiter dictum*** by the US Supreme Court in its controversial opinion in the case *Jesner v. Arab Bank*.[8] According to the majority in *Jesner* (led by Justice Kennedy), the history of Nuremberg evidences the 'conscious decision' of the international community to reject the idea of corporate liability under international law in favour of a purely individualistic approach to international criminal liability.[9] The view follows in the footsteps of the decision of the US Court of Appeal for the Second Circuit in *Kiobel v. Royal Dutch Petroleum Co.* where the majority considered the lack of inclusion of legal entities within the jurisdiction of the International Military Tribunal of Nuremberg (IMT) – and, later on, within the jurisdiction of the US Military Tribunals established by Control Council Law No. 10[10] (CCL10) – 'not a matter of happenstance or oversight' but a firm refusal of the concept of corporate liability for international crimes.[11] The *I.G. Farben* case,[12] in particular, was used to reinforce such a conclusion. According to the majority:

> In declining to impose corporate liability under international law in the case of the most nefarious corporate enterprise known to the civilized world, while prosecuting the men who led I.G. Farben, the military tribunals established under Control Council Law No. 10 *expressly* defined liability under the law of nations as liability that could not be divorced from individual moral responsibility.[13]

5 *Jesner v. Arab Bank, PLC*, 138 S. Ct. 1386 (2018), 'Brief of Amici Curiae Nuremberg Scholars in Support of Petitioners' (27 June 2017) 5.

6 Ibid.

7 *Kiobel v. Royal Dutch Petroleum Co.*, 621 F.3d 111, at 134-136 (2d Cir. 2010). *Jesner v. Arab Bank, PLC*, 138 S. Ct. 1386, at 1399-1402 (2018).

8 *Jesner v. Arab Bank, PLC*, 138 S. Ct. 1386 (2018).

9 *Jesner v. Arab Bank, PLC*, 138 S. Ct. 1386, at 1400-1 (2018).

10 Ibid.

11 Ibid.

12 United States Military Tribunal at Nuremberg, *The United States of America vs. Carl Krauch et al.*, 'The I.G. Farben Case', Case No. 6, in *Trials of War Criminals Before the Nuremberg Military Tribunals Under Control Council Law No. 10* ("Green Series") (Washington 1952) Vol. VIII.

13 *Kiobel v. Royal Dutch Petroleum Co.*, 621 F.3d 111, at 134 (2d Cir. 2010) (emphasis added)

This interpretation of the *Farben* case was used by the *Kiobel* majority to support the conclusion that the Nuremberg trials deliberately refused to recognise the liability of corporate entities for any serious breach of international law.[14]

Considering these conflicting views, it is of primary importance to shed light on the implication of Nuremberg and the post-World War II trials on the development of an international criminal liability of corporations. This chapter thus looks at the history of Nuremberg to investigate the extent to which the criminal liability of corporate entities was discussed at that time. It begins by looking at the role played by groups and organisations during the trial conducted by the IMT in the aftermath of World War II. Starting with an analysis of the drafting of Articles 9 and 10 of the London Charter, the first part of the chapter considers the characteristics of the model of criminal organisation adopted in the Charter to contrast it with the modern concept of corporate criminal liability. Following this investigation, the chapter looks at the subsequent trials conducted by the US Military Tribunals pursuant to CCL10. The analysis focuses specifically on the *I.G. Farben* case as a pivotal example of corporate involvement in international crimes. The aim of the chapter is to provide a better contextualisation of the Nuremberg experience in today's debate on corporate criminal liability for international crimes to avoid future misinterpretations.

1.2 Criminal Organisations at Trial: The Nuremberg Experience

Established for the purpose of prosecuting crimes committed by the Nazis during World War II, the IMT represents a milestone in the history of international law and marks the origins of the concept of individual criminal responsibility at the international level.[15] The Nuremberg Tribunal departed from the ancient Act of State doctrine[16] and inaugurated a new era of international law by acknowledging that 'individuals have international duties which transcend the national obligations of obedience imposed by the individual state'.[17]

The Tribunal's most quoted statement, '[c]rimes against international law are committed by men, not by abstract entities, and only by punishing individuals who commit such crimes can the provisions of international law

14 Ibid at 135-136.

15 Antonio Cassese and Paola Gaeta, *Cassese's International Criminal Law*, 3rd (edn, OUP 2013) 4 et ss.

16 Elies van Sliedregt, *Individual Criminal Responsibility in International Law* (Oxford Monographs in International Law 2012) 18. On the 'Act of State' doctrine in connection with the Nuremberg Trial see, e.g., Stefan Glaser, 'The Charter of the Nuremberg Tribunal and New Principles of International Law', in Guénaël Mettraux (ed), *Perspectives on the Nuremberg Trial* (OUP 2008) 55, 58 et ss.

17 *United States et al. v Goering et al.*, Judgment, 30 September–1 October 1946 (1948) 1 IMT 171, 223.

be enforced',[18] crystallises the idea that individuals can and should be held accountable for the most serious violations of international law and lays the foundations of contemporary international criminal law.[19] For the first time, individuals were brought to trial before an international tribunal and punished for their involvement in serious violations of international law.[20]

In an article published in 1947, the eminent Austrian jurist and legal philosopher, Hans Kelsen, commented on the value of the London Agreement and of the IMT by stating that:

> [i]ts greatest merit is that it puts into force the idea of individual criminal responsibility for violations of international law and thus improves-though not in general but for some particular cases-the primitive technique of general international law with its collective responsibility.[21]

However, even though individuals were the main focus of the Allies in drafting the IMT's Charter, they were not the only one facing prosecution at Nuremberg. A number of groups or organisations were also an important part of the prosecution's case.[22] Six groups or organisations were indicted before the IMT: (i) the Reich Cabinet; (ii) the Leadership Corps of the Nazi Party; (iii) the Schutzstaffeln Der Nationalsozialistischen Deutschen Arbeiterparte (commonly known as the SS), including the Sicherheitsdienst (commonly known as the SD); (iv) the Gestapo; (v) the Die Sturmabteilungen Der N.S.D.A.P. (commonly known as the SA); and (vi) the General Staff of the High Command of the German Armed Forces.[23] Each of these groups or organisations was charged on all counts listed in Article 6 of the London Charter, namely crimes against peace, war crimes, and crimes against humanity.[24] It would be therefore a mistake to interpret Nuremberg as the triumph of individual criminal liability as the *only* form of liability accepted and acceptable under international law.

18 Ibid.

19 Applying the Principles of Nuremberg in the ICC, Keynote Address at the Conference 'Judgment at Nuremberg' held on the 60th Anniversary of the Nuremberg Judgment, Judge Philippe Kirsch President of the International Criminal Court, Washington University, St. Louis, USA 30 September 2006, para 3.

20 Elizabeth Borgwardt, 'Bernath Lecture: Commerce and Complicity: Corporate Responsibility for Human Rights Abuses as a Legacy of Nuremberg' (2010) 34(4) Journal of the Society for Historians of American Foreign Relations – Diplomatic Relations 627, 628.

21 Hans Kelsen, 'Will the Judgment in the Nuremberg Trial Constitute a Precedent in International Law?' (1947) 1 International Law Quarterly 153, 165.

22 David Fraser, '(De)Constructing the Nazi State: Criminal Organisations and the Constitutional Theory of the International Military Tribunal' (2017) 39 The Loyola of Los Angeles International and Comparative Law Review 117, 120.

23 *Trial of the Major War Criminals before the International Military Tribunal*, Vol. I – Official Documents (14 November 1945–1 October 1946), Library of Congress, 28.

24 Ibid 29 et ss.

The following paragraphs highlight the role of organisations and groups in the prosecution's case and discuss to what extent the concept of criminal organisation employed at Nuremberg might resemble (or might not) the modern notion of corporate criminal liability.

1.2.1 The Origin of the Prosecution's Case against Organisations

The case against groups and organisations developed as one of the pillars of the American strategy to tackle the unprecedented magnitude of Nazi crimes. Its genesis can be traced back to late 1944. At the time one of the main concerns among U.S. officials was how to deal with the hundreds of thousands of war criminals responsible for the atrocities committed in Europe.[25] On 15 September 1944, Lieutenant Colonel Murray C. Bernays – chief of the Special Projects Office of the Personnel Branch – presented a Memorandum on the 'Trial of European War Criminals' in which he set forth an innovative solution to the problem.[26] The four-page long Memorandum opened with a brief overview of the challenges involved in proceeding against Nazi criminals on an 'individual basis, and by old modes and procedures' and with a criticism of some of the solutions so far proposed.[27] Bernays' criticism focused, in particular, on the proposal made by the Secretary of Treasury, Henry Morgenthau Jr., that involved the execution by firing squads of those Nazi criminals generally recognised as guilty by the United Nations.[28] On this regard, Bernays observed that:

> [T]his suggestion would not solve the problem of punishing the thousands of less outstanding culprits. Furthermore, it would do violence to the very principles for which the United Nations have taken up arms, [...]. The suggested procedure would taint an essential act of justice with false color of vindictiveness.[29]

In light of these deficiencies, Bernays proposed an alternative solution structured in two phases. At first, an 'appropriately constituted' international tribunal would proceed against 'the Nazi Government and its Party and State agencies', such as the Gestapo, SS, and SA, for the crimes of 'conspiracy to commit murder, terrorism, and the destruction of peaceful populations in

25 Bradley F Smith, *The American Road to Nuremberg: Documentary Record 1944–1945* (Hoover Inst Press, 1982), 5 et ss. See also Jonathan A Bush, 'The Prehistory of Corporations and Conspiracy in International Criminal Law: What Nuremberg Really Said' (2009) 109(5) Columbia Law Review 1094, 1140; Richard Arens, 'Nuremberg and Group Prosecution', (1951) 1951(3) Washington University Law Review 329, 345.

26 Smith (n 12) 33, van Sliedregt (n 3) 22.

27 Smith (n 12) 33-36.

28 Ibid 27.

29 Ibid 35.

violation of the law of war.'[30] During this first phase, only those individuals 'considered to be representative of the defendant organisations' would be brought to justice.[31] Once the international tribunal established the 'guilt' of the accused organisations, subsequent proceedings would be opened at the national level against individual members on the basis of their adherence to the organisation's aim and methods.[32] Indeed, according to Bernays:

> Behind each Axis war criminal ... lays the basic criminal instigation of the Nazi doctrine and policy. It is the guilty nature of this instigation that must be established, for only thus will conviction and punishment of the individuals concerned achieve their true moral and juristic significance. [...], *this approach throws light on the nature of the individual's guilt, which is not dependent on the commission of specific criminal acts, but follows inevitably from the mere fact of voluntary membership in organisations devised solely to commit such acts.*[33]

Bernays' plan found the support of the Secretary of War, Henry L. Stimson, who endorsed the proposal on 27 October 1945.[34] In the course of the following months, Bernays' Memorandum was closely examined and discussed within the US Administration.[35] Ultimately, a refined version of the initial proposal was incorporated into the Memorandum of Proposals for the Prosecution and Punishment of Certain War Criminals and other Offenders, submitted by the U.S. to the representatives from the United Kingdom, the Provisional Government of France, and the Soviet Union ahead of the San Francisco Conference of 3 May 1945.[36] In the days that followed the Conference, the draft Proposal was further revised following observations made by legal experts of the four Allied Powers.[37] The core of Bernays proposal, however, remained unchanged.

On 26 June 1945, representatives of the four victorious nations met in London to finalise their plan of action regarding the prosecution and punishment of Nazi leaders and organisations. Supreme Court Justice Robert H. Jackson, appointed Chief of Counsel for the Prosecution of Axis Criminality by President Truman on 2 May 1945, led the US delegation throughout the

30 Ibid 36.
31 Ibid.
32 Ibid.
33 Ibid 35 (emphasis added).
34 Ibid 11.
35 Ibid 11-12.
36 Robert Jackson, *Report of Robert H. Jackson, United States Representative to the International Conference on Military Trials* (London 1945), Doc. V, 'American Memorandum Presented at San Francisco (April 30, 1945)' 28.
37 Smith (n 12) 140, Telford Taylor, The Nuremberg War Crimes Trials (1949) 27 International Conciliation 243, 249.

negotiations.[38] During the Conference, participants expressed divergent views on the opportunity to confer the power to declare the criminality of groups and organisations upon the Tribunal, with the Soviet prosecutor – Gen. Nikitchenko – strongly against it.[39]

It was ultimately due to Justice Jackson's perseverance that a compromise was reached and the proposal on criminal organisations was incorporated – with minor adjustments – into the final text of the Charter of the International Military Tribunal (London Charter).[40]

1.2.2 The London Charter

The London Charter was formally adopted on 8 August 1945 as an Annex to the Agreement for the Prosecution and Punishment of the European Axis.[41] It outlined the law and procedure governing the constitution, jurisdiction, and functions of the newly established International Military Tribunal. In particular, the Charter vested the IMT with the power to prosecute and punish individuals 'who, acting in the interests of the European Axis countries', committed one of the crimes listed in Article 6 of the Charter, namely crimes against peace, war crimes and crimes against humanity.[42] Also, as mentioned above, it granted the Tribunal authority over groups or organisations, alongside individuals.

With specific regard to groups and organisations, the legal framework was provided for by Articles 9 and 10 of the Charter:

> **Article 9**
> At the trial of any individual member of any group or organisation, the Tribunal may declare (in connection with any act of which the individual may be convicted) that the group or organisation of which the individual was a member was a criminal organisation.
> After the receipt of the Indictment the Tribunal shall give such notice as it thinks fit that the prosecution intends to ask the Tribunal to make such declaration and any member of the organisation will be entitled to apply to the Tribunal for leave to be heard by the Tribunal upon the question of

38 Bradley F Smith, *Reaching Judgment at Nuremberg: The Untold Story of How the Nazi War Criminals Were Judged* (Basic Books 1977) 46 et ss.

39 Jackson (n 23) 134-135. See also Arens (n 25) 347-349, Taylor (n 23) 253.

40 UNWCC, Development of the Law Respecting Criminal Groups and Organisations in History of the United Nations War Crimes Commission and the Development of the Laws of War, Ch. XI (H.M. Stationery Office 1948) 303. See also Stoitchkova (n 1) 47-48.

41 United Nations, *Agreement by the Government of the United Kingdom of Great Britain and Northern Ireland, the Government of the United States of America, the Provisional Government of the French Republic and the Government of the Union of Soviet Socialist Republics for the prosecution and punishment of the major war criminals of the European Axis ('London Agreement')*, 8 August 1945, 82 U.N.T.S. 279.

42 Ibid Article 6.

the criminal character of the organisation. The Tribunal shall have power to allow or reject the application. If the application is allowed, the Tribunal may direct in what manner the applicants shall be represented and heard.[43]

Article 10
In cases where a group or organisation is declared criminal by the Tribunal, the competent national authority of any Signatory shall have the right to bring individuals to trial for membership therein before national, military or occupation courts. In any such case the criminal nature of the group or organisation is considered proved and shall not be questioned.[44]

Overall, these articles represent a ***unicum*** in the panorama of international criminal law: no similar provisions can be found in the statutes of subsequent international criminal tribunals or courts. Article 9 of the Charter conferred to the Tribunal the power to declare the criminality of a group or organisation on the condition that at least one of its individual members is also facing prosecution, while Article 10 provided the basis for subsequent proceedings against individuals for membership in groups and organisations declared criminal at Nuremberg. The language employed in both articles was deliberately vague and left many legal issues unresolved. Neither Article 9 nor Article 10 provided for a definition of the terms 'group' or 'organisation'.[45] Left to the interpretation of the Tribunal were also questions concerning the legal nature of a declaration of criminality and the effects of such an 'unquestionable' declaration.[46] As will be observed in the following section, all these questions were discussed at length during the trial and ultimately resolved by the judges in the final Judgment.

1.2.3 The Nuremberg Trial and Judgment

The Trial of the Major War Criminals before the International Military Tribunal began on 20 November 1945. The proceedings lasted for about nine months, from November 1945 to August 1946. The Judgment was rendered on 30 September – 1 October 1946. Twenty-four individuals and six groups and organisations were named in the Indictments. Out of the twenty-four individual defendants, twelve were sentenced to death, seven jailed, three acquitted, one committed suicide while in custody, and another was declared

43 Ibid Article 9.

44 Ibid Article 10.

45 Smith, *Reaching Judgment at Nuremberg: The Untold Story of How the Nazi War Criminals Were Judged* (n 25) 61, Stoitchkova (n 1) 48.

46 UNWCC, 'Development of the law respecting criminal groups and organisations' in *The History of the UN War Crimes Commission.*, Chapter XI, 289, 299; digitalized and available on Human Rights after Hitler: The History of the UNWCC Website. See also Smith, *Reaching Judgment at Nuremberg: The Untold Story of How the Nazi War Criminals Were Judged* (n 25) 61; Stoitchkova (n 1) 48.

unfit to stand trial. The Tribunal declared the criminality of three groups and organisations, namely the Leadership Corps of the Nazi Party, the Gestapo/SD, and the SS, while the Reich Cabinet, the SA, and the General Staff and High Command of the German Forces were acquitted.[47]

Since the beginning, the case against groups and organisations represented a challenge for the Tribunal, first of all for the massive amount of evidence submitted by both sides. Over the course of the proceedings, the Prosecution submitted several thousand documents demonstrating the inherent criminality of the accused groups and organisations.[48] The Tribunal also received 38,000 affidavits on behalf of the Political Leaders, 136,213 on behalf of the SS, 10,000 on behalf of the SA, 7,000 on behalf of the SD, 3,000 on behalf of the General Staff, and 2,000 on behalf of the Gestapo.[49] The evidence in defence of the organisations was so extensive that most of it was taken before Commissioners appointed by the Tribunal in accordance with Article 17(e) of the London Charter. Only the most important witnesses were heard by the judges themselves.[50]

The trial of groups and organisation challenged the Tribunal also for the complex issues of law it raised.[51] American historian Bradley F. Smith so described the Tribunal's troublesome approach to groups and organisations:

> The problem that never seemed to leave [the judges] alone was that of criminal organisations. Some of the Tribunal members had begun to fuss about it long before the trial opened, and all through the trial it kept coming back to present new difficulties to the Court. [...] The reasons that the controversies and uncertainties over the organisations had such a long life are not difficult to see. This was the most novel of the prosecutions, with no precedents in international law and a few, if any, in the domestic laws of the major states.[52]

On 14 January 1946, in an attempt to shed some light on the scope of the procedure set out by Articles 9 and 10 of the Charter, the Tribunal invited arguments from both the Prosecution and the Defence on the criteria the judges should apply in determining the criminal nature of a group or organisation.[53]

47 *United States et al. v Goering et al.*, Judgment, 30 September–1 October 1946 (1948) 1 IMT 171.
48 Ibid 172.
49 Ibid.
50 Ibid.
51 Telford Taylor, *The Anatomy of the Nuremberg Trials. A Personal Memoir* (first published 1992, Skyhorse Pub Co Inc. 2013) 276.
52 Smith, *Reaching Judgment at Nuremberg: The Untold Story of How the Nazi War Criminals Were Judged* (n 25) 156.
53 *Trial of the Major War Criminals before the International Military Tribunal*, Vol. V - Proceedings (9 January–21 January 1946), Library of Congress, 238-239.

The Prosecution and the Defence presented their arguments in a series of open sessions held from 28 February to 2 March 1946.[54]

The arguments for the Prosecution were presented by Justice Jackson, the main promoter of the case against groups and organisations. The U.S. Chief Prosecutor argued that, for the purpose of Article 9 of the Charter, a group or organisation should be 'an aggregation of persons associated in identifiable relationship with a collective, general purpose'.[55] The general purpose pursued by the group or organisation should have been criminal 'in that it was designed to perform acts denounced as crimes in Article 6 of the Charter' and it should have been of such character 'that its membership in general may properly be charged with knowledge' of it.[56] Justice Jackson also clarified that membership in such a group or organisation must have been 'intentional and voluntary', not due to legal compulsion.[57] During the discussion, Jackson also touched upon the issue of the legal nature of the declaration of criminality and its effects on individual members by stating that a declaration pursuant Article 9 of the Charter should be considered as a 'declaratory judgement' concerning only the 'collective criminality of the organisation or group' and not the individual guilt of its members.[58]

On the other side, the Defence strongly contested the legitimacy of the procedure established by Articles 9 and 10 of the Charter. According to the Defence, indeed, by issuing a declaration of criminality binding for subsequent courts, the Tribunal would have acted as a legislator and not as a judicial body, so infringing the principle of separation of powers.[59] Also, even assuming the legitimacy of such a procedure, the defence counsels contested its applicability to the groups and organisations they represented. First of all, they argued that a declaration pursuant to Article 9 could not be issued against the indicted entities considering that all groups and organisations had already been dissolved by the time the trial began.[60] Moreover, they denied the validity of the criteria set forth by the Prosecution, considered too vague and inapplicable to the indicted groups and organisations.[61]

In the end, the thesis of the Prosecution prevailed. In the final judgment, the Tribunal embraced the criteria proposed by Justice Jackson during the

54 *Trial of the Major War Criminals before the International Military Tribunal*, Vol. VIII - Proceedings (20 February 1946–7 March 1946), Library of Congress, 359 et ss.

55 Ibid 367.

56 Ibid 367-8.

57 Ibid 367.

58 Ibid 358.

59 Ibid 398 et ss. Similar doubts were raised also by the American Judge, Mr Biddle, and the French Judge, M de Vabres, see ibid 450-4.

60 Ibid 391, 427.

61 Ibid 390 et ss.

course of the trial.[62] The judges started by acknowledging that Articles 9 and 10 of the Charter provided for a 'far-reaching and novel procedure' that may produce 'great injustice' if applied without certain safeguards.[63] Therefore, according to the Tribunal, a declaration of criminality should be made 'in a manner to ensure that innocent persons will not be punished'.[64] To guarantee the respect of the principle of 'personal guilt', the Tribunal provided a clear definition of the 'criminal organisation', stating that:

> A criminal organisation is analogous to a criminal conspiracy in that the essence of both is co-operation for criminal purposes. There must be a group bound together and organized for a common purpose. The group must be formed or used in connection with the commission of crimes denounced by the Charter. Since the declaration with respect to the organisations and groups will, as has been pointed out, fix the criminality of its members, that definition should exclude persons who had no knowledge of the criminal purposes or acts of the organisation and those who were drafted by the State for membership, unless they were personally implicated in the commission of acts declared criminal by Article 6 of the Charter as members of the organisation.[65]

The judges also emphasised that '[m]embership alone is not enough to come within the scope of these declarations', so highlighting the need to evaluate the individual guilt of each member on a case-by-case basis.[66] Also, the Tribunal set forth a number of recommendations to be followed by subsequent courts in the trial of individual members of the convicted groups and organisations.[67]

As for the accused groups and organisations, the Tribunal issued a declaration of criminality against three of the indicted organisations: the Leadership Corps of the Nazi Party, the Gestapo/SD, and the SS. The basis of the Tribunal's finding was the participation of these organisations 'in War Crimes and Crimes against Humanity connected with the war', in particular in the persecution of the Jews, the administration of the slave labour programme, and the mistreatment of prisoners of war.[68] With regard to the other indicted groups and organisations, namely the Reich Cabinet, the SA, and the General

62 UNWCC, 'Development of the law respecting criminal groups and organisations' in *The History of the UN War Crimes Commission.*, Chapter XI, 289, 303; digitalized and available on Human Rights after Hitler: The History of the UNWCC Website, http://www.unwcc.org/wp-content/uploads/2017/04/UNWCC-history-ch11-pt1.pdf.

63 *United States et al. v Goering et al.*, Judgment, 30 September–1 October 1946 (1948) 1 IMT 171, 256.

64 Ibid.

65 Ibid.

66 Ibid.

67 Ibid 256-7.

68 Ibid 257-73.

Staff and High Command of the German Forces, the Tribunal refrained from declaring their criminality on various grounds. The SA was acquitted because, after 1934, '[it] was reduced to the status of a group of unimportant Nazi hangers-on' and the Tribunal had no jurisdiction over the criminal actions committed before that date.[69] The Reich Cabinet was considered too small a group of individuals to require a declaration of criminality; all its members could easily be tried individually even without a declaration against the group as a whole.[70] Lastly, the judges acquitted the General Staff and High Command of the German Forces on the basis that it was 'neither an 'organisation' nor a 'group' within the meaning of those terms as used in Article 9 of the Charter'.[71]

1.2.4 Crimes of Membership v Corporate Criminal Liability

The analysis conducted so far allows drawing a first conclusion concerning the legacy of the Nuremberg Trial and the criminal liability of legal entities under international criminal law. Even though groups and organisations played an important role in the IMT proceedings, the legal basis for their indictment at Nuremberg greatly differs from the rationale underlying the modern concept of corporate criminal liability. Indeed, as observed in the previous sections, the theory of criminal organisations was developed to facilitate the rapid prosecution of the thousands of individual members of these groups and organisations deemed the 'repositories of all power in the Nazi regime'.[72] By bestowing the IMT with the authority to declare a group or an organisation 'criminal', the London Charter laid the foundations for the subsequent prosecution and punishment of individuals for the specific crime of 'membership in categories of a criminal group or organisation declared criminal by the International Military Tribunal'.[73] The purpose was, therefore, the criminalisation of individual membership in organisations whose aim was the performance of criminal activities.[74]

The Tribunal's finding in the case against the Reich Cabinet is indicative of this approach. In dismissing the Prosecution's request to declare the criminality of such an entity, the judges observed:

69 Ibid 275.

70 Ibid 276.

71 Ibid 278.

72 *Trial of the Major War Criminals before the International Military Tribunal*, Vol. VIII - Proceedings (20 February 1946–7 March 1946), Library of Congress, 374.

73 Control Council Law No. 10, Punishment of Persons Guilty of War Crimes, Crimes Against Peace and Against Humanity, December 20, 1945 (1946) 3 Official Gazette Control Council for Germany 50-55.

74 Jeßberger (n 1) 337. See also Kyriakakis (n 1) 90 and Stoitchkova (n 1) 52.

> It is estimated that there are forty-eight members of the group, that eight of these are dead and seventeen are now on trial, leaving only twenty-three at the most as to whom the declaration could have any importance. Any others who are guilty should also be brought to trial; but nothing would be done to expedite or facilitate their trials by declaring the Reich Cabinet to be a criminal organisation. *Where an organisation with a large membership is used for such purposes, a declaration obviates the necessity of inquiring as to its criminal character in the later trial of members who are accused of participating through membership in its criminal purposes and thus saves much time and trouble.* There is no such advantage in the case of a small group like the Reich Cabinet.[75]

Moreover, another aspect differentiates the Nuremberg case against criminal organisations from the modern concept of corporate criminal liability. None of the indicted accused groups and organisations were a private company pursuing economic profit. Indeed, only public entities were indicted during the main trial. As it has been observed:

> [...] at every step, the term 'organisations' was meant to include government agencies and security and party formations only. The entire goal of the war was to crush the Nazi regime and its institutional levers. [...] 'Organisations' were meant to include party, government, and security formations, and not business entities.[76]

The procedure established by Articles 9 and 10 of the Charter, therefore, was designed to deal with political organisations or militia which solely pursued criminal purposes.[77] It was never meant to address the involvement of profit-oriented entities in atrocities committed by the Third Reich.

Understood in these terms, the theory of criminal organisations as developed at Nuremberg could not be considered a valid legal precedent for corporate criminal liability under international criminal law.[78] Indeed, the modern principle of corporate criminal liability theorises a form of criminal liability that applies to the corporation *itself* and that does not cascade on the posi-

75 *United States et al. v Goering et al.*, Judgment, 30 September–1 October 1946 (1948) 1 IMT 171, 276 (emphasis added).

76 *Kiobel v. Royal Dutch Petroleum Co.*, 569 U.S. 108 (2013), Brief Nuremberg Historians and International Law Lawyers in Support of Neither Party, September 2011, pp. 19-20.

77 Jørgensen (n 65), 'A reappraisal of the abandoned Nuremberg Concept of Criminal Organisations in the Context of Justice in Rwanda', 397.

78 Jeßberger (n 1) 337. A more nuance reading of the concept of 'criminal organisations' *à la Nuremberg* is proposed by Kyriakakis who observed that '[u]ltimately, the concept of criminal organisations occupies an uneasy place between individual and collective responsibility, and in this sense reflects perhaps most starkly the ambivalence of the Nuremberg trial framework to this distinction'. See Kyriakakis (n 1) 94.

tion of each individual employee, whose liability can be established solely in cases where they are individual perpetrators or accomplices for the same crime. Conversely, as highlighted by Jørgensen, 'the concept of criminal organisation was designed as a method of dealing with mass, organised criminality where there were numerous willing participants' in the criminal conduct.[79] As such, its end goal is to facilitate the trial of the individual members of the organisation and not to impose criminal liability on the organisation *in itself*.[80]

This being said, it is relevant to mention that an attempt to draw a parallel between the theory of criminal organisations and corporate criminal liability was made already during the main Nuremberg Trial. In raising the point of the prior dissolution of the accused groups and organisations, two counsel for the accused groups and organisations – Dr. Egon Kubuschok, for the Reich Cabinet, and Dr. Hans Laternser, for General Staff and High Command – referred to the novel concept of corporate criminal liability, developed in the Anglo-American system, as the notion upon which Article 9 of the Charter was modelled. It is worth including here the pertinent passages of the speeches of both defence counsels:

> **DR. KUBUSCHOK:**
> The six organisations under Indictment are, according to the request of the Prosecution, to be declared criminal organisations in their entirety. A request of that kind and the proceedings pertaining to it would represent something unprecedented in the jurisprudence of all states. As we know, this request is not uninfluenced by the fact that, contrary to other nations, in England and even more so in the United States, even companies and corporations as such can be prosecuted in some cases for reasons of expediency. This is a legal development called for by the dominant position which companies and corporations have acquired, above all, in economic life. This position made their punishment seem desirable in certain cases. They were affected by this punishment, however, only to the extent to which they could be affected in their economic sphere, that is to say, by the imposition of fines. .... the organisations under Indictment have been dissolved by a law of the Military Government, and therefore, no longer exist. What still exists are only the individual

79 Nina H. B. Jørgensen, 'A reappraisal of the abandoned Nuremberg Concept of Criminal Organisations in the Context of Justice in Rwanda' (2001) 12 Criminal Law Forum 371, 397. See also Nina H B Jørgensen, *The Responsibility of States for International Crimes* (OUP 2000), 69-71.

80 On the challenges posed by the concept of criminal organisations, especially in relation to the perceived risk of collective criminalisation, see, *inter alia*, Shane Darcy, Collective Responsibility and Accountability under International Law (Brill 2007), 257-291, David Fraser, '(De) Constructing the Nazi State: Criminal Organisations and the Constitutional Theory of the International Military Tribunal' (2017) Loyola of Los Angeles International and Comparative Law Review 117, and Arens (n 25).

former members who, therefore, in reality, are the actual defendants and have simply been brought together under the name of the former organisation as a collective designation.'[81]

DR. LATERNSER:
If in England and America – as exceptions – associations as such can be punished, that can be done only on account of certain groups of offenses and only to the effect that either the dissolution of the corporation may be pronounced or fines imposed. Naturally in such proceedings it is a necessary condition for the Prosecution and the Defense that the corporation as such be represented during the proceedings by its functionaries and representatives and be able to defend itself; whereas in this Trial the groups and organisations as such are summoned before the Court, although they do not exist any longer and although their functionaries are absent.[82]

The Prosecution's rebuttal on this point was left to Sir David Maxwell-Fyfe – Deputy Chief Prosecutor for the United Kingdom – who unequivocally stated that the sole purpose of a declaration under Article 9 was to facilitate subsequent trials against individual members. In particular:

The first point that Dr Kubuschok made was that the procedure of asking for a declaration against the organisations was objectionable for two reasons: First, because it was founded on the limited phenomenon in Anglo-Saxon jurisprudence, that a corporation may be convicted in certain limited spheres; and secondly, that the organisations were in fact dissolved some time ago.

I think it is important to stress that *that is not the legal conception which underlies this portion of the Charter*. It is really based, in my submission, on a doctrine found in most systems of law, either *res adjudicata* or the conception of the judgment *in rem* as opposed to the judgment *in personam*. That is, that it is in the general and public interest that litigation on a particular point should not be interminable, and that, if the appropriate tribunal has come to a decision on a point of general interest and importance, that point should not thereafter be litigated many times.[83]

Considering the above, it is clear that the Prosecution at Nuremberg never intended that Articles 9 and 10 of the Charter be interpreted as a *sui generis* procedure to apply corporate criminal liability.

This notwithstanding, it would be a mistake to assume that Nuremberg has nothing to teach in regard to the prosecution of corporate entities at the international level. From a procedural perspective, indeed, Nuremberg

81 *Trial of the Major War Criminals before the International Military Tribunal*, Vol. VIII - Proceedings (20 February 1946–7 March 1946), Library of Congress, 390-1.
82 Ibid 435.
83 Ibid 455 (emphasis added).

demonstrates that entities can fit in the context of an international criminal trial. During the trial, the position of the accused groups and organisations was not dissimilar from that of the individual defendants.[84] Even though the procedural rules at Nuremberg were quite rudimentary, attention was paid to the respect of the procedural guarantees of the accused groups and organisations. Indeed, in accordance with Rule 2 of the IMT Rules of Procedure, each of the accused groups or organisations had the right to be represented by a counsel, to submit evidence in support of their defence and to present arguments on legal issues of their concern.[85] Ultimately, although the case against criminal organisations presented a number of challenges, most of them related to the sheer amount of evidence, the Tribunal was nonetheless able to deal with it in an effective way.

1.3 Post-World War II Trials: The Industrialist Cases

In the wake of the main international trial at Nuremberg, the Allies undertook a series of subsequent trials against representatives of the German public and private sectors for their involvement in crimes perpetrated by the Nazi Regime. The legal framework for these subsequent proceedings was provided by CCL10, enacted on 20 December 1946.[86] CCL10 authorised each of the four Allied powers to proceed against suspected war criminals in their respective zone of occupation.[87] The list of crimes punishable pursuant to CCL10 was mostly modelled on that of the London Agreement, with the significant addition of the crime of '(d) Membership in categories of a criminal group or organisation declared criminal by the International Military Tribunal'.[88]

Out of all the trials carried out under the umbrella of CCL10, the so-called 'industrialist cases' are by far the most relevant in the context of this book. These proceedings were the first to touch upon the issue of business involvement in international crimes and, to a certain extent, the question of

84 Telford Taylor, 'The Nuremberg War Crimes Trials', (1949) 27 Int'l Conciliation 243, 261. In his speech on 28 February 1946, Justice Robert Jackson expressed a different view stating that '[u]nder the Charter, the groups and organisations named in the Indictment are not on trial in the conventional sense of that term. They are more nearly under investigation as they might be before a grand jury in Anglo-American practice'. See *Trial of the Major War Criminals before the International Military Tribunal*, Vol. VIII - Proceedings (20 February 1946–7 March 1946), Library of Congress, 358. See van den Herik (n 1) 350-368, 352.

85 *Trial of the Major War Criminals before the International Military Tribunal*, Vol. I – Official Documents (14 November 1945–1 October 1946), Library of Congress, 19-23.

86 Control Council Law No. 10, Punishment of Persons Guilty of War Crimes, Crimes Against Peace and Against Humanity, 20 December 1945 (1946) 3 Official Gazette Control Council for Germany 50-55.

87 Ibid Article 3.

88 Ibid Article 2(1)(d).

the liability of legal entities for complicity in mass atrocities.[89] These trials were conducted by the US Military authorities against directors and executives of three powerful German concerns, namely Flick, I.G. Farben, and Krupp.[90] The following sections investigate to what extent corporate criminal liability was discussed in the months preceding the opening of these trials and how business entities were portrayed in the context of these proceedings. Regarding this latter aspect, particular attention will be paid to the *I.G. Farben* case (*United States v Carl Krauch et al.*, Case No. 6), the biggest and most complicated of the industrialist cases.[91]

1.3.1 Business Complicity in International Crimes: From the Failure of the Krupp Case at Nuremberg to the US Industrialist Trials

The idea of addressing the complicity between the German business sector and the Third Reich pre-dated the end of World War II. During the war, the US had looked with concern to the relationship between German industrialists and the Nazi Party.[92] From 1943 to the end of the conflict, a series of public hearings were held by the US Senate Subcommittee on War Mobilization to discuss the role of German industry in the consolidation of Hitler's power since the mid-1930s.[93] On 13 November 1944, the Subcommittee – chaired by Senator Harley M. Kilgore – presented a Report on Cartel and National Security in which it highlighted the link between international cartels and 'the

89 Clapham (n 1) 140. See also Nadia Bernaz, *Business and Human Rights: History, Law and Policy – Bridging the Accountability Gap* (Routledge – 2017) 63; Jernej Letnar Cernic, *Human Rights Law and Business. Corporate Responsibility for Fundamental Human Rights* (Groningen: Europa Law Publishing, 2010) 62-3; Wolfgang Kaleck and Miriam Saage-Maaβ, 'Corporate Accountability for Human Rights Violations Amounting to International Crimes The Status Quo and its Challenges' (2010) 8 Journal of International Criminal Justice 699, 702; Steven R. Ratner, 'Corporations and Human Rights: A Theory of Legal Responsibility.' (2001) 111 Yale Law Journal 443, 477-8.

90 United States Military Tribunal at Nuremberg, *The United States of America vs. Alfried Krupp et al.*, 'The Krupp Case', Case No. 10, in *Trials of War Criminals Before the Nuremberg Military Tribunals Under Control Council Law No. 10* ("Green Series") (Washington 1952) Vol. IX, United States Military Tribunal at Nuremberg, *The United States of America vs. Friedrich Flick et al.*, 'The Flick Case', Case No. 5, in *Trials of War Criminals Before the Nuremberg Military Tribunals Under Control Council Law No. 10* ("Green Series") (Washington 1952) Vol. VI, United States Military Tribunal at Nuremberg, *The United States of America vs. Carl Krauch et al.*, 'The I.G. Farben Case', Case No. 6, in *Trials of War Criminals Before the Nuremberg Military Tribunals Under Control Council Law No. 10* ("Green Series") (Washington 1952) Vol. VIII.

91 Telford Taylor, *Final Report to the Secretary of Army on the Nuernberg War Crimes Trials Under Control Council Law No.10*, (Washington D.C. 1949) 195.

92 Grietje Baars, 'Capitalism's Victor's Justice? The Hidden Stories Behind the Prosecution of Industrialists Post-WWII' in Kevin Heller and Gerry Simpson, *The Hidden Histories of War Crimes Trials* (OUP Oxford 2013) 165.

93 Ibid. Mira Wilkins, *The History of Foreign Investment in the U.S., 1914–1945* (Harvard University Press 2004) 534.

problem of national defence and the establishment of world peace'.[94] It was the Subcommittee's opinion that German industrialists had colluded with the Nazi Regime to plan, organise and launch an aggressive war to pursue their own business interests.[95]

In particular, the Subcommittee considered that:

> A study of the evidence which has been accumulated discloses how the cartel system of international economic relations operated in the period between the two world wars and shows by what means our Axis enemies engaged in systematic economic warfare against the United States as a prelude to their military aggressions. These economic aspects of war and peace have received far less public notice than the political and military aspects.[96]

This concern regarding the role played by industrialists before and during World War II was shared also by the Soviet Union and France.[97]

For this reason, when the time came to draft a list of individuals to indict in the international trial at Nuremberg, it was suggested to include Gustav Krupp von Bohlen und Halbach, head of Krupp Industries, among the possible defendants.[98] Unfortunately, the prosecutors failed to consider Krupp's medical conditions. At 75 years old, Gustav Krupp was in no way fit for trial due to his poor mental and physical state.[99] In light of that, on 4 November 1945, the defence counsel for Krupp presented a motion for the postponement of the trial against the businessman.[100] On 15 November 1945, the Tribunal granted the defence's request of postponement and ordered 'that the charges in the indictment against Gustav Krupp von Bohlen shall be retained upon the docket of the Tribunal for trial hereafter, if the physical and mental condition of the defendant should permit'.[101] To no avail the US Chief Prosecutor

94 United States, Senate, Committee on Military Affairs, *Cartels and national security: report from the Subcommittee on War Mobilization to the Committee on Military Affairs, United States Senate, pursuant to S. Res. 107, a resolution authorizing a study of the possibilities of better mobilizing the national resources of the United States* (Washington 1944).

95 Ibid 6-7; see also Baars (n 92) 165-6.

96 United States, Senate, Committee on Military Affairs, *Cartels and national security: report from the Subcommittee on War Mobilization to the Committee on Military Affairs, United States Senate, pursuant to S. Res. 107, a resolution authorizing a study of the possibilities of better mobilizing the national resources of the United States* (Washington 1944), 2.

97 Baars (n 92) 169.

98 Smith, *Reaching Judgment at Nuremberg: The Untold Story of How the Nazi War Criminals Were Judged* (n 25) 68. See also Bush (n 12) 1111; Joseph Borkin, *The Crime and Punishment of I.G. Farben* (Andre Deutsch 1978) 135.

99 Bernaz (n 73) 67; See also Bush (n 12) 1112.

100 *Trial of the Major War Criminals before the International Military Tribunal*, Vol. I – Official Documents (14 November 1945–1 October 1946), Library of Congress, 124.

101 Ibid 143.

Jackson requested the bench to replace Gustav Krupp with his son Alfred, formally in charge of the Krupp Industries since 1943.[102] In the end, Gustav Krupp's medical conditions never improved and his trial never took place.

Notwithstanding the failure of the Gustav Krupp case, the Allies did not set aside their resolution to proceed against representatives of the German industry. For months, the Allies debated the feasibility of conducting a second international trial only against German businessmen.[103] The proposal, raised immediately after the dismissal of the Krupp case by the British and the French delegations,[104] was seriously considered in Spring 1946.[105] However, the project was eventually abandoned, mostly due to a lack of political support by the governments of the United States.[106]

After the derailment of the plan for a second international trial, the Allies resolved to address the issue of the complicity of German industrialists with the Nazi regime in a series of subsequent proceedings to be conducted under the umbrella of CCL10.[107] Overall, four cases against industrialists were conducted in compliance with CCL10: three in the US zone (the 'industrialist cases') and one in the French zone (the *Roechling* case[108]). The UK also opened a case against *Bruno Tesch et al.* for complicity in the murder of interned allied civilians by means of poison gas (the so-called Zyklon B case),[109] but the trial was conducted outside the scope of CCL10.[110] There is evidence that trials against industrialists were also conducted by the Soviet Union, even though it is difficult to gauge the numbers and scope of such proceeding as 'most [Soviet] trials took place in secret and were not reported'.[111] An example is provided by the case against top officials of Topf & Söhne – the builders of the crematory

102 Ibid 134-138. See also Bernaz (n 73) 67-68; Bush (n 12) 1112.

103 Taylor, *Final Report to the Secretary of Army on the Nuernberg War Crimes Trials Under Control Council Law No.10* (n 75) 22 et ss. See also Bush (n 12) 1123 et ss.

104 *Trial of the Major War Criminals before the International Military Tribunal*, Vol. I – Official Documents (14 November 1945–1 October 1946), Library of Congress, 147.

105 Taylor, *Final Report to the Secretary of Army on the Nuernberg War Crimes Trials Under Control Council Law No.10* (n 75) 24-26.

106 It is beyond the scope of this book to address all the reasons that led to the abandonment of this project. For an in-depth analysis of the issue see Bush (n 12) 1123 et ss.

107 Taylor, *Final Report to the Secretary of Army on the Nuernberg War Crimes Trials Under Control Council Law No.10* (n 75) 24-26.

108 *The Case against Herman Roechling and other,* General Tribunal of the Military Government of the French Zone of Occupation in Germany, 30 June 1948.

109 *Trial of Bruno Tesch et al.*, British Military Court, Hamburg, Germany, 1–8 May 1946.

110 The British authorities never implemented Control Council Law No. 10, opting for proceeding against war criminals in strictly military courts pursuant to Royal Warrant. See Taylor, *Final Report to the Secretary of Army on the Nuernberg War Crimes Trials Under Control Council Law No.10* (n 75) 8, 254-257.

111 Grietje Baars, *The Corporation, Law and Capitalism: A Radical Perspective on the Role of Law in the Global Political Economy* (Brill 2019) 192-193.

ovens employed at Auschwitz.[112] However, information on the legal proceedings remains limited.[113]

The following section focuses on the preparation of the subsequent trials carried out by the Americans in their own zone of occupation.

1.3.2 The Preparatory Phase of the U.S. Industrialist Cases: Pomerantz's Memorandum

In the US controlled zone, the preparation of subsequent proceedings against German war criminals began in the early months of 1946. With the first international trial still underway, on 12 January 1946, Justice Jackson established within the Office, Chief of Counsel for the Prosecution of Axis Criminality (OCCPAC) a 'Subsequent Proceeding Division' tasked to start collecting evidence and material to conduct future trials under CCL10.[114] Immediately after, on 16 January 1946, US President Harry S. Truman signed Executive Order No. 9679, officially authorising Justice Jackson 'to proceed before United States military or occupational tribunals, in proper cases, against other Axis adherents' and, for this purpose, 'to designate a Deputy Chief of Counsel' responsible for 'organizing and planning the prosecution of charges of atrocities and war crimes, other than those … being prosecuted … in the international military tribunal'.[115] At the end of March 1946, the position of Deputy Chief of Counsel was assigned to Brigadier General Telford Taylor, already a member of Jackson's team at Nuremberg.[116]

As Justice Robert Jackson had been the main promoter and strong supporter of the first international trial, Brigadier General Telford Taylor became the driving force behind the subsequent proceedings conducted by the US under CCL10. As Deputy Chief of Counsel, Brig. Gen. Taylor took charge of the Subsequent Proceedings Division, which later on became the Office, Chief of Counsel for War Crimes (OCCWC),[117] and began recruiting new staff members to prepare future cases against German war criminals.[118] The new team of lawyers and legal experts recruited by Brig. Gen. Taylor was

112 The case has been investigated from a criminological perspective in Annika Van Baar and Wim Huisman, 'The Oven Builders of The Holocaust: A Case Study of Corporate Complicity in International Crimes' (2012) 52(6) The British Journal of Criminology 1033.

113 Baars, *The Corporation, Law and Capitalism: A Radical Perspective on the Role of Law in the Global Political Economy* (n 111) 192-193.

114 The Division was created by General Memorandum n. 13 of 12 January 1946, as stated in General Memorandum n. 15 of 29 March 1946, published in Taylor, *Final Report to the Secretary of Army on the Nuernberg War Crimes Trials Under Control Council Law No.10* (n 75) 268.

115 Ibid 267.

116 Ibid 268.

117 Ibid 14.

118 Ibid 14-15. See also Bush (n 12) 1130.

organised into five groups, each of them tasked to develop different aspects of the subsequent proceedings programme. Of the five groups or 'trial teams', two were charged with preparing the cases against German industrialists, while the others focused on cases involving military leaders, SS and police officials, diplomats, and other high government functionaries.[119]

Under Taylor's direction, the Subsequent Proceedings Division worked on the preparation of the subsequent trials, assembling evidence and developing legal theories for the prosecution. Between June and September 1946, a significant part of the work carried out by the Subsequent Proceedings Division involved the preparation of the industrialist cases.[120] As a distinguished scholar observed:

> In the summer of 1946, the challenge for American prosecutors was … how to start the [subsequent proceedings] program, and the questions were legal more than evidentiary or political. Surrounded by businesses and businessmen whose crimes were immense and numbers far too large to permit more than a handful to be tried, the Americans needed legal theories that might allow the worst of the worst to be tried efficiently and fairly.[121]

It was precisely during that time that a proposal to indict corporations in their own capacity was brought to the attention of Brig. Gen. Taylor.[122] In a Memorandum dated 27 August 1946, Abraham L. Pomerantz, Taylor's senior deputy in charge of economic cases, presented his views on the 'feasibility and propriety to indict I.G. Farben and Krupp as corporate entities'.[123] To date, Pomerantz's Memorandum represents the only available evidence that corporate criminal liability was indeed considered as a possible solution to address the involvement of business entities in international crimes.[124]

In his Memorandum, Pomerantz firstly highlighted a number of reasons in support of the idea of charging I.G. Farben and Krupp for their complicity in Nazi crimes.[125] He argued that, from a tactical point of view, the indictment of these corporations would have increased the prospects of obtaining a conviction also against the individual defendants, '[f]or the much greater guilt of

119 Ibid 15.
120 Ibid 63.
121 Bush (n 12) 1134-5.
122 Bush (n 12) 1149; Beth Van Schaack, 'Symposium: The lessons of Nuremberg' (SCOTUS blog, 25 July 2017) https://www.scotusblog.com/2017/07/symposium-lessons-nuremberg/ Accessed 26 March 2023.
123 Memorandum of 27 August 1946, reprinted as an annex in Bush (n 12) 1247-8.
124 *Kiobel v. Royal Dutch Petroleum Co.*, 569 U.S. 108 (2013), Brief Nuremberg Historians and International Law Lawyers in Support of Neither Party, September 2011, 10.
125 Memorandum of 27 August 1946, reprinted as an annex in Bush (n 12) 1247.

the entity will tend to enhance the culpability of the individual defendants'.[126] Indeed, according to Pomerantz, a case against these corporations would have stood on more solid grounds than a case against individual defendants. He also observed that a ruling on the criminal liability of these corporate entities for war crimes would have laid 'a legal and moral foundation for the expropriation of all or any part of these properties'. Lastly, he claimed that a decision against these industrial giants would have demonstrated 'to the German people the real powers behind Hitler and the NSDAP'.[127]

In the second half of his Memorandum, Pomerantz took the time to briefly address the issue of whether the legal framework created by the London Agreement, the London Charter, and CCL10 'precludes indictment of corporations'.[128] It is worth noting that, in Pomerantz's opinion, neither the London Charter nor CCL10 foreclosed corporate criminal liability.[129] Indeed, he stated that, although '[d]escription of defendants as "individuals" and "persons" would ... seem to buttress a contention that only natural persons were envisaged by the Charter and the Law ... when the words are read contextually, *it is clear that the draftsmen did not intend to exclude criminal corporations from its scope*'.[130] To support this argument, he observed that:

> Art. 1 of the quadripartite agreement provides for the trial of war criminals, "whether they be accused individually or in their capacity as members of organisations or groups or in both capacities". Here the word "individually" is clearly intended to contradistinguish "representative" liability. Certainly, it is not used to distinguish "individual" from "corporate" liability. The same formulation appears in Art. 6 of the Charter, this time, however, prefaced by a reference to potential defendants as "persons". However (in the absence of law dictionaries and encyclopaedias), I believe the word "person" in statutes has consistently been held to embrace corporations.[131]

Pomerantz's interpretation of the London Agreement and of the Charter was most certainly influenced by his legal background. As a lawyer specialising in US commercial litigations, Pomerantz had in-depth knowledge of the US legal system. His view on the interpretation of the word 'person' followed the provisions of the recently adopted US Dictionary Act of 30 July 1947,[132] which provided that:

126 Ibid.
127 Ibid.
128 Ibid 1248.
129 Ibid.
130 Ibid (emphasis added).
131 Ibid.
132 The Dictionary Act, Ch. 388, 61 Stat 633 (1947).

> In determining the meaning of any Act or resolution of Congress ... the word "person" may extend and be applied to partnerships and corporations, and the reference to any officer shall include any person authorized by law to perform the duties of such office, unless the context shows that such words were intended to be used in a more limited sense.[133]

Such an interpretation, however, was in direct contrast with Justice Jackson's understanding of the scope of the London Charter. According to Justice Jacksons, indeed, '[t]he power of the Tribunal to try is confined to "persons", and the Charter does not expand that term by definition, as statutes sometimes do, to include other than natural persons'.[134] It is unclear whether Pomerantz deliberately disregarded Jackson's position or, more realistically, was not aware of it.[135] Whichever the case, Pomerantz's view provided an alternative, and interesting, interpretation of the scope of the London Charter that could have opened the door to the prosecution of corporate entities, alongside natural persons.

Unfortunately, it is unclear how this proposal to indict corporate defendants was received by Brig. Gen. Taylor or why it was ultimately dismissed in favour of the prosecution of individual defendants. As observed by Jonathan A. Bush, '[t]he likelihood is that someone noted that since no corporations were charged at the first Nuremberg trial, it might seem odd to introduce a new theory now'.[136] Nothing indicates that the decision not to pursue corporate criminal liability was based on a 'legal determination that it was impermissible under international law'.[137] In December 1946, Abraham L. Pomerantz resigned from his position in Nuremberg and returned to the States.[138] There is no evidence that his proposal was ever discussed following his departure.

Having set aside the idea of proceeding against corporate defendants, US officials directed all their efforts to the preparation of the trials against a selected group of businessmen closely linked to Hitler and his circle of allies. By February 1947, when the indictment in the first of the industrialist cases (the Flick case) was being finalised, the proposal to proceed against corporations as separate legal entities had been long forgotten.

133 Ibid § 1.

134 *Trial of the Major War Criminals before the International Military Tribunal*, Vol. VIII - Proceedings (20 February 1946–7 March 1946), Library of Congress, 359.

135 No record survived on how Pomerantz's proposal was received by Taylor and his staff. It is therefore unclear whether the inconsistency between Pomerantz's and Jackson's approach to the interpretation of the Charter had ever been addressed.

136 Bush (n 12) 1151.

137 Ibid 1239. See also Borgwardt (n 7) 632; Van Schaack (n 104).

138 Bush (n 12) 1171-2.

1.3.3 The Industrialist Cases

The three industrialist cases were conducted between April 1947 and July 1948 at the Palace of Justice of Nuremberg. These trials involved the prosecution of a total of forty-two individual defendants from the Flick, I.G. Farben, and Krupp firms, charged with crimes against peace, war crimes, crimes against humanity, and – to a minor extend – membership in criminal organisations.[139]

The Flick case (*U.S. vs. Friedrich Flick et al.* – Case No. 5) was the first of the industrialist cases.[140] It began on 19 April 1947 and concerned the prosecution of Friedrich Flick and five other leading officials of the Flick Concern.[141] Under the Nazi regime, the Flick Concern rose to be one of the largest coal, steel, and manufacturing companies of the Reich and took part in a series of 'aryanisation' projects to consolidate its business position.[142] The prosecution charged the defendants with forced deportation and enslavement for the use in slave labour, plunder and spoliation of property in occupied territories, 'aryanisation' or the illegal acquisition of Jewish properties during the pre-war years, and membership in, and support of, the SS and the 'Circle of Friends of Himmler'.[143] The judgement was rendered on 22 December 1947. The US Military Tribunal found Friedrich Flick guilty of forced deportation and enslavement for use in slave labour of prisoners of war, plunder and spoliation of property, and of membership in criminal organisations.[144] The Tribunal also convicted two of his associates, defendant Bernhard Weiss and defendant Otto Steinbrinck, for forced deportation and enslavement for use in slave labour of prisoners of war and membership in criminal organisations, respectively. Accordingly, the convicted were sentenced to terms of imprisonment

139 Taylor, *Final Report to the Secretary of Army on the Nuernberg War Crimes Trials Under Control Council Law No.10* (n 25) 184-202; Bernaz (n 73) 68-69; Kyle R Jacobson, 'Doing Business with the Devil: The Challenges of Prosecuting Corporate Officials Whose Business Transactions Facilitate War Crimes and Crimes Against Humanity' (2005) Air Force Law Review 167, 177-191

140 United States Military Tribunal at Nuremberg, *The United States of America vs. Friedrich Flick et al.*, 'The Flick Case', Case No. 5, in *Trials of War Criminals Before the Nuremberg Military Tribunals Under Control Council Law No. 10* ("Green Series") (Washington 1952), Vol. VI, 3.

141 Ibid 11-2.

142 L M Stallbaumer, 'Big Business and the Persecution of the Jews: The Flick Concern and the Aryanization of Jewish Property before the War' (1999) 13 Holocaust and Genocide Studies 1.

143 United States Military Tribunal at Nuremberg, *The United States of America vs. Friedrich Flick et al.*, 'The Flick Case', Case No. 5, in *Trials of War Criminals Before the Nuremberg Military Tribunals Under Control Council Law No. 10* ("Green Series") (Washington 1952), Vol. VI, 3.

144 Ibid. 1222-1223.

ranging from seven to three and a half years.[145] The Tribunal acquitted the other defendants on all counts.[146]

The Farben case (*U.S. vs. Carl Krauch et al.* – Case No. 6), the 'biggest and most complicated'[147] of the industrialist cases, opened on 12 August 1947.[148] Twenty-four defendants – twenty members of the 'Vorstand' and four directors and executives – stood trial for planning and waging aggressive war, plunder and spoliation of property in occupied territories, enslavement, and mistreatment of prisoners of war, deportees, and concentration camp inmates, membership in criminal organisations and conspiracy to commit aggressive war.[149] The judgement was rendered on 30 July 1948.[150] None of the defendants were found guilty of the crimes of planning and waging aggressive war and conspiracy to commit aggressive war.[151] Thirteen defendants were found guilty of one or both of the crimes of plunder and spoliation of property in occupied territories, and enslavement and mistreatment of prisoners of war, deportees and concentration camp inmates.[152] As in the Flick case, the Tribunal sentenced the convicted to terms in prison varying from eight to one and a half years.[153] Ten defendants were acquitted on all counts.[154] One of the defendants, Max Brüggemann, was declared unfit for trial due to medical reasons and his case was discontinued in September 1947.[155]

Third – and last – of the industrialist cases, the Krupp case (*U.S. vs. Alfred Krupp et al.* – Case No. 10) opened on 9 December 1947 and involved the prosecution of Alfred Krupp von Bohlen und Halbach alongside eleven officers of the Krupp concern.[156] The defendants were charged with planning and waging aggressive war, plunder and spoliation of occupied territories, enslavement and mistreatment of prisoners of war, deportees, and concentration camp inmates, and conspiracy to commit aggressive war.[157] The judgement,

145 Ibid 1223.
146 Ibid 1222-3.
147 Telford Taylor, *Final Report to the Secretary of Army on the Nuernberg War Crimes Trials Under Control Council Law No.10*, (n 25) 195.
148 United States Military Tribunal at Nuremberg, *The United States of America vs. Carl Krauch et al.*, 'The I.G. Farben Case', Case No. 6, in *Trials of War Criminals Before the Nuremberg Military Tribunals Under Control Council Law No. 10* ("Green Series") (Washington 1952) Vol. VIII, 3.
149 Ibid 2.
150 Ibid 3.
151 Ibid 1206-1209.
152 Ibid.
153 Ibid 1206-1208.
154 Ibid 1206-1209.
155 Ibid 1083
156 United States Military Tribunal at Nuremberg, *The United States of America vs. Alfried Krupp et al.*, 'The Krupp Case', Case No. 10, in *Trials of War Criminals Before the Nuremberg Military Tribunals Under Control Council Law No. 10* ("Green Series") (Washington 1952) Vol. IX,1
157 Ibid 2.

rendered on 31 July 1948, convicted eleven defendants for one or both of the crimes of enslavement and mistreatment of prisoners of war, deportees, and concentration camp inmates and spoliation of property in occupied territories.[158] As in the *I.G. Farben* case, all defendants were acquitted of the crimes of planning and waging aggressive war and conspiracy to commit aggressive war.[159] The sentences imposed by the Tribunal ranged from a maximum of twelve to a minimum of two years of imprisonment.[160]

Overall, the outcome of these proceedings was quite disappointing.[161] In all three cases, the judges were particularly lenient towards the defendants and often ruled in their favour. In his personal account on the Farben case, *The Devil's Chemists*, Josiah E. DuBois, Jr. – head of the prosecution team for the Farben case – bitterly observed that '[t]he sentences were light enough to please a chicken thief, or a driver who irresponsibly run down a pedestrian'.[162]

To the disappointment of the prosecution teams, in both the Flick and Farben case the judges accepted the defence of necessity raised by the defendants, recognising that the 'reign of terror' created by Hitler did not allow those businessmen to act contrary to the Reich's policy.[163] The decision to allow such a defence stood in open contrast with CCL10 which explicitly stated that '[t]he fact that any person acted pursuant to the order of his Government or of a superior does not free him from responsibility for a crime'.[164] On this regard, the Flick Tribunal clarified:

> In our opinion, it is not intended that these provisions [of Control Council Law 10] are to be employed to deprive a defendant of the defence of necessity under such circumstances as obtained in this case with respect to defendants Steinbrinck, Burkart, Kaletsch, and Terberger. This Tribunal might be reproached for wreaking vengeance rather than

158 Ibid 1373, 1448.

159 Ibid 390-400.

160 Ibid 1449-52.

161 Baars, 'Capitalism's Victor's Justice? The Hidden Stories Behind the Prosecution of Industrialists Post-WWII' (n 92) 179; *Kiobel v. Royal Dutch Petroleum Co.*, 569 U.S. 108 (2013), Brief Nuremberg Historians and International Law Lawyers in Support of Neither Party, September 2011, 12.

162 Josiah E DuBois, Jr., *The Devil's Chemists: 24 Conspirators of the International Farben Cartel Who Manufacture Wars* (Beacon Press 1952) 339.

163 United States Military Tribunal at Nuremberg, *The United States of America vs. Friedrich Flick et al.*, 'The Flick Case', Case No. 5, in *Trials of War Criminals Before the Nuremberg Military Tribunals Under Control Council Law No. 10* ("Green Series") (Washington 1952) Vol. VI, 1200-1201; United States Military Tribunal at Nuremberg, *The United States of America vs. Carl Krauch et al.*, 'The I.G. Farben Case', Case No. 6, in *Trials of War Criminals Before the Nuremberg Military Tribunals Under Control Council Law No. 10* ("Green Series") (Washington 1952) Vol. VIII, 1173-1178.

164 Control Council Law No. 10, Punishment of Persons Guilty of War Crimes, Crimes Against Peace and Against Humanity, 20 December 1945 (1946) 3 Official Gazette Control Council for Germany 50-55, Article 2(4)(b).

> administering justice if it were to declare as unavailable to defendants the defence of necessity here urged in their behalf. ... The defendants lived within the Reich. The Reich, through its hordes of enforcement officials and secret police, was always "present," ready to go into instant action and to mete out savage and immediate punishment against anyone doing anything that could be construed as obstructing or hindering the carrying out of governmental regulations or decrees.[165]

Perhaps an even bigger disappointment came from the judges' refusal to ascribe any responsibility to the Farben and Krupp defendants for crimes against peace. From the perspective of the prosecution, indeed, the 'aggressive war' charges against both the Farben and Krupp defendants stood on solid grounds.[166] Nonetheless, the Farben and Krupp Tribunals completely dismissed these charges. In this regard, the majority in the Farben case observed that:

> In this case we are faced with the problem of determining the guilt or innocence with respect to the waging of aggressive war on the part of men of industry who were not makers of policy but who supported their government during its period of rearmament and who continued to serve that government in the waging of war, ... The defendants now before us were neither high public officials in the civil government nor high military officers. Their participation was that of followers and not leaders. If we lower the standard of participation to include them, it is difficult to find a logical place to draw the line between the guilty and the innocent among the great mass of German people.[167]

Marginally more successful was the prosecution's case on the crimes of slave labour and spoliation of property.[168] In all three cases the prosecution teams were able to achieve the conviction of some of the defendants for one or both charges. However, even in those cases where the judges found the defendants

165 United States Military Tribunal at Nuremberg, *The United States of America vs. Friedrich Flick et al.*, 'The Flick Case', Case No. 5, in *Trials of War Criminals Before the Nuremberg Military Tribunals Under Control Council Law No. 10* ("Green Series") (Washington 1952) Vol. VI, 1200-1.

166 Telford Taylor, *Final Report to the Secretary of Army on the Nuernberg War Crimes Trials Under Control Council Law No.10*, (n 25) 196-7.

167 United States Military Tribunal at Nuremberg, *The United States of America vs. Carl Krauch et al.*, 'The I.G. Farben Case', Case No. 6, in *Trials of War Criminals Before the Nuremberg Military Tribunals Under Control Council Law No. 10* ("Green Series") (Washington 1952) Vol. VIII, 1124-5.

168 Harmen Van der wilt, 'Corporate Criminal Responsibility for International Crimes: Exploring the Possibilities' (2013) 12 Chinese Journal of International Law 43, 54-5.

guilty of slave labour or spoliation their criminal liability was always narrowly defined.[169]

As for the significance of these trials in the context of the development of a norm of corporate criminal liability for international crimes, it has already been mentioned above that none of the industrialist cases involved the prosecution of corporate entities. Despite this, the issue of corporate liability for violation of international law was constantly on the judges' minds. Indeed, in each of these cases, the US Military Tribunals put strong emphasis on the role played by the company itself in the commission of the crimes charged.[170] As observed by Steven R. Ratner, 'the courts … routinely spoke in terms of corporate responsibilities and obligations'.[171]

An example of this can be found, *inter alia*, in the Krupp judgement. In addressing the role of the Krupp firm in the spoliation of property in occupied France (Count Two of the Indictment), the Krupp Tribunal observed that:

> We conclude from the credible evidence before us that the confiscation of the Austin plant based upon German inspired anti-Jewish laws and its subsequent detention by the Krupp firm constitute a violation of Article 43 of the Hague Regulations which requires that the laws in force in an occupied country be respected; that it was also a violation of Article 46 of the Hague Regulations which provides that private property must be respected; *that the Krupp firm*, through defendants Krupp, Loeser, Houdremont, Mueller, Janssen, and Eberhardt, *voluntarily and without duress participated in these violations by purchasing and removing the machinery and leasing the property of the Austin plant and in leasing the Paris property* …[172]

This systematic allusion to the role and responsibility of the corporation alongside that of its directors and managers was a constant feature in the Farben case. As observed by Jonathan Bush, '[u]nlike Krupp and Flick, whose lead defendants were more important than their corporate vehicles … with Farben the gulf between the notorious firm and its large cast of grey managers and directors made it inevitable that the firm itself was always being discussed in court and the press.'[173] Over the course of the trial, both the Prosecution and the Defence devoted a considerable amount of time to the discussion of

169 Alberto L Zuppi, 'Slave Labor in Nuremberg 's I.G. Farben Case: The Lonely Voice of Paul M. Hebert' (2006) Louisiana Law Review 510.

170 Clapham (n 1) 140.

171 Ratner (n 73) 81.

172 United States Military Tribunal at Nuremberg, *The United States of America vs. Alfried Krupp et al.*, 'The Krupp Case', Case No. 10, in *Trials of War Criminals Before the Nuremberg Military Tribunals Under Control Council Law No. 10* ("Green Series") (Washington 1952) Vol. IX, 1352-3 (emphasis added).

173 Bush (n 12) 1223.

the 'enormous and intricate industrial complex of I.G. Farben'.[174] The goals pursued by the parties were, of course, the opposite. From the perspective of the Prosecution, the arguments concerning the structure and organisation of Farben aimed at demonstrating the instrumentality of the legal entity in the commission of the crimes charged.[175] Contrarily, the Defence used the organisational structure of the company as a shield to deflect the defendants' responsibility for acts not strictly related to their scope of employment.[176]

Testimony of the prominent role of Farben in the proceedings is provided by the Tribunal's decision to allow one of the defence counsel, Dr. Silcher, to make a closing statement on behalf of the company itself.[177] In his address to the bench, Dr. Silcher stated that:

> In this trial formally only the twenty-three defendants in the dock are indict[ed] and not the firm I.G. Farben. *However this firm from a moral point of view is the invisible defendant who in addition to those twenty three men has been mentioned time and again in this trial.* Your Honors only need to read the indictment in order to gather therefrom this inescapable impression. *Therefore in the world's public opinion as well, this is really a trial against the firm I.G. Farben.* For this reason alone it seems necessary to speak once in the course of the defense of I.G. Farben and to defend this firm. Therefore the defense has deemed it proper to draw in addition to all the other pleadings an overall-picture of I.G. Farben.[178]

The 'invisible defendant' – as referred by Dr. Silcher – occupied a central role also in the judgement. Even though the bench conceded that 'the corporate defendant, Farben, is not before the bar of this Tribunal and cannot be subjected to criminal penalties in these proceedings',[179] nonetheless it often referred to the liability of the business entity as distinct for that of its managers and directors. This attitude is particularly evident in the judgement's section on Count Two – plunder and spoliation of property. While discussing the

174 United States Military Tribunal at Nuremberg, *The United States of America vs. Carl Krauch et al.*, 'The I.G. Farben Case', Case No. 6, in *Trials of War Criminals Before the Nuremberg Military Tribunals Under Control Council Law No. 10* ("Green Series") (Washington 1952) Vol. VIII, 108.

175 Ibid 378.

176 Ibid.

177 United States Military Tribunal at Nuremberg, *United States of America vs. Carl Krauch et al.* (Case 6), Transcript of Proceedings, National Archives Microfilm Publication M895, Roll 15, Vol. 42, June 7–9, 1948, 15400-15441.

178 Ibid 15400 (emphasis added).

179 United States Military Tribunal at Nuremberg, *The United States of America vs. Carl Krauch et al.*, 'The I.G. Farben Case', Case No. 6, in *Trials of War Criminals Before the Nuremberg Military Tribunals Under Control Council Law No. 10* ("Green Series") (Washington 1952) Vol. VIII, 1153.

provisions of the Hague Regulations of 1907 pertinent to the charges,[180] the Tribunal preliminarily observed that:

> [T]he Hague Regulations are broadly aimed at preserving the inviolability of property rights to both public and private property during military occupancy. ... Where private individuals, ***including juristic persons***, proceed to exploit the military occupancy by acquiring private property against the will and consent of the former owner, such action, not being expressly justified by any applicable provision of the Hague Regulations, is in violation of international law. ... Similarly where a private individual or ***a juristic person*** becomes a party to unlawful confiscation of public or private property by planning and executing a well-defined design to acquire such property permanently, acquisition under such circumstances subsequent to the confiscation constitutes conduct in violation of the Hague Regulations.[181]

Applying this reasoning to the case at hand, the judges concluded that:

> With reference to the charges in the present indictment concerning Farben's activities in Poland, Norway, Alsace-Lorraine, and France, we find that the proof establishes beyond a reasonable doubt that offenses against property as defined in Control Council Law No. 10 were committed by Farben, ... The action of Farben and its representatives, under these circumstances, cannot be differentiated from acts of plunder or pillage committed by officers, soldiers, or public officials of the German Reich.[182]

With regard to the charge of economic spoliation of property, therefore, the Farben Tribunal recognised that the activities of the corporation itself constituted a breach of the Hague Regulations. Not just the individual defendants, but also the corporation in its own capacity was considered responsible for the violation of international norms. However, the same Tribunal acknowledged that one thing is the responsibility of the corporation, other than the individual criminal liability of the defendants indicted in the proceedings:

> One cannot condone the activities of Farben in the field of spoliation. If not actually marching with the Wehrmacht, Farben at least was not far

180 The Tribunal referred, in particular, to Articles 46, 47, 52, 53, and 55 of the Hague Regulations of 1907. See ibid, 1131-2.

181 Ibid 1131-1132.

182 Ibid 1139.

> behind. But translating the criminal responsibility to personal and individual criminal acts is another matter.[183]

Although the judges recognised responsibility on the part of Farben for the commission of the war crimes charged under count two, they refused to consider this circumstance sufficient *per se* to establish the criminal liability of the individuals in the dock.

This dichotomy between the responsibility of the corporation, on one side, and the individual criminal liability of the defendants, on the other, is evident also in the separate concurring opinion filled by Judge Paul Macarius Hebert on counts one and five (crimes against peace and conspiracy to commit crimes against peace). Judge Hebert concurred with the majority in the acquittal of all defendants for the charges on the aggressive war, but his reasoning greatly differed from the one adopted by the majority. In one of the passages of his separate opinion, Judge Hebert distinguished between the knowledge attributable to the company and this imputable to the single individuals. In particular, he observed that:

> The record abundantly establishes a substantial participation by certain of the individual defendants who were members of the Vorstand of Farben, in the action of Farben in furthering the armament activities which constituted preparation for the aggressive wars launched by Hitler. The corporate defendant is not under indictment before this Tribunal. *If a single individual had combined the knowledge attributable to the corporate entity and had engaged in the course of action under the same circumstances as that attributable to the corporate entity, it is extremely doubtful that a judgment of acquittal could properly be entered.*[184]

Judge Hebert's statement echoed the considerations expressed by Pomerantz more than two years prior to the Farben judgement.[185] Had the Prosecution indicted Farben in its corporate capacity, the outcome of the whole proceeding could have been very different. The indictment of the company would have indeed enhanced the prospects of a conviction. From a tactical perspective, the decision not to proceed against Farben probably cost the Prosecution the first historic conviction of a corporation for participation in international crimes.

To conclude, even though all the allusions to the liability of the corporation mentioned above are mere *obiter dicta*, they nonetheless indicate that already at the time of Nuremberg it was to some extent accepted that corporations

183 Ibid 1153.
184 Ibid 1214 (emphasis added).
185 Memorandum of 27 August 1946, reprinted as an annex in Bush (n 12) 1247-1248.

themselves may violate international law and – as a consequence – incur some form of responsibility.

1.4 Extra-Judicial Sanctioning of Farben

In recent years, several scholars have argued that a discussion on the early development of a norm on corporate accountability for international crime should not focus exclusively on the jurisprudence of the IMT and of the Military Tribunals established under CCL10. According to those authors, consideration should be given also to the various measures implemented by the Allies against German corporations 'outside of the courtroom'.[186] This view was expressed, in particular, by a number of Nuremberg scholars in their *Brief of Amici Curiae in Support of Petitioners* submitted to the US Supreme Court in the case *Kiobel et al. vs Royal Dutch Petroleum*.[187] In the Brief, those authors argued that:

> The international criminal trials of Nazi officials and individual industrialists were only one part of Allied efforts to punish those responsible for Nazi-era atrocities. ... Control Council Law No. 10, putting individuals on trial - whether German doctors, jurists, industrialists, or various members of the SS - was only a small part of the Allied plan for postwar Germany that also included the dissolution of private corporations, the seizure of industrial facilities, restitution of confiscated properties, and reparations to both the states and natural persons who had suffered harm.[188]

Reference was made, in particular, to Control Council Law No. 9 (from now on CCL9), titled 'Providing for the Seizure of Property Owned by I.G. Farbenindustrie and the Control Thereof', adopted on 30 November 1945.[189] The objectives pursued through CCL9 were the destruction of Farben's 'monopolistic control over German industry'[190] and the elimination of 'the war potential which it represented'.[191] In light of the prominent role played by Farben in building up and maintaining the German war machine, CCL9

186 *Kiobel v. Royal Dutch Petroleum Co.*, 569 U.S. 108 (2013), Brief of Amici Curiae Nuremberg Scholars in Support of the Petitioners, September 2011, 3.

187 *Kiobel v Royal Dutch Petroleum Co.* 133 S.Ct. 1659 (2013).

188 *Kiobel v. Royal Dutch Petroleum Co.*, 569 U.S. 108 (2013), Brief of Amici Curiae Nuremberg Scholars in Support of the Petitioners, September 2011, 12.

189 Control Council Law No. 9, 'Providing for the Seizure of Property Owned by I.G. Farbenindustrie and the Control Thereof' (30 November 1945), reprinted in Enactments and Approved Papers of the Control Council and Coordinating Committee, 225.

190 Military Government of Germany, Control of I.G. Farben, Special Report of Military Governor U.S. Zone (1 October 1945), 1.

191 Ibid.

affected the seizure of '[a]ll plants, properties and assets of any nature situated in Germany which were, on or after 8 May, 1945, owned or controlled by I.G Farbenindustrie A.G.' and the transfer of the legal title over those property to Control Council.[192]

The extra-judicial sanction imposed on Farben by CCL9 has been seen as proof that, at the time of Nuremberg, international law provided for the accountability of business entities for international crimes. In particular, it has been observed that:

> This ultimate sanction was as drastic as any that could be imposed on a juristic entity: death through seizure and was as much a pronouncement of international law as Control Council Law No. 10 which was used to prosecute individuals. The extreme sanction of dissolution imposed by Control Council No. 9 is clearly inconsistent with … [the] conclusion that international law at the time of Nuremberg did not consider corporations liable for violations of international law norms.[193]

Moreover, it has been argued that the dissolution of Farben in late 1945 justified the subsequent decision taken by the U.S. prosecutors not to pursue the corporation itself during the trial against its managers and directors: 'when the international trial of individual Farben defendants took place pursuant to Control Council Law No. 10, there was no need to put I.G. Farben itself on trial, since it had already suffered corporate death pursuant to Control Council Law No. 9'.[194]

Even though such an argument has its allure and can be used in support of the idea that international law could (and should) impose some form of liability to companies for international crimes,[195] nonetheless it has limited relevance in the context of today's debate over the development of an international criminal liability of corporations. Indeed, the imposition of a sanction (as severe as the dissolution of the company) outside the courtroom could not justify the conclusion that a similar sanction could be also applied in the context of an international criminal trial. Surely, the relevance of the seizure and dissolution of Farben by an international body such as the Control Council could demonstrate that sanctions can be imposed on legal entities at the international level. However, such conclusion should be tempered by

192 Control Council Law No. 9, 'Providing for the Seizure of Property Owned by I.G. Farbenindustrie and the Control Thereof' (30 November 1945), reprinted in Enactments and Approved Papers of the Control Council and Coordinating Committee, 225.

193 *Kiobel v. Royal Dutch Petroleum Co.*, 569 U.S. 108 (2013), Brief of Amici Curiae Nuremberg Scholars in Support of the Petitioners, September 2011, 14.

194 Ibid 3.

195 *Contra* see *Kiobel v. Royal Dutch Petroleum Co.*, 569 U.S. 108 (2013), Brief Nuremberg Historians and International Law Lawyers in Support of Neither Party, September 2011, 26 et ss.

the acknowledgement of the exceptional circumstances of the Farben case. Indeed, the special treatment reserved for Farben was mostly due to political considerations. As observed above, US authorities contemplated the idea of putting a limit to the monopolistic power of Farben even before the end of the Second World War.[196]

Therefore, even though the seizure and dissolution of Farben represents an interesting and relevant case study in the field of corporate accountability, its relevance with regard to the development of a norm on 'international' corporate criminal liability should not be overstated.

1.5 Conclusion

This chapter has examined to what extent the idea of holding corporations criminally accountable for international crimes was discussed at Nuremberg in the immediate aftermath of World War II. Conflicting readings of the precedential value of the Nuremberg trials have been presented to either support or dismiss the concept of corporate criminal liability for international crimes. The analysis conducted in the chapter sheds light on the relevance of the Nuremberg experience in today's debate on the international criminal liability of corporations.

The chapter first looked at the origin and significance of the case against groups and organisations to consider whether the concept of 'criminal organisation' *à la* Nuremberg may share some commonalities with the modern concept of corporate criminal liability. In this regard, it has been argued that the theoretical underpinning of Articles 9 and 10 of the London Charter differs from that of the modern concept of corporate criminal liability. Indeed, the chapter demonstrated how the concept of 'criminal organisation' was developed to address the phenomenon of mass criminality that characterised the Nazi regime and it was ultimately directed to facilitate the establishment of individual criminal liability on a large scale. As such, it represented a hybrid form between individual and collective liability. Its scope and function are thus different from that of corporate criminal liability. The latter concept rests on the idea that the corporate entity, as separate from its individual members, can be held criminally accountable for its involvement in criminal activities. Therefore, it would be erroneous to conflate the concept of corporate criminal liability with that of criminal organisation. That being said, the chapter does not entirely dismiss the precedential value of the Nuremberg trial against groups and organisations. Conversely, it suggests a recontextualization of such precedent that focuses more on the ability of the IMT to deal with the procedural challenges arising from the trial against groups and organisations. Read in this sense, Nuremberg demonstrates that complex entities can fit within the

196 Bush (n 12) 1114.

context of an international criminal trial and that the challenges posed by the trial of such entities are not without solution.

The focus of the analysis then shifted to the subsequent trials of German industrialists conducted by the US under the aegis of CCL10. These cases feature prominently in the contemporary debate on corporate liability for international crimes. The chapter took the view that, despite the lack of prosecution of corporate entities, these cases offer relevant insights into the way in which corporate liability for international crimes was perceived in the immediate aftermath of World War II. Looking at the preparatory phase of the US industrialist cases, it appears evident that an attempt was made to include corporations among the list of defendants for the trials. Even though it ultimately failed, this attempt confirms the conclusion that already at Nuremberg, the question of corporate criminal liability was part of the debate on how to address business involvement in international crimes. This conclusion is further supported by the analysis of the cases against corporate officials of Krupp, Flick, and I.G. Farben. While the corporations were not directly indicted in any of these subsequent trials, they nonetheless found their way inside the courtroom as 'invisible defendants'. Indeed, in all three judgements, the courts repeatedly spoke in terms of corporate liability and acknowledged the ability of legal persons to commit international crimes. The relevance of the industrialist cases, thus, cannot be ignored.

Lastly, the chapter considered the significance of the Allies' decision to impose severe administrative sanctions on I.G. Farben as a punishment for the role played by the industrial conglomerate during World War II. This argument has been repeatedly used in support of corporate liability for international crimes, especially in the context of corporate litigations under the Alien Tort Statute. It is argued that, while interesting, this presents relevant limitations. Indeed, the fact that corporations such as Farben were subjected to extra-judicial sanctioning says nothing about whether similar sanctions could have been applied as the result of an international criminal trial. Conversely, the argument under consideration may even be interpreted as evidence against corporate criminal liability under international criminal law as the decision of the Allied Powers to sanction corporations out of the courtroom may be seen as an implicit recognition of the difficulties of addressing corporate wrongdoing in the trial setting. The chapter, thus, suggested a cautious approach to this argument.

Overall, the investigation of the Nuremberg experience demonstrated that most of the questions that still plague academics and practitioners debating the feasibility of prosecuting corporations under international criminal law were already in the minds of the Nuremberg judges and prosecutors. The relationship between corporate criminal liability and individual criminal liability, the evidentiary problems related to the investigation and prosecution of complex legal entities, and the tactical advantages (and disadvantages) of indicting corporate defendants were only some of the issues addressed at Nuremberg. It is, therefore, necessary to acknowledge the precedential value of the Nuremberg experience, without overestimating its impact on the development of a norm of international corporate criminal liability for international crimes.

References

Primary sources

Conventions and Treaties

United Nations, *Agreement by the Government of the United Kingdom of Great Britain and Northern Ireland, the Government of the United States of America, the Provisional Government of the French Republic and the Government of the Union of Soviet Socialist Republics for the prosecution and punishment of the major war criminals of the European Axis ('London Agreement')*, 8 August 1945, 82 U.N.T.S. 279

International Military Tribunal and Subsequent Trials

British Military Court, *Trial of Bruno Tesch et al.*, Hamburg, Germany, 1-8 May 1946

General Tribunal of the Military Government of the French Zone of Occupation in Germany, *The Case against Herman Roechling and other*, Judgment, 30 June 1948

United States Military Tribunal at Nuremberg, *The United States of America vs. Alfried Krupp et al.*, 'The Krupp Case', Case No. 10, in *Trials of War Criminals Before the Nuremberg Military Tribunals Under Control Council Law No. 10* ("Green Series") (Washington 1952) Vol. IX

United States Military Tribunal at Nuremberg, *The United States of America vs. Friedrich Flick et al.*, 'The Flick Case', Case No. 5, in *Trials of War Criminals Before the Nuremberg Military Tribunals Under Control Council Law No. 10* ("Green Series") (Washington 1952) Vol. VI

United States Military Tribunal at Nuremberg, *The United States of America vs. Carl Krauch et al.*, 'The I.G. Farben Case', Case No. 6, in *Trials of War Criminals Before the Nuremberg Military Tribunals Under Control Council Law No. 10* ("Green Series") (Washington 1952) Vol. VIII

United States Military Tribunal at Nuremberg, *United States of America vs. Carl Krauch et al.* (Case 6), Transcript of Proceedings, National Archives Microfilm Publication M895, Roll 15, Vol. 42, June 7-9, 1948

United States et al. v Goering et al., Judgment, 30 September-1 October 1946 (1948) 1 IMT 171

Official Publications

Control Council Law No. 10, Punishment of Persons Guilty of War Crimes, Crimes Against Peace and Against Humanity, 20 December 1945 (1946) 3 Official Gazette Control Council for Germany 50-55

Control Council Law No. 9, Providing for the Seizure of Property Owned by I.G. Farbenindustrie and the Control Thereof, 30 November 1945, in *Enactments and Approved Papers of the Control Council and Coordinating Committee*, Library of Congress

Military Government of Germany, *Control of I.G. Farben*, Special Report of Military Governor U.S. Zone (1 October 1945)
Trial of the Major War Criminals before the International Military Tribunal, Vol. I – Official Documents (14 November 1945 – 1 October 1946), Library of Congress
Trial of the Major War Criminals before the International Military Tribunal, Vol. V - Proceedings (9 January – 21 January 1946), Library of Congress
Trial of the Major War Criminals before the International Military Tribunal, Vol. VIII - Proceedings (20 February 1946 -7 March 1946), Library of Congress
United States, Senate, Committee on Military Affairs, Cartels and national security: report from the Subcommittee on War Mobilization to the Committee on Military Affairs, United States Senate, pursuant to S. Res. 107, a resolution authorizing a study of the possibilities of better mobilizing the national resources of the United States (United States Government Printing Office 1944)
UNWCC, Development of the Law Respecting Criminal Groups and Organisations in *History of the United Nations War Crimes Commission and the Development of the Laws of War*, Ch. XI (H.M. Stationery Office 1948)

Domestic cases

Jesner v. Arab Bank, PLC, 138 S. Ct. 1386 (2018)
Jesner v. Arab Bank, PLC, 138 S. Ct. 1386 (2018), 'Brief of Amici Curiae Nuremberg Scholars in Support of Petitioners' (27 June 2017)
Kiobel v. Royal Dutch Petroleum Co., 621 F.3d 111 (2d Cir. 2010)
Kiobel v. Royal Dutch Petroleum Co., 569 U.S. 108 (2013), 'Brief Nuremberg Historians and International Law Lawyers in Support of Neither Party' (September 2011)
Kiobel v. Royal Dutch Petroleum Co., 569 U.S. 108 (2013), 'Brief of Amici Curiae Nuremberg Scholars in Support of the Petitioners' (September 2011)

Domestic Laws

Alien's Action for Tort, 28 U.S. Code § 1350 (1948)
The Dictionary Act, Ch. 388, 61 Stat 633 (1947)

Secondary sources

Books

Baars G, *The Corporation, Law and Capitalism: A Radical Perspective on the Role of Law in the Global Political Economy* (Brill 2019)
Bernaz N, *Business and Human Rights: History, Law and Policy – Bridging the Accountability Gap* (Routledge 2017)
Borkin J, *The Crime and Punishment of I.G. Farben* (Andre Deutsch 1978)
Cassese A and Gaeta P, *Cassese's International Criminal Law* (3rd edn, OUP 2013)
Cernic J L, *Human Rights Law and Business. Corporate Responsibility for Fundamental Human Rights* (Europa Law Publishing 2010)
Darcy S, *Collective Responsibility and Accountability under International Law* (Brill 2007)

DuBois Jr. J E, *The Devil's Chemists: 24 Conspirators of the International Farben Cartel Who Manufacture Wars* (Beacon Press 1952)

Jackson R, *Report of Robert H. Jackson, United States Representative to the International Conference on Military Trials* (London 1945)

Jørgensen N H B, *The Responsibility of States for International Crimes* (OUP 2000)

Kyriakakis J, *Corporations, Accountability and International Criminal Law. Industry and Atrocity* (Edward Elgar 2021)

Smith B F, *Reaching Judgment at Nuremberg: The Untold Story of How the Nazi War Criminals Were Judged* (Basic Books 1977)

Smith B F, *The American Road to Nuremberg: Documentary Record 1944–1945* (Hoover Inst Press, 1982)

Stoitchkova D, *Towards Corporate Liability in International Criminal Law* (Intersentia 2010)

Taylor T, *Final Report to the Secretary of Army on the Nuernberg War Crimes Trials Under Control Council Law No.10* (Washington, D.C.: U.S. G.P.O 1949)

Taylor T, *The Anatomy of the Nuremberg Trials. A Personal Memoir* (first published 1992, Skyhorse Pub Co Inc. 2013)

van Sliedregt E, *Individual Criminal Responsibility in International Law* (Oxford Monographs in International Law 2012)

Wilkins M, *The History of Foreign Investment in the U.S., 1914–1945* (Harvard University Press 2004)

Contribution to Edited Books

Baars G, 'Capitalism's Victor's Justice? The Hidden Stories Behind the Prosecution of Industrialists Post-WWII' in Kevin Heller and Gerry Simpson (eds), *The Hidden Histories of War Crimes Trials* (OUP 2013)

Clapham A, 'The Question of Jurisdiction under International Criminal Law over Legal Persons: Lessons from the Rome Conference on an International Criminal Court' in Menno T. Kamminga and Saman Zia-Zarifi (eds), *Liability of Multinational Corporations under International Law* (Kluwer Law International 2000)

Glaser S, 'The Charter of the Nuremberg Tribunal and New Principles of International Law', in Guénaël Mettraux (ed), *Perspectives on the Nuremberg Trial* (OUP 2008)

van den Herik L, 'Corporations as Future Subject of the International Criminal Court: An Exploration of the Counterarguments and Consequences' in Carsten Stahn and Larissa van den Herik (eds), *Future Perspectives on International Criminal Justice* (T.M.C. Asser Press 2010)

Journal Articles

Arens R, 'Nuremberg and Group Prosecution' (1951) 3 Washington University Law Review 329

Borgwardt E, 'Bernath Lecture: Commerce and Complicity: Corporate Responsibility for Human Rights Abuses as a Legacy of Nuremberg' (2010) 34(4) Journal of the Society for Historians of American Foreign Relations – Diplomatic Relations 627

Bush J A, 'The Prehistory of Corporations and Conspiracy in International Criminal Law: What Nuremberg Really Said' (2009) 109(5) Columbia Law Review 1094

Fraser D, '(De)Constructing the Nazi State: Criminal Organisations and the Constitutional Theory of the International Military Tribunal' (2017) 39 The Loyola of Los Angeles International and Comparative Law Review 117

Jacobson K R, 'Doing Business with the Devil: The Challenges of Prosecuting Corporate Officials Whose Business Transactions Facilitate War Crimes and Crimes Against Humanity' (2005) Air Force Law Review 167

Jeßberger F, 'Corporate Involvement in Slavery and Criminal Responsibility under International Law' (2016) Journal of International Criminal Justice 327

Jørgensen N H B, 'A Reappraisal of the Abandoned Nuremberg Concept of Criminal Organisations in the Context of Justice in Rwanda' (2001) 12 Criminal Law Forum 371

Kaleck W and Saage-Maaβ M, 'Corporate Accountability for Human Rights Violations Amounting to International Crimes The Status Quo and its Challenges' (2010) 8 Journal of International Criminal Justice 699

Kelsen H, 'Will the Judgment in the Nuremberg Trial Constitute a Precedent in International Law?' (1947) 1 International Law Quarterly 153

Ratner S R, 'Corporations and Human Rights: A Theory of Legal Responsibility' (2001) 111 Yale Law Journal 443

Stallbaumer L M, 'Big Business and the Persecution of the Jews: The Flick Concern and the Aryanization of Jewish Property before the War' (1999) 13 Holocaust and Genocide Studies 1

Taylor T, 'The Nuremberg War Crimes Trials' (1949) 27 International Conciliation 243

Van Baar A and Huisman W, 'The Oven Builders of The Holocaust: A Case Study of Corporate Complicity in International Crimes' (2012) 52(6) The British Journal of Criminology 1033

Van der wilt H, 'Corporate Criminal Responsibility for International Crimes: Exploring the Possibilities' (2013) 12 Chinese Journal of International Law 43

Zuppi A L, 'Slave Labor in Nuremberg 's I.G. Farben Case: The Lonely Voice of Paul M. Hebert' (2006) Louisiana Law Review 510

Miscellaneous

Applying the Principles of Nuremberg in the ICC, Keynote Address at the Conference 'Judgment at Nuremberg' held on the 60th Anniversary of the Nuremberg Judgment, Judge Philippe Kirsch President of the International Criminal Court, Washington University, St. Louis, USA 30 September 2006

Van Schaack B, 'Symposium: The lessons of Nuremberg' (SCOTUSblog, 25 July 2017), https://www.scotusblog.com/2017/07/symposium-lessons-nuremberg/ Accessed 26 March 2023

2 The Question of Corporations in the Aftermath of the Nuremberg Trials

2.1 Introduction

Chapter 1 evaluated the Nuremberg experience and its precedential value in the context of the contemporary debate on the feasibility of holding corporations accountable under international criminal law. The analysis contrasted the concept of 'criminal organisation' under Articles 9 and 10 of the London Charter with the modern construct of corporate criminal liability to re-assess the narrative surrounding the Nuremberg case against groups and organisations. While the case against Nazi organisations undoubtedly shows the feasibility of prosecuting complex entities at the international level, the investigation into the scope and purpose of the concept of 'criminal organisation' casts doubt on its value as a precedent for corporate criminal liability. Chapter 1 also considered to what extent the liability of corporations was addressed in the context of the subsequent trials against German industrialists. The cases against corporate officials of Flick, Krupp, and I.G. Farben shed light on the role played by businesses in the commission of Nazi atrocities. They demonstrated the struggles faced by the US judges and prosecutors in distinguishing between the individual liability of businessmen, on the one side, and the liability of the corporate entity, on the other. While it is true that no company was indicted in the subsequent trials, the analysis of the courts' records and final judgements evidenced how the question of the liability of corporations for international crimes was a central theme at Nuremberg.

This chapter looks at the immediate aftermath of the Nuremberg experience to demonstrate how the question of corporate liability remained a feature of the debate on the scope of international criminal law from the late 1940s to the early 1950s. The Nuremberg judgements brought a wave of great enthusiasm for international justice. Fuelled by the achievements of the IMT, many international lawyers and scholars embarked on a series of initiatives to promote the development and codification of international criminal law as an autonomous branch of international law. Carried out under the aegis of the United Nations, these initiatives addressed some of the questions left unanswered by the Nuremberg judgments, such as the definition of genocide, the concept of international criminal liability, and the possibility of establishing

DOI: 10.4324/9781003390534-3

a permanent international criminal tribunal to ensure accountability at the international level.[1]

So far, scholars have generally disregarded the contribution made by these early initiatives to the development of an international norm on corporate criminal liability. As a matter of fact, the vast majority of the existing literature on the international criminal liability of corporate entities focuses on two pivotal moments in the history of international criminal law: the Nuremberg experience and the 1998 Rome Diplomatic Conference for an International Criminal Court.[2] What happened in between remains mostly overlooked.[3] This chapter, thus, fills a gap in the existing literature on the liability of legal persons for international crimes and contributes to the current debate on whether corporations should be included among the subjects of international criminal law.

2.2 The 1948 Convention on the Prevention and Punishment of the Crime of Genocide

To fully understand the way in which the issue of the liability of corporations for international crimes was integrated within the broader debate on the scope and limitation of international criminal law, it is fundamental to look at the work conducted by various UN bodies in the immediate aftermath of Nuremberg. Such an analysis should necessarily start by considering one of the most important conventions adopted in the field of human rights

1 William A Schabas, *The International Criminal Court: A Commentary on the Rome Statute*, (2nd edn, OUP 2016) 6-8; Antonio Cassese, Paola Gaeta, John R W D Jones (eds), The Rome Statute of the International Criminal Court: A Commentary (OUP 2002) 9.

2 Joanna Kyriakakis, Corporations, *Accountability and International Criminal Law. Industry and Atrocity* (Edward Elgar 2021), Nadia Bernaz, *Business and Human Rights: History, Law and Policy – Bridging the Accountability Gap* (Routledge 2017), Leora Yedida Bilsky, *The Holocaust, Corporations, and the Law: Unfinished Business (Law, Meaning, and Violence)* (The University of Michigan Press 2017), Desislava Stoitchkova, *Towards Corporate Liability in International Criminal Law* (Intersentia 2010), Elizabeth Borgwardt, 'Bernath Lecture: Commerce and Complicity: Corporate Responsibility for Human Rights Abuses as a Legacy of Nuremberg' (2010) 34 Diplomatic History 627, Joanna Kyriakakis, 'Corporate Criminal Liability and the ICC Statute: The Comparative Law Challenge' (2009) 56(3) Netherlands International Law Review 333.

3 In one of his contributions on the liability of corporations under international law, Andrew Clapham briefly touched upon the early debate on the liability of legal entities which take place in the context of the 1951 and 1953 Committees on International Criminal Jurisdiction: see Andrew Clapham, 'The Question of Jurisdiction under International Criminal Law over Legal Persons: Lessons from the Rome Conference on an International Criminal Court' in Menno T Kamminga and Saman Zia-Zarifi (eds), *Liability of Multinational Corporations under International Law* (Kluwer Law International 2000). Similarly, in his recent book, Michael J Kelly addressed the question of whether corporations were considered in the *travaux prèparatoires* of the Genocide Convention: see Michael J Kelly, *Prosecuting Corporations for Genocide* (OUP 2016).

and international criminal law: The 1948 *Convention of the Prevention and Punishment of the Crime of Genocide* (hereinafter Genocide Convention or Convention).[4]

Although over the last 80 years, the Convention has been the subject of an ever-growing body of academic literature,[5] its contribution to the debate on the feasibility of holding corporations criminally accountable at the international level has been largely overlooked. The text of the Convention, indeed, makes no reference to the liability of legal entities for the crime of genocide.[6] This notwithstanding, in recent years, a number of scholars have argued that the liability of corporations for genocide, although not expressly provided for in the text, could nonetheless be inferred from the wording of the Convention.[7]

The starting point of their analysis is Article IV of the Genocide Convention which stated:

> Persons committing genocide or any of the other acts enumerated in Article III shall be punished, whether they are constitutionally responsible rulers, public officials or private individuals.[8]

Article IV does not provide a clear indication of whether the word 'persons' should be interpreted to include only natural persons or could embrace also legal persons. According to some authors, therefore, 'while natural persons are the more relevant category, a proper reading [of Article IV] suggests that the provision does not preclude states from imposing criminal liability for genocide also on corporations'.[9] In particular, Michael J. Kelly observed that:

4 *Convention on the Prevention and Punishment of the Crime of Genocide* (adopted 9 December 1948, entered into force 12 January 1951) 78 U.N.T.S. 277.

5 See, *inter alia*, John Quigley, *The Genocide Convention. An International Law Analysis* (Routledge 2016) Christian J Tams, Lars Berster and Björn Schiffbauer, *Convention on the Prevention and Punishment of the Crime of Genocide: A Commentary* (C H Beck Hart Nomos 2014), Paola Gaeta (ed), *The UN Genocide Convention. A Commentary* (OUP 2009), William A Schabas, *Genocide in International Law: The Crime of Crimes*, (2nd edn,, Cambridge University Press 2009) Jérémie Gilbert, 'Perspectives on Cultural Genocide. From Criminal Law to Cultural Diversity' in Margaret M deGuzman and Diane Marie Amann (eds) *Arcs of Global Justice: Essays in Honour of William A. Schabas* (OUP 2018).

6 A/CN.4/690, para 44.

7 Kelly, *Prosecuting Corporations for Genocide* (n 3), Christian J Tams, Lars Berster and Björn Schiffbauer, *Convention on the Prevention and Punishment of the Crime of Genocide: A Commentary* (C H Beck Hart Nomos 2014) 19, Michael J Kelly, 'Never Again: German Chemical Corporation Complicity in the Kurdish Genocide' (2103) 31 Berkeley Journal of International Law 348, 380-2, Harold Hongju Koh, 'Separating Myth from Reality about Corporate Responsibility Litigation' (2004) 7 Journal of International Economic Law 263, 266.

8 *Convention on the Prevention and Punishment of the Crime of Genocide* (adopted 9 December 1948, entered into force 12 January 1951) 78 U.N.T.S. 277, Article IV.

9 Tams, Berster and Schiffbauer (n 7) para 19; Koh (n 7) 266.

> There is no artificial distinction between natural or legal (juridical) in either the reference to 'persons' or 'private individuals,' whereas such distinction is specifically made in later international criminal treaties. Thus, corporate liability could therein lurk.[10]

To corroborate his view, Kelly referred to the *travaux preparatoires* of the Convention, noting that '[a]n exploration of what the treaty drafters were thinking does not dampen this prospect'.[11] Indeed, he noted a certain ambiguity by the drafters in the use of the terms 'persons' and 'private individuals' that may justify a broad interpretation of Article IV so as to include private corporations.[12] He concluded that, while 'any indication of inclusion [of corporations within the scope of the Convention] is merely speculative … there is equally no definitive exclusion apparent in the *travaux*'.[13]

This interpretation of the Genocide Convention is interesting and adds to the growing literature supporting the recognition of corporate criminal liability for international crimes. However, it may prove overly speculative. To evaluate whether such an interpretation may be justified under the existing international law framework, it is necessary to start by looking at the rules on treaty interpretation provided by the *Vienna Convention on the Law of Treaties* (hereafter the Vienna Convention).[14]

According to Article 31(1) of the Vienna Convention, '[a] treaty shall be interpreted in good faith in accordance with the ordinary meaning to be given to the terms of the treaty'.[15] The discussion on Article IV of the Genocide Convention, and its applicability to corporations, therefore, should necessarily start with an investigation of the literal meaning of the term 'person' used in the provision. In its ordinary meaning, a 'person' is defined as a 'human, individual – sometimes used in combination especially by those who prefer to avoid man in compounds applicable to both sexes' or 'one (such as a human being, a partnership, or a *corporation*) that is recognized by law as the subject of rights and duties'.[16] While the former definition adopts an anthropomorphic approach to the term 'person', the latter considers a person from a legal point of view, looking at its status within a legal system. The literal interpretation of the term 'person', thus, does not seem to provide a definitive answer to the question of whether Article IV of the Genocide Convention could be constructed to include corporations, as suggested by Kelly.

10 Kelly, *Prosecuting Corporations for Genocide* (n 3) 61.
11 Ibid.
12 Ibid 62-4.
13 Ibid 64.
14 Vienna Convention on the Law of Treaties (adopted 1969, entered into force 1980) 1155 U.N.T.S 331.
15 Ibid Article 31(1).
16 Merriam-Webster Online Dictionary, Person, https://www.merriam-webster.com/dictionary/person Accessed 26 March 2023.

A similar conclusion can be reached when looking at the 'grammatical construction of the provision or phrase' within which the term 'person' is located.[17] Article IV establishes that persons committing genocide or any of the acts listed under Article III of the Genocide Convention shall be punished 'whether they are constitutionally responsible rulers, public officials or private individuals'.[18] In this context, the reference to 'private individuals', in the second part of the provision, cannot be considered decisive evidence in favour of the anthropomorphic definition. Indeed, literally interpreted, the noun 'individual' can indicate either 'a particular being or thing as distinguished from a class, species, or collection such as a single human being or a single organism' or 'an indivisible entity'.[19] An investigation of the whole Convention seems to lead to a similar conclusion. In the whole body of the Convention, the term 'person' is used only three times in the document – in Article IV, as already discussed, and in Articles V and VI, which do not offer any further clarification on the way in which such terms should be constructed.[20]

As the analysis of the text of the Genocide Convention does not provide conclusive evidence on whether legal persons can be included in the scope of Article IV, an investigation of the preparatory works of the treaty, as supplementary means of interpretation, must be conducted to assess the validity of Kelly's thesis. On this regard, a reading of the preparatory work shows that, while Kelly is correct in stating that none of the delegations has ever vetoed the inclusion of private corporations in the list of persons liable under Article IV, an opportunity to express such a position never presented itself during the negotiation of the Convention.

Indeed, looking at the drafting history of the Genocide Convention, and in particular of Article IV, it emerges that the liability of legal entities was debated solely in relation to the potential responsibility of States and Governments. The issue of the criminal liability of legal entities was discussed on 5 November 1948, when the Sixth Committee opened the debate on the Article V of the *Ad Hoc* Committee Draft Convention, titled 'Persons Liable'.[21] The initial text provided that '[t]hose committing genocide or any of the other acts enumerated in Article IV shall be punished whether they are heads of State, public officials or private individuals'.[22]

17 Ibid 199.

18 *Convention on the Prevention and Punishment of the Crime of Genocide* (adopted 9 December 1948, entered into force 12 January 1951) 78 U.N.T.S. 277, Article IV.

19 Merriam-Webster Online Dictionary, Individual, https://www.merriam-webster.com/dictionary/individual Accessed 26 March 2023.

20 *Convention on the Prevention and Punishment of the Crime of Genocide* (adopted 9 December 1948, entered into force 12 January 1951) 78 U.N.T.S. 277, Articles IV, V and VI.

21 A/C.6/SR.92

22 Ad Hoc Committee on Genocide, Report of the Committee and Draft Convention drawn up by the Committee, (24 May 1948), E/794, Article V. The text of Article V adopted by the Ad Hoc Committee mostly followed Article IV of the Secretariat Draft which stated: 'Those

Ahead of the discussion, five delegations submitted amendments to the text.[23] In the context of the present analysis, the proposal submitted by the United Kingdom is of particular relevance. The UK delegation proposed a completely new text of Article V which emphasised the role of States and Governments in the commission of acts of genocide.[24] The new version of Article V would have read as follows:

> Criminal responsibility for any act of genocide as specified in Articles II and IV shall extend not only to all private persons or associations, but also to States and Governments, or organs or authorities of the State or Government, by whom such acts are committed. Such acts committed by or on behalf of States or Governments constitute a breach of the present Convention.[25]

In presenting the amendment, the British delegate explained that:

> when a head of State was guilty of genocide, it was in reality the State itself or the Government which committed the crime. In those circumstances, it was useless to say that 'heads of State' should be punished. The fact to be established was the penal responsibility of the State or the Government itself.[26]

The British amendment generated an animate debate on the feasibility of including States and Governments, as legal entities, among those potentially liable for the crime of genocide. The majority of the delegates were very sceptical towards the idea that States and Governments could be held criminally accountable for genocide.[27] The main argument advanced against this idea pertained to the limited recognition, at the national level, of the applicability of criminal law on entities other than individuals. On this regard, the French delegate opposed the amendment by pointing out that 'French law did not recognize the criminal responsibility of States or Governments, which were legal entities. While such entities could have financial responsibility, they could not be held criminally responsible'.[28] Similar positions were expressed by the

committing genocide shall be punished, be they rulers, public officials or private individuals.' UN Secretary-General, 'Draft Convention on the Crime of Genocide' (26 June 1947) E/447, Article IV.

23 Amendments to that text were proposed by the delegations of the USSR (A/C.6/215/Rev.1), Belgium (A/C.6/217), France (A/C.6/224), the United Kingdom (A/C.6/236), Syria (A/C.6/246), and Sweden (A/C.6/247).

24 A/C.6/236.

25 Ibid.

26 A/C.6/SR.92.

27 See the opinion expressed by Spiropoulos and Pérez Perozo in A/C.6/SR.95.

28 Ibid.

delegates of the Dominican Republic and Sweden.[29] The latter, in particular, explained that:

> The United Kingdom amendment raised a ... question, that of the provision for criminal sanctions. [...] The Swedish delegation was prepared to discuss the inclusion in the convention of a clause regarding the reparations to be paid to victims by a State of which the heads had committed genocide, but it wished to point out that, strictly speaking, a criminal penalty would not be involved. For those reasons and also because the *Swedish criminal code did not recognize the idea of the penal responsibility of legal persons,* the Swedish delegation was of the opinion that it was inappropriate to refer to the penal responsibility of States and Governments and that article V should provide only for the punishment of individuals. [30]

Firmly against the UK proposal was also the delegate from the United States, Maktos. Coming from a State where the liability of legal entities was deeply embedded in the national legal system, Maktos' argument against the inclusion of the liability of States and Governments in the Convention was more a matter of principle. Indeed, according to him, 'judicial entities such as the State' could not commit genocide because '*in reality genocide was always committed by individuals*'.[31]

In the end, the British amendment was rejected by 24 votes to 22 and the final version of Article V referred exclusively to 'constitutionally responsible rulers, public officials or private individuals' as those potentially liable for genocide.[32]

The brief analysis conducted so far confirms that, during the drafting of the Genocide Convention, the question of the criminal liability of legal entities was addressed essentially from the perspective of the liability of States. Private corporations remained outside the scope of the debate. As observed by Andrew Clapham, the 'opposition to the idea of State crimes seems to have eclipsed discussion of international criminal responsibility of other entities such as corporations'.[33] Therefore, arguing in favour of the applicability of the Convention to private legal entities, and using the Convention as evidence of an early recognition of corporate criminal liability for international crimes, may be hazardous.

The Genocide Convention represents, thus, a missed opportunity to launch a genuine debate on the international criminal liability of corporations as

29 A/C.6/SR.92.
30 Ibid (emphasis added).
31 A/C.6/SR.93 (emphasis added).
32 A/C.6/256.
33 Clapham (n 3) 171, footnote 62.

separate from the responsibility of political entities such as the State. As will be demonstrated in the following sections, this lack of consideration towards private legal entities – this inability, or unwillingness, to recognise their distinctiveness – would remain, for decades, a glaring feature of the debate on the international criminal liability of corporate entities.

2.3 The ILC Draft Code of Offences against Peace and Security of Mankind: An Early Debate on the Criminal Liability of Legal Entities

Another initiative undertaken by the UN General Assembly in the aftermath of Nuremberg concerned the drafting of a *Code of Offences against Peace and Security of Mankind*. The task of working on an international criminal code was initially assigned to the Committee on the Codification of International Law by UNGA Resolution 95 (I) of 11 December 1946.[34] The following year, the responsibility of preparing a Draft Code was passed to the newly established International Law Commission (hereinafter ILC or Commission) by means of Resolution 177 (II).[35] The Commission's work on the Draft Code then began in 1949 and, although interrupted on several occasions, lasted till 1996.[36]

In the literature on the international criminal liability of corporations, the Draft Code is scarcely considered – if not completely ignored. However, it is worth noticing that it was precisely in the context of the Commission's study on the Code's scope *ratione personae* that the issue of the international criminal liability of corporations was first addressed independently from the question of the liability of States.[37]

The question was firstly addressed in the First Report on the Draft Code prepared by Jean Spiropoulos, which addressed the issue of the identification of the 'subjects of criminal responsibility under the draft code'.[38] The Report considered three possible subjects of criminal responsibility: individuals, organisations, and States.[39] The liability of each of these subjects was analysed using the Nuremberg precedent as the point of reference. Consequently, Spiropoulos concluded that only individuals should be subjects of interna-

34 UNGA Res 95 (I) (11 December 1946). See also M Cherif Bassiouni, 'The History of the Draft Code of Crimes against the Peace and Security of Mankind' (1993) 27 Israel Law Review 247.

35 UNGA Res 177 (II) (21 November 1947).

36 Rosemary Rayfuse, 'The Draft Code of Crimes Against the Peace and Security of Mankind: Eating Disorders at the International Law Commission' (1997) 8(1) Criminal Law Forum 43, 44-49. See also Bassiouni (n 34); Benjamin B Ferencz, 'Current Developments. The Draft Code of Offences Against the Peace and Security of Mankind' (1981) 75(3) American Journal of International Law 674.

37 A/CN.4/39.

38 A/CN.4/25, paras 46-56.

39 Ibid.

tional criminal liability,[40] thus excluding corporations or other organisations. Indeed, according to the Special Rapporteur, only the criminal liability of individuals found recognition within the legal framework provided for by the London Charter and the Nuremberg judgment.[41] Moreover, for what concerned the liability of organisations, another consideration weighed on the decision to exclude the international criminal liability of these entities: the lack of a general agreement on the possibility of imposing criminal liability to legal persons at the domestic level. Indeed, in his Report, the Special Rapporteur observed that:

> In our opinion the question [of] whether organisations within a State shall be subjects of international penal responsibility ought to be answered negatively. *The grounds for the answer are provided by the fact that the various municipal laws, with rare exceptions, do not establish the penal responsibility of legal persons*, and by the position taken, in this respect, by the Nürnberg Tribunal.[42]

Conversely, a different perspective on the matter was suggested in another document made available to the Commission ahead of its second discussion on the Draft Code. In 1949, the Secretariat presented a *Memorandum Concerning a Draft Code of Offences against the Peace and Security of Mankind* to provide some insights into the possible scope and content of the Draft Code.[43] Written by Vespasian V. Pella, President of the Association Internationale de Droit Penal (AIDP), the Memorandum analysed issues such as the concept of international crime, the general principles related to the punishment of these crimes, and the necessity to adopt an international code as a way to enhance State compliance with international law. More importantly, in one of its sections, the Memorandum considered the question of the 'responsibility of legal entities other than the State'.[44] Even though the issue was addressed as part of a broader analysis on the 'active subjects of international crimes' – including individuals and States – the criminal liability of corporations was approached as a separate concept, not overshadowed by considerations of States' liability.[45] As observed above, this ability to distinguish between States and other legal entities was quite uncommon at that time.

The section on legal persons other than the State opened with a brief overview of the role played by corporate entities in the context of the Second World War.[46] On this regard, Pella pointed out how, during the conflict,

40 Ibid paras 46, 51-52 and 56.
41 Ibid para 46.
42 Ibid para 51 (emphasis added).
43 A/CN.4/39.
44 Ibid para 80.
45 Ibid paras 68-81.
46 Ibid para 80.

private corporations often participated in international crimes perpetrated by the Third Reich.[47] In particular, he observed that:

> Some companies facilitated – or organized – monstrous experiments of so-called scientific character made on human beings in concentration camps. Others have provided funds to carry out war propaganda and to prepare aggressive war.[48]

Their complicity in such atrocities was indeed well documented. Pella observed that in such cases, 'in addition to the criminal liability of the individuals who acted as organs of the legal person, *the international criminal responsibility of the latter is perfectly conceivable*'.[49] Pella recalled how, in 1929, the Second Congress of the International Association of Criminal Law had recognised the necessity of imposing criminal liability on business entities in all cases in which their activities 'endanger[ed] the national legal order'.[50] According to Pella, the same considerations which may justify the application of criminal sanctions to corporations at the domestic level, were equally valid at the international level.[51]

In his Memorandum, Pella examined also the criminal sanctions potentially applicable to such entities. On this regard, he observed that:

> It is obvious that, against legal persons, one can apply only those penal sanctions and security measures suitable for their nature; such as warning, fine, prohibition to open branches within a country or abroad, prohibition to carry out activities in certain fields, limitation on the amount of capital invested and/or the number of employees, special surveillance and control measures and, finally, dissolution.[52]

No obstacle to the application of such sanctions at the international level was identified by the Memorandum's author. In light of the above, Pella invited the Commission to take into serious consideration the possibility of including a provision on the criminal liability of corporate bodies in the context of *Draft Code for Offences against the Peace and Security of Mankind*.[53]

Unfortunately, Pella's position was mostly ignored by the Commission. Indeed, when the question of the subjects of international criminal liability was discussed on 26 June 1950, none of the members of the Commission even

47 Ibid.
48 Ibid. Original in French. Translation provided by the author.
49 Ibid. Original in French. Translation provided by the author (emphasis added).
50 Ibid.
51 Ibid.
52 Ibid. Original in French. Translation provided by the author.
53 Ibid para 81.

mentioned Pella's considerations.[54] Overall, the discussion on the issue was extremely brief. Even though some members of the Commission supported the idea of including States and organisations within the scope of the Draft Code,[55] the majority accepted the view expressed by the Special Rapporteur that the debate on the Draft Code should be confined to the sole criminal responsibility of individuals.[56] The shared concern was that a discussion on the criminal liability of legal entities, such as States and organisations, would have been time-consuming.[57] As observed by the Special Rapporteur, indeed, by limiting the discussion to the criminal responsibility of individuals, 'the Commission was embarking upon the only path which could ensure reasonably brief discussion'.[58]

In the end, thus, the Commission decided to proceed with its analysis of the Draft Code focusing only on the liability of natural persons.[59] Such a decision was described in the Final Report as merely 'provisional', seemingly implying a willingness on the side of the Commission to leave the door open to further considerations on the matter.[60] However, when in 1983, the time did come to reconsider the question of the subjects of international criminal law, it became clear that the liability of corporate entities was not among the Commission's priorities.

Indeed, even though the newly appointed Special Rapporteur, Doudou Thiam, recognised the relevance of the issue of the criminal liability of 'commercial companies', he quickly dismissed it to focus his attention on the sole liability of States.[61] The following extract of the Rapporteur's First Report is explanatory of that:

> The question of the criminal responsibility of legal entities is posed not only in international law, but also in municipal law. Under the laws of some countries today, commercial companies, for example, may be tried for criminal offences, such as economic crimes, and are liable to financial penalties. In its draft articles on State responsibility, the Commission itself has adopted the aforementioned article 19 (see para. 39 above), paragraph 2 of which refers to international crimes. [...] The inclusion of article 19 in the draft on State responsibility has reopened the debate. *The question is whether the Commission's position, which was to exclude States from the scope of the 1954 draft code, can still be maintained today. If it cannot, the Commission will have to reshape the 1954 draft substantially,*

54 A/CN.4/SR.54, paras 74-96.
55 Ibid paras 77 and 85. See, in particular, the position expressed by François and Hudson.
56 Ibid para 94.
57 Ibid para 82.
58 Ibid para 91.
59 A/CN.4/34, para 151.
60 A/CN.4/SR.54, paras 94-96.
61 A/CN.4/364, paras 42-44.

> *thus putting an end to the long-drawn-out theoretical debate—no doubt extremely interesting, but apparently interminable—between advocates and opponents of the theory of criminal responsibility of States.*[62]

Albeit the Rapporteur initially distinguished between the (highly controversial) criminal liability of States and the (slightly less controversial) criminal liability of business entities, considerations on the former completely overshadowed those on the latter. This approach weighed on the subsequent debate on the matter and resulted, yet again, in the Commission's decision to confine the scope of the Draft Code to natural persons.[63]

Once more, the impracticability of conceiving the criminal responsibility of States foreclosed any evaluation on the feasibility of including private companies among the subject of international criminal law. The Draft Code, thus, constitutes another missed opportunity for the development of a more genuine debate on the international criminal liability of business companies.

2.4 The Liability of Legal Persons in the Early Stage of the Debate on an International Criminal Court: The Role of the 1951 and 1953 Committees on International Criminal Jurisdiction

As discussed above, the direct relevance of the 1948 Genocide Convention in the development of a norm of international criminal liability of corporations is still controversial. However, its *indirect* influence cannot be questioned. Indeed, by setting into motion the modern debate on the feasibility of establishing an international criminal court, the Genocide Convention has indeed provided the context for further consideration of the question of the international criminal liability of corporate entities.

The question of an international criminal court with jurisdiction over genocide arose repeatedly during the two-year negotiation of the Genocide Convention. The idea of creating an international institution with the power to investigate and prosecute those responsible for genocide was a matter of great contention among delegations.[64]

Ultimately, after considerable discussion, a reference to an international criminal jurisdiction was incorporated in the final text of the Convention under Article VI which reads:

> Persons charged with genocide or any of the other acts enumerated in article III shall be tried by a competent tribunal of the State in the territory of which the act was committed, *or by such international penal*

62 Ibid para 44 (emphasis added).
63 A/38/10, paras 50-61.
64 Schabas, *The International Criminal Court: A Commentary on the Rome Statute* (n 1) 6.

> *tribunal as may have jurisdiction with respect to those Contracting Parties which shall have accepted its jurisdiction.*[65]

The adoption of the Genocide Convention did not exhaust the debate on the feasibility of establishing an international criminal court. Acknowledging the necessity to give further consideration to the question, the General Assembly instructed the ILC 'to study the desirability and possibility of establishing an international judicial organ for the trial of persons charged with genocide or other crimes over which jurisdiction will be conferred upon that organ by international convention'.[66]

The ILC began its work on the question of an international criminal court in 1949 and proceeded in its evaluation for only two sessions.[67] During this early stage of the debate, the ILC approached the issue of a permanent criminal jurisdiction mostly from a theoretical perspective, refusing to consider the political and diplomatic implications pertaining to the creation of such mechanisms.[68] The decision to approach the issue only *in abstracto* limited the value of the Commission's initial consideration of the question of international criminal jurisdiction. When the Commission's Final Report was discussed by the Sixth Committee of the UN General Assembly, the lack of concrete proposals concerning a draft statute for an international criminal court prevented many delegations from expressing a definitive opinion on whether such an institution could have been concretely established.[69]

Conscious of the need to adopt a more practical approach to the issue, the General Assembly decided not to refer the question back to the ILC.[70] Following the Sixth Committee's suggestion, the General Assembly adopted Resolution 489 (V) of 12 December 1950 setting up an *ad hoc* Committee tasked to prepare a draft statute for an international criminal court to be used as a base for further discussion on the subject matter.[71] This Committee – known as the 1951 Committee on International Criminal Jurisdiction – was composed of representatives of seventeen Member States and operated throughout August 1951.[72]

The analysis of the 1951 Committee's work – and the work of its successor, the 1953 Committee on International Criminal Jurisdiction – is particularly relevant in the context of this book. Indeed, both Committees' debate on

65 *Convention on the Prevention and Punishment of the Crime of Genocide* (adopted 9 December 1948, entered into force 12 January 1951) 78 U.N.T.S. 277, Article VI.

66 UNGA Res 260(B)(III) (9 December 1948).

67 A/CN.4/13 and Corr. 1-3, paras 1-2.

68 A/CN.4/SR.43, para 43.

69 Yuen-Li Liang, 'Notes on Legal Questions Concerning the United Nations' (1951) 45 American Journal of International Law 509, 524-525.

70 The decision was strongly criticised by Bassiouni. See Bassiouni (n 34) 252.

71 UNGA Res 489 (V) (12 December 1950).

72 Ibid.

the scope of an international criminal court's jurisdiction *ratio personae* offers valuable insights on States' attitudes towards the feasibility of holding legal entities criminally liable at the international level. Even though the outcome of the Committees' work once again excluded corporations from the jurisdiction *ratione personae* of the proposed international criminal court, it is still worth observing how the Committees' discussion on the subject matter presents a deeper level of understanding of the difference between corporate liability and State liability. To a certain extent, the debate carried out within the 1951 and 1953 Committees can be considered the first mature analysis of the idea of holding private legal entities accountable at the international level.

2.4.1 The 1951 Committee on International Criminal Jurisdiction

The 1951 Committee on International Criminal Jurisdiction convened for the first time o 1 August, in Geneva.[73] As per Resolution 489 (V) of 12 December 1950, its mandate was to prepare 'one or more preliminary draft conventions and proposals relating to the establishment and the statute of an international criminal court'.[74] In pursuance of the task received, the Committee produced a 55-article draft statute for an international criminal court covering issues such as the appropriate procedures for the establishment of the proposed court, the law it will apply, its internal organisation and functioning and, most importantly, its jurisdiction.[75]

Discussion on the scope of the court's jurisdiction began on 3 August 1951.[76] For the better part of a week, the Committee examined under which conditions the proposed court would have been authorised to exercise its jurisdiction.[77] It was only on 13 August that the focus of the discussion shifted to the issue of the court's jurisdiction *ratione personae*.[78] The basis for the debate was provided by a *Memorandum on the Creation of an International Criminal Court* submitted by the Secretariat in early July 1951.[79] The memorandum touched upon some of the pivotal issues related to the scope of the court's jurisdiction and suggested some solutions to inform the Committee's discussion. With regard to the categories of subjects upon which the proposed court should be allowed to exercise its jurisdiction, the memorandum adopted a clear – and narrow – position. As stated in the document:

73 A/2136, 1.
74 UNGA Res 489 (V) (12 December 1950), 1.
75 A/2136, Annex I. See also Quincy Wright, 'Proposal for an International Criminal Court' (1952) 46 American Journal of International Law 60.
76 A/AC.48/SR.3, para 44 et ss.
77 A/AC.48/SR.3, A/AC.48/SR.4, A/AC.48/SR.5, A/AC.48/SR.6, A/AC.48/SR.7, A/AC.48/SR.8, A/AC.48/SR.9.
78 A/AC.48/SR.9.
79 A/AC.48/1.

> It is noteworthy that the general opinion is in favour of limiting the jurisdiction of the Court to the trial of natural persons only. [...] it could quite well be made optional for juristic persons to be arraigned before the court on the grounds of criminal responsibility.
>
> [However] in view of the difficulties in setting up the Court, *there is no point in increasing those difficulties by extending the Court's jurisdiction to a particularly controversial matter when there is no necessity to do so.*[80]

As emerged from the Memorandum, at the time of the discussion, the international criminal liability of corporate bodies was perceived as an issue too complex to be solved within a reasonable amount of time.[81] Hence, expanding the court's jurisdiction beyond natural persons was considered a hazard, a risk too high to be taken.

Notwithstanding the Secretariat's position, some of the Committee's members felt the need to consider adopting a broader approach to the subject matter. The representative from Australia, Wynes, was particularly sceptical towards the idea of excluding legal persons from the scope of the draft statute of the proposed international criminal court.[82] Even though he conceded that, at the time of the discussion, the criminal liability of legal entities was an unknown concept in many domestic legal systems, he prompted the Committee to take into consideration the possibility of including at least *private entities* within the scope of the court's jurisdiction.[83] As emerged from the summary record of the Committee's 9th meeting, Wynes pointed out that:

> [...] if, as might well be, confiscation of property was one of the penalties prescribed in the statute [of the proposed court], consideration might be given to the possibility of the imposition of such penalty on a *corporation*, the head of which, acting on behalf of that corporation, had committed a crime. [In deciding to exclude legal entities from the statute], the Secretariat has concentrated largely on the responsibility of States, but [Wynes] was thinking more of *private institutions.*[84]

Besides acknowledging the diversity between State liability and corporate liability, it suggested for the first time a specific model of attribution of international criminal liability to corporations. In particular, Wynes proposed to link

80 Ibid p. 25 (emphasis added).
81 A/CN.4/SR.54, para 82.
82 A/AC.48/SR.9, para 73.
83 Ibid.
84 Ibid (emphasis added).

the company's liability with that of its 'head' – i.e. the managing director – , making the former *dependent* on the latter.[85]

It is unclear whether Wynes' suggestion was grounded in a specific legal theory of corporate criminal liability. It may be possible that, in making his statement, the Australian representative had in mind the common law doctrine of 'identification' according to which the criminal liability of a company derives from that of the individual who carried out the criminal activity where the natural person is 'of a sufficient standing' that he or she is 'identified' with the entity.[86] Such a doctrine was first elaborated in the United Kingdom in the early 1940s and was then adopted – with some adjustments – by many other common law systems, including Australia.[87] Regardless of this, Wynes' proposal represents the first effort to open up a more mature debate on the criminal liability of 'private institutions'.

Unfortunately, this attempt did not find the favour of other members of the Committee. Soon after Wynes' intervention, the focus of the discussion shifted back to the liability of States closing the door to any consideration of his proposal on the international criminal liability of corporations.[88] Overshadowed by the much more pressing issue of State criminality, the liability of corporations was once again excluded from the scope of the draft statute for an international criminal court.[89] In its final Report, the 1951 Committee commented on its decision in the following way:

> With respect to other legal entities, it was pointed out that the penal responsibility of private corporations was not unknown in some national systems of penal law. Punishments, such as payment of fines or confiscation of property, might be inflicted upon legal entities found to be responsible for illegal acts. Other national legal systems, however, did not recognise such a penal responsibility on the part of legal entities, and it was therefore felt by most members of the Committee that *the introduction of such a responsibility in international law would be a matter of considerable controversy*.[90]

85 Ibid.

86 Celia Wells, *Corporations and Criminal Responsibility*, (2nd edn, OUP 2005) 93-99, Celia Wells, 'Corporations Culture, Risk and Criminal Liability' (1993), Criminal Law Review 551, 559, Richard Mays, 'Towards Corporate Fault as the Basis of Criminal Liability of Corporations' (1998) Mountbatten Journal of Legal Studies 31, 39.

87 Mays (n 85) 39.

88 A/AC.48/SR.9, paras 77 et ss.

89 A/2136, para 89.

90 Ibid para 88.

2.4.2 The 1953 Committee on International Criminal Jurisdiction

The 1951 Committee's decision to limit the proposed court's jurisdiction to 'natural person only'[91] did not foreclose further discussion on the question of the international criminal liability of corporations. Less than two years later, the issue was once again addressed by its successor, the 1953 Committee on International Criminal Jurisdiction. Established by Resolution 687 (VII) of 5 December 1952, the 1953 Committee was tasked to resume the work on a statute for an international criminal court using the 1951 Draft as a base for discussion.[92] During the Committee's sessions, held in New York in the summer of 1953, the issue of the liability of legal entities was addressed on two separate occasions: briefly, in connection with Article 1 (Purpose of the court) and, more in the detail, as part of the debate on the scope of Article 25 (Jurisdiction as to persons).[93] Both debates offer some relevant insights into the Committee's position on the question of the accountability of private companies for international crimes.

The discussion on Article 1 (Purpose of the court) began on 5 August 1953.[94] The text under examination read as follows:

> There is established an International Criminal Court to try persons accused of crimes under international law, as may be provided in the conventions or special agreements among States parties to the present Statute.[95]

Among the various proposals submitted to amend Article 1, two were concerned specifically with the use of the word 'persons' in its initial formulation. According to some members of the Committee, the term 'persons' used in the English text created some confusion as to the exact scope of the court's judicial power.[96] Indeed, broadly interpreted, the English word 'persons' could have indicated not only individuals but also legal entities such as corporations and States. Considering that, the British representative proposed to substitute 'persons' with 'individuals' so as to make the English text more in line with the French version, which used the term 'individu'.[97] Alternatively, the Israeli representative suggested adding 'natural' before the word 'persons' so as to avoid any misunderstanding.[98]

91 Ibid, Annex I, Article 1, Article 25.
92 UNGA Res 687 (VII) (5 December 1952), 3.
93 A/AC.65/SR.8 and A/AC.65/SR.11.
94 A/AC.65/SR.8.
95 A/2136, Annex I, Article 1.
96 A/AC.65/SR.8, pp. 7 to 14.
97 Ibid p. 7.
98 Ibid p. 13.

Both suggestions were briefly considered by the Committee and found the support of those members who were concerned that a lack of clarity in the English text of Article 1 would have affected the level of consistency of the Draft Statute.[99] Conversely, other members expressed some scepticism towards the British and Israeli proposals. The Argentinian and Dutch representatives, in particular, deemed it unnecessary to amend the wording of Article 1 considering that such a provision was only a general statement on the overall purpose of the court.[100] It was therefore correct to formulate it in broader terms.

A different – and more interesting – objection to the rewording of Article 1 was raised by Loomes, the Australian representative. In his intervention, he firmly stated that:

> [I]f the Israeli proposal was put to the vote, he would abstain from voting. The word 'persons' included companies and he asked that it should be mentioned in the summary record of the meeting that *he was in favour of that interpretation*.[101]

While other members of the Committee contested the Israeli (and British) proposal on the basis that Article 1 was to be considered as a statement of general principles, Loomes' opposition pertained to the concrete scope of the court's jurisdiction. In stating his support to the idea of extending the court's jurisdiction beyond individuals, Loomes brought the question of the international criminal liability of corporations back to the attention of the Committee, regardless of the fact that such a concept was previously excluded from the 1951 Draft Statute. It is also worth noting that Loomes' statement was clearly formulated so as to separate the liability of private companies from this of other public legal entities, such as the State. Only the former was considered adoptable at the international level.

Acknowledging the complexity of the issue raised by the Australian representative, the Committee felt that the discussion on the wording of Article 1 was not the appropriate context to address the question of the criminal liability of corporate entities.[102] Consequently, the debate was deferred until the Committee re-examined Article 25 (Jurisdiction as to persons).[103]

The time for the discussion on the court's jurisdiction *ratione personae* came two days later, on 7 August. In its original formulation, Article 25 stated

99 See position of the United States representative. Ibid p. 14.
100 Ibid p. 13.
101 Ibid p. 14 (emphasis added).
102 Ibid.
103 Ibid.

that '[t]he Court shall be competent to judge natural persons only, including persons who have acted as Head of State or agent of government'.[104]

In opening the debate on the scope of the provision, Loomes once again advanced the idea of expanding the proposed court's jurisdiction to include 'private corporations' alongside individuals.[105] Immediate was the opposition of the representative for the Philippines, Mendez, who firmly stated that:

> [p]rivate corporations fell strictly within the jurisdiction of domestic courts, which conferred certain privileges upon them. Moreover, should a private corporation engage in criminal activities, the individual responsibility of its officers could easily be determined.[106]

Mendez's refusal to recognise an international criminal liability of corporations stemmed from two different sets of considerations. On one side, he viewed private companies as 'creatures of the State' thus relegating them to the domestic legal sphere. Regulation on the nature and scope of their legal personality, and consequently of their liability, was solely a State's prerogative. On the other hand, Mendez considered corporate criminal liability as an unnecessary addition to the individual criminal liability of those individuals acting on behalf of the corporation. In the Philippines' representative's opinion, individual criminal liability was enough to cover all the possible forms of corporate involvement in criminal activities. Both sets of arguments had their roots in a general scepticism towards the idea of corporate criminal liability probably due to the unfamiliarity of such a legal concept. Indeed, at the time of the discussion, the Philippines' legal system did not recognise the possibility of holding private companies as subjects of criminal law.[107]

Contrary to the Australian proposal was also Roling, the Dutch representative. His opposition, however, focused more on the 'international' side of the question. Indeed, even though he recognised that 'private corporations were subject to criminal law' at the domestic level, he observed that 'the experience of the Nuremberg and Tokyo trials led him to believe that it was *premature* to extend the jurisdiction of the international criminal court to private corporations'.[108] This opinion was also shared by the Argentinian and French representatives.[109]

In replying to the aforementioned objections, Loomes firstly recalled how 'the criminal responsibility of private corporations was not excluded either by

104 A/2136, Annex I, Article 25.
105 A/AC.65/SR.11, p. 8.
106 Ibid p. 8.
107 Alex Manolito C Labador, 'Corporate Crime and the Criminal Liability of Corporate Entities in the Philippines' (2008) UNAFEI Resource Material Series No. 76, 73.
108 A/AC.65/SR.11, p. 9 (emphasis added).
109 Ibid pp. 7 and 9.

doctrine and jurisprudence'.[110] According to the Australian representative, the liability of corporations was an autonomous legal concept – distinct from the criminal liability of individuals – which was firmly embedded in a number of common law legal systems. As a matter of principle, therefore, nothing was preventing the Committee from adopting such a concept at the international level.

As for the specific concern raised by the Dutch representative, Loomes considered it 'not convincing'.[111] On this regard, he observed that the mere fact that formal recognition of the international criminal liability of corporations might have been considered *at that time* 'premature' – but not legally unsound – was not a reason enough to oppose the inclusion of such a concept within the statute of the proposed court. Indeed, he stated that:

> The statute of the court would, in fact, remain in force for many years and international criminal law would be developed during that period. A provision relating to the criminal responsibility of private corporations should be included in the statute now.[112]

The consideration made by the Australian representative was particularly forward-looking. It rested on the idea that international criminal law was still in its infancy and thus expected to further develop over the years. In light of that, Loomes considered it fundamental to create an international criminal court able to face both present and future challenges, including those deriving from the involvement of private legal entities in international crimes.

Regretably, the Australian proposal did not meet the favour of the Committee. Put to vote, it was ultimately rejected 11 votes to 1, with 4 abstentions.[113] The failure of Loomes' proposal marked the end of the debate on the opportunity to include private companies within the scope of the statute of the proposed international criminal court. It would have taken more than 40 years for the question to arise again in the context of the negotiation of a statute for an international criminal court.

This notwithstanding, the value of the 1951 and 1953 Committees' discussion on the issue cannot be ignored. For the first time, the liability of business entities was discussed separately from the responsibility of States and proposals were put forward on how such a concept should have been defined within the framework of a statute for an international court. The overall quality of the debate, the variety of the arguments raised in favour and against corporate criminal liability, demonstrates a more mature understanding of the complexity of the issue under consideration. Understood in these terms, the work of

110 Ibid p. 10.
111 Ibid.
112 Ibid.
113 Ibid.

the 1953 Committee represents a fundamental step in the progression of the discussion on the feasibility of holding corporations criminally accountable at the international level.

2.5 Conclusion

This chapter explored to what extent the idea of including corporate liability within the scope of international criminal law was discussed in the aftermath of the Nuremberg trials. The analysis started with an evaluation of the contribution made by the Genocide Convention to the debate on the international criminal liability of corporations. The chapter considered the argument according to which the liability of corporations for genocide, although not expressly provided for in the Convention, could nonetheless be inferred from the wording of Article IV. While this argument is interesting, the analysis of the preparatory work of the Convention seems to cast doubts on the possibility of using the Convention as evidence of the early recognition of corporate criminal liability for international crimes. Indeed, in the year that led to the adoption of the Convention, the question of the criminal liability of legal entities was addressed essentially from the perspective of the liability of States, while other legal entities were left outside the scope of the debate.

The chapter showed that this inability to distinguish between private entities, on the one side, and the State, on the other, remained a glaring feature of the debate on the international criminal liability of corporate entities in the years following the Nuremberg trials. Evidence of this is provided by the analysis of the ILC's work on the Draft Code of Offences against the Peace and Security of Mankind. Even though an express reference to the liability of corporations was made by Vespasian V. Pella, the Commission struggled with the idea of extending the Draft Code's scope *ratione personae* beyond natural persons. This reticence seems to rest on two main concerns: on the one side, a difficulty to conceive corporate liability as separate from State liability; on the other, the novelty of the concept of corporate criminal liability. These concerns ultimately hindered the debate on the international criminal liability of corporations and prevented the Commission from fully engaging with the topic.

An effort to differentiate between corporate liability and State liability was finally made in the context of the 1951 and 1953 Committees on International Criminal Jurisdiction, discussed in the final part of the chapter. The work of the two Committees signalled an evolution in the debate on the international criminal liability of corporations. No longer overshadowed by the question of State liability, the liability of corporations became the centre of a lively debate where several arguments were put forward to support or contest its relevance in the context of a statute of an international criminal court. Even though proposals on corporate liability were ultimately set aside by the Committees, the work of the 1951 and 1953 Committees offered a fundamental contribution to the discussion on the feasibility of holding corporations accountable under international criminal law.

Overall, the analysis of the post-Nuremberg efforts to recognise corporate criminal liability is a recollection of failed attempts. From the late 1940s to the early 1950s, the question of the criminal liability of legal persons was raised and dismissed, over and over again. This notwithstanding, each one of these (failed) attempts demonstrated that the issue of corporate criminal liability has constantly been a feature of the debate on the scope of international criminal law. This chapter has thus built a bridge between the Nuremberg experience and the Rome Conference – so far, the only two moments in time considered relevant for the discussion on the liability of corporations – and helped paint a more accurate picture of the historical development of the debate on the international criminal liability of private companies.

References

Primary Sources

1951 Committee on International Criminal Jurisdiction, 1st session: summary record of the 3rd meeting held at the Palais des Nations, Geneva, on Friday, 3 August 1951, A/AC.48/SR.3

1951 Committee on International Criminal Jurisdiction, 1st session: summary record of the 4th meeting held at the Palais des Nations, Geneva, on Monday, 6 August 1951, A/AC.48/SR.4

1951 Committee on International Criminal Jurisdiction, 1st session: summary record of the 5th meeting held at the Palais des Nations, Geneva, on Tuesday, 7 August 1951, A/AC.48/SR.5

1951 Committee on International Criminal Jurisdiction, 1st session: summary record of the 6th meeting held at the Palais des Nations, Geneva, on Wednesday, 8 August 1951, A/AC.48/SR.6

1951 Committee on International Criminal Jurisdiction, 1st session: summary record of the 7th meeting held at the Palais des Nations, Geneva, on Thursday, 9 August 1951, A/AC.48/SR.7

1951 Committee on International Criminal Jurisdiction, 1st session: summary record of the 8th meeting held at the Palais des Nations, Geneva, on Friday, 10 August 1951, A/AC.48/SR.8

1951 Committee on International Criminal Jurisdiction, 1st session: summary record of the 9th meeting held at the Palais des Nations, Geneva, on Monday, 13 August 1951, A/AC.48/SR.9

1951 Committee on International Criminal Jurisdiction, Creation of an International Criminal Court, Report, A/AC.48/1, 2 July 1951

1953 Committee on International Criminal Jurisdiction: summary record of the 11th meeting held at Headquarters, New York, on Friday, 7 August 1953, A/AC.65/SR.11

1953 Committee on International Criminal Jurisdiction: summary record of the 8th meeting held at Headquarters, New York, on Wednesday, 5 August 1953, A/AC.65/SR.8 A/C.6/215/Rev.1

Ad Hoc Committee on Genocide, Report of the Committee and draft Convention drawn up by the Committee, (24 May 1948), E/ 794, Article V.

Convention on the Prevention and Punishment of the Crime of Genocide (adopted 9 December 1948, entered into force 12 January 1951) 78 U.N.T.S. 277

Genocide: draft Convention (E/794) and report of the Economic and Social Council: amendments to the draft Convention / Belgium, A/C.6/217, 5 October 1948

Genocide: draft Convention (E/794) and report of the Economic and Social Council: amendments to the draft Convention / France, A/C.6/224, 8 October 1948

Genocide: draft Convention and report of the Economic and Social Council: further amendments to the draft Convention (E/794) / United Kingdom, A/C.6/236, 16 October 1948

Genocide: draft Convention and report of the Economic and Social Council: amendment to Article 5 of the draft Convention on Genocide (E/794) / Syria, A/C.6/246, 26 October 1948

Genocide: draft Convention and report of the Economic and Social Council: amendment to Article 5 of the draft Convention (E/794) / Sweden, A/C.6/247, 27 October 1948A/C.6/256

International Law Commission, Draft Code of Crimes against the Peace and Security of Mankind, Report by J. Spiropoulos, Special Rapporteur, A/CN.4/25, 26 April 1950

International Law Commission, First report on the Draft Code of Offences against the Peace and Security of Mankind / by Doudou Thiam, Special Rapporteur, A/CN.4/364, 18 March 1983

International Law Commission, Memorandum Concerning a Draft Code of Offences Against the Peace and Security of Mankind, presented by the Secretariat, A/CN.4/39, 254 November 1950

International Law Commission, Second Report on Crimes Against Humanity by Sean D. Murphy, Special Rapporteur (21 January 2016) A/CN.4/690

International Law Commission, Summary record of the 43rd meeting, held on Friday, 9 June 1950, A/CN.4/SR.43

International Law Commission, Summary record of the 54th meeting, held on Monday, 26 June 1950, A/CN.4/SR.54

Report of the Committee on International Criminal Jurisdiction on its session held from 1 to 31 August 1951, A/2136, 16 July 1952

Report of the International Law Commission, 1st session, 12 April–9 June 1949, A/CN.4/13, 12 April 1949

Report of the International Law Commission, 2nd session, 5 June-29 July 1950, A/CN.4/34, July 1950

Report of the International Law Commission, 35th session, 3 May-22 July 1983, A/38/10, 3 August 1983

UN Secretary-General, 'Draft Convention on the Crime of Genocide' (26 June 1947) E/447

UNGA Res 177 (II), Formulation of the principles recognized in the Charter of the Nurnberg Tribunal and in the judgement of the Tribunal, A/RES/177(II), 21 November 1947

UNGA Res 260(B)(III), Study by the International Law Commission of the question of an international criminal jurisdiction, A/RES/260(III)[B], 9 December 1948

UNGA Res 489 (V), International criminal jurisdiction, A/RES/489(V), 12 December 1950

UNGA Res 687 (VII), International criminal jurisdiction, A/RES/687(VII), 5 December 1952

UNGA Res 95 (I) Affirmation of the Principles of International Law recognized by the Charter of the Nurnberg Tribunal, A/RES/95(I), 11 December 1946

UNGA, 6th Committee, Summary record of the 92nd meeting, held on Friday, 5 November 1948, A/C.6/SR.92

UNGA, 6th Committee, Summary record of the 93rd meeting, held on Saturday, 6 November 1948, A/C.6/SR.93

UNGA, 6th Committee, Summary record of the 95th meeting, held on Monday, 8 November 1948, A/C.6/SR.95

Vienna Convention on the Law of Treaties (adopted 1969, entered into force 1980) 1155 UNTS 331

Secondary Sources

Books

Bernaz N, *Business and Human Rights: History, Law and Policy – Bridging the Accountability Gap* (Routledge 2017)

Bilsky L Y, *The Holocaust, Corporations, and the Law: Unfinished Business (Law, Meaning, and Violence)* (The University of Michigan Press 2017)

Cassese A, Gaeta P, and Jones J R W D (eds), *The Rome Statute of the International Criminal Court: A Commentary* (OUP 2002)

Gaeta P (ed), *The UN Genocide Convention.* A Commentary (OUP 2009)

Kelly M J, *Prosecuting Corporations for Genocide* (OUP 2016)

Kyriakakis J, *Corporations, Accountability and International Criminal Law. Industry and Atrocity* (Edward Elgar 2021)

Quigley J, *The Genocide Convention. An International Law Analysis* (Routledge 2016)

Schabas W A, *Genocide in International Law: The Crime of Crimes* (2nd edn, Cambridge University Press 2009)

Schabas W A, *The International Criminal Court: A Commentary on the Rome Statute* (2nd edn, OUP 2016)

Stoitchkova D, *Towards Corporate Liability in International Criminal Law* (Intersentia 2010)

Tams C J, Berster L, and Schiffbauer B, *Convention on the Prevention and Punishment of the Crime of Genocide: A Commentary* (C.H. Beck Hart Nomos 2014)

Wells C, *Corporations and Criminal Responsibility* (2nd edn, OUP 2005)

Contribution in Edited Books

Clapham A, 'The Question of Jurisdiction under International Criminal Law over Legal Persons: Lessons from the Rome Conference on an International Criminal Court' in Menno T. Kamminga and Saman Zia-Zarifi (eds), *Liability of Multinational Corporations under International Law* (Kluwer Law International 2000)

Journal Articles

Bassiouni M C, 'The History of the Draft Code of Crimes against the Peace and Security of Mankind' (1993) 27 Israel Law Review 247

Borgwardt E, 'Bernath Lecture: Commerce and Complicity: Corporate Responsibility for Human Rights Abuses as a Legacy of Nuremberg' (2010) 34 Diplomatic History 627

Ferencz B B, 'Current Developments. The Draft Code of Offences Against the Peace and Security of Mankind' (1981) 75(3) American Journal of International Law 674

Gilbert J, 'Perspectives on Cultural Genocide. From Criminal Law to Cultural Diversity' in Margaret M. deGuzman and Diane Marie Amann (eds), *Arcs of Global Justice: Essays in Honour of William A. Schabas* (OUP 2018)

Kelly M J, 'Never Again: German Chemical Corporation Complicity in the Kurdish Genocide' (2013) 31 Berkeley Journal of International Law 348

Koh H H, 'Separating Myth from Reality about Corporate Responsibility Litigation' (2004) 7 Journal of International Economic Law 263

Kyriakakis J, 'Corporate Criminal Liability and the ICC Statute: The Comparative Law Challenge' (2009) 56(3) Netherlands International Law Review 333

Labador A M C, 'Corporate Crime and the Criminal Liability of Corporate Entities in the Philippines' (2008) UNAFEI Resource Material Series No. 76

Liang Y, 'Notes on Legal Questions Concerning the United Nations' (1951) 45 American Journal of International Law 509

Mays R, 'Towards Corporate Fault as the Basis of Criminal Liability of Corporations' (1998) 2(2) Mountbatten Journal of Legal Studies 31

Rayfuse R, 'The Draft Code of Crimes Against the Peace and Security of Mankind: Eating Disorders at the International Law Commission' (1997) 8(1) Criminal Law Forum 43

Wells C, 'Corporations Culture, Risk and Criminal Liability' (1993) Criminal Law Review 551

Wright Q, 'Proposal for an International Criminal Court' (1952) 46 American Journal of International Law 60

Online sources

Merriam-Webster Online Dictionary, Person, https://www.merriam-webster.com/dictionary/person Accessed 3 March 2023

Merriam-Webster Online Dictionary, Individual, https://www.merriam-webster.com/dictionary/individual Accessed 3 March 2023

3 The Adoption of the Rome Statute

Corporate Criminal Liability's Swan Song?

3.1 Introduction

Chapter 2 investigated to what extent corporate liability was discussed in the aftermath of the Nuremberg experience. The chapter focused on three major initiatives carried out under the aegis of the United Nations, specifically the adoption of the Genocide Convention, the ILC's work on the Draft Code of Offences Against the Peace and Security of Mankind, and the 1951 and 1953 Committees on International Criminal Jurisdiction. In the scholarship on the international criminal liability of corporations, these initiatives are often overlooked. However, this book argues that a consideration of these early initiatives is necessary to establish a continuity between Nuremberg and the Rome Conference and to provide a more accurate narrative on the development of the debate on the liability of corporations under international criminal law. Chapter 2 showed how concerns relating to the liability of the State cast a shadow on the discussion on whether corporations could be held liable for international crimes. While this line of arguments had already started to lose cogency in the early 1950s, it nonetheless affected the possibility of promoting a genuine debate on corporate liability in the context of the negotiation of the Genocide Convention and the ILC's work on the Draft Code of Offences Against the Peace and Security of Mankind. A more mature understanding of the differences between State liability and corporate liability characterised the work of the 1951 and 1953 Committees on International Criminal Jurisdiction. As the arguments put forward to support or contest corporate liability for international crimes became more refined, discussions started on possible models of attribution of criminal liability to corporate entities and on the purpose that such a form of liability may serve.

This chapter further develops the historical analysis of the debate on corporate liability by focusing on the preparatory works that led to the adoption of the Statute of the International Criminal Court (ICC). By the mid-1950s, after almost a decade of work to promote the concept of international justice, all attempts to establish an international criminal court reached a dead end. Concerns over the precariousness of the international political order ended up diverting the attention of the international community away from the project

DOI: 10.4324/9781003390534-4

of a permanent criminal jurisdiction, stunting the development of international criminal law for almost 30 years.[1] It was only in the 1980s that the situation started to change. In 1982, the International Law Commission tentatively resumed its work on the Draft Code of Crimes against the Peace and Security of Mankind with the support of the UN General Assembly (UNGA).[2] Six years later, on 9 November 1989, the fall of the Berlin Wall signalled the end of the Cold War and inaugurated a new phase in the development of international criminal law in some respect similar to the one that occurred in the aftermath of Nuremberg.[3]

It was the sudden collapse of previously multi-ethnic societies that acted as a major catalyst in accelerating the debate on the opportunity to establish a permanent international criminal court. The conflicts in the former Yugoslavia and, later on, in Rwanda 'rekindle the sense of outrage felt at the closing stage of the Second World War', forcing the international community to consider new solutions to fight impunity for international crimes.[4] The subsequent establishment of the two *ad hoc* tribunals accelerated the process which led to the establishment of the first (and only) permanent international criminal court in July 1998.

By retracing the developments that occurred from the 1980s to July 1998, this chapter considers the extent to which the question of the liability of corporate entities was integrated into the discussion on the scope and limitation of an international criminal jurisdiction. This chapter concludes the historical analysis of the debate on an international criminal liability of corporations by covering the final phase that led to its (apparent) dismissal.

3.2 Resuming the Drafting of the Statute of the ICC: The ILC's Work (1982-1994)

After almost 30 years of a hiatus, the question of the feasibility of establishing a permanent international criminal court came back to the attention of the international community in the 1980s. The context for the discussion was once again provided by the ILC's work on the Draft Code of Crimes against the Peace and Security of Mankind, which resumed in 1982.[5]

Already in 1983, the Commission raised the question of whether its mandate on the Draft Code should have been extended to include 'the preparation

1 Philippe Kirsch and John T Holmes, 'The Birth of the International Criminal Court: The 1998 Rome Conference' (1998) 36 Canadian Yearbook of International Law 3, 4.

2 UNGA Res 36/106 (10 December 1981).

3 William A Schabas, *The International Criminal Court: A Commentary on the Rome Statute*, (2nd edn, OUP 2016) 10 et ss.; Antonio Cassese, *Cassese's International Criminal Law*, (3rd edn, OUP 2013) 258; M Cherif Bassiouni, *The Statute of the International Criminal Court: A Documentary History* (M Cherif Bassiouni ed 1998), 13.

4 Schabas (n 1) 17; Cassese (n 1), 259.; Bassiouni (n 1) 19.

5 UNGA Res 36/106 (10 December 1981).

of the statute of a competent international criminal jurisdiction for individuals', seeking the opinion of the General Assembly on the matter.[6] Acknowledging the ILC's request, the General Assembly asked the Secretary-General 'to seek the views of Member States and intergovernmental organizations' on the question of an international criminal jurisdiction and to submit them to the Assembly at its 39th session 'with a view to adopting, at the appropriate time, the necessary decision thereon'.[7]

However, it was not until the late 1980s that the question of an international criminal jurisdiction became, once again, a central topic of discussion within the ILC. In 1987, a reference to the possibility of establishing an international criminal court with jurisdiction over the crimes covered in the Draft Code was included by the Special Rapporteur, Doudou Thiam, in his Fifth Report.[8] The mention was incorporated into draft Article 4 on the principle of *aut dedere aut punier*. According to draft paragraph 2, the State obligation to 'try or extradite' did not 'prejudge the establishment of an international criminal jurisdiction' with the authority to prosecute individuals accused of perpetrating a crime included in the draft code.[9]

In 1988, the provision of draft Article 4 was discussed within the ILC Drafting Committee which adopted it in the following formulation:

1. Any State in whose territory an individual alleged to have committed a crime against the peace and security of mankind is present shall try or extradite him.
2. If extradition is requested by several States, special consideration shall be given to the request of the State in whose territory the crime was committed.
3. The provisions of paragraphs 1 and 2 of this article shall not prejudge the establishment and the jurisdiction of an international criminal court.[10]

The Commentary to draft Article 4 stated that, even though the initial approach was to consider national courts as the appropriate *fora* for the prosecution of those crimes, the Commission deemed it advisable not to rule out other available options – including the creation of an international criminal court.[11]

The discussion on an international criminal jurisdiction was further propelled by the adoption, in December 1989, of UNGA Resolution 44/39 on the 'international criminal responsibility of individuals and entities engaged in illicit trafficking in narcotic drugs across national frontiers and other transnational criminal activities: establishment of an international criminal court

6 A/38/10, para 69.
7 UNGA Res 38/132 (19 December 1983), para 2.
8 A/CN.4/404, p. 3.
9 Ibid.
10 A/CN.4/L.422, p. 272 at par. 36; A/43/10, p. 67.
11 A/43/10, pp. 67-68.

with jurisdiction over such crimes'.[12] Sponsored by Trinidad and Tobago, Resolution 44/39 explicitly requested the ILC:

> to address the question of establishing an international criminal court or other international criminal trial mechanism with jurisdiction over persons alleged to have committed crimes which may be covered under such a code, including persons engaged in illicit trafficking in narcotic drugs across national frontiers, and to devote particular attention to that question in its report on that session.[13]

In light of these developments, in 1990 the Special Rapporteur presented to the Commission a draft Statute of an International Criminal Court with the aim of offering 'some choices among the various possible solutions and to elicit responses' on key aspects of the functioning of an international criminal jurisdiction.[14]

The Special Rapporteur's draft Statute elicited an extensive debate within the Commission. Opinions expressed covered a wide range of issues, such as the procedure for appointing judges, submissions of cases, penalties, and financial provisions.[15] It is already at this early stage that the question of whether the proposed Court should be able to assert its jurisdiction over legal entities arose to the attention of the members of the Commission.

In a number of meetings held between 9–16 May 1990, the issue of the international criminal liability of corporations was addressed by some members of the Commission who questioned the restrictive approach adopted by the Special Rapporteur.[16] Interestingly, one of the first Commissioners to advocate for a broader approach to the question of the Court's jurisdiction was Bernhard Graefrath from the (then) German Democratic Republic, a country historically reluctant to recognise legal entities as subjects of criminal law. In his statement, he observed that:

> While the Special Rapporteur was right to say that the competence of the court should be limited to trying individuals, the Commission should none the less consider whether it might not also be necessary to establish competence to try legal persons or entities other than States, at least in the case of certain crimes.[17]

12 UNGA Res 44/39 (4 December 1989).

13 Ibid para 1.

14 A/CN.4/430 and Add.1 para 77 et ss.

15 A/45/10, para 29.

16 See A/CN.4/SR.2154, A/CN.4/SR.2155, A/CN.4/SR.2156, A/CN.4/SR.2157, and A/CN.4/SR.2158.

17 A/CN.4/SR.2154, para 39.

Professor of international law at the Humboldt University in Berlin from 1963 to 1982, Graefrath clearly differentiated between the State and other legal persons/entities, considering only the latter as subjectable to international criminal prosecution.[18] Unfortunately, it is impossible to determine the basis of which legal theory he claimed the responsibility of legal entities such as corporations could have been constructed. The summary records of the meeting do not provide any clarification on the matter. Similarly, Graefrath's scholarship does not offer a clear insight into his view on corporate criminal liability, as it focuses almost entirely on the controversy over the concept of State responsibility for international wrongdoing.[19]

Graefrath's opinion was echoed by Husain M. Al-Baharna, who expressed some reservations about the use of the term 'natural persons' in the draft statute 'since there was some cogency in the argument that the jurisdiction of the court could properly be extended to "legal entities", some of which should not be exempt from culpability in the case of certain crimes'.[20] These views were shared also by other members such as Motoo Ogiso[21] and Ahmed Mahiou.[22]

More aligned with the position of the Special Rapporteur was the opinion of Jiuyong Shi who praised the Rapporteur's Report by observing that:

> With regard to the jurisdiction of the court, the Special Rapporteur proposed a remarkably concise and precise text [...] which dealt with both jurisdiction *ratione personae* and jurisdiction *ratione materiae*. According to that text, only natural persons would be subject to the jurisdiction of the court. Having started from the assumption that the code could deal only with the criminal responsibility of individuals, the Commission could hardly extend the jurisdiction of the court to crimes committed by public or private entities—as some members of the Commission had suggested during the debate—before knowing the position of Governments on the question of the criminal responsibility of the State.[23]

18 Bernhard Graefrath, 'International Crimes — A Specific Regime of International Responsibility of States and its Legal Consequences' in Joseph H H Weiler et. al. (eds), *International Crimes of States: A Critical Analysis of the ILC's draft Article 19 on State Responsibility* (Walter de Gruyter 1988) 162.

19 Ibid. See also Bernhard Graefrath, 'Völkerrechtliche Konsequenzen aus der Anwendung der Aggressionsdefinition durch den UN-Sicherheitsrat', Neue Justize 30 (1976), 732; Bernhard Graefrath, Edith Oeser, Peter Alfons Steiniger, *Völkerrechtliche Verantwortlichkeit der Staaten* (Berlin, Staatsverlag der Deutschen Demokratischen Republik, 1977).

20 A/CN.4/SR.2157, para 68.

21 A/CN.4/SR.2155, para 10.

22 A/CN.4/SR.2154, para 61.

23 A/CN.4/SR.2157, para 50.

In closing the discussion, the Special Rapporteur, Thiam, once again maintained his position on the Court's jurisdiction *ratione personae*, reiterating the need to adopt a more cautious approach while, at the same time, conceding that any final decision on 'the criminal responsibility of States or of legal entities in general, to which some members [of the Commission] attached great importance, could be taken up at a later stage'.[24]

For the overall quality of the views expressed, this first discussion on the liability of legal persons quite resembled the one carried out almost 40 years earlier in the aftermath of the Nuremberg trials. None of the opinions shared by the members of the Commission fully considered the legal implications of holding corporations criminally accountable for international crimes nor proposed a feasible model to establish such liability. Also, some of the comments still seem to blur the line between the responsibility of the State, on one side, and that of private entities, on the other.[25] However, this is not entirely surprising considering the early stage of the discussion. It would have taken six more years for the debate to reach a new level of maturity.

In the following days, the question of the international criminal liability of legal entities was further discussed within the Working Group (WG) set up by the Commission on 16 May 1990.[26] Evidence of the discussion is provided in the final Report produced by the Group.[27] Unfortunately, it is unclear to what extent the issue was considered as no record of the WG's sessions is currently available. Similarly, the liability of legal entities was also addressed during the analysis of the *Report of the International Law Commission on the work of its 42nd session* conducted by the UN General Assembly's Sixth Committee.[28] During the debate, several members expressed their support or scepticism towards the proposal to include legal persons in the jurisdiction of an international criminal court.[29] Once again, the level of the discussion remained mostly superficial, but it still indicated a willingness among the Committee's members to further consider the status of legal entities under international criminal law.

Despite this initial interest, the question of the international liability of legal entities was quickly set aside. In its ninth report on the Draft Code, submitted the following year, the Special Rapporteur failed to include any reference to legal persons in its overview of the issue of the Court's jurisdiction *ratione*

24 A/CN.4/SR.2158, para 62.
25 See comment made by Jiuyong Shi, A/CN.4/SR.2157, para 50.
26 A/45/10, para 7.
27 A/CN.4/L.454 [and Corr.1], para 129.
28 The discussion over the relevant part of the ILC Report (Chapter III) started during the Committee's 23rd meeting and lasted until the 39th meeting.
29 Opinions favourable to the inclusion of legal entities were expressed by representatives of Jamaica (A/C.6/45/SR.31, para 87), Guinea (A/C.6/45/SR.33, para 22), Trinidad and Tobago (A/C.6/45/SR.33, para 26), Algeria (A/C.6/45/SR.34, para 65), Libya (A/C.6/45/SR.37, para 61), and Guatemala (A/C.6/45/SR.36, para 59). A more sceptical view was shared by a representative of China (A/C.6/45/SR.34, para 11).

personae, referring exclusively to individuals.[30] The Rapporteur's 'prudent' approach was swiftly endorsed by the ILC which limited its consideration of the Court's personal jurisdiction to 'private persons', an expression that, even though quite misleading, was understood by the Commission as referring exclusively to individuals.[31]

In the following years, the ILC continued to work on the statute of an international criminal court, producing the first comprehensive draft in 1993, which was then revised in 1994.[32] The 1994 Draft Statute was positively received by the UN General Assembly which welcomed the Commission's recommendation to 'convene an international conference of plenipotentiaries to study the draft statute and to conclude a convention on the establishment of an international criminal court'.[33] This officially concluded the Commission's work on the draft statute of an international criminal court. After years of joint evaluation, the question of an international criminal jurisdiction was separated from the work on the Draft Code of Crimes against the Peace and Security of Mankind and started its four-year journey towards the Rome Diplomatic Conference for an International Criminal Court.

3.3 The Establishment of the Ad Hoc Tribunals for the Former Yugoslavia and Rwanda

Before proceeding with the analysis of the work of the 1995 *ad hoc* Committee on the Establishment of an International Criminal Court – and of its successor, the 1996 Preparatory Committee – it is important to consider another major development which occurred in the early 1990s: the establishment of the *ad hoc* International Criminal Tribunal for the former Yugoslavia (ICTY) in 1993. Followed one year later by a second *ad hoc* tribunal – the International Criminal Tribunal for Rwanda (ICTR) – the ICTY represents the first example of a functioning international criminal jurisdiction of the post-Nuremberg era. Its creation played a fundamental role in the acceleration of the process that led to the adoption of the Rome Statute five years later.[34]

The conflict in the former Yugoslavia began in 1991 when internal tensions in the six republics forming the then Socialist Federal Republic of Yugoslavia irremediably compromised the political stability of the country. Over the first 18 months, the hostilities spread from Slovenia and Croatia to Bosnia, which became the main focus of the conflict.[35] Concerned by the level of brutality

30 A/CN.4/435 & Corr.1 and Add.1 & Corr.1, para 38, p. 41.

31 This emerges from the analysis of the ILC's Final *Reports* produced from 1992 to 1994. See A/47/10; A/48/10; A/49/10.

32 For a detailed overview of the legislative history of the ICC see Bassiouni (n 1) 19.

33 UNGA Res 49/51 (17 February 1995), para 2 and UNGA Res 49/53 (17 February 1995).

34 Schabas (n 1) 17; Cassese (n 1) 259; Bassiouni (n 1) 19.

35 Daphna Shraga and Ralph Zacklin, 'The International Criminal Tribunal for the Former Yugoslavia' (1994) 5 European Journal of International Law 360, 360.

which characterised the conflict, the United Nations took action to ensure the prosecution of those responsible for international crimes in the Balkans. On 22 February 1993, the Security Council adopted Resolution 808 in which it was decided that 'an international tribunal shall be established for the prosecution of persons responsible for serious violations of international humanitarian law committed in the territory of the former Yugoslavia since 1991'.[36] Contextually, the Security Council mandated the Secretary-General 'to submit ... a report on all aspects of this matter, including specific proposals and where appropriate options for the effective and expeditious implementation of the decision [to establish an international tribunal]'.[37]

The Secretary-General presented his Report pursuant to paragraph 2 of Security Council Resolution 808 (1993) on 3 May 1993.[38] The Report incorporated the suggestions put forward by numerous Member States and it was heavily influenced by the documentation produced by the United Nations and by other bodies involved in the drafting of a statute for an international criminal court, including the two Committees on International Criminal Jurisdiction and the International Law Commission.[39] It touched upon a number of pivotal issues related to the creation and functioning of an international criminal tribunal, first and foremost, the legal basis upon which such a jurisdiction should have been established.[40] Questions related to the Tribunal's jurisdiction *ratione materiae*, *temporis*, *loci*, and *personae* were also addressed by the Secretary-General.[41] With regard to the Tribunal's personal jurisdiction, the Report made it immediately clear that a narrow interpretation of the term 'persons' was to be preferred in the context of the statute of the *ad hoc* Tribunal. In particular, it stated that:

> 50. By paragraph 1 of resolution 808 (1993), the Security Council decided that the International Tribunal shall be established for the prosecution of persons responsible for serious violations of international humanitarian law committed in the territory of the former Yugoslavia since 1991. In the light of the complex of resolutions leading up to resolution 808 (1993) (see paras. 5–7 above), the ordinary meaning of the term 'persons responsible for serious violations of international humanitarian law' would be natural persons *to the exclusion of juridical persons.*[42]

Paragraph 51 then also addressed the question of whether the *ad hoc* tribunal should have followed Nuremberg's approach to the concept of criminal

36 UNSC Res 808 (22 February 1993), para 1.
37 Ibid para 2.
38 S/25704 of 3 May 1993.
39 Ibid paras 13-17.
40 Ibid para 6-8.
41 Ibid paras 31-63.
42 Ibid para 50 (emphasis added).

organisation as an instrument to trigger the Tribunal's jurisdiction over its members. On this regard, the *Report* stated that:

> 51. The question arises, however, whether a juridical person, such as an association or organisation, may be considered criminal as such and thus its members, for the reason alone, be made subject to the jurisdiction of the International Tribunal. The Secretary-General believes that this concept should not be retained in regard to the International Tribunal. The criminal acts set out in this statute are carried out by natural persons; such persons would be subject to the jurisdiction of the International Tribunal irrespective of membership in groups.[43]

This interpretation reflected the position of most of the Member States involved in the consultation phase which led to the draft of the ICTY Statute. Indeed, the analysis of the documentation submitted by Member States pursuant to Resolution 808 (1993) reveals that great emphasis was put on the concept of individual criminal responsibility. Letters submitted, *inter alia*, by the Russian Federation, the United States, and representatives of the Organisation of the Islamic Conference (IOC) systematically referred to the term 'individuals' when discussing the scope of the Tribunal's jurisdiction.[44] Not even once the term 'legal person' was mentioned in those documents – either with reference to the State or to other private entities.

The only instance in which the question of the liability of entities was addressed – albeit briefly – was in a letter submitted by the Permanent Mission of Canada to the Secretary-General on 1 April 1993.[45] The letter enclosed the *Report of the International Meeting of Experts on the Establishment of an International Criminal Tribunal.* Hosted by the International Centre for Criminal Law Reform and Criminal Justice Policy, the meeting was held in Vancouver in late March 1993 and brought together experts from 28 countries to discuss 'the short-term issue of the creation of an *ad hoc* tribunal ... and the longer term aim of the establishment of a permanent court'.[46] With regard to the jurisdiction *ratione personae* of both the *ad hoc* tribunal and a permanent court, the Report observed that:

> There appeared to be consensus that the jurisdiction of the ad hoc tribunal and, *in its first years at least*, of the permanent court would be limited to individuals, including state officials notwithstanding their functions and immunities, as opposed to states.[47]

43 Ibid para 51.
44 S/25537 of 6 April 1993; S/25575 of 12 April 1993; S/25512 of 5 April 1993.
45 S/25504 of 1 April 1993.
46 Ibid p. 3.
47 Ibid p. 14 (emphasis added).

The *Report* did not completely foreclose the possibility of including legal persons within the jurisdiction of an international criminal tribunal or court but considered the issue of secondary importance in the grand scheme of things.

As emerged from the analysis conducted above, the drafting history of the Statute of the International Criminal Tribunal for the former Yugoslavia scarcely contributed to the debate on the international criminal liability of corporations, if not in a negative way. Indeed, the decision not to address the liability of legal entities as part of the discussion on the Tribunal's jurisdiction *ratione personae* seems to indicate a disregard towards the issue and ignores the numerous references made to such a liability by the two Committees on an international criminal jurisdiction and the ILC. Such an approach has been interpreted by some as a dismissal of the idea that entities can be held criminally accountable at the international level.[48] However, it needs to be acknowledged that, at the time of the creation of the ICTY, the international community was working to a tight deadline. The need to come up with a prompt and strong solution to the mass atrocities committed in the Balkans greatly influenced the work of those involved in the drafting of the ICTY Statute. It is therefore not entirely surprising that a complex and innovative concept such as the international criminal liability of corporations was not considered as a priority.

A similar conclusion can be drawn with regard to the drafting history of the Statute of the International Criminal Tribunal for Rwanda. The Statute of the second *ad hoc* Tribunal – which followed almost verbatim the provisions of the first – also excluded the possibility to prosecute legal entities for their involvement in the crimes committed in Rwanda in 1994.[49] Like the ICTY, the International Criminal Tribunal for Rwanda was established as a matter of urgency to prosecute those responsible for the heinous crimes committed in the African country. Once again, it is possible to conclude that time constraints reduced any chance to discuss alternative solutions to those already implemented in the context of the ICTY.

3.4 The Negotiation of the Statute of the ICC (1995-1998)

If the analysis of the drafting history of the ICTY and ICTR's statutes seems to demonstrate a general disregard towards the liability of legal entities, the final stages of the preparatory works of the Statute of the ICC tell a different story and prove that the question of the criminal liability of corporations was far from settled. The following sections investigate to what extent the

48 *Jesner v. Arab Bank, PLC*, 138 S. Ct. 1386, at 1401 (2018). See also Ole Kristian Fauchald and Jo Stigen, 'Corporate Responsibility before International Institutions' (2009) 40 George Washington International Law Review 1025, 1037; Daniel Thurer, 'Vom Nurnberger Tribunal zum Jugoslawien-Tribunal und Weiter zu Einem Weltstrafgerichtshof' (1993) 3 Swiss Review of International and European Law 491, 498.

49 UN Security Council, Statute of the International Criminal Tribunal for Rwanda (8 November 1994), Article 5.

international criminal liability of corporations was discussed in the context of the 1995 *ad hoc* Committee and of the 1996 Preparatory Committee. This analysis aims to clarify how the famous French proposal on the liability of legal persons came to be and its journey to the Diplomatic Conference of 1998.

3.4.1 From the 1995 Ad Hoc Committee to the 1996 Preparatory Committee

Following the conclusion of the ILC's work on the question of an international criminal jurisdiction, the task to develop a draft statute for an international criminal court was assigned to the 1995 *ad hoc* Committee on the Establishment of an International Criminal Court.[50] In its 20 days of activity, the *ad hoc* Committee reviewed most of the major substantive and administrative problems linked to the establishment of a permanent international criminal court. As observed by M. Cherif Bassiouni, the work of the Committee 'had the positive effect of allowing states to familiarise themselves with the issues involved in the creation of an international criminal court' but failed to produce a sufficiently agreed-upon draft to be presented to a conference of plenipotentiaries.[51]

Although it is difficult to ascertain to what extent the *ad hoc* Committee considered the question of the liability of legal entities, a reference to the 'criminal liability of corporations' was incorporated into the *Guidelines for consideration of the question of general principles of criminal law* annexed to the Committee's Final Report.[52] The inclusion of such an item seems to imply that the international criminal liability of corporate entities was indeed addressed by the Committee. Unfortunately, not much can be inferred from the Committee's Final Report as it made no specific reference to corporations or other legal entities in any other sections aside from the *Guidelines*.[53]

The work of the 1995 *ad hoc* Committee provided the basis for the establishment of another body tasked to draft a statute of an international criminal court, the 1996 Preparatory Committee, set up by the UN General

50 UNGA Res 49/53 (17 February 1995), para 2.

51 Bassiouni (n 1) 19-20.

52 A/50/22, p. 58.

53 The term 'juridical persons' appeared also in an Informal Paper Submitted by the Bureau Substantive Law and Jurisdiction, UD/A/AC-244/IP-1, which reported various provisions of international instruments concerning the definition of crimes potentially falling within the jurisdiction of the Court. In particular, the term was included in (i) Article 1 of the *International Convention against the Taking of Hostages* (adopted 17 December 1979, entered into force 3 June 1983), 1316 U.N.T.S. 205, (ii) Article 3 of the *Convention for the Suppression of Unlawful Act against the Safety of Maritime Navigation* (adopted 10 March 1988, entered into force 1 March 1992), 1678 U.N.T.S. 222, and (iii) Article 2 of the *Protocol for the Suppression of Unlawful Act against the Safety of Fixed Platforms Located on the Continental Shelf* (adopted 10 March 1988, entered into force 1 March 1992), 1678 U.N.T.S. 222. In those provisions, however, 'juridical persons' are mentioned as third parties in the crime, not as perpetrators.

Assembly with Resolution 50/46 of 11 December 1995.[54] The mandate of the 1996 Preparatory Committee was 'explicit and goal-oriented'[55] and was finalised to the drafting of 'a widely acceptable consolidated text of a convention for an international criminal court as a next step towards consideration by a conference of plenipotentiaries'.[56]

The Preparatory Committee convened for the first time in late March 1996 and proceeded in its work on a draft statute for an international criminal court until mid-1998. The work of the Preparatory Committee is significant to evaluate the evolution of the debate on the international criminal liability of corporations. Indeed, it is in August 1996 that a new attempt was made to include corporate criminal liability within the scope of an international criminal court. On 6 August 1996, ahead of the Preparatory Committee's second session (12–30 August 1996), the French delegation submitted a working paper presenting a detailed 154-article long draft statute for an international criminal court.[57] The French draft included a number of original provisions which had no equivalent in the ILC 1994 draft.[58] Among those stood Article 78 titled, 'Physical persons and juridical persons'.[59] This provision represented the first articulate endeavour to define the scope of the liability of legal entities, its underlining principle of attribution, and the key aspect of the relationship between corporate liability – on the one side – and individual liability – on the other. Amended more than once, the French provision on corporate criminal liability remained a controversial matter throughout the two years which separated its original formulation from the adoption of the Statute of the ICC in 1998.

Over the last two decades, the proposal has played a key role in the narrative of the development (or lack thereof) of an international norm of corporate criminal liability. Similarly to the Nuremberg experience, the French proposal – and the discussion it elicited in the final stage of the negotiation of the Rome Statute – has captured the attention of both those in favour and against the recognition of an international criminal liability of corporations.[60] The vast

54 UNGA Res 50/46 (11 December 1995).
55 Bassiouni (n 1) 20.
56 UNGA Res 50/46 (11 December 1995), para 2.
57 A/AC.249/L.3.
58 Ibid pp. 7-22.
59 Ibid p. 59.
60 For a judicial interpretation of the dismissal of the French proposal see *Jesner v. Arab Bank, PLC*, 138 S. Ct. 1386 (2018). For an academic analysis, see, *inter alia*, Nadia Bernaz, *Business and Human Rights: History, Law and Policy – Bridging the Accountability Gap* (Routledge – 2017) 107-109; Caroline Kaeb, 'The Shifting Sands of Corporate Liability under International Criminal Law' (2016) 49 George Washington International Law Review 351, 396 et ss.; Joanna Kyriakakis, 'Corporations before International Criminal Courts: Implications for the International Criminal Justice Project' (2016) Leiden Journal of International Law 1; David Scheffer, 'Corporate Liability under the Rome Statute' (2016) 57 Harvard International Law Journal 35; Harmen van der Wilt, 'Corporate Criminal Responsibility for Interna-

majority of the existing literature orbits around the final version of the proposal – as developed in the summer of 1998 in the context of the Working Group on General Principle – devolving only marginal attention to its previous formulations. Such a narrow approach fails to appreciate the complexity linked to the definition of the liability of legal entities and the difficulties faced by promoting its inclusion within the Rome Statute. Contrary to this approach, the following section retraces the provision's journey, from its original formulation in 1996 to its dismissal in 1998, to provide a comprehensive analysis of the debate surrounding the international criminal liability of corporations.

3.4.2 The French Proposal on Corporate Criminal Liability: Origin and Early Debate

Included under Title II (Persons Liable to Punishment) of Part 5. (Criminal Law and Criminal Responsibility), Article 78 reads as follows:

1. The Court shall be competent to take cognizance of the criminal responsibility of:
   (a) Physical persons;
   (b) Juridical persons, with the exception of States, when the crimes committed were committed on behalf of such juridical persons or by their agencies or representatives.
2. The criminal responsibility of juridical persons shall not exclude the criminal responsibility of physical persons who are perpetrators of or accomplices in the same crimes.
3. These provisions shall be without prejudice to the responsibility of States with respect to international law.[61]

Article 78 was complemented by Article 95 which clarified the sanctioning system applicable to juridical persons specifically. In particular, Article 95 listed the following penalties as applicable to legal entities:

(a) Fines, the amount of which shall be freely set by the Court;
(b) Dissolution;

tional Crimes: Exploring the Possibilities' (2013) 12 Chinese Journal of International Law 43; Joanna Kyriakakis, 'Corporate Criminal Liability and the ICC Statute: The Comparative Law Challenge' (2009) 56 Netherlands International Law Review 333; Andrew Clapham, *Human Rights Obligations of Non-State Actors* (OUP 2006) 244-247; Andrew Clapham, 'The Question of Jurisdiction under International Criminal Law over Legal Persons: Lessons from the Rome Conference on an International Criminal Court' in Menno T Kamminga and Saman Zia-Zarifi (eds), *Liability of Multinational Corporations Under International Law* (Martinus Nijhoff 2000), 139.

61 A/AC.249/L.3, p. 59.

(c) Prohibition, in perpetuity or for a period freely determined by the Court, of the direct or indirect exercise of one or more professional or social activities;
(d) Closure, in perpetuity or for a period freely determined by the Court, of the establishments used in the commission of the crimes;
(e) Confiscation of any item used in the commission of the crimes or which is a product of the crimes. [...].[62]

In its original formulation, the French proposal replicated almost verbatim the (then) recently adopted Articles 121–2 of the 1994 *Code Pénal* which introduced, for the first time, the principle of corporate criminal liability within the French legal system.[63] Indeed, Articles 121–2 of the French Penal Code recognised (and still recognises) the criminal liability of 'legal persons, with the exclusion of the state, ... for offences committed on their behalf by their organs or by their representatives'.[64]

Like Articles 121–2, draft Article 78 of the French draft maintained the separation between States and other legal entities providing that only the latter could be subjected to criminal prosecution at the international level. However, draft Article 78 also clarified that the exclusion of States from the scope of international criminal liability in no way exonerated them from other forms of responsibility under international law.[65]

Similar to Articles 121–2, the model of attribution proposed linked the liability of the entities to that of a natural person who materially perpetrated the crime, yet without making the former entirely dependent on the latter. On this point, however, the wording of draft Article 78 slightly deviated from the terminology used in Articles 121–2 of the French Penal Code. Indeed, while the national provision indicates the entity's organs and representatives as the only natural persons who can trigger the corporate liability, the formulation of draft Article 78 used the disjunctive 'or' to separate those committing a crime 'on behalf' the juridical person, on one side, from its 'agencies or representatives', on the other.[66] This latter approach seems to expand the scope of the provision beyond the limits set by Articles 121–2, so as to include all employees acting on behalf of the company among those who can prompt the entity's criminal liability.

62 Ibid p. 64.
63 Katrin Deckert, 'Corporate Criminal Liability' in France in Mark Pieth and Radha Ivory (eds) *Corporate Criminal Liability: Emergence, Convergence, and Risk* (Springer 2011), Jean-Yves Maréchal, 'Responsabilité pénale des personnes morales' (2009) 80 JurisClasseur Pénal Code 1, Leonard Orland and Charles Cachera, 'Corporate Crime and Punishment in France: Criminal Responsibility of Legal Entities (Personnes Morales) under the New French Criminal Code (Nouveau Code Penal)' (1995) 11 Conn J Int'l L 111, 114.
64 French Criminal Code, Article 121-2.
65 A/AC.249/L.3, p. 59, Article 78(3).
66 Ibid p. 59, Article 78(1)(b).

This interpretation would put draft Article 78 more in line with the US doctrine of *respondeat superior* than with the narrower approach to corporate criminal liability embraced by France.[67] Developed by the US federal courts since 1909,[68] the doctrine of *respondeat superior* has its roots in the agency model adopted in tort law and established that a corporation may be held criminally liable for the acts of any of its employees, irrespective of their position within the company's hierarchy.[69] Conversely, the French approach – more in line with the principle of identification embraced in the English legal system – limits the categories of individuals who can trigger the liability of the entity to those in an apical position as only they can embody the will of the legal person.[70]

This broader approach to the liability of the entity would also represent a change from the narrow 'model' of attribution suggested, years before, by Wynes – the Australian representative at the 1951 Committees on International Criminal Jurisdiction – who referred to the 'head' of the corporation – i.e. the managing director(s) – as the only natural person(s) who may trigger the corporate liability.[71] Unfortunately, the documents available do not allow to determine whether this difference in the formulation of draft Article 78 was actually based on a conscious decision to propose a broader model of attribution for an international corporate liability as no commentary or explicatory note was included in the 1996 French draft.

Similarly, the documentation produced by the 1996 Preparatory Committee does not offer any clarification on the matter. The 1996 French proposal was examined by the Informal Group on General Principles of Criminal Law – chaired by Per Saland – which included the provision of Article 78 among those 'examples of … possible texts' to be considered for the Statute of an international criminal court.[72] No official records of the debate are available. The only indication of the quality of the debate on the liability of legal entities is provided by the complementary note to Article 78 which stated:

> Some delegations indicated that the expression 'juridical persons' should extend to organizations lacking a legal status.
>
> Some delegations expressed doubts about including the criminal responsibility of juridical persons into the Statute.

67 For a comparative analysis of models of attribution of corporate criminal liability adopted by US and France see Cristina de Maglie, 'Models of Corporate Criminal Liability in Comparative Law' (2005) 4 Washington University Global Studies Law Review 547, 553-554.
68 *New York Central & Hudson River R.R. v. United States*, 212 U.S. 481 (1909).
69 Celia Wells, *Corporations and Criminal Responsibility*, (2nd edn, OUP 2005) 134.
70 Pascal Beauvais, 'Country Report: France' in James Gobert and Ana-Maria Pascal (eds), *European Developments in Corporate Criminal Liability* (Routledge 2011), 241.
71 A/AC.48/SR.9, para 74.
72 A/AC.249/CRP.13, p. 1.

> It was proposed as an alternative the possibility of referring to the 'responsibility' of the juridical persons without including the word 'criminal'.[73]

Similar observations were expressed in the Preparatory Committee's 1996 Final Report. In summarising the Committee's position on the proposal concerning the 'Criminal liability of corporations', the Report observed that:

> Some delegations held the view that it would be more useful to focus attention on individual responsibility, noting at the same time that corporations were in fact controlled by individuals. Several delegations stated that such liability ran counter to their domestic law.[74]

Nonetheless, the Committee conceded that 'the liability of a corporation could be important in the context of restitution' and therefore may be worthy of further consideration.[75] Interestingly, the 1996 Report also recalled that 'the principle had been applied in the Nürnberg Judgment' to justify additional discussion on the concept of corporate liability.[76] Most probably, this statement had its roots in the misconception over the qualification of the legal regime applicable to 'criminal organisations and groups', as defined in Articles 9 and 10 of the London Charter. As previously observed, such a misconception has characterised the debate on the liability of legal entities since its origin in the 1940s and even today it plays an important role in the discussion on an international corporate criminal liability.

In December 1996, the UN General Assembly renewed the Committee's mandate for nine more weeks in 1997–98 with the goal of developing a final draft to be submitted to a diplomatic conference to be held in mid-1998.[77] The prorogation of the Committee's mandate offered further opportunity to consider the implication of extending the new Court's jurisdiction to legal entities. In 1997, the original version of the French proposal was discussed – and refined – during the Preparatory Committee's third session, held from 11 to 21 February.[78] In the Report produced by the Working Group on General Principles of Criminal Law and Penalties, the liability of legal persons

73 Ibid p. 4. The compilation produced by the Informal Group on General Principles of Criminal Law was then integrated into the Report of the Preparatory Committee on the Establishment of an International Criminal Court, Vol. II, A/51/22, p. 81.

74 A/51/22, para 194, p. 44.

75 Ibid.

76 Ibid.

77 UNGA Res 51/207 (17 December 1996).

78 Preparatory Committee on Establishment of International Criminal Court to Meet at Headquarters, 11–21 February, L/2819, 7 February 1997.

was incorporated under Article B a., (Individual Criminal Responsibility), paragraphs 5 and 6.[79] Those provisions – included in brackets – read as follows:

> [5. The Court shall also have jurisdiction over juridical persons, with the exception of States, when the crimes committed were committed on behalf of such juridical persons or by their agencies or representatives.
>
> 6. The criminal responsibility of juridical persons shall not exclude the criminal responsibility of natural persons who are perpetrators or accomplices in the same crimes.][80]

The core of the proposal remained the same with the exclusion of any reference to the international responsibility of States. Once again, the provision was complemented by a footnote which highlighted the conflicting views that emerged during the discussion over the liability of legal entities. In particular, the note stated that:

> There is a deep divergence of views as to the advisability of including criminal responsibility of juridical persons in the Statute. Many delegations are strongly opposed, whereas some strongly favour its inclusion. Others have an open mind. Some delegations hold the view that providing for only the civil or administrative responsibility/liability of juridical persons could provide a middle ground. This avenue, however, has not been thoroughly discussed. Some delegations, who favour the inclusion of juridical persons, hold the view that this expression should be extended to organizations lacking legal status. Some prefer the term 'legal entities'.[81]

In an attempt to bridge the gap between the conflicting views on the liability of legal persons, on 2 April 1998, the French delegation submitted a new proposal which strayed away from the model originally proposed.[82] Abandoning any resemblance to the concept of corporate criminal liability, the new document shifted the focus from the notion of legal entities to this of 'criminal organisations', suggesting an approach *á la* Nuremberg. Indeed, the new proposal read as follows:

> **Par. 5 and 6 (~~legal persons~~ criminal organizations)**
> [5. When the crime was committed by a natural person on behalf or with the assent of a group or organization of every kind, the Court may declare that this group or organization is a criminal organization.

79 A/AC.249/1997/WG.2/CRP.2; A/AC.249/1997/L.5, p. 20-1.
80 A/AC.249/1997/WG.2/CRP.2; A/AC.249/1997/L.5, p. 20-1. See also A/AC.249/1998/L.13, pp. 52-53.
81 A/AC.249/1997/WG.2/CRP.2; A/AC.249/1997/L.5, p. 20-1.
82 A/AC.249/1998/DP.14.

6. In the cases where a group or organization is declared criminal by the Court, this group or organization shall incur the penalties referred in article 69, and the relevant provision of articles 66 and 72 are applicable.

In any such case, the criminal nature of the group or organization is considered proved and shall not be questioned, and the competent national authorities of any State party shall take the necessary measures to ensure that the judgment of the Court shall have binding force and to implement it.][83]

Perhaps due to time constraints, the new French proposal was not discussed during the last session of the Preparatory Committee (held from 16 March to 3 April 1998) and, therefore, not included in the final document prepared by the Informal Group on General Principles of Criminal Law – which retained the 1997 formulation instead.[84] Nonetheless, the revised proposal found its way into the Rome Conference where it was discussed during the first meeting of the Committee of the Whole, opening the door to further consideration of the possibility to create a space for legal entities within the new international criminal justice system.

3.5 The 1998 Rome Conference for an International Criminal Court

The United Nations Diplomatic Conference of Plenipotentiaries on the Establishment of an International Criminal Court led off in Rome, Italy, on 15 June 1998 and lasted until 17 July 1998. Defined by the UN Secretary-General, Kofi Annan, as 'an opportunity to take a monumental step in the name of human rights and the rule of law',[85] the Conference brought together delegations from 160 States, alongside representatives from numerous inter-governmental organisations and NGOs.[86] The Conference's work was mostly carried out under the direction of the Committee of the Whole, which coordinated the activities of 'a myriad of thematic working groups' tasked to elaborate different sections of the draft statute.[87]

The issues the delegations in Rome were called to resolve were countless. Interestingly, the first one to be addressed by the Committee of the Whole was the question of the liability of legal entities.[88] On 16 June 1998, on the occasion of the Committee's first session, Ms Le Fraper du Hellen took the floor to introduce the debate over the French proposal on the liability of legal

83 Ibid.
84 A/AC.249/CRP.13.
85 A/CONF.183/SR.1, para 12.
86 Schabas (n 1) 22.
87 Ibid.
88 A/CONF.183/C.1/SR.1, para 32 et ss.

persons.[89] Instead of focusing on the draft text of Article 23 paragraphs 5 and 6 – as included in the final document submitted by the Preparatory Committee – the discussion centred on the new French proposal of April 1998.

In presenting the new text, the French delegation started by explaining the reasons for the change in the formulation by referring to the arguments raised by those against the recognition of the responsibility of legal persons. In particular, Ms Le Fraper du Hellen identified two main objections that moved against the proposal on legal entities: the lack of recognition of corporate criminal liability at the domestic level, on one side, and the scepticism towards the possibility of applying such forms of liability at the international level, on the other.[90] While the French delegation acknowledged the relevance of such arguments, it nonetheless 'felt that the Statute should go at least as far as the Nuremberg Charter, which had provided for the criminal responsibility of "criminal organizations"'.[91]

The French delegation then proceeded to clarify the 'principles' underlining the new proposal on criminal organisations. All those principles aimed to highlight the similarities between the French proposal and Articles 9 and 10 of the London Charter.[92] As explained by Le Fraper du Hellen, paragraph 5 of the new proposal was formulated in a way to mirror the provision of Article 9(1) of the London Charter which bestowed on the Nuremberg Tribunal the power to declare the criminality of a 'group or organisation' in connection with the conviction of any of its individual members by the Tribunal itself.[93] Like in Article 9(1) of the London Charter, the French proposal considered the responsibility of a group or organization as 'consequent on the previous commission by a natural person of a crime falling within the jurisdiction of the Court'.[94] This would have made sure that, under no circumstance, the individual would have been allowed to conceal his or her responsibility 'behind that of an organization'.[95]

If paragraph 5 was modelled over Article 9(1) of the London Charter, the second section of paragraph 6 echoed Article 10 of the London Charter. Both provisions, indeed, affirmed the 'unquestionable' nature of a decision by the Court concerning the criminality of an organisation.[96] On this point, however,

89 Ibid.

90 A/CONF.183/C.1/SR.1, para 32.

91 Ibid.

92 Ibid para 33.

93 United Nations, *Agreement by the Government of the United Kingdom of Great Britain and Northern Ireland, the Government of the United States of America, the Provisional Government of the French Republic and the Government of the Union of Soviet Socialist Republics for the prosecution and punishment of the major war criminals of the European Axis ('London Agreement')*, 8 August 1945, 82 U.N.T.S. 279, Annex, Article 9(1).

94 A/CONF.183/C.1/SR.1, para 33.

95 Ibid.

96 Ibid. United Nations, *Agreement by the Government of the United Kingdom of Great Britain and Northern Ireland, the Government of the United States of America, the Provisional Gov-*

the French delegate conceded that such an approach – already criticised at Nuremberg – may have required 'further discussion'.[97]

Probably the most interesting aspect of the French proposal – and the sole point of contrast with the model designed in Articles 9 and 10 of the London Charter – pertained to the first section of paragraph 6 which subjected criminal organisations to a specific sanctioning system. This system was defined by draft Article 69 – also included in the document submitted by France on 3 April 1998 – which read as follows:

> **Article 69 - Penalties applicable to ~~legal persons~~ criminal organisations**
> A criminal organization shall incur the one or more of the following penalties.
>
> (i) fines,
> (ii) *deleted.*
> (iii) *deleted.*
> (iv) *deleted.*
> (v) forfeiture of [instrumentalities of crime and] proceeds, property and assets obtained by criminal conduct;] [and]
> [(vi) appropriate forms of reparation].][98]

Draft Article 69 proposed a revisited version of the provision originally submitted in 1996 (then draft Article 95) with the significant exclusion of some of the penalties, namely dissolution, prohibition (in perpetuity or for a period determined by the Court) of the direct or indirect exercise of one or more professional or social activities, and closure (in perpetuity or for a period determined by the Court) of the establishment used in the commission of the crime.[99] The decision to limit the range of penalties applicable to criminal organisations was once again justified by the attempt to 'build a bridge between the countries that accept criminal responsibility for organisations or groups and those that did not'.[100] Still, even if limited in its scope, the sanctioning system referred to in the first section of paragraph 6 of the French proposal represented an interesting deviation from the approach adopted at Nuremberg. Articles 9 and 10 of the London Charter, indeed, did not provide the Tribunal with the power to impose any kind of penalty on the criminal organisation or group – a

ernment of the French Republic and the Government of the Union of Soviet Socialist Republics for the prosecution and punishment of the major war criminals of the European Axis ('London Agreement'), 8 August 1945, 82 U.N.T.S. 279, Annex, Article 10.

97 A/CONF.183/C.1/SR.1, para 33.

98 A/AC.249/1998/DP.14, p. 2-3 (emphasis in original).

99 A/AC.249/L.3, p. 64.

100 A/CONF.183/C.1/SR.1, para 33.

power that, in itself, would have been useless considering that all organisations and groups indicted at Nuremberg had been disbanded ahead of the trial.[101]

The new proposal received mixed reactions from the delegations sitting in the Committee.[102] A number of delegations – including Egypt, Tunisia, Japan, Argentina, Ukraine, Jordan, and Australia – expressed 'interest' towards the new French proposal, considering it an improvement from the original formulation of Article 23 paragraphs 5 and 6. Nonetheless, even among those more open to the responsibility of criminal organisations, a lingering scepticism persisted. The Egyptian delegation, in particular, observed that '[a]lthough the French proposal was an improvement on the existing text of paragraphs 5 and 6, it did not solve the underlying problems' raised by the concept of criminal liability of fictional entities.[103] Similarly, the Australian representative conceded that, even though Australia recognised the criminal liability of organisations, 'that was not the case in all countries, and Australia's doubts about the enforcement of any finding of criminal responsibility in relation to organizations remained'.[104]

Entirely against the recognition of a liability of legal entities were the delegations from China, Mexico, Sweden, Lebanon, Denmark, Syria, Greece, El Salvador, Yemen, and Iran.[105] Specific concerns were raised, among others, by the delegates from Slovenia and Poland who referred, respectively, to time constraints and evidentiary issues as reasons not to proceed with the adoption of the French proposal.[106] The representative from China, Hu Bin, urged caution in providing for an international criminal liability of legal entities in light of 'the sensitive political issues involved'.[107] In referring to the Nuremberg precedent, he drew attention to 'the specific historical background and the special characteristics' of the Nuremberg trials and highlighted how '[t]he Court under discussion would be established against the background of a complex international political situation that differed sharply from the situation prevailing in 1945'.[108] Any attempt to draw a parallel between Nuremberg and Rome was, therefore, dangerous and based on an incorrect understanding of the context in which the International Military Tribunal operated.

Sceptical towards the adoption of an approach *á la* Nuremberg was also Yee, from Singapore, who opposed the new French proposal advocating for

101 *Trial of the Major War Criminals before the International Military Tribunal*, Vol. VIII - Proceedings (20 February 1946–7 March 1946), Library of Congress, 391, 427.

102 A/CONF.183/C.1/SR.1, paras 34-66. See also Clapham, 'The Question of Jurisdiction under International Criminal Law over Legal Persons: Lessons from the Rome Conference on an International Criminal Court' (n 60) 147 et ss.

103 A/CONF.183/C.1/SR.1, para 59.

104 Ibid para 35.

105 Ibid paras 36, 43, 44, 46, 55, 56, 57, 63, 64 and 65.

106 Ibid paras 60-61.

107 Ibid para 36.

108 Ibid.

the return to its original formulation.[109] According to Yee, the adoption of the Nuremberg model raised a number of 'conceptual difficulties', in particular in relation to the 'procedural safeguards' applicable to organisations. Therefore, he stated that his delegation would rather maintain the original formulation of paragraphs 5 and 6, which established the 'criminal responsibility for legal persons in the same way as for individuals', instead of adopting 'the approach of a blanket declaration that an organization was criminal and using that as a basis for the treatment or trial of individuals'.[110] A similar opinion was expressed by Manogi, from the United Republic of Tanzania, who observed that 'paragraphs 5 and 6 should be retained as they stood, rather than the more broadly worded French proposal' and referred to allegations of corporate crimes in Rwanda to justify the adoption of a provision on international corporate criminal liability:

> To take a specific example, one of the allegations concerning the genocide in Rwanda was that there had been companies in whose warehouses arms bought with the profits of those companies had been stored and from which they had been distributed, with the full knowledge of the representatives of those companies. Tanzania believed, therefore, that not only should criminal responsibility be attributed to representatives in their individual capacity, but that the entity itself should be held criminally liable, if only by paying fines or by being liquidated.[111]

The position of the Singaporean representative was also partially endorsed by Harris, a member of the US delegation, who shared the opinion that the new French proposal might create more problems than its original version. In his statement, Harris indicated that the US delegation was prepared to 'work towards an acceptable definition of the concepts involved' in the establishment of an international criminal liability of legal persons, but he was sceptical that a consensus could have been reached on the matter.[112] On this regard, he observed that '[f]ailure to reach a consensus must be readily acknowledged in view of the time constraints, and would not in any event seriously undermine the effectiveness of the Court'.[113] Even though the US delegation was open to the idea of an international criminal liability of legal entities, it did not consider the topic in itself essential to the functioning of an international criminal court.

The conflicting views that emerged during the debate within the Committee of the Whole, once again, demonstrated the 'substantive difficulties' involved in the definition of a criminal liability of legal persons. In an attempt to bridge

109 Ibid paras 45 and 52.
110 Ibid para 45.
111 Ibid para 52.
112 Ibid para 54.
113 Ibid.

the gap between the opposite positions emerging during the discussion, the proposal on the liability of legal entities was referred to the Working Group on General Principles (hereafter WGGP) for further consideration.[114]

For three weeks, the proposal was considered in a number of informal meetings led by the French delegation, with the support of the representatives from the Solomon Islands.[115] During this time, one rolling text and three working papers were circulated among the delegations to facilitate the discussion.[116] While some differences in the terminology can be identified (e.g. the terms 'legal persons and other organisations', adopted in the rolling text and in the first working paper, were replaced with 'juridical persons' in the second and third versions),[117] the core elements covered in these documents mostly remained the same. The following section focuses on the last and more comprehensive text formulated in the context of the Rome Conference to provide an analysis of its key features and elements.

3.5.1 The Final Working Paper on the Liability of Juridical Persons: The Last Stage of the Debate

The third and final working paper on the criminal liability of juridical persons was presented on 3 July 1998 and reads as follows:

> 5. Without prejudice to any individual criminal responsibility of natural persons under this Statute, the Court may also have jurisdiction over a juridical person for a crime under this Statute. Charges may be filed by the Prosecutor against a juridical person, and the Court may render a judgment over a juridical person for the crime charged, if:
>
> (a) The charges filed by the Prosecutor against the natural person and the juridical person allege the matters referred to in subparagraphs (b) and (c); and
> (b) The natural person charged was in a position of control within the juridical person under the national law of the State where the juridical person was registered at the time the crime was committed; and
> (c) The crime was committed by the natural person acting on behalf of and with the explicit consent of that juridical person and in the course of its activities; and
> (d) The natural person has been convicted of the crime charged.

114 Ibid para 66.

115 Clapham, 'The Question of Jurisdiction under International Criminal Law over Legal Persons: Lessons from the Rome Conference on an International Criminal Court' (n 60) 147.

116 A/CONF.183/C.1/WGGP/L.5; A/CONF.183/C.1/WGGP/L.5/Rev.1; A/CONF.183/C.1/WGGP/L.5/Rev.2.

117 Ibid.

For the purpose of this Statute, 'juridical person' means a corporation whose concrete, real or dominant objective is seeking private profit or benefit, and not a State or other public body in the exercise of State authority, a public international body or an organization registered, and acting under the national law of a State as a non-profit organization.

6. The proceedings with respect to a juridical person under this article shall be in accordance with this Statute and the relevant Rules of Procedure and Evidence. The Prosecutor may file charges against the natural and juridical persons jointly or separately. The natural person and the juridical person may be jointly tried. If convicted, the juridical person may incur the penalties referred to in article 76. These penalties shall be enforced in accordance with the provisions of article 99.[118]

The final text of the French proposal is, without a doubt, the most advanced attempt to define a model of corporate criminal liability applicable at the international level and 'demonstrates how far the concept had developed over the three weeks of discussion'.[119]

In line with its original formulation, the working paper adopted a derivative approach to the criminal liability of the entity making it contingent upon the conviction of the natural person who materially committed the crime (draft Article 23(5)(d)).[120] This approach differed from the model of criminal organisation embodied in the Charter of the International Military Tribunal of Nuremberg according to which the declaration of the criminality of a group or organisation was instrumental to the establishment of the liability of its members.[121] As observed by Clapham, by reversing the relationship between the individual and the juridical entity, the proposal seemed to consider the juridical person 'as a sort of "accessory" to the individual's crime'[122], constructing its liability as an addition to the criminal responsibility of the individual.

Draft Article 23(5) also indicated which natural persons can trigger the liability of a juridical entity. Departing from the broader model adopted in draft Article 78, draft Article 23(5)(b) established that the Court would have been able to exercise its jurisdiction over an entity only when the crime

118 A/CONF.183/C.1/WGGP/L.5/Rev.2. (footnotes in original omitted).

119 Clapham, 'The Question of Jurisdiction under International Criminal Law over Legal Persons: Lessons from the Rome Conference on an International Criminal Court' (n 60) 150.

120 A/CONF.183/C.1/WGGP/L.5/Rev.2.

121 United Nations, *Agreement by the Government of the United Kingdom of Great Britain and Northern Ireland, the Government of the United States of America, the Provisional Government of the French Republic and the Government of the Union of Soviet Socialist Republics for the prosecution and punishment of the major war criminals of the European Axis ('London Agreement')*, 8 August 1945, 82 U.N.T.S. 279, Annex, Articles 9 and 10.

122 Clapham, 'The Question of Jurisdiction under International Criminal Law over Legal Persons: Lessons from the Rome Conference on an International Criminal Court' (n 60) 153.

was committed by a natural person 'in a position of control'.[123] While draft Article 78 related more to the model embraced by the US federal courts, the final version of the French proposal seemed more in line with the approach found in the 1994 French Penal Code and in the legal system of England and Wales.[124] As mentioned above, indeed, under Articles 121–2 of the French Penal Code, a corporation can be held liable for the acts committed by the entity's organs or representatives who are deemed to express the corporation's will.[125] Similarly, in England and Wales, the identification doctrine establishes that only the acts of those individuals 'who [are] really the directing mind and will of the corporation, the very ego and centre of the personality of the corporation' can trigger the liability of the entity.[126] According to the case law developed by the English courts, only 'a person who is in actual control of the operations of a company or of part of them and who is not responsible to another person in the company for the manner in which he discharges his duties in the sense of being under his orders' can be deemed to be the directing mind of a company.[127]

The provision of draft Article 23(5)(b), thus, would have narrowed the scope of the liability of the entity to those crimes committed by an individual in an apical position, excluding it every time the criminal act was perpetrated by a mere subordinate. At the same time, though, the provision established that the identification of those 'in a position of control' would have been determined based on 'the national law of the State where the juridical person was registered at the time the crime was committed'. In doing so, draft Article 23(5)(b) would have prevented a company from falling under the Court's jurisdiction 'through the actions of someone unauthorised under the relevant national law'.[128]

In addition to the condition set by draft Article 23(5)(b), the working paper also required that, in committing the crime, the natural person was 'acting on behalf of and with the explicit consent of that juridical person and in the course of its activities'.[129] If the element of the 'position of control' was most likely influenced by the legal tradition of England and Wales, the provision of draft Article 23(5)(c) seems to find its roots in the legal approach to corporate

123 A/CONF.183/C.1/WGGP/L.5/Rev.2.

124 Guy Stessens, 'Corporate Criminal Liability: A Comparative Perspective' (1994) 43(3) International and Comparative Law Quarterly 493, 507.

125 For an analysis of the interpretation of the concepts of corporate 'organ' and 'representative' under French law, see Deckert (n 63) 158-161.

126 *Lennard's Carrying Co v. Asiatic Petroleum Co.* [1915] A.C. 705, 713. A similar approach has been followed also by Canada. See Stessens (n 126) 510.

127 *Tesco Supermarkets v. Nattrass* [1971] UKHL 1, 187 (per Viscount Dilhorne). See also Mark Dsouza, 'The Corporate Agent in Criminal Law – An Argument for Comprehensive Identification' (2020) 79 The Cambridge Law Journal 91, 96; Stessens (n 124) 508.

128 Clapham, 'The Question of Jurisdiction under International Criminal Law over Legal Persons: Lessons from the Rome Conference on an International Criminal Court' (n 60) 154.

129 A/CONF.183/C.1/WGGP/L.5/Rev.2.

criminal liability adopted by the federal courts of the United States.[130] In the US jurisprudence, a corporation may be held accountable for the acts committed by one of its employees when he or she acted 'within the scope of his [or her] employment'.[131] To trigger the liability of the entity, the employee must have the actual or apparent authority to perform the activity resulting in the commission of the crime.[132] As explained in the case *United States v. Cincotta*:

> A corporation may be convicted for the criminal acts of its agents, under a theory of respondent superior. But criminal liability may be imposed on the corporation only where the agent is acting within the scope of employment. That, in turn, requires that the agent be performing acts of the kind which he is authorized to perform, and those acts must be motivated – at least in part – by an intent to benefit the corporation.[133]

In the opinion of Clapham, the inclusion of such a requirement would have shielded the juridical entity from prosecution in cases where the natural person was 'acting solely for his or her own benefit'.[134] In these instances, he observed, 'the corporation could be considered the victim of the crime rather than the perpetrator, and the case for corporate liability as such is weak'.[135] Quite surprisingly, however, the working paper did not explicitly refer to the element of the 'intent to benefit the corporation' as one of the requirements to establish the entity's liability. In the absence of a clear indication, it would have been left to the judge's interpretation to determine whether such an element could have been considered implicitly included in the formulation of draft Article 23(5).

In its final paragraph, draft Article 23(5) then provided a definition of the concept of 'juridical person' adopted in the provision. According to the working paper, the term 'juridical persons' covered solely those corporations whose 'concrete, real or dominant objective' was to seek 'private profit or benefit'.[136] In accordance with this narrow interpretation, other legal entities such as the State, public entities 'in the exercise of State authority', public international

130 Clapham, 'The Question of Jurisdiction under International Criminal Law over Legal Persons: Lessons from the Rome Conference on an International Criminal Court' (n 60) 154.

131 See, inter alia, *United States v. A & P Trucking Co.*, 358 U.S. 121, at 126 (1958); *A.I. Credit Corp. v. Legion Ins. Co.*, 265 F.3d 630, at 637 (7th Cir. 2001).

132 Wells (n 71) 135; Annie Geraghty, 'Corporate Criminal Liability' (2002) 39 American Criminal Law Review 327, 329 et ss.

133 *United States v. Cincotta*, 689 F.2d 238, at 242 (1st Cir., 1982).

134 Clapham, 'The Question of Jurisdiction under International Criminal Law over Legal Persons: Lessons from the Rome Conference on an International Criminal Court' (n 60) 154.

135 Ibid.

136 A/CONF.183/C.1/WGGP/L.5/Rev.2.

bodies and non-profit organisations were to be excluded from the jurisdiction of the Court.[137]

While draft Article 23(5) defined the scope of application of the international criminal liability of corporations, draft Article 23(6) was concerned with the procedural implications of establishing such a liability. Less detailed than paragraph 5, draft Article 23(6) provided that the charges against a juridical person could have been filed jointly with these against the natural person accused of perpetrating the crime and that, consequently, the juridical person and the individual could have been 'jointly tried'.[138] The provision, however, did not provide any indication of how such a joint trial could have been managed, in particular with regard to the question of the legal representation at the trial of the private company. Lastly, draft Article 23(6) briefly touched upon the issue of sentencing by referring to the provisions of draft Article 76 and draft Article 99 which respectively concerned the determination of the penalties applicable to the legal person – specifically fines and forfeitures[139] – and their enforcement.[140]

As emerged, the working paper combined elements from different legal systems in an attempt to define a model of international corporate criminal liability able to be accepted by the majority of the delegations. The efforts made, however, were not enough. When the working paper was finally discussed in the WGGP, on 7 July 1998[141], it became clear that the proposal was far from providing an answer to all the questions arising from the definition of such a complex form of criminal liability. With less than two weeks left before the end of the Conference, the French delegation recognised the impossibility of reaching an agreement on the text of the proposal and ultimately decided to withdraw it.[142]

In his comprehensive account of the last stage of the negotiation of draft Article 25(5) and (6), Clapham so summarises the positions of the various delegations in Rome:

> Many delegations worked to support the various versions of the proposal. ... Many delegations felt there simply was no time to elaborate such a provision during the five-week negotiating process. For some delegations the whole notion of corporate criminal responsibility was simply 'alien', raising problem of complementarity. In addition there were perceived procedural problems relating to who would represent the legal

137 Ibid.
138 Ibid.
139 A/CONF.183/C.1/L.3, Article 76.
140 A/CONF.183/C.1/WGGP/L.5/Rev.2.
141 A/CONF-183/JOURNA -16.
142 Bernaz (n 60) 108; Desislava Stoitchkova, *Towards Corporate Liability in International Criminal Law* (Intersentia 2010), 16.

person in Court and how assets could be taken without affecting the rights of third persons.[143]

A similar view of the drafting history of draft Article 23(5) and (6) provided by David J. Scheffer, who attended the Conference as a member of the US delegation. In recalling his experience in Rome, Scheffer observed that:

> [The] exclusion of corporations from International Criminal Court prosecution was inevitable *not because States agreed that corporations are above the law as a matter of right or principle*, but because a fundamental underpinning of the Rome treaty is the preference for and deference to domestic prosecution (the principle of complementarity) and the obligation of states parties to undertake the capacity to prosecute. If a legal system did not hold juridical persons liable under criminal law, then under the Rome Treaty that national system likely would fail the test of complementarity. Given that diversity, it was not possible to negotiate a new standard of corporate criminal liability with universal application in the time frame permitted for concluding the Rome Treaty in light of such differences in criminal liability for juridical persons among so many national jurisdictions.[144]

Time constraints, complementarity concerns, and procedural difficulties were the main reasons which made the project to include corporations within the scope of the Rome Statute derail.[145] Nothing in the preparatory works seems to indicate a complete rejection of the concept as a matter of principle. Indeed, even delegations from countries that – at the time of the Conference – did not incorporate corporate criminal liability in their domestic systems seemed to recognise the value of holding private entities accountable for their involvement in international crimes. Italy, for example, voiced in favour of the French proposal on legal persons even though it did not recognise legal persons as subjects of criminal law in its national system.[146]

The analysis conducted so far, thus, demonstrates that the failure of the French proposal did not rest on theoretical grounds but on practical

143 Clapham, 'The Question of Jurisdiction under International Criminal Law over Legal Persons: Lessons from the Rome Conference on an International Criminal Court' (n 60) 157.

144 David Scheffer, 'Keynote Address: Is the Presumption of Corporate Impunity Dead?' (2018) 50 Case Western Reserve Journal of International Law 213, 216–217 (emphasis added). See also Doug Cassel, 'Corporate Aiding and Abetting of Human Rights Violations: Confusion in the Courts' (2008) 6 Northwestern University Journal of International Human Rights 304, 316.

145 Per Saland, 'International Criminal Law Principles' in Roy Lee (ed), *The International Criminal Court: The Making of the Rome Statute* (Martinus Nijhoff Publishers 1999), 199.

146 Clapham, 'The Question of Jurisdiction under International Criminal Law over Legal Persons: Lessons from the Rome Conference on an International Criminal Court' (n 60) 158.

considerations, linked to the specific historical context in which the negotiations took place. As a result, the decision not to include corporations within the scope of the Statute of the ICC cannot be considered a definitive statement against the recognition of an international corporate criminal liability. Like Nuremberg, Rome provides valuable insights on the complexity of holding corporations accountable under international criminal law but in itself does not exhaust the debate on the issue.

3.6 Conclusion

This chapter examined the way in which the criminal liability of corporations was discussed in the years that led to the adoption of the Statute of the ICC. During the negotiation of the Rome Statute, the question of the international criminal liability of corporate entities featured prominently in the debate on the scope and function of an international criminal court. The chapter focused specifically on the debate surrounding the French proposal on the liability of legal persons. Presented for the first time in 1996, the French proposal represents the first attempt to draft a detailed model of corporate criminal liability for international crimes. The chapter discussed the theoretical underpinning of such a proposal and followed its evolution over the two years that led to its dismissal in 1998. In its initial formulation, the proposal adopted a broad approach to corporate criminal liability by combining elements of the doctrine of identification with that of the doctrine of *respondeat superior*. As a result, the 1996 proposal would have allowed the ICC to establish the liability of the corporation for criminal acts committed on behalf of the entity or by its agencies or representatives, irrespective of their hierarchical position. The proposal divided the delegations and generated a heated debate on the opportunity of including corporations among the subjects of international criminal law. To foster the discussion, the proposal was radically amended in 1998. It first regressed to a model of criminal organisation *à la* Nuremberg to then develop into a narrow model of corporate criminal liability where only the conduct of a person in a position of control within the legal entity could have triggered the liability of the corporation.

The analysis of the evolution of the proposal highlighted the complexity of the task of defining a provision on corporate criminal liability. At the same time, it demonstrated a willingness on the side of several delegations to engage with the question of corporate criminal liability and to question the individualistic model of responsibility traditionally embraced under international criminal law. Furthermore, the examination of the preparatory works of the Statute of the ICC supports the conclusion that the exclusion of corporate criminal liability from the Statute did not rest on theoretical grounds or on an incompatibility between the concept and international criminal law. Conversely, the withdrawal of the proposal was due to practical considerations such as the lack of sufficient time to properly discuss the issue and to solve the challenges posed by the (then) limited recognition of corporate criminal liability at the domestic level. Accordingly, it is submitted that the failure of the French proposal should be interpreted in this context without overestimating its impact on future discussions on the subject matter. Far from representing the 'swan song' of corporate criminal liability, the withdrawal of the French proposal should be seen solely as a setback in the debate on the feasibility of including corporations within the domain of international criminal law.

References

Primary sources

Conventions and Treaties

Convention for the Suppression of Unlawful Act against the Safety of Maritime Navigation (adopted 10 March 1988, entered into force 1 March 1992) 1678 UNTS 222

International Convention against the Taking of Hostage (adopted 17 December 1979, entered into force 3 June 1983) 1316 UNTS 205

Protocol for the Suppression of Unlawful Act against the Safety of Fixed Platforms Located on the Continental Shelf (adopted 10 March 1988, entered into force 1 March 1992) 1678 UNTS 222

United Nations, *Agreement by the Government of the United Kingdom of Great Britain and Northern Ireland, the Government of the United States of America, the Provisional Government of the French Republic and the Government of the Union of Soviet Socialist Republics for the prosecution and punishment of the major war criminals of the European Axis ('London Agreement')*, 8 August 1945, 82 U.N.T.S. 279

UN Documents

1951 Committee on International Criminal Jurisdiction, 1st session: summary record of the 9th meeting held at the Palais des Nations, Geneva, on Monday, 13 August 1951, A/AC.48/SR.9

Informal Paper Submitted by the Bureau Substantive Law and Jurisdiction, UD/A/AC-244/IP-1

International Law Commission, Draft Code of Crimes against the Peace and Security of Mankind: draft articles on the draft Code of Crimes against the Peace and Security of Mankind: titles and texts / adopted by the Drafting Committee, A/CN.4/L.422, 15 July 1988

International Law Commission, Eighth report on the draft Code of Crimes against the Peace and Security of Mankind / by Doudou Thiam, Special Rapporteur, A/CN.4/430, 8 March 1990

International Law Commission, Fifth report on the draft Code of Offences against the Peace and Security of Mankind / by Doudou Thiam, Special Rapporteur, A/CN.4/404, 17 March 1987

International Law Commission, Ninth report on the draft Code of Crimes against the Peace and Security of Mankind, by Mr Doudou Thiam, Special Rapporteur, A/CN.4/435, 8 February 1991

International Law Commission, Ninth report on the draft Code of Crimes against the Peace and Security of Mankind, by Mr Doudou Thiam, Special Rapporteur, A/CN.4/435/Add.1, 15 March 1991

International Law Commission, Ninth report on the draft Code of Crimes against the Peace and Security of Mankind, by Mr Doudou Thiam, Special Rapporteur, A/CN.4/435/Corr.1, 6 May 1991

International Law Commission, Summary record of the 2154th meeting, held on Wednesday, 9 May 1990, A/CN.4/SR.2154
International Law Commission, Summary record of the 2155th meeting, held on Thursday, 10 May 1990, A/CN.4/SR.2155
International Law Commission, Summary record of the 2156th meeting, held on Friday, 11 May 1990, A/CN.4/SR.2156
International Law Commission, Summary record of the 2157th meeting, held on Tuesday, 15 May 1990, A/CN.4/SR.2157
International Law Commission, Summary record of the 2158th meeting, held on Wednesday, 16 May 1990, A/CN.4/SR.2158
Letter dated 31 March 1993 from the Charge d'Affaire a.i. of the Permanent Mission of Canada to the United Nations addressed to the Secretary-General, S/25504, 1 April 1993
Letter dated 93/03/31 from the representatives of Egypt, the Islamic Republic of Iran, Malaysia, Pakistan, Saudi Arabia, Senegal and Turkey to the United Nations addressed to the Secretary-General, S/25512, 5 April 1993
Letter dated 93/04/05 from the Permanent Representative of the Russian Federation to the United Nations addressed to the Secretary-General, S/25537, 6 April 1993
Letter dated 93/04/05 from the Permanent Representative of the United States of America to the United Nations addressed to the Secretary-General, S/25575, 12 April 1993
Preparatory Committee on Establishment of International Criminal Court to Meet at Headquarters, 11 - 21 February, L/2819, 7 February 1997
Report of the Ad Hoc Committee on the Establishment of an International Criminal Court, A/50/22, 6 September 1995
Report of the International Law Commission, 35th session, 3 May-22 July 1983, A/38/10, 3 August 1983
Report of the International Law Commission, 40th session, 9 May-29 July 1988, A/43/10, 19 August 1988
Report of the International Law Commission, 42nd session, 1 May-20 July 1990, A/45/10, 29 August 1990
Report of the International Law Commission, 44th session 4 May-24 July 1992, A/47/10, 1 September 1992
Report of the International Law Commission, 45th session, 3 May-23 July 1993, A/48/10, 1993
Report of the International Law Commission, 46th session, 2 May-22 July 1994, A/49/10, 1 September 1994
Report of the Preparatory Committee on the Establishment of an International Criminal Court, Vol. II, A/51/22, 13 September 1996
Report of the Preparatory Committee on the Establishment of an International Criminal Court, Vol. II, A/51/22
Report of the Secretary-General pursuant to Paragraph 2 of the Security Council Resolution 808 (1993), S/25704, 3 May 1993
Report of the Working Group Established by the Commission pursuant to the request from the General Assembly in paragraph 1 of its resolution 44/39, A/CN.4/L.454, 2 July 1990
UN Preparatory Committee on the Establishment of an International Criminal Court, Decisions taken by the Preparatory Committee at its session held from 11 to 21 February 1997, A/AC.249/1997/L.5, 12 March 1997

UN Preparatory Committee on the Establishment of an International Criminal Court, Working Group on General Principles of Criminal Law and Penalties, Chairman, *Article B b., c. and d.: Individual criminal responsibility: Chairman's text*, A/AC.249/1997/WG.2/CRP.2, 19 February 1997

UN Preparatory Committee on the Establishment of an International Criminal Court, *Article 17, Individual criminal responsibility: proposal / submitted by France*, A/AC.249/1998/DP.14, 2 April 1998

UN Preparatory Committee on the Establishment of an International Criminal Court, *Report of the inter-sessional meeting from 19 to 30 January 1998 in Zutphen, the Netherlands*, Zutphen Report, A/AC.249/1998/L.13, 4 February 1998

UN Preparatory Committee on the Establishment of an International Criminal Court, *Informal Group on General Principles of Criminal Law: proposed new Part (III bis) for the Statute of an International Criminal Court*, A/AC.249/CRP.13, 26 August 1996

UN Preparatory Committee on the Establishment of an International Criminal Court, *Draft statute of the International Criminal Court: working paper / submitted by France*, A/AC.249/L.3, 6 August 1996

UN Security Council, Statute of the International Criminal Tribunal for Rwanda (8 November 1994)

UNGA Res 36/106, Draft Code of Offences against Peace and Security of Mankind, A/RES/36/106, 10 December 1981

UNGA Res 38/132, Draft Code of Offences against Peace and Security of Mankind, A/RES/38/132, 19 December 1983

UNGA Res 44/39, International Criminal Responsibility of Individuals and Entities Engaged in Illicit Trafficking in Narcotic Drugs Across National Frontiers and other Transnational Criminal Activities, A/RES/44/39, 4 December 1989

UNGA Res 49/51, Report of the International Law Commission on the work of its forty-sixth session, A/RES/49/51, 17 February 1995

UNGA Res 49/53, Establishment of an International Criminal Court, A/RES/49/53, 17 February 1995

UNGA Res 50/46, Establishment of an International Criminal Court, A/RES/50/46, 11 December 1995

UNGA Res 51/207, Establishment of an International Criminal Court, A/RES/51/207, 17 December 1996

UNGA, 6th Committee, Summary record of the 31st meeting, held on Tuesday, 6 November 1990, New York, General Assembly, 45th session, A/C.6/45/SR.31

UNGA, 6th Committee, Summary record of the 33rd meeting, held on Wednesday, 7 November 1990, New York, General Assembly, 45th session, A/C.6/45/SR.33

UNGA, 6th Committee, Summary record of the 34th meeting, held on Thursday, 8 November 1990, New York, General Assembly, 45th session, A/C.6/45/SR.34

UNGA, 6th Committee, Summary record of the 36th meeting, held on Friday, 9 November 1990, New York, General Assembly, 45th session, A/C.6/45/SR.36

UNGA, 6th Committee, Summary record of the 37th meeting, held on Friday, 9 November 1990, New York, General Assembly, 45th session, A/C.6/45/SR.37

United Nations Diplomatic Conference of Plenipotentiaries on the Establishment of an International Criminal Court, Article 23, Individual Criminal Responsibility: Legal Persons: Proposal / Submitted By France, A/CONF.183/C.1/L.3, 16 June 1998

United Nations Diplomatic Conference of Plenipotentiaries on the Establishment of an International Criminal Court, Committee of the Whole, Summary Record of the

1st Meeting Held at the Headquarters of the Food and Agriculture Organization of the United Nations on Tuesday, 16 June 1998, A/CONF.183/C.1/SR.1

United Nations Diplomatic Conference of Plenipotentiaries on the Establishment of an International Criminal Court, Working Paper on Article 23, Paragraphs 5 and 6: [Draft Statute of an International Criminal Court], A/CONF.183/C.1/WGGP/L.5/Rev.1, 25 June 1998

United Nations Diplomatic Conference of Plenipotentiaries on the Establishment of an International Criminal Court, Working Paper on Article 23, Paragraphs 5 and 6: [Draft Statute of an International Criminal Court], A/CONF.183/C.1/WGGP/L.5/Rev.2, 4 July 1998

United Nations Diplomatic Conference of Plenipotentiaries on the Establishment of an International Criminal Court, Working Paper on Article 23, Paragraphs 5 and 6, A/CONF.183/C.1/WGGP/L.5, 20 June 1998

United Nations Diplomatic Conference of Plenipotentiaries on the Establishment of an International Criminal Court, Summary Record of the 1st Plenary Meeting Held at the Headquarters of the Food and Agriculture Organization of the United Nations on Monday, 15 June 1998, A/CONF.183/SR.1

United Nations Diplomatic Conference of Plenipotentiaries on the establishment of an International Criminal Court Rome, Italy 15 June17 July 1998 - JOURNAL No. 16, A/CONF-183/JOURNAL -16, 7 July 1998

UNSC Res 808 (1993), On establishment on an International Tribunal for the Prosecution of Persons Responsible for Violations of International Humanitarian Law Committed in the Territory of the Former Yugoslavia, S/RES/808 (1993) 22 February 1993

Domestic cases

A.I. Credit Corp. v. Legion Ins. Co., 265 F.3d 630 (7th Cir. 2001)

Jesner v. Arab Bank, PLC, 138 S. Ct. 1386

Lennard's Carrying Co v. Asiatic Petroleum Co. [1915] A.C. 705

New York Central & Hudson River R.R. v. United States, 212 U.S. 481 (1909)

Tesco Supermarkets v. Nattrass [1971] UKHL 1

United States v. A & P Trucking Co., 358 U.S. 121 (1958)

United States v. Cincotta, 689 F.2d 238, at 242 (1st Cir., 1982)

Secondary sources

Books

Bassiouni M C, *The Statute of the International Criminal Court: A Documentary History* (Transnational Pub Inc; 1998)

Bernaz N, *Business and Human Rights: History, Law and Policy – Bridging the Accountability Gap* (Routledge 2017)

Cassese A, *Cassese's International Criminal Law* (3rd edn, OUP 2013)

Clapham A, *Human Rights Obligations of Non-State Actors* (OUP 2006)

Graefrath B, Oeser E, and Steiniger P A, *Völkerrechtliche Verantwortlichkeit der Staaten* (Staatsverlag der Deutschen Demokratischen Republik 1977)

Schabas W A, *The International Criminal Court: A Commentary on the Rome Statute* (2nd edn, OUP 2016)

Stoitchkova D, *Towards Corporate Liability in International Criminal Law* (Intersentia 2010)
Wells C, *Corporations and Criminal Responsibility* (2nd edn, OUP 2005)

Contribution in edited books

Beauvais P, 'Country Report: France' in James Gobert and Ana-Maria Pascal (eds), *European Developments in Corporate Criminal Liability* (Routledge 2011)
Clapham A, 'The Question of Jurisdiction under International Criminal Law over Legal Persons: Lessons from the Rome Conference on an International Criminal Court' in Menno T. Kamminga and Saman Zia-Zarifi (eds), *Liability of Multinational Corporations Under International Law* (Martinus Nijhoff 2000)
Graefrath B, 'International Crimes – A Specific Regime of International Responsibility of States and its Legal Consequences' in J H H Weiler, A Cassese and M Spinedi (eds), *International Crimes of States: A Critical Analysis of the ILC's draft Article 19 on State Responsibility* (Walter de Gruyter 1988)
Saland P, 'International Criminal Law Principles' in Roy Lee (ed), *The International Criminal Court: The Making of the Rome Statute* (Martinus Nijhoff Publishers 1999)

Journal Articles

Cassel D, 'Corporate Aiding and Abetting of Human Rights Violations: Confusion in the Courts' (2008) 6 Northwestern University Journal of International Human Rights 304
de Maglie C, 'Models of Corporate Criminal Liability in Comparative Law' (2005) 4 Washington University Global Studies Law Review 547
Deckert K, 'Corporate Criminal Liability' in France in Mark Pieth and Radha Ivory (eds), *Corporate Criminal Liability: Emergence, Convergence, and Risk* (Springer 2011)
Dsouza M, 'The Corporate Agent in Criminal Law – An Argument for Comprehensive Identification' (2020) 79 The Cambridge Law Journal 91
Fauchald O K and Stigen J, 'Corporate Responsibility before International Institutions' (2009) 40 George Washington International Law Review 1025
French Criminal Code, Article 121-2
Geraghty A, 'Corporate Criminal Liability' (2002) 39 American Criminal Law Review 327
Graefrath B, 'Völkerrechtliche Konsequenzen aus der Anwendung der Aggressionsdefinition durch den UN-Sicherheitsrat' (1976) 30 Neue Justize 732
Maréchal Jean-Yves, 'Responsabilité pénale des personnes morales' (2009) 80 JurisClasseur Pénal Code 1
Kaeb C, 'The Shifting Sands of Corporate Liability under International Criminal Law' (2016) 49 George Washington International Law Review 351
Kirsch P and Holmes J T, 'The Birth of the International Criminal Court: The 1998 Rome Conference' (1998) 36 Canadian Yearbook of International Law 3
Kyriakakis J, 'Corporate Criminal Liability and the ICC Statute: The Comparative Law Challenge' (2009) 56 Netherlands International Law Review 333

Kyriakakis J, 'Corporations before International Criminal Courts: Implications for the International Criminal Justice Project' (2016) 30(1) Leiden Journal of International Law 1

Orland L and Cachera C, 'Corporate Crime and Punishment in France: Criminal Responsibility of Legal Entities (Personnes Morales) under the New French Criminal Code (Nouveau Code Penal)' (1995) 11 Connecticut Journal of International Law 111

Scheffer D, 'Corporate Liability under the Rome Statute' (2016) 57 Harvard International Law Journal 35

Scheffer D, 'Keynote Address: Is the Presumption of Corporate Impunity Dead?' (2018) 50 Case Western Reserve Journal of International Law 213

Shraga D and Zacklin R, 'The International Criminal Tribunal for the Former Yugoslavia' (1994) 5 European Journal of International Law 360

Stessens G, 'Corporate Criminal Liability: A Comparative Perspective' (1994) 43(3) International and Comparative Law Quarterly 493

Thurer D, 'Vom Nurnberger Tribunal zum Jugoslawien-Tribunal und Weiter zu Einem Weltstrafgerichtshof' (1993) 3 Swiss Review of International and European Law 491

van der Wilt H, 'Corporate Criminal Responsibility for International Crimes: Exploring the Possibilities' (2013) 12 Chinese Journal of International Law 43

Miscellaneous

Trial of the Major War Criminals before the International Military Tribunal, Vol. VIII - Proceedings (20 February 1946–7 March 1946), Library of Congress

4 Corporate Criminal Liability after Rome

International Developments in the Aftermath of the Adoption of the ICC Statute

4.1 Introduction

Chapter 3 analysed the preparatory work of the Statute of the ICC to outline to what extent the idea of including corporations within the scope of the Court's jurisdiction *ratione personae* was discussed in the 1990s. The chapter demonstrated that the question of the international liability of corporations has remained a key feature of the debate since 1990, when the ILC resumed its work on a draft statute of an international criminal court. Over the years, more and more attention was paid to the idea of corporate liability as the proposals to include such a form of liability at the international level became increasingly more refined. The analysis conducted in the previous chapter focused in particular on the French proposal on the liability of legal persons. The investigation followed the evolution of the proposal, from its origin to its final formulation, to highlight the several attempts made to define a model of corporate criminal liability that could have won the favour of the delegations in Rome. The analysis of the preparatory work of the Rome Statute shed light on the arguments raised to discuss the French proposal on legal persons and evidenced how the obstacles that prevented the adoption of the proposal rest primarily on practical considerations and not, as often suggested, on a (perceived) incompatibility between corporate liability and international criminal law.[1] To those against the recognition of an international criminal liability of corporations, the position adopted in Rome located corporations outside the scope of international criminal law, closing the door to future discussion on the subject matter.[2] This interpretation, however, conflicts with the analysis conducted in Chapter 3 and fails to recognise the dynamic nature of the international legal system and its ability to evolve and adjust to the needs of the international community.

1 *Kiobel v. Royal Dutch Petroleum Co.*, 621 F.3d 111, at 120 (2d Cir. 2010), *Jesner v. Arab Bank, PLC*, 138 S. Ct. 1386, at 1400-1 (2018).
2 Ibid.

DOI: 10.4324/9781003390534-5

Thus, an investigation of the status of corporate criminal liability for international crimes necessarily needs to look beyond the adoption of the Rome Statute and consider the national and international developments that have occurred over the past 20 years. These developments have become more and more significant in the discussion of the international criminal liability of corporations. Advancements in the field of international criminal law have called for a reconsideration of the role of legal persons within the international criminal justice system and have drawn attention to the need for effective mechanisms to hold legal entities accountable for international crimes. This chapter focuses specifically on the developments that have occurred at the international level in the area of international criminal law. Interestingly, all the events here considered have a common denominator of the year of 2014.

Indeed, the chapter begins with an analysis of the decisions adopted by the Special Tribunal for Lebanon (hereafter STL) at various stages of the proceedings opened, in 2014, against two corporations: New TV S.A.L. and Akhbar Beirut S.A.L.[3] While these decisions present relevant limitations as they were adopted in the context of contemptuous offences, they still represent a first attempt from an international criminal tribunal to assert its jurisdiction over corporate entities. The chapter then looks at the initiative promoted by the African Union to create a regional criminal chamber within the (proposed) African Court of Justice and Human Rights with jurisdiction over international and transnational crimes perpetrated by individuals and corporations alike.[4] The model proposed by the 2014 Malabo Protocol – even though still far from entering into force – provides food for thought regarding a possible approach to impose international criminal liability on corporations. Lastly, the Draft Articles on Crimes Against Humanity occupy an important part in the investigation of the post-1998 developments involving the liability of corporations.[5] Elaborated by the ILC in a span of five years – from 2014 to 2019 – , the Draft Articles represent the first attempt to produce a specialised convention on crimes against humanity to complement the Genocide Convention. In the chapter, particular attention is paid to draft Article 6(8) which proposed the inclusion of the liability of legal entities for their involvement in the crimes listed in the proposed convention. The investigation of these three key developments is essential to appreciate how the arguments in support of the

3 *New TV S.A.L. and Ms Khayat*, Redacted Version of Decision in Proceedings for Contempt with Orders in Lieu of an Indictment, STL-14-05/1/CJ, Contempt Judge, 31 January 2014; *Akhbar Beirut S.A.L. and Mr Al-Amin*, Redacted Version of Decision in Proceedings for Contempt with Orders in Lieu of an Indictment, STL-14-06/1/CJ, Contempt Judge, 31 January 2014.

4 African Union, Protocol on Amendments to the Protocol on the Statute of the African Court of Justice and Human Rights, 27 June 2014.

5 International Law Commission, Draft articles on Prevention and Punishment of Crimes against Humanity, A/74/10, para 44.

inclusion of corporations within the framework of international criminal law have evolved over the past twenty years.

4.2 The Special Tribunal for Lebanon's Jurisdiction over Legal Persons: An Analysis of the 2014 Contempt Cases

In July 2016, the STL became the first international tribunal to issue a judgment against a corporate entity. The guilty verdict was entered against the newspaper company Akhbar Beirut S.A.L. and its editor-in-chief and chairman of the board of directors, Mr Ibrahim Mohamed Al-Amin, for interfering with the Tribunal's administration of justice.[6] In particular, the company (and its editor-in-chief) stood accused of breaching the confidentiality of several Prosecution witnesses in the case of *Ayyash, et al.* The conviction of Akhbar Beirut S.A.L. followed the previous acquittal of another corporate entity, New TV S.A.L., also accused of contemptuous conduct against the administration of justice.[7]

Both cases attracted the attention of scholars in the field of business and human rights for the novelty of the arguments discussed and for the potential impact that such cases could have had in the field of corporate accountability.[8] While the overall relevance of these two cases may be questionable due to their limited scope, their procedural history offers interesting insight into the evolution of the debate on corporate criminal liability at the international level. The following sections look at the decisions that, in 2014, paved the way to the first 'historic' judgment delivered by an international criminal tribunal against a corporation. Specifically, the next sections considered the decisions issued in the *New TV S.A.L. case* by the two contempt judges – Judge Baragwanath and Judge Lettieri – respectively in January and June 2014, and by the Appeals Panel, in the October of the same year. These decisions provided the legal arguments that were subsequently applied in the twin case against Akhbar Beirut S.A.L. and Al-Amin and laid the foundation for both contempt trials.

6 *Akhbar Beirut S.A.L. and Mr Al-Amin*, Public Redacted Version of the Judgment, STL-14-06/T/CJ, Contempt Judge, 15 July 2016.

7 *New TV S.A.L. and Khayat*, Public Redacted Version of Judgment on Appeal, STL-14-05/A/AP, Appeals Panel, 8 March 2016.

8 Osama Alkhawaja, 'In Defense of the Special Tribunal for Lebanon and the Case for International Corporate Accountability' (2020) 20 Chicago Journal of International Law 450, Nadia Bernaz, 'Corporate Criminal Liability under International Law. The New TV S.A.L. and Akhbar Beirut S.A.L. Cases at the Special Tribunal for Lebanon' (2015) 13 Journal of International Criminal Justice 313; Russell Hopkins, 'Forth, back and forth on corporate criminal liability at the Special Tribunal for Lebanon' (Corporate War Crimes 2015) https://corporatewarcrimes.com/author/corporatewarcrimes/page/27/ Accessed 26 March 2023.

4.2.1 *The First Contempt Decision: Judge Baragwanath's View on Corporate Criminal Liability*

Established in the wake of the terrorist attack in 2005 that killed former Lebanese Prime Minister, Rafiq Hariri, together with 22 others, the STL is a unique example of a modern hybrid or internationalised criminal tribunal.[9] From its narrow scope, limited to a specific attack and to a restricted number of connected cases, to its 'innovative' Statute, which for the first time covers the crime of terrorism[10] and introduces provisions for trials in absentia[11], the STL has proved to be an interesting case study in international criminal law. The decision to directly address the question of corporate criminal liability further contributed to increasing the 'uniqueness' of the Tribunal.

The proceedings that led to the first trials against two (business) corporate entities started in 2013 when Judge Baragwanath, then STL Contempt Judge, ordered the opening of an investigation on allegations of contempt and interference with the administration of justice in relation to the publication of information relating to the identity of alleged confidential witnesses before the Ttribunal.[12] The investigation was conducted by an *amicus curiae*, Stephane Bourgon, appointed by the Tribunal Acting Registrar and resulted in a final report that was presented to Judge Baragwanath on 23 October 2013.[13] The report offered 'sufficient grounds to proceed for contempt' against four persons, two individuals, and two corporations.

On 31 January 2014, Judge Baragwanath delivered a Decision in Proceedings for Contempt in which he issued orders in lieu of an indictment against (a) New TV S.A.L., the company operating Al Jadeed TV, and its deputy head of news, Ms Karma Khayat, and (b) the newspaper company Akhbar Beirut S.A.L. and its editor-in-chief and chairman of the board of directors.

9 For an analysis of the 'peculiar' nature of the STL see contributions in Amal Alamuddin, Nidal Nabil Jurdi, and David Tolbert (eds), *The Special Tribunal for Lebanon: Law and Practice* (OUP 2014).

10 See Nidal Nabil Jurdi, 'The Crime of Terrorism in Lebanese and International Law in Amal Alamuddin' in Nidal Nabil Jurdi, and David Tolbert (eds), *The Special Tribunal for Lebanon: Law and Practice* (OUP 2014).

11 See Caleb H Wheeler, *The Right to be Present at Trial in International Criminal Law* (Brill | Nijhoff 2019) 133-163; Paola Gaeta, 'Trial *in Absentia* Before the Special Tribunal for Lebanon' in Amal Alamuddin, Nidal Nabil Jurdi, and David Tolbert (eds), *The Special Tribunal for Lebanon: Law and Practice* (OUP 2014).

12 *Ayyash et al.*, Public Redacted Version of Decision on Allegations of Contempt, STL-11-01//PT/CJ/R60bis.1, Contempt Judge, 29 April 2013.

13 *New TV S.A.L. and Ms Khayat*, Redacted Version of Decision in Proceedings for Contempt with Orders in Lieu of an Indictment, STL-14-05/1/CJ, Contempt Judge, 31 January 2014, para 8; *Akhbar Beirut S.A.L. and Mr Al-Amin*, Redacted Version of Decision in Proceedings for Contempt with Orders in Lieu of an Indictment, STL-14-06/1/CJ, Contempt Judge, 31 January 2014, para 8.

Mr Ibrahim Mohamed Al-Amin.[14] The decision began with an analysis of the scope of the Tribunal's contempt jurisdiction. As explained by the Judge, such jurisdiction does not derive from the Tribunal's Statute – which remains silent on the subject – but from the Tribunal's 'inherent jurisdiction to protect the integrity of the judicial process and to ensure the proper administration of justice'.[15]

In its jurisprudence, the STL has defined its 'inherent jurisdiction' as the power 'to determine incidental legal issues which arise as a direct consequence of the procedures of which the Tribunal is seized by reason of the matter falling under its primary jurisdiction'.[16] Such jurisdiction is therefore considered 'ancillary or incidental to the [Tribunal's] primary jurisdiction' and it is deemed pivotal 'to ensure a good and fair administration of justice'.[17]

In instances of contempt, the International Criminal Tribunal for the former Yugoslavia also relied upon the concept of inherent jurisdiction in the case *Prosecutor v Dusko Tadic* where the judges observed that even though the Tribunal's Statute makes no mention of the issue of contempt:

> [t]he Tribunal does, however, possess an inherent jurisdiction, deriving from its judicial function, to ensure that its exercise of the jurisdiction which is expressly given to it by that Statute is not frustrated and that its basic judicial functions are safeguarded. As an international criminal court, the Tribunal must therefore possess the inherent power to deal with conduct which interferes with its administration of justice.[18]

The STL has incorporated such a concept into Rule 60bis of the Rules of Procedure and Evidence which recognises that '[t]he Tribunal, in the exercise of its inherent power, may hold in contempt those who knowingly and wilfully interfere with its administration of justice, upon assertion of the Tribunal's jurisdiction according to the Statute'.[19] Rule 60bis, thus, provides the legal framework for the exercise of the Tribunal's power in cases of contempt of court.

14 *New TV S.A.L. and Ms Khayat*, Redacted Version of Decision in Proceedings for Contempt with Orders in Lieu of an Indictment, STL-14-05/1/CJ, Contempt Judge, 31 January 2014; *Akhbar Beirut S.A.L. and Mr Al-Amin*, Redacted Version of Decision in Proceedings for Contempt with Orders in Lieu of an Indictment, STL-14-06/1/CJ, Contempt Judge, 31 January 2014.

15 Ibid para 10.

16 *In the matter of El Sayed*, Decision on Appeal of Pre-Trial Judge's Order Regarding Jurisdiction and Standing, CH/AC/201 0/02, Appeals Chamber, 10 November 2010, para 45.

17 Ibid.

18 *Prosecutor v. Tadić*, Judgment on Allegations of Contempt Against Prior Counsel, Milan Vujin, IT-94-1-A-R77, 31 January 2000, para 13. See also *Prosecutor v. Simić et al.*, Judgment in the Matter of Contempt Allegations Against an Accused and his Counsel, IT-95-9-R77, 30 June 2000, para 91.

19 Special Tribunal for Lebanon, Rules of Procedure and Evidence, Rule 60bis (A).

If the applicability of such a provision to contemptuous conducts of natural persons did not raise specific concerns, more controversial was the question of 'whether the Tribunal's inherent power to prosecute cases of contempt [extended] to legal persons' as well.[20] Judge Baragwanath considered the issue in section I(D) of the Decision, presenting his reasoning in a quite brief way.[21]

The five-page long section mostly centred on the juxtaposition of the Tribunal's primary jurisdiction – defined by its Statute – and contempt jurisdiction – which regulatory framework was provided by Rule 60bis.[22] According to Judge Baragwanath, while several elements in the Statute of the STL impose an interpretation of the Tribunal's primary jurisdiction limited to natural persons only, 'the logic demanding this conclusion does not call for such limitation in the case of contempt'.[23]

Looking at the provisions of the Statute, the Contempt Judge observed that:

> In confining the primary jurisdiction of the Tribunal to persons 'individually responsible for crimes' set forth in Article 2, Article 3(1) does not distinguish between natural and legal persons. There is no question that an 'individual' person can, by definition, be a distinct legal person. However, Article 3 (2)(3) expressly declares superiors criminally responsible for the crimes of subordinates under 'his or her effective authority and control' and provides that the 'fact that [a subordinate] acted pursuant to an order of a superior shall not relieve him or her of criminal responsibility'. Article 16 also repeatedly refers to natural persons in spelling out the rights of an accused. Moreover, there is no reference to an 'it' in the context of an accused anywhere in the Statute.[24]

20 *New TV S.A.L. and Ms Khayat*, Redacted Version of Decision in Proceedings for Contempt with Orders in Lieu of an Indictment, STL-14-05/1/CJ, Contempt Judge, 31 January 2014, para 18; *Akhbar Beirut S.A.L. and Mr Al-Amin*, Redacted Version of Decision in Proceedings for Contempt with Orders in Lieu of an Indictment, STL-14-06/1/CJ, Contempt Judge, 31 January 2014, para 18.

21 Hopkins (n 8).

22 *New TV S.A.L. and Ms Khayat*, Redacted Version of Decision in Proceedings for Contempt with Orders in Lieu of an Indictment, STL-14-05/1/CJ, Contempt Judge, 31 January 2014, paras 18-28; *Akhbar Beirut S.A.L. and Mr Al-Amin*, Redacted Version of Decision in Proceedings for Contempt with Orders in Lieu of an Indictment, STL-14-06/1/CJ, Contempt Judge, 31 January 2014, paras 18-28. See also Hopkins (n 8).

23 *New TV S.A.L. and Ms Khayat*, Redacted Version of Decision in Proceedings for Contempt with Orders in Lieu of an Indictment, STL-14-05/1/CJ, Contempt Judge, 31 January 2014, para 21; *Akhbar Beirut S.A.L. and Mr Al-Amin*, Redacted Version of Decision in Proceedings for Contempt with Orders in Lieu of an Indictment, STL-14-06/1/CJ, Contempt Judge, 31 January 2014, para 21.

24 Ibid para 22.

Lacking proper evidence of the drafters' intention to include legal persons in the primary jurisdiction of the Tribunal, the logical solution – according to Judge Baragwanath – was to presume the applicability of the principle *societas delinquere non potest*.[25] 'Since both the language of the Statute and that principle pull in the same direction', the Contempt Judge felt compelled to conclude that Articles 2 and 3 of the Statute do not apply to legal persons.[26]

As will be discussed *infra*, this gendered interpretation of the Tribunal's Statute was subsequently criticised by the Appeals Panel who proposed a broader reading of the Statute based on the French and Arabic versions of the document.[27] At this stage, however, the question of a potential conflict between the terminology used in the three official languages of the Tribunal was not taken into consideration by the Contempt Judge. In Judge Baragwanath's view, the provisions of the Statute (as worded in its English version) were simply drafted in a way that did not offer any room for doubt on how they should be interpreted.

However, Rule 60bis of the Rules of Procedure and Evidence allows for a different conclusion. In this regard, the Judge observed that, while Rule 60bis complements the provisions of the Statute of the Special Tribunal, 'it is not necessarily limited by them'.[28] In particular, Judge Baragwanath considered that:

> The Tribunal's inherent power to hold persons in contempt, necessary to ensure the administration of justice, is ancillary to its primary purposes. Whether a legal person can be an accused under Articles 2 and 3 of the Statute is a very different question from whether a legal person can be held in contempt for knowingly and wilfully interfering with the administration of justice. ... [I]n order to ensure the administration of justice ..., Rule 60bis must be read to cover acts of contempt allegedly undertaken by legal persons. Under the highest procedural standards, corporate entities cannot be any more entitled than natural persons to interfere with the judicial process.[29]

25 Ibid para 23.

26 Ibid para 23.

27 *New TV S.A.L. and Ms Khayat*, Decision on Interlocutory Appeal Concerning Personal Jurisdiction in Contempt Proceedings, STL-14-05/PT/AP/ARI26.1, Appeals Panel, 2 October 2014 paras 37-39.

28 *New TV S.A.L. and Ms Khayat*, Redacted Version of Decision in Proceedings for Contempt with Orders in Lieu of an Indictment, STL-14-05/1/CJ, Contempt Judge, 31 January 2014, para 24; *Akhbar Beirut S.A.L. and Mr Al-Amin*, Redacted Version of Decision in Proceedings for Contempt with Orders in Lieu of an Indictment, STL-14-06/1/CJ, Contempt Judge, 31 January 2014, para 24.

29 Ibid.

In justifying this conclusion, the Judge recognised the novelty of his position and the lack of precedents at the international criminal justice level.[30] However, he considered that developments at the domestic level justify a change in the perspective on corporate liability, at least concerning contempt cases.[31] Indeed, the Judge pointed out that as corporations 'have assumed ever greater prominence as actors in legal and commercial affairs, domestic jurisdictions have progressively recognized the need to hold them criminally accountable for their conduct'.[32]

This emphasis put on the progressive acceptance of corporate criminal liability at the national level is particularly relevant and evidences a shift in the argumentation used to discuss such a legal construct at the international level. If in 1998 the limited recognition of corporate criminal liability at the domestic level represented one of the main obstacles to the inclusion of corporations within the jurisdiction of the ICC, in 2014 the comparative law argument became a major argument *in favour* of the international recognition of such legal construct.

This shift in the use of the comparative law argument certainly did not occur overnight. As will be discussed *infra*, this change of perspective gradually emerged in the late 2000s to become a central feature in nowadays debate on the international criminal liability of corporations.[33] In Judge Baragwanath's decision, the comparative law argument based on the domestic developments on corporate criminal liability was only briefly addressed and was mostly used to provide a context for the analysis of the provision of Article 210 of the Lebanese Criminal Code which recognised such a form of liability in the Lebanese legal system.[34] Modelled on Article 121 of the French Criminal Code, Article 210 establishes that a legal person is criminally liable for the offences committed by its 'directors, management staff, representatives and employees' when such offences are committed 'on behalf of or using the means provided by such legal person'.[35]

In the decision under consideration, Article 210 evidenced Lebanon's openness towards the concept of corporate criminal liability and its rejection

30 Ibid para 25.

31 Ibid para 26.

32 Ibid para 27.

33 Jendrik Adam, *Die Strafbarkeit juristischer Personem im Volkerstrafrecht* (Nomos 2015), 95 et ss.; Caroline Kaeb, 'The Shifting Sands of Corporate Liability Under International Criminal Law' (2016) George Washington International Law Review 351; Joanna Kyriakakis, 'Corporate Criminal Liability and the Comparative Law Challenge' (2009) Netherland International Law Review 333.

34 *New TV S.A.L. and Ms Khayat*, Redacted Version of Decision in Proceedings for Contempt with Orders in Lieu of an Indictment, STL-14-05/1/CJ, Contempt Judge, 31 January 2014, para 26; *Akhbar Beirut S.A.L. and Mr Al-Amin*, Redacted Version of Decision in Proceedings for Contempt with Orders in Lieu of an Indictment, STL-14-06/1/CJ, Contempt Judge, 31 January 2014, para 26.

35 Lebanese Criminal Code, Article 210.

of the principles of *societas delinquere non potest*. As such, Judge Baragwanath deemed it would have been 'bizarre for [the] Tribunal to deny protection of its due process against corporate interference because of an ancient maxim that the State it serves has rejected'.[36] The emphasis put on Article 210 of the Lebanese Criminal Code in the Judge's reasoning may find a justification in the provision of Rule 3 of the Rules of Procedure and Evidence which listed the Lebanese Code of Criminal Procedure as one of the elements that judges should consider when interpreting the Rules.[37] While the reference is specific to the Code of Criminal Procedure, the undeniable link between the Code of Criminal Procedure and the Criminal Code of a country justifies a reading of Rule 3 that encompasses both documents as interpretative sources.

Lastly, Judge Baragwanath observed that the applicability of the Tribunal's contempt jurisdiction to legal persons was also justified by the power that corporate entities wield in modern society. According to the Contempt Judges:

> [i]t would not only be naive but dangerous to accept that only natural persons can interfere with the administration of justice. To limit criminal liability for contempt to individual natural persons risks undermining the justice process; for the actual and most powerful culprits of any proved interference with justice would go untried. ... I decline to impute to the Plenary an intention to immunize legal persons against liability for interfering with due process.[38]

Undoubtedly, the reasoning followed by Judge Baragwanath presents several shortcomings as some of the arguments are not sufficiently elaborated. As mentioned above, more consideration should have been paid to the comparative law argument prosed by the Judge. Due to the role it plays in the reasoning, the argument should have been better substantiated with more thought given to the domestic developments under consideration. Additionally, the Judge's application of Rule 3 to determine the scope of Rule 60bis lacks a proper degree of accuracy. Indeed, to support the inclusion of corporations in the contempt jurisdiction of the Tribunal, the Contempt Judge merely relied on Rule 3(A)(iv) which imposes that the Tribunal's Rules 'shall be interpreted

36 *New TV S.A.L. and Ms Khayat*, Redacted Version of Decision in Proceedings for Contempt with Orders in Lieu of an Indictment, STL-14-05/1/CJ, Contempt Judge, 31 January 2014, para 26; *Akhbar Beirut S.A.L. and Mr Al-Amin*, Redacted Version of Decision in Proceedings for Contempt with Orders in Lieu of an Indictment, STL-14-06/1/CJ, Contempt Judge, 31 January 2014, para 26.

37 Special Tribunal for Lebanon, Rules of Procedure and Evidence, Rule 3.

38 *New TV S.A.L. and Ms Khayat*, Redacted Version of Decision in Proceedings for Contempt with Orders in Lieu of an Indictment, STL-14-05/1/CJ, Contempt Judge, 31 January 2014, para 28; *Akhbar Beirut S.A.L. and Mr Al-Amin*, Redacted Version of Decision in Proceedings for Contempt with Orders in Lieu of an Indictment, STL-14-06/1/CJ, Contempt Judge, 31 January 2014, para 28.

in a manner consonant with the spirit of the Statute and, …, as appropriate, [with] (iv) the Lebanese Code of Criminal Procedure'.[39] Conversely, no attention is paid to the other interpretative guidelines provided under Rule 3(A), specifically the 1969 Vienna Convention on the Law of the Treaties (Rule 3(A)(i)), international standards on human rights (Rule 3(A)(ii)) and the general principles of international criminal law and procedure (Rule 3(A)(iii)).[40]

Still, Judge Baragwanath's decision can be considered 'ground-breaking' as it represents the first attempt made by an international judge to offer an innovative reading of the role of corporations under international criminal law. Indeed, even though limited in scope, the decision presents new arguments in favour of the inclusion of corporate actors within the scope of international criminal law – especially regarding domestic developments – which should not be overlooked.

4.2.2 Challenging Corporate Criminal Liability: The Point of View of Judge Lettieri

In January 2014, contextually to Judge Baragwanath's decision, the contempt cases against New TV S.A.L. and Ms Karma Khayat, on the one side, and Akhbar Beirut S.A.L. and Mr Ibrahim Mohamed Al-Amin, on the other, were assigned to a new Contempt Judge: Judge Nicola Lettieri.

On 16 June 2014, New TV S.A.L. and Ms Karma Khayat presented a Preliminary Motion Challenging Jurisdiction in which the defence contested the Tribunal's jurisdiction over legal persons and asked the Judge to drop all the charges against the broadcasting company.[41] In particular, the defence criticised Judge Baragwanath's conclusion on corporate criminal liability for contempt as 'fundamentally flawed and illogical'.[42] According to the defence, the argument based on a perceived distinction between 'those who can be charged under Rule 60bis as opposed to Articles 1–3 of the Statute … is wholly unsustainable' as the scope of Rule 60bis should not extend any further than that of Articles 1–3 of the Tribunal's Statute.[43] The defence contested as well the Judge's reference to Article 210 of the Lebanese Code and the developing trend to recognise corporate criminal liability at the domestic level as entirely irrelevant in the context of the case under consideration.[44]

39 Special Tribunal for Lebanon, Rules of Procedure and Evidence, Rule 3.

40 Ibid.

41 *New TV S.A.L. and Khayat*, Defence Preliminary Motion Challenging Jurisdiction, STL-14-05/PT/CJ, 16 June 2014.

42 Ibid para 12.

43 Ibid.

44 Ibid paras 43-51 and paras 52-66.

On 24 July 2014, Judge Lettieri granted the Defence Motion and ordered all charges against New TV S.A.L. to be dismissed.[45] Judge Lettieri's reasoning on the issue of corporate criminal liability is opposite to that of Judge Baragwanath but equally short (once again, five pages).[46]

After reaffirming the Tribunal's inherent jurisdiction over contempt and obstruction of justice,[47] Judge Lettieri started his analysis of Rule 60bis to determine whether the provision may contemplate corporate criminal liability for contempt.[48] The Judge observed that to answer such a question, 'a clear and determinative distinction must be made between jurisdiction *ratione materiae/temporis/loci* and jurisdiction *ratione personarum*'.[49] While the Tribunal's contempt jurisdiction 'certainly broaden the scope of the Tribunal's *authority ratione materiae* (and *ratione temporis/loci*)' by allowing it to address conduct not directly criminalised by the Statute and occurred after 2005, the same cannot be said about the Tribunal's jurisdiction *ratione personae.*[50]

Indeed, according to Judge Lettieri, if the Tribunal's jurisdiction *ratione materiae/temporis/loci* for contempt were limited by the Statute, 'no interference with the administration of the Tribunal's justice could be prosecuted; the inherent power of contempt, and Rule 60bis, would effectively be rendered meaningless'.[51] Conversely, when looking at the jurisdiction *ratione personae*, the Contempt Judge considered that 'the fact that the Tribunal is not allowed to prosecute legal persons does not as such render its contempt power meaningless'.[52] While Judge Lettieri conceded that he 'could even agree with Judge Baragwanath *de lege ferenda*', an interpretation of Rule 60bis on the basis of what the law should be 'does not suffice to solidly ground the Tribunal's jurisdiction *de lege lata*'.[53]

Rule 60bis, recalled the Contempt Judge, does not provide any explicit reference to the Tribunal's authority over legal persons for contemptuous offences.[54] In considering whether such authority may be inferred implicitly, Judge Lettieri took a different approach from that adopted by Judge Baragwanath in the January decision. Per Rule 3 of the Rules of Procedure and Evidence, Judge Lettieri referred in his analysis to Article 31(1) of the 1969 Vienna

45 *New TV S.A.L. and Khayat*, Decision on Motion Challenging Jurisdiction and on Request for Leave to Amend Order in Lieu of an Indictment, STL-14-05/PT/CJ, Contempt Judge, 24 July 2014.

46 Hopkins (n 8).

47 *New TV S.A.L. and Khayat*, Decision on Motion Challenging Jurisdiction and on Request for Leave to Amend Order in Lieu of an Indictment, STL-14-05/PT/CJ, Contempt Judge, 24 July 2014, para 56.

48 Ibid paras 57 et ss.

49 Ibid para 65.

50 Ibid.

51 Ibid para 66.

52 Ibid para 67.

53 Ibid para 68.

54 Ibid para 69.

Convention on the Law of Treaties which states that treaty provisions 'shall be interpreted in good faith in accordance with the ordinary meaning to be given to the terms of the treaty in their context and in light of its object and purpose'.[55] In this regard, the Judge observed that:

> The spirit of the Statute, given its terms, supports an interpretation limiting personal jurisdiction in contempt cases to natural persons only. In cases where the legislator (in this case, Lebanon and the United Nations, which discussed the terms of the Statute) did not explicitly foresee criminal jurisdiction for legal persons, it is impermissible to proceed by analogy. On the basis of the principle *ubi lex voluit dixit, ubi noluit tacuit*, which requires judges to infer precise consequences from the legislator's silence, it would therefore be inappropriate to expand the interpretation of the term 'person' to cover legal persons.[56]

By applying 'the basic canons of treaty interpretation', the Contempt Judge considered that the term 'person' used in the Rules of Procedure and Evidence should be interpreted 'in consonance with the Statute's understanding of the same term' therefore reading it as including natural persons only.[57] Judge Lettieri contended as well that this literal interpretation of the term 'person' under Rule 60bis is the most appropriate in the international criminal law as:

> [n]o international criminal court or tribunal has ever been granted explicit authority to or found that it had authority to try legal persons. Further, there is no general principle of international criminal law, international treaty or customary law supporting corporate liability, or an interpretation of 'person' that encompasses corporations. At most, one could say that international law does not prohibit the imposition of criminal liability for corporations; but this cannot translate into an expansion of the meaning of the term 'person' to include entities beyond natural persons.[58]

This narrow interpretation of the history of international criminal law disregards the Nuremberg experience concerning the trial of criminal organisations. While it is correct to say that no business entity has ever been convicted by an international criminal court or tribunal, it is not entirely accurate to affirm that '[n]o international criminal court or tribunal has ever been granted explicit authority to … try legal persons'.[59] As analysed in Chapter 1, in 1945,

55 Ibid para 70.
56 Ibid para 71.
57 Ibid para 72.
58 Ibid para 75.
59 Ibid para 74.

six legal entities stood accused in front of the International Military Tribunal of Nuremberg in the context of the trial of the major Nazi war criminals.[60] The position of these six groups and organisations was of course different from that of the two corporations indicted by the STL and the legal framework applied by the International Military Tribunal to criminalise organisations (provided by Articles 9 and 10 of the London Charter) is not comparable to the modern concept of corporate criminal liability.[61] Notwithstanding, the Nuremberg precedent offers evidence of the ability of an international criminal tribunal to exert its authority to try legal persons and, as such, it should have not been so easily dismissed by the Contempt Judge.

Further, on the contextual interpretation, Judge Lettieri also considered the central argument proposed by Judge Baragwanath: the domestic developments in the field of corporate criminal liability. In this regard, the Judge saw no evidence that a consensus has emerged with respect to corporate liability to justify an interpretation of the term 'person' to include corporations.[62] A mere 'trend' towards a broader recognition of corporate criminal liability in 'most countries' should be deemed as insufficient 'to establish the existence of [a] consensus on a specific principle' as it disregards 'the many important legal systems where corporate liability is not accepted'.[63] In the notes, Judge Lettieri referred in particular to countries such as Germany and Italy where corporate criminal liability remains a contested legal concept – especially in the former.[64]

It is plausible that the focus put by Judge Lettieri on the German and Italian jurisdictions may have been determined by his national background. Judges' viewpoints may consciously or unconsciously be influenced by their own national and professional experience and by how certain legal constructs are interpreted at the domestic level.[65] In the case at hand, Judge Lettieri's opinion may have been moulded by the specific legal approach embraced by the Italian doctrine which rejects the concept of corporate criminal liability on the premise that only individuals can be held criminally accountable.[66] While a system of quasi-criminal liability of legal entities has been implemented in the

60 *United States et al. v Goering et al.*, Judgment, 30 September–1 October 1946 (1948) 1 IMT 171.

61 See Chapter I, section 2.4.

62 *New TV S.A.L. and Khayat,* Decision on Motion Challenging Jurisdiction and on Request for Leave to Amend Order in Lieu of an Indictment; STL-14-05/PT/CJ, Contempt Judge, 24 July 2014, para 74.

63 Ibid.

64 Ibid, footnote 116.

65 James Meernik et al., 'Judicial Decision Making and International Tribunals: Assessing the Impact of Individual, National, and International Factors' (2005) 86 Social science quarterly 683, 693.

66 Republic of Italy, Constitution, Article 27. See also Elisa Pavanello, *La Responsabilitá Penale delle Persone Giuridiche di Diritto Pubblico. Societas publica delinquere potest* (Padova University Press 2011) 266 et ss; Vincenzo Militello, 'The Basis for Criminal Responsibility of Collective Entities in Italy', in Albin Eser, Günter Heine, Barbara Huber (eds), *Criminal*

country since 2001,[67] this model has been seen by a part of the Italian doctrine as distinct from the traditional form of criminal liability.[68] This understanding of corporate criminal liability is directly in contrast with the approach adopted by New Zealand – the home country of Judge Baragwanath – which has recognised such a form of liability since 1976.[69] It is plausible, therefore, that the different emphasis put by the two Contempt Judges on domestic laws on corporate criminal liability may have had its roots in the (opposite) legal tradition embraced by their home countries.

Lastly, Judge Lettieri dismissed the argument based on Article 210 of the Lebanese Criminal Code and the recognition of corporate criminal liability within the Lebanese legal system. On this point, Judge Lettieri's reasoning is particularly brief as he deemed it sufficient to recall that, according to Article 2 of the Tribunal's Statute, the provisions of the Lebanese Criminal Code shall be applicable only 'subject to the provisions of this Statute'.[70] Thus, missing any reference in the Statute 'to an "it" with respect to an accused' and considering the 'lack of consensus in the international system and among domestic systems on corporate criminal liability', the concept of corporate criminal liability under Lebanese law remains 'inapplicable' to the case under consideration.[71]

Judge Lettieri's decision entirely overturned the order in lieu of an indictment issued by Judge Baragwanath against the New TV SAL by adopting a narrow stance to the question of the Tribunal's contempt jurisdiction. As observed by Alkhawaja, Judge Lettieri 'attempted to follow his mandate as narrowly as possible and not to make a judgment on evolving standards of international corporate liability'.[72] Unsurprisingly, the prosecution promptly challenged the Contempt Judge's decision placing the case into the hands of

---

Responsibility of Legal and Collective Entities (Freiburg im Breisgau, edition iuscrim 1999) 181 et ss.

67 Italian Legislative Decree No. 231 of 8 June 2001 (Decreto Legislativo n. 231/2001 'Disciplina della responsabilità amministrativa delle persone giuridiche, delle società e delle associazioni anche prive di personalità giuridiche').

68 Luigi Foffani, 'Responsabilitá degli Enti da Reato in Italia' in Antonio Fiorella and A. M. Stile (eds), *Corporate Criminal Liability and Compliance Programs, First Colloquium* (Jovene Editore 2012) 97; Contrary, Cristina de Maglie, 'Country report: Italy' in James Gobert and Ana-Maria Pascal (eds), *European Developments in Corporate Criminal Liability* (Routledge 2011) 253.

69 *Nordik Industries v Regional Controller of Inland Revenue* [1976] 1 NZLR 194 at 199-201 (SC). See also Rebecca Rose, 'Corporate Criminal Liability: A Paradox of Hope' (2006) 14 Waikato Law Review 52.

70 Special Tribunal for Lebanon, Statute, Article 2.

71 *New TV S.A.L. and Khayat,* Decision on Motion Challenging Jurisdiction and on Request for Leave to Amend Order in Lieu of an Indictment, STL-14-05/PT/CJ, Contempt Judge, 24 July 2014, para 78.

72 Alkhawaja (n 8) 471.

the Appeals Panel for a final decision on the matter of the Tribunal's jurisdiction over legal persons.

4.2.3 The Decision of the Appeals Panel in the New TV S.A.L. Case

On 2 October 2014, the Appeals Panel of the STL issued its *Decision on Interlocutory Appeal Concerning Personal Jurisdiction in Contempt Proceedings* reversing Judge Lettieri's decision and confirming the Tribunal's contempt jurisdiction over legal entities.[73] The main question examined by the Appeals Panel concerned 'whether the Contempt Judge erred in excluding legal persons when interpreting Rule 60bis pursuant to Rule 3'.[74] The Panel answered this question in the affirmative, rejecting Judge Lettieri's arguments against the recognition of a corporate criminal liability for contempt offences.

To do so, the Appeals Panel started by focusing on the interpretation of the term 'person' included in Rule 60bis. Following the principles set by the Vienna Convention on the Law of Treaties, which require that terms used in a treaty should be given their ordinary meaning, the Panel observed that 'the term "person" in a legal context can include a natural human being or a legal entity (such as a corporation) that is recognized by law as the subject of rights and duties'.[75] In rejecting Judge Lettieri's narrow interpretation of the word 'person', the Appeal Panel focused in particular on the language used in the three official versions of the Statute and Rules of the Tribunal. Recalling that both documents were drafted in three official languages – Arabic, English, and French – the majority pointed out that all three versions of Rule 60bis adopted a gender-neutral terminology which allows concluding that it was not in the drafters' intention to limit the scope of the provision to individuals only.[76] According to the Panel, this conclusion was further supported by the fact that, when the drafters had indeed intended to restrict the scope of a Rule to natural persons, they had done so explicitly 'as exemplified by the definition of a victim under Rule 2 of the Rules'.[77]

Then, the Appeals Panel observed that in their respective decisions both contempt judges – Judge Baragwanath, first, and Judge Lettieri, later – referred to the gendered language contained in the English version of Articles 3(2) and (3) ('his or her/him or her') and Article 16 (he or she) to discuss the Tribunal's jurisdiction *ratione personae*. However, as observed above, while Judge Baragwanath refused to see in the gendered terminology used in the Statute a limitation to the Tribunal's contempt jurisdiction, Judge Lettieri

73 *New TV S.A.L. and Al Khayat,* Decision on Interlocutory Appeal Concerning Personal Jurisdiction in Contempt Proceedings, STL-14-05/PT/AP/ARI26.1, Appeals Panel, 2 October 2014.

74 Ibid paras 33-74.

75 Ibid para 36.

76 Ibid para 37.

77 Ibid.

considered the words used by the drafters as indicative of a clear intention to exclude legal persons from the jurisdiction of the Tribunal, including in cases of contempt. In the Appeal Decision, the Panel rejected Judge Lettieri's interpretation as erroneous and contrary to the spirit of the Statute.[78]

In its reasoning, the Appeals Panel noted in particular that the Contempt Judge's interpretation failed to consider the linguistic approach adopted in the Arabic and French versions of the Statute.[79] In this regard, it observed that 'unlike the English version, the Arabic and French versions of the Statute do not contain gendered language'.[80] To resolve this discrepancy among the texts of the Statute, the judges looked at Article 33(4) of the Vienna Convention on the Law of the Treaties which establishes that 'when a comparison of the authentic texts discloses a difference of meaning which the application of articles 31 and 32 does not remove, the meaning which best reconciles the texts, having regard to the object and purpose of the treaty, shall be adopted'.[81] Following this provision, the Appeals Panel considered that a gender-neutral interpretation of the Statute – in line with the language used in the Arabic and French versions – better served the purpose of the Statute itself.[82] As observed by Bernaz, the Appeals Panel did not provide a clear explanation for its decision to favour the Arabic and French versions over the English version.[83] It is possible to agree with the view expressed by the author according to which:

> it seems as though what the judges meant was that in this context, drawing conclusions from the gendered language in the English version, as the Contempt Judge had done, leads to ignoring the neutral, wider language of the other two versions. By contrast, embracing the Arabic and French versions, as the Appeal Panel did, does not lead to ignoring the English version, as natural persons clearly remain included. Thus, a wider interpretation, one that does not rely on the gendered language of English 'best reconcile[s]' the texts.[84]

Echoing the opinion expressed by Bernaz, 'more clarity on the part of the Panel would have been welcomed'.[85]

The Appeals Panel also considered the extent to which international and domestic developments may influence a decision to extend the Tribunal's

78 Ibid para 38.
79 Ibid para 39.
80 Ibid.
81 *Vienna Convention on the Law of Treaties*, 23 May 1969, 1155 U.N.T.S. 331, art 33(4).
82 *New TV S.A.L. and Al Khayat*, Decision on Interlocutory Appeal Concerning Personal Jurisdiction in Contempt Proceedings, STL-14-05/PT/AP/AR126.1, Appeals Panel, 2 October 2014, para 39.
83 Bernaz (n 8) 323.
84 Ibid.
85 Ibid.

contempt jurisdiction to legal persons. Both developments are discussed under the title 'International Standards on Human Rights'. Preliminarily, the Appeals Judges observed that, in recent years, the issue of corporate accountability for human rights abuses has become a central item in the international human rights agenda.[86] The Panel recalled in particular the work conducted by the United Nations in the field of corporate accountability which culminated with the adoption, in 2011, of the *UN Guiding Principles on Business and Human Rights.*[87] To the judges, 'the substance of these efforts is an indicator of the evolving practice in relation to corporations at the global level, in particular with respect to remedies for their transgressions'.[88]

In the decision, the Panel did not further elaborate on the relevance of recent developments in international human rights law in the context of contempt offences that do not qualify as human rights violations *per se.* Once again, the 'audacious' approach adopted by the Appeals Panel appears to lack substance and to rest on precarious grounds. As observed by Bernaz:

> [w]hile there is indeed an international trend towards more corporate accountability in general, this does not necessarily mean that such accountability … should include corporate liability for contempt, a precise offence – at least when this type of responsibility is not explicitly foreseen in writing beforehand.[89]

This argument, thus, raises legitimate concerns as it seems to disregard 'the need for strict legality in the construction of criminal provisions, to the detriment of the rights of the (corporate) accused'.[90]

The Appeals Panel then moved to consider the domestic developments in the field of corporate criminal liability. In the decision, this argument represented the 'one factor … that overwhelmingly supports a broader interpretation of Rule 60bis'.[91] As discussed above, both Contempt Judges looked at domestic developments to justify their (opposite) conclusions on the Tribunal's contempt jurisdiction *ratione personae.* In the view of Judge Lettieri, recent domestic developments in the area of corporate criminal liability did not evidence an emerging consensus on the applicability of criminal law to legal persons as certain countries still reject such a concept. Conversely,

86 *New TV S.A.L. and Al Khayat,* Decision on Interlocutory Appeal Concerning Personal Jurisdiction in Contempt Proceedings, STL-14-05/PT/AP/ARI26.1, Appeals Panel, 2 October 2014, para 46.

87 Ibid para 46.

88 Ibid para 47.

89 Bernaz (n 8) 324.

90 Ibid.

91 *New TV S.A.L. and Al Khayat,* Decision on Interlocutory Appeal Concerning Personal Jurisdiction in Contempt Proceedings, STL-14-05/PT/AP/ARI26.1, Appeals Panel, 2 October 2014, para 44.

Judge Baragwanath saw in the progressive adoption of domestic laws on corporate criminal liability the proof that countries were now ready to move away from the principle of *societas delinquere non potest.*

In the Appeals Decision, the Panel embraced Judge Baragwanath's perspective and provided a more detailed analysis of the argument under consideration.[92] The analysis began with a consideration of the legislation of eighteen European countries that provide for 'genuine corporate criminal liability'.[93] The judges considered as well 24 countries from outside the European geographical area, to ensure a wide representation of various legal traditions.[94] For each country, the Panel identified the relevant national law on corporate criminal liability to evidence the evolution of such a concept at the domestic level.[95] The effort made by the Panel to ground its analysis in specific domestic laws is certainly a welcomed development compared to the approach adopted by Judge Baragwanath. Indeed, the Panel's extensive comparative analysis offers a solid foundation for the conclusion that a trend has emerged in relation to corporate criminal liability. While acknowledging that state practice 'varies in national systems', the judges concluded that 'it is apparent that in a majority of the legal systems in the world, corporations are not immune from accountability merely because they are a legal – and not a natural – person'.[96] Thus, this allowed the Panel to 'interpret the term "person" [in Rule 60bis] to include legal entities in the exercise of the Tribunal's inherent power over contempt proceedings'.[97]

The Panel's reliance on domestic developments as a factor informing the interpretation of Rule 60bis has been criticised as contrary to the provision of Rule 3 of the Tribunal's Rules of Procedure and Evidence.[98] Indeed, Rule 3 does not list state practice as one of the interpretation aids the Tribunal should consider in determining the meaning and scope of the Rules. According to McDermott, the Panel failed to provide any 'solid reasoning ... as to why the contempt judge should have taken [domestic criminal laws] into account'.[99] While conceding that the Panel could have better justified its decision to rely

92 Andrew Clapham, 'Human Rights Obligations for Non-State Actors. Where Are We Now?' in Fannie Lafontaine and François Larocque (eds), *Doing Peace the Rights Way: Essays in International Law and Relations in Honour of Louise Arbour* (Intersentia 2019) 29; Bernaz (n 8) 324.

93 *New TV S.A.L. and Al Khayat,* Decision on Interlocutory Appeal Concerning Personal Jurisdiction in Contempt Proceedings, STL-14-05/PT/AP/ARI26.1, Appeals Panel, 2 October 2014, para 52.

94 Ibid para 55.

95 Ibid footnotes 97-150.

96 Ibid para 58.

97 Ibid paras 59-60.

98 Yvonne McDermott Rees, 'Criminal Liability for Legal Persons for Contempt returns to the STL' (PhD studies in human rights, 8 October 2014) http://humanrightsdoctorate.blogspot.com/2014/10/corporate-liability-for-legal-persons.html Accessed 26 March 2023.

99 Ibid.

on domestic laws, it is possible to argue that the development of state practice on corporate criminal liability has significant importance in the wider debate on corporate accountability for human rights abuses. As recalled by Bernaz, state practice in the area of corporate criminal liability has constantly featured the work of the former UN Special Representative on Business and Human Rights, John Ruggie, on the drafting of the UN Guiding Principles on Business and Human Rights.[100] As such, the Panel's examination of state practice can be deemed relevant in the context of the decision on the Tribunal's jurisdiction over legal persons.

Following the analysis of domestic developments, the Panel then briefly considered instances where legal entities and international criminal law intersected. The investigation looked specifically to the Nuremberg experience and the negotiation of the Rome Statute to assess the status of legal persons under international criminal law. Firstly, the Panel referred to the provisions on criminal organisations included in Articles 9 and 10 of the Statute of the International Military Tribunal of Nuremberg which bestowed the Tribunal with the power to declare Nazi organisations and groups as criminal. According to the majority, the inclusion of such provisions was 'evidence that legal persons did not escape accountability'.[101] The Panel's brief examination of the Nuremberg experience is laudable if compared to the approach adopted by Judge Lettieri who entirely dismissed it. Nonetheless, the Panel should have attempted to provide a better contextualisation of the system introduced by Articles 9 and 10 of the London Charter to highlight its peculiar characteristics (see Chapter 2). While the Nuremberg experience undoubtedly offers relevant insight into the role of corporate actors in international criminal law, the Panel could have elaborated more on the relevance of such a precedent.

The majority's analysis of the Rome Statute is equally brief. In this regard, the Panel simply noted that the Statute of the ICC 'did not purport to codify existing principles emanating from customary international law or to be applicable outside the confines of the ICC'.[102] As such, the omission of corporate criminal liability from the Statute could not be seen as 'a concerted exercise that reflected a legal view that legal persons are completely beyond the purview of international criminal law'.[103] Instead, 'it is a reflection of the lack of a *political* (rather than legal) consensus to provide such jurisdiction in the Rome Statute'.[104] As such, the Panel's interpretation on this point supports the analysis previously conducted in Chapter 3 and confirms the reading of the

100 Bernaz (n 8) 325.

101 *New TV S.A.L. and AI Khayat*, Decision on Interlocutory Appeal Concerning Personal Jurisdiction in Contempt Proceedings, STL-14-05/PT/AP/ARI26.1, Appeals Panel, 2 October 2014, para 63.

102 Ibid para 66.

103 Ibid.

104 Ibid (emphasis in original).

drafting history of the Rome Statute proposed by numerous authors, including Clapham and Scheffer (who personally attended the Rome Conference).[105]

Linking together the analysis conducted on the domestic developments and the evaluation of the drafting history of the Rome Statute, the Panel then proceeded to make what is perhaps its boldest statement:

> While it remains true that no post-World War II international criminal court or tribunal has previously found that it had the authority to try legal persons, this singular fact does not convince the Appeals Panel that the term 'person' under Rule 60bis excludes legal persons ... Indeed, corporate liability for serious harms is a feature of most of the world's legal systems and therefore *qualifies as a general principle of law*. ... the Appeals Panel considers that, given all the developments outlined above, corporate criminal liability is on the verge of attaining, at the very least, the status of a *general principle of law* applicable under international law.[106]

The qualification of corporate criminal liability as an emerging general principle of law under international law was used by the Panel to justify its interpretation of the Statute and Rules of Procedure and Evidence to include corporations within the scope of the Tribunal's contempt jurisdiction. However, such a conclusion could have been better supported as it seems to be based solely on the investigation of the status of corporate criminal liability at the domestic level. While the level of recognition at national level is the necessary starting point of any analysis on general principles of law, the Panel should have elaborated more on the reasoning adopted to its conclusion on this point – in particular about the transposition of such a form of liability at the international level. As will be further discussed, the argument on corporate criminal liability as a general principle of law has developed as an evolution of the comparative law argument that sees the growing recognition of such a form of liability at the domestic level as evidence of the possibility of its inclusion within the international legal framework. Due to the importance of both of these arguments in the current debate on corporate criminal liability, their advantages and limitations will be further discussed in Chapter 6.

105 David Scheffer, 'Corporate Liability under the Rome Statute' (2016) 57 Harvard International Law Journal 35, Andrew Clapham, 'The Question of Jurisdiction under International Criminal Law over Legal Persons: Lessons from the Rome Conference on an International Criminal Court' in Menno T Kamminga and Saman Zia-Zarifi (eds), *Liability of Multinational Corporations under International Law* (Kluwer Law International 2000).

106 *New TV S.A.L. and Al Khayat*, Decision on Interlocutory Appeal Concerning Personal Jurisdiction in Contempt Proceedings, STL-14-05/PT/AP/AR126.1, Appeals Panel, 2 October 2014, para 67 (emphasis added).

Lastly, the Panel reaffirmed the relevance of the Lebanese approach to corporate criminal liability in the context of the interpretation of Rule 60bis.[107] According to the Appeals Panel, the circumstance that Article 210(2) of the Lebanese Criminal Code explicitly recognises the criminal liability of legal entities makes it foreseeable under Lebanese law that a company – particularly a journalistic publication or a television station – 'could be criminally liable provided that actual complicity in the crime committed is proven'.[108]

***

The decision of the Appeals Panel of the STL has elicited mixed reactions. As the first international decision of its kind, it has to be welcomed as it represents a tentative attempt by an international criminal tribunal to promote a broader interpretation of the scope of international criminal law to include corporate entities. Nonetheless, as observed by Bernaz, it is undeniable that 'the New TV SAL case is not the one business and human rights advocates might have dreamed of as they were patiently waiting for an international breakthrough in their field'.[109] The main critique moved against the decision concerns, in particular, its limited applicability due to its focus on contempt crimes and the specific reference to the Lebanese context.

Against these scepticisms, Alkhawaja observed that 'all of the arguments, justifications, and examples' used by the Tribunal to justify an expansion in the definition of 'person' under the Statute 'were not limited to contempt cases'. Rather, the Appeals Panel:

> surveyed cases in the Military Tribunals of Nuremberg, the statute of the ICC ... and domestic laws that deal with corporate liability more broadly. When the STL declared that corporate liability had become a general principle of law, it did not limit this holding to contempt crimes. It issued a broad principle that could apply to any criminal violation.[110]

107 Ibid para 69.

108 Ibid para 71.

109 Bernaz (n 8), 329; Fé de Jonge, 'International Corporate Criminal Liability at the Special Tribunal for Lebanon: Prosecutor v. Karma Al Khayat and Al Jadeed' (Peace Palace Library, 8 May 2015); Anne-Marie Verwiel and Karlijn van der Voort, 'Some further thoughts on the STL Appeals Chamber decision on criminal liability for legal entities' (Special Tribunal for Lebanon Blog, 16 October 2014); McDermott Rees (n 98), Dov Jacobs, 'A Molotov Cocktail on the Principle of Legality: STL confirms contempt proceedings against legal persons' (Blog at Spread the Jam, 6 October 2014) https://dovjacobs.com/2014/10/06/a-molotov-cocktail-on-the-principle-of-legality-stl-confirms-contempt-proceedings-against-legal-persons/ Accessed 26 March 2023.

110 Alkhawaja (n 8) 483-484.

While Alkhawaja's view has the merit of recognising the general relevance of the arguments embraced by the Appeals Panel – and thus their potential applicability in other contexts besides contempt cases – it is still undeniable that so far, the 2014 decision has had a relatively limited impact on the development of a norm on the international criminal liability of corporations. While the case has indeed been cited in several scholarly publications and mentioned in domestic cases, it has yet to be formally accepted as evidence of a shift in the international approach to corporate criminal liability.[111]

4.3 Corporate Criminal Liability within the Statute of the (Proposed) African Court of Justice and Human Rights

At about the same time as the decision of the STL to open the two twin contempt cases against New TV S.A.L. and Akhbar Beirut S.A.L., the African Union adopted the 2014 *Protocol on Amendments to the Protocol on the Statute of the African Court of Justice and Human Rights* (better known as the 'Malabo Protocol') which vested the (proposed) African Court of Justice and Human Rights with criminal jurisdiction over international and transnational crimes.[112] As such, the Protocol allows for the creation of the first regional criminal court with jurisdiction over international crimes that would represent a 'novel phenomenon in the landscape of international courts and tribunals'.[113]

The Protocol presented numerous innovative elements that reflect the peculiarity of the African context in which the proposed Court will operate. One of the most relevant novelties introduced by the Protocol concerns the inclusion in the Statute of the African Court of Justice and Human Rights of a provision on corporate criminal liability for international crimes (Article 46C). This element makes the Statute of the proposed Court unique compared to the statutes of other international and hybrid criminal courts and tribunals.[114]

The inclusion of such a provision is not entirely surprising considering the number of allegations made against multinational corporations for their involvement in human rights violations committed in the African continent.[115]

111 *Jesner v. Arab Bank, PLC*, 138 S. Ct. 1386 (2018).

112 African Union, Protocol on Amendments to the Protocol on the Statute of the African Court of Justice and Human Rights, 27 June 2014, Annex, Article 16.

113 Gerhald Werle and Morits Vornbaum, 'Creating an African Criminal Court' in Gerhald Werle and Morits Vornbaum (eds), *The African Criminal Court, A Commentary on the Malabo Protocol* (Springer 2017), 3-9.

114 Clapham, 'Human Rights Obligations for Non-State Actors. Where Are We Now?' (n 91) 27-29; Chantal Meloni, 'Modes of Responsibility (Article 28N), Individual Criminal Responsibility (Article 46B) and Corporate Criminal Liability (Article 46C)' in Gerhald Werle and Morits Vornbaum (eds), *The African Criminal Court, A Commentary on the Malabo Protocol* (Springer 2017) 3-9.

115 Elies van Sliedregt, 'Regional Criminal Justice, Corporate Criminal Liability and the Need for Non-Doctrinal Research' in Marina Aksenova, Elies van Sliedregt and Stephan Parmentier (eds) *Breaking the Cycle of Mass Atrocities: Criminological and Socio-Legal Approaches in*

Indeed, as observed by Meloni, the fact that corporations are often involved in 'massive human rights violations amounting to international crimes is beyond dispute' and as such 'the attempt by the [Malabo Protocol] drafters to hold corporations directly accountable under international criminal law has to be welcomed'.[116]

The provision of Article 46C reads as follows:

1. For the purpose of this Statute, the Court shall have jurisdiction over legal persons, with the exception of States.
2. Corporate intention to commit an offence may be established by proof that it was the policy of the corporation to do the act which constituted the offence.
3. A policy may be attributed to a corporation where it provides the most reasonable explanation of the conduct of that corporation.
4. Corporate knowledge of the commission of an offence may be established by proof that the actual or constructive knowledge of the relevant information was possessed within the corporation.
5. Knowledge may be possessed within a corporation even though the relevant information is divided between corporate personnel.
6. The criminal responsibility of legal persons shall not exclude the criminal responsibility of natural persons who are perpetrators or accomplices in the same crimes.[117]

The first paragraph of Article 46C addresses the question of which kind of legal persons may fall under the scope of the Court's jurisdiction. Similarly to the approach adopted during the negotiation of the Rome Statute, the provision introduced by the Malabo Protocol excludes States from the competence of the proposed African Court.[118] However, while the draft text of Article 23(5) discussed in Rome offered a clear indication of the scope of the term 'juridical person',[119] Article 46C, paragraph 1, remains entirely vague on this point. Indeed, no specific definition of the concept of 'legal person' is included in the text of the Article. As such, it is unclear whether the African Court will have jurisdiction solely over corporations or whether additional

International Criminal Law (Hart Publishing, Oxford, 2019) 224-227; Amissi Melchiade Manirabona, 'The Jurisdiction of the Proposed African Criminal Court over Corporations: Proposals to Strengthen a Novel Mechanism' (2017) 55 Canadian Yearbook of International Law 293, 296 and 299 et ss.

116 Meloni (n 114) 153; Joanna Kyriakakis, 'Article 46C: Corporate Criminal Liability at the African Criminal Court' in C Jalloh, K Clarke, V Nmehielle (eds) *African Court of Justice and Human and People's Rights in Context* (Cambridge University Press 2019) 794.

117 African Union, Protocol on Amendments to the Protocol on the Statute of the African Court of Justice and Human Rights, 27 June 2014, Annex, Article 46C.

118 Ibid paragraph 1.

119 A/CONF.183/C.1/WGGP/L.5/Rev.2.

categories of entities, such as non-governmental organisations, trade unions, and other unincorporated associations, will also fall under the scope of the Court's jurisdiction.[120]

In this book, it is argued that a more restrictive interpretation of Article 46C, paragraph 1, is to be preferred as it better adheres to the principles of interpretation under Articles 31(1) and (2) of the Vienna Convention on the Law of Treaties. Indeed, looking at the text of Article 46C – its title and the wording used in its other paragraphs – it is evident how the provision repeatedly uses the word 'corporation' or 'corporate' to define the different aspects of the principle of attribution adopted in the Statute. This can suggest the intention of the drafters to limit the jurisdiction of the Court to incorporated entities only, meaning those legal persons that are granted a separate legal personality from that of their individual members.[121]

This narrow understanding of the concept of legal person, however, does not solve all the doubts raised by the wording of Article 46C, paragraph 1. In particular, it does not address whether state-owned corporations, as public entities, can fall under the scope of the provision. On this point, Article 46C should be read in a manner consistent with the approach suggested by draft Article 23(5) which proposed the exclusion from the jurisdiction of the ICC of public entities insofar they exercise State authority.[122] This interpretation is in line with the provisions of the ILC's *Draft Articles on State Responsibility for Internationally Wrongful Acts* which recognise that certain acts of public entities equate to acts of the State.[123] Draft Article 5, in particular, establishes that the conduct of a public entity 'shall be considered an act of the State under international law' provided that the entity is exercising 'elements of governmental authority'.[124] Consequently, activities of a public entity that fall outside the public sphere may legitimately be included under the scope of the proposed African Court's International Criminal Law Section.

Overall, while the lack of clarity regarding the definition of legal persons leaves many questions unanswered, it has correctly been observed that 'the fact that the Protocol is not restrictive in relation to the entities under its scope bestows on the Court the necessary flexibility to deal with evolving corporate structure'.[125] This is particularly welcomed as it may offer an effective tool to

120 Kyriakakis, 'Article 46C: Corporate Criminal Liability at the African Criminal Court' (n 116) 806-807, Manirabona (n 113) 309.

121 In support see Kyriakakis, 'Article 46C: Corporate Criminal Liability at the African Criminal Court' (n 116) 808.

122 A/CONF.183/C.1/WGGP/L.5/Rev.2.

123 Taygeti Michalakea, 'Article 46C of the Malabo Protocol: A Contextually Tailored Approach to Corporate Criminal Liability and Its Contours' (2018) 7 International Human Rights Law Review 225, 237.

124 International Law Commission, Draft Articles on Responsibility of States for Internationally Wrongful Acts, November 2001, Supplement No. 10, A/56/10, chp.IV.E.1, Article 5.

125 Michalakea (n 123) 237.

address modern forms of corporate involvement in violations of international law in the African context.

4.3.1 Article 46C and the Principle of Attribution: An Organisational Approach to Corporate Criminal Liability

The core provisions of Article 46C define the model of attribution of corporate criminal liability adopted by the Statute of the proposed African Court. In this regard, Article 46C offers an alternative model of attribution to that proposed in 1998 during the negotiation of the Statute of the ICC. As discussed above, draft Article 23(5) of the Rome Statute embraced a narrow identification approach to corporate criminal liability, establishing that the liability of the corporation could have been established solely in cases where the offence was committed by an individual 'in a position of control' who was 'acting on behalf of and with the explicit consent of that juridical person and in the course of its activities'.[126] Conversely, Article 46C departs from this traditional (and restrictive) view to adopt an 'organisational model' to attribute criminal liability to legal entities.

According to the organisational model of corporate criminal liability, the fault of a legal entity does not derive from the conduct of a single individual or organ of the corporation but is the result of the complex interplay of corporate policies, regulations, and institutionalised practices.[127] Such an approach has its roots in the 'realist' theories of corporate personality.[128] As observed by Colvin:

> '[r]ealist' theories ... assert that corporations have an existence that is, to some extent, independent of their members. Corporations can act and be at fault in ways that are different from the ways in which their members can act and be at fault. [...] On the realist approach, the responsibility of the corporation is primary. It is not dependent on the responsibility of any individual. Responsibility is analysed within a realist framework by examining directly questions about what the corporation did or did not do, as an organization; what it knew or ought to have known about its conduct; and what it did or ought to have done to prevent harm from being caused.[129]

126 A/CONF.183/C.1/WGGP/L.5/Rev.2.

127 Neil Cavanagh, 'Corporate Criminal Liability: An Assessment of the Models of Fault' (2011) 75 The Journal of Criminal Law 414, 415.

128 Eli Lederman, 'Models for Imposing Corporate Criminal Liability: From Adaptation and Imitation Toward Aggregation and the Search for Self-Identity' (2001) 4 Buffalo Criminal Law Review 641, 680.

129 Eric Colvin, 'Corporate Personality and Criminal Liability' (1995) 6 Criminal Law Forum 1, 2.

The Australian Criminal Code Act of 1995 offers a prime example of the organisational approach to corporate criminal liability.[130] Alongside the traditional forms of corporate accountability, the 1995 Criminal Code Act provides that criminal liability can be imputed to the corporation for those 'actions previously described as 'company practice' and [thus] previously considered beyond the reach of criminal law'.[131] Specifically, Section 12.3(1) of the Criminal Code Act establishes that, for offences requiring proof of intention, knowledge or recklessness, criminal liability can be imposed on the corporation where the offence has been 'expressly, tacitly or implicitly authorised or permitted' by the corporate body.[132] Furthermore, Section 12.3(2), letters (c) and (d), clarifies that:

> (2) The means by which such an authorisation or permission may be established include: [...]
>
> (c) proving that a corporate culture existed within the body corporate that directed, encouraged, tolerated or led to noncompliance with the relevant provision; or
>
> (d) proving that the body corporate failed to create and maintain a corporate culture that required compliance with the relevant provision.[133]

By referring to the concept of 'corporate culture', the Australian legislator allows the courts to take into consideration all those attitudes, policies, rules, and practices developed by the corporation when assessing the criminal liability of the corporate entity.[134]

Similarly to the Australian's approach to the organisational model, Article 46C does not derive corporate criminal liability from the act and state of mind of a single individual (or a group of specific individuals) but 'situate corporate culpability within the corporate policies and corporate knowledge that enabled the offence'.[135]

With regard to the mental element of intent, paragraph 2 of Article 46C establishes that 'corporate intention to commit an offence may be established by proof that it was the policy of the corporation to do the act that constituted the offence'.[136] As such, the provision refers to the existence of a relevant policy that contemplates the commission of specific offences, not to the con-

130 Australian Criminal Code Act, 1995 § 12.1-12.6.

131 Alan Rose, 'Developments in Criminal Law and Criminal Justice, 1995 Australian Criminal Code Act: Corporate Criminal Provisions' (1995) 6 Criminal Law Forum 129, 129.

132 Australian Criminal Code Act 1995, § 12.3(1).

133 Ibid § 12.3(2), let. (c) and (d).

134 Ibid § 12.3(6).

135 Kyriakakis, 'Article 46C: Corporate Criminal Liability at the African Criminal Court' (n 116) 816.

136 African Union, Protocol on Amendments to the Protocol on the Statute of the African Court of Justice and Human Rights, 27 June 2014, Annex, Article 46C, para 2.

duct of specific natural persons. Furthermore, paragraph 3 clarifies that 'a policy may be attributed to a corporation where it provides the most reasonable explanation of the conduct of that corporation'.[137]

Scholars have raised some concerns in relation to the wording of paragraph 2 of Article 46C.[138] In particular, the provision under consideration does not offer any indication on whether the term 'policy' has to be interpreted in a formal way – encompassing solely the official policies adopted by the legal person – or, more generally, it should cover also all those uncodified practices followed by the corporation. Kyriakakis argued against a too restrictive approach to the definition of 'policy', observing that 'formal corporate policies may denote one position while corporate attitudes, unwritten rules, or previous practices and courses of conduct, de facto authorise something quite different'.[139] In support of a broader interpretation of Article 46C, Kyriakakis refers to the wording used in paragraph 3 where the Article establishes that policy may be attributed to a legal person where it offers 'the most reasonable explanation' of the corporation's conduct.[140] According to the author, paragraph 3 'is intended to convey that a Court is entitled to infer that corporate members understood something to be 'an implied directive' (and hence a policy of the corporation) in those circumstances where the corporate practices are so flagrantly against the law that 'they made more sense if viewed as embodying a determination to avoid the regulations, rather than as a product of inadvertent negligence or even recklessness'.[141]

Even so, while a broader understanding of the term 'policy' may better reflect the reality of corporate behaviour, elements in the drafting history of Article 46C may evidence the drafters' intention to adopt a more restrictive approach instead. In the original formulation of the provision, the drafters made explicit reference to the concept of 'corporate culture' as provided in the Australian Criminal Code Act.[142] Specifically, draft Article 46C, paragraph 4, recognised that '[c]orporate knowledge of the commission of an offence may be established by proof that the relevant knowledge was possessed within the corporation and that the *culture of the corporation* caused or encouraged the commission of the offence'.[143]

137 Ibid para 3.
138 Kyriakakis, 'Article 46C: Corporate Criminal Liability at the African Criminal Court' (n 116) 817.
139 Ibid.
140 Ibid.
141 Ibid citing Colvin (n 129) 33-34.
142 African Union, Meeting of Government Experts and Ministers of Justice/Attorneys General on Legal Matters 7 to 11 and 14 to 15 May 2012, Addis Ababa, Ethiopia, Draft Protocol on Amendments to the Protocol on the Statute of the African Court of Justice and Human Rights, Exp/Min/IV/Rev.7, Article 46C, para 4.
143 Ibid (emphasis added).

Draft paragraph 7 further clarified that:

> 7. For the purpose of this section:
> 'Corporate culture' means an attitude, policy, rule, course of conduct or practice existing within the body corporate generally or within the area of the body corporate in which the relevant activities take place.[144]

This mention of the 'culture of the corporation', read together with the provisions of paragraphs 2 and 3 of Article 46C, may have allowed for a more expansive interpretation of the concept of policy as it recognised the existence of a specific culture within a corporation which is only partially determined by the official policies and regulations codified by the entity. As such, it would have confirmed the view supported by Kyriakakis.

However, the final formulation of Article 46C, paragraph 4, makes no mention of the concept of corporate culture. This change in the language may imply the drafters' preference for a 'more formal manifestation of the organisational model' based on the evidence provided by the official policies adopted by the corporation.[145] If this is the case, compliance programmes and human rights due diligence may end up playing a central role in the evaluation of corporate intent. Indeed, national legislations already recognise the significance of due diligence and compliance programmes as elements to exclude or mitigate the criminal liability of the corporation.[146] The proposed African Court will be called to shed some light on these fundamental aspects of the provision.

Paragraph 4 of Article 46C addresses the question of corporate knowledge and its attribution to the legal entity. Specifically, the provision provides that corporate knowledge 'may be established by proof that the actual or constructive knowledge of the relevant information was possessed within the corporation'.[147] Paragraph 5 further clarifies that corporate knowledge can be imputed to the corporation through aggregation in cases where 'the relevant information is divided between corporate personnel'.[148] The aggregation model of corporate criminal liability is based on the assumption that corporate knowledge can be inferred 'by linking the thoughts of different agents of the legal body and in thus creating the required mental element'.[149] According to this model, knowledge of an event may be imputed to the corporation even when it is not possible to identify an individual who possesses the same level of knowledge of the specific fact or event.

144 Ibid para 7.
145 Michalakea (n 123) 239.
146 See, e.g., Australian Criminal Code Act 1995 § 12.3(3) and United States Sentencing Commission, Guidelines Manual, §8B2.1. (Nov. 2021).
147 African Union, Protocol on Amendments to the Protocol on the Statute of the African Court of Justice and Human Rights, 27 June 2014, Annex, Article 46C, par 4.
148 Ibid para 5.
149 Lederman (n 128) 662.

The adoption of the aggregation model in the Protocol can be seen as a positive attempt to acknowledge the multi-layered structure of modern corporations and their ability to establish information-sharing systems that, collectively examined, determine the corporation's knowledge. Nonetheless, the wording of Article 46C raises some questions concerning the scope of application of such a model. Indeed, paragraph 5 of the provision, in conjunction with paragraph 4, establishes that aggregate knowledge can be imputed to the entity in cases where evidence is provided that 'the actual or *constructive* knowledge of the relevant information was possessed within the corporation'.[150] The concept of constructive knowledge refers to situations where knowledge of certain information is presumed on the assumption that the responsible person should have acquired such information by exercising reasonable care.[151]

The decision to 'widen the kind of knowledge that can be attributed to a corporation might [create an incentive for] good corporate management by making the corporation responsible for failures among personnel to inquire where they ought'.[152] Once again, compliance programmes and human rights due diligence processes will play a fundamental role in determining the existence of constructive corporate knowledge. Indeed, they will provide evidence of the mechanisms adopted by the corporations to ensure that proper information sharing occurs and that accountability procedures are established to promote good practice and transparency within the corporation.

However, constructive knowledge – based on the 'should have known' standard – may end up lowering the bar to establish the criminal liability of corporations in contrast with the standard usually applied to individual defendants. Generally, international criminal law requires intent and knowledge as the mental elements for attributing individual criminal liability. Article 30 of the Rome Statue, for example, established that '[u]nless otherwise provided, a person shall be criminally responsible and liable for punishment only if the material elements [of the crime] are committed with intent and knowledge'.[153] Regarding 'knowledge', the Statute further clarifies that such an element is understood as requiring the defendant's 'awareness that a circumstance exists or a consequence will occur in the ordinary course of events'.[154] The standard adopted by Article 30 of the Rome Statute, thus, limits the meaning of the

150 African Union, Protocol on Amendments to the Protocol on the Statute of the African Court of Justice and Human Rights, 27 June 2014, Annex, Article 46C, para 4 (emphasis added).

151 On the concept of constructive knowledge see, e.g., Simon Stern, 'Constructive Knowledge, Probable Cause, and Administrative Decisionmaking' (2007) 82 Notre Dame Law Review 1085.

152 Kyriakakis, 'Article 46C: Corporate Criminal Liability at the African Criminal Court' (n 116) 819-820.

153 Rome Statute of the International Criminal Court (opened for signature 17 July 1998, entered into force 1 July 2002) 2187 UNTS 90, Article 30(1).

154 Ibid Article 30(3).

mental element of knowledge to 'actual knowledge' as opposed to the wider concept of 'constructive knowledge' embraced in Article 46C of the Statute of the proposed African Court.[155]

The ICC's Elements of Crimes contemplate some exceptions to this principle but they remain limited to specific crimes. An example is provided by the war crime of 'conscripting or enlisting children under the age of fifteen years into the national armed forces or using them to participate actively in hostilities'.[156] The Elements of Crimes Article 8(2)(b)(xxvi) provide that liability can be established when the defendant 'knew or should have known' that a child was under the age of 15 years.[157] The 'should have known' standard embraced in the Elements allows the Court to apply a 'constructive knowledge' test when inferring the mental element regarding this specific circumstance of the crimes.[158] This example, however, constitutes a departure from the general approach to the mental element in relation to individual criminal liability.

Conversely, constructive knowledge is commonly recognised in the context of command responsibility.[159] Pursuant to Article 28 of the Rome Statute, a military commander is criminally responsible for crimes committed by forces under their effective command or authority where they 'either knew or ... *should have known* that the forces were committing or about to commit such crimes'.[160] As observed by various commentators on the Rome Statute, the 'should have known' standard included in the provision of Article 28(1)(a) introduces a test of negligence as a mental element for the attribution of criminal liability to military commanders.[161] This has been confirmed by the Pre-Trial Chamber II in the Bemba Gombo case where the judges stated that '[t]he 'should have known' standard requires the superior to 'ha[ve] merely been negligent in failing to acquire knowledge' of his or her subordinates' illegal conduct'.[162]

155 Mohamed Badar, 'The Mental Element in the Rome Statute of the International Criminal Court: A Commentary from a Comparative Criminal Law Perspective' (2008) 19 Criminal Law Forum 19 473, 496.

156 Rome Statute of the International Criminal Court (opened for signature 17 July 1998, entered into force 1 July 2002) 2187 UNTS 90, Article 8(2)(b)(xxvi).

157 International Criminal Court, Elements of Crimes (last amended 2011), Article 8(2)(b)(xxvi), para 3.

158 Ibid, Article 6(3), para 6, Article 8(2)(b)(vii)-1, para 3, and Article 8(2)(b)(vii)-4, para 3.

159 Stuart E Hendin, 'Command Responsibility and Superior Orders in the Twentieth Century – A Century of Evolution' (2003) 10 Murdoch University Electronic Journal of Law.

160 Rome Statute of the International Criminal Court (opened for signature 17 July 1998, entered into force 1 July 2002) 2187 UNTS 90, Article 28(1)(ii).

161 Chantal Meloni, *Command Responsibility in International Criminal Law* (T.M.C. Asser Press, 2010) 182-186. See also Antonio Cassese, *International Criminal Law*, 2nd (edn, OUP, 2008), 74 and 251-252; Kai Ambos, 'Superior Responsibility' in Antonio Cassese et al., (eds), *The Rome Statute of the International Criminal Court: A Commentary*, Volume 1 (OUP, 2002), 823.

162 *Prosecutor v. Jean-Pierre Bemba Gombo*, Decision Pursuant to Article 61(7)(a) and (b) of the Rome Statute on the Charges of the Prosecutor Against Jean-Pierre Bemba Gombo; ICC-

In the context of Article 46C, therefore, the inclusion of constructive knowledge to attribute the *mens rea* of a crime to the corporation introduces an element of negligence not dissimilar to that proper of command responsibility. The corporation might thus be considered criminally liable where it fails to supervise its personnel or to acquire relevant information that may allow it to prevent the commission of a crime. As observed by Kyriakakis, this low standard provided by Article 46C may create a risk of over-criminalisation.[163] To avoid that, the Court should elaborate clear criteria for the evaluation of internal oversight procedure and compliance and due diligence mechanisms to indicate what can be reasonably expected from the corporation in the fulfilment of its 'duty of knowledge'.[164]

Lastly, another question left open by the final formulation of Article 46C concerns the interpretation of the term 'corporate personnel' included in the provision of paragraph 5 relevant to the determination of how aggregate corporate knowledge can be established. In the absence of any indication, it remains unclear whether 'corporate personnel' should include solely the corporate employees or whether it may encompass also corporate agents, contractors and even subsidiaries. In this regard, Kyriakakis observed that:

> The wider the net is cast, the more amenable the model will be to corporate prosecutions, particularly in transnational settings where business is often transacted through local subsidiaries and contract chains and where parent company control can be and is often exercised. But at the same time, and particularly given the permissive grounds for attributing knowledge to the corporation, the wider the net the further determinations may move from genuine situations of corporate misfeasance.[165]

As there is a lot of scope for discretion in the implementation of the provision of Article 46C, the Court will be called to provide some guidance on the interpretation of key legal concepts in the area of corporate crimes.

Finally, it is relevant to point out another element that makes the provision of Article 46C quite dissimilar from the French proposal on legal persons discussed in Rome i.e. the relationship between corporate criminal liability and individual criminal liability. While draft Article 23(5)(d) adopts a narrow derivative approach, making corporate liability contingent upon the conviction

---

01/05-01/08-424, Pre-Trial Chamber II, 15 June 2009, para 432.

163 Kyriakakis, 'Article 46C: Corporate Criminal Liability at the African Criminal Court' (n 116) 820.

164 The expression 'duty of knowledge' is used by Meloni in her analysis of the implications of the 'should have known' standard in the context of command responsibility. Meloni, *Command Responsibility in International Criminal Law* (n 161) 183.

165 Kyriakakis, 'Article 46C: Corporate Criminal Liability at the African Criminal Court' (n 116) 822.

of the individual perpetrator,[166] Article 46C implies a clear separation between the liability of the corporate entity, on one side, and that of the natural person, on the other. Indeed, according to Article 46C, paragraph 6, '[t]he criminal responsibility of legal persons shall not exclude the criminal responsibility of natural persons who are perpetrators or accomplices in the same crimes'.[167] As such, unlike draft Article 23(5)(d), the provision introduced by the Malabo Protocol does not subordinate the criminal liability of the corporation to the previous conviction of the individual defendant(s). This is of course in line with the organisational model embraced by the drafters as it recognises corporate liability as distinct from the liability of its personnel.

4.3.2 Sentencing System

A final aspect of the model of corporate criminal liability embraced in the Statute of the (proposed) African Court concerns the sentencing system defined by Article 43A.[168] According to paragraph 2 of Article 43A 'the penalties imposed by the Court shall be limited to prison sentences and/or pecuniary fines'.[169] In addition to that, paragraph 5 further allows the Court to 'order the forfeiture of any property, proceeds or any asset acquired unlawfully or by criminal conduct, and their return to their rightful owner or to an appropriate Member State'.[170] The applicability of Article 43A to both individual and corporate defendants makes it evident that the drafters of the Statute of the (proposed) African Court did not introduce a separate sanctioning regime for corporations, equating their position to that of natural persons.

The prudent approach adopted in the Statute of the (proposed) African Court differs from the more progressive view that emerged during the negotiation of the Statute of the ICC. Indeed, in the Draft Statute submitted by the Preparatory Committee on the Establishment of an International Criminal Court, the drafters included a specific provision on the penalties applicable to legal persons (draft Article 76) which, in its original formulation, provided as follows:

> A legal person shall incur one or more of the following penalties:
>
> (i) fines;
> [(ii) dissolution;]
> [(iii) prohibition, for such period as determined by the Court, of the exercise of activities of any kind;]

166 A/CONF.183/C.1/WGGP/L.5/Rev.2.

167 African Union, Protocol on Amendments to the Protocol on the Statute of the African Court of Justice and Human Rights, 27 June 2014, Annex, Article 46C.

168 Ibid Article 43A.

169 Ibid para 2.

170 Ibid para 5.

[(iv) closure, for such a period as determined by the Court, of the premises used in the commission of the crime;]
[(v) forfeiture of [instrumentalities of crime and] proceeds, property and assets obtained by criminal conduct;] [and]
[(vi) appropriate forms of reparation.][171]

Draft Article 76 would have allowed the Court to impose a wide range of sanctions – including the equivalent of a 'death penalty' for a corporation (i.e. 'dissolution') – to tackle corporate crimes and deter future misbehaviour. Even though the draft Article was subsequently amended and limited to pecuniary sanctions only,[172] the original formulation still offered an interesting example of how a sanctioning regime for corporations can be constructed to include non-pecuniary measures that can affect directly the operation of the company (e.g. temporary prohibition of the exercise of activities of any kind) and, as such, prompt significant change in its organisation and policy.

In the context of the Statute of the (proposed) African Court, the decision to allow pecuniary fines only to be applicable in the case of corporate liability may be justified by pragmatic reasons. Indeed, pecuniary sanctions are generally recognised as the most common response to corporate wrongdoing;[173] as such, they may facilitate States' cooperation in the enforcement of a judgment against a corporation. Still, this narrow approach may undermine the Court's ability to effectively condemn corporate wrongdoing. As observed by Michaleka, this limited range of sanctions may be 'inadequate to capture the whole range of operations of modern corporations'.[174] This is particularly true in the African context where multinational corporations operate through a web of subsidiaries scattered around the continent. A more progressive approach – based on a combination of pecuniary fines and interdictions – may have provided a more robust system to address the issue of corporate involvement in international (and transnational) crimes in Africa.

Ultimately, the effectiveness of this model of corporate sanctioning will depend on the guidelines that the (proposed) Court will develop in its Rules of Procedure and Evidence and, most importantly, in its jurisprudence on the subject matter.

***

Overall, Article 46C proposes a new and unique model to address corporate criminal liability at the international level. In comparison with previous proposals, it departs from the traditional approaches to corporate criminal

171 A/CONF.183/2/Add.1, p. 121.
172 A/CONF.183//C.1/L.3, p. 2.
173 Kyriakakis, 'Article 46C: Corporate Criminal Liability at the African Criminal Court' (n 116) 824.
174 Michalakea (n 123) 244.

liability based on derivative theories such as *respondeat superior* and the doctrine of identification, to embrace a modern model of corporate accountability grounded on the concept of organisational fault. As such, it must be recognised as a step forward from the proposals discussed in the context of the negotiation of the Statute of the ICC.

However, the model proposed by Article 46C does display relevant limitations. As observed in the previous sections, the provision often lacks proper clarity and leaves key terms open to the interpretation of the Court. While this is not to be seen as a negative in itself as it is a common trait of many provisions of the statutes of international criminal courts and tribunals, nonetheless it may render the application of Article 46C entirely unpredictable to the detriment of the rights of the corporate defendant. Therefore, it would be pivotal for the (proposed) African Court to include in its Rules of Procedure and Evidence clear definitions regarding fundamental concepts such as 'legal person', 'policy', and 'corporate personnel' to fill the existing gaps in the provision of Article 46C.

To date, the Malabo Protocol has been signed by 15 countries but has not been ratified by any of the Member States of the African Union.[175] This, unfortunately, casts a shadow on the impact that such a Protocol may have on the development of international criminal law and corporate accountability for international crimes. Nonetheless, it should still be seen as a tentative step toward the recognition of an international criminal liability of corporations and, as such, it cannot be ignored.

4.4 The ILC's Draft Articles on Crimes against Humanity

The final development addressed in this chapter relates to the work conducted by the ILC on the topic of crimes against humanity. While those core crimes have been recognised since Nuremberg[176] and are ingrained in the statutes of all international criminal tribunals and courts established since 1991,[177] they have yet to be codified into a multilateral convention that can provide a uniform definition of such crimes and identify States' obligations regarding national criminalisation and mutual assistance.

175 African Union, List of Countries Which Have Signed, Ratified/Acceded to the Protocol on Amendments to the Protocol on the Statute of the African Court of Justice and Human Rights (last updated on 20 May 2019).

176 United Nations, *Agreement by the Government of the United Kingdom of Great Britain and Northern Ireland, the Government of the United States of America, the Provisional Government of the French Republic and the Government of the Union of Soviet Socialist Republics for the prosecution and punishment of the major war criminals of the European Axis ('London Agreement')*, 8 August 1945, 82 U.N.T.S. 279, Annex, Article 6(c).

177 UN Security Council, Statute of the International Criminal Tribunal for the Former Yugoslavia (25 May 1993), Article 5; UN Security Council, Statute of the International Criminal Tribunal for Rwanda (8 November 1994), Article 3; UN Security Council, Statute of the Special Court for Sierra Leone (16 January 2002), Article 2.

In 1994, M. Cherif Bassiouni observed that:

> Almost half a century after the horrors of World War II, the legal precedents of Nuremberg, Tokyo, and the Subsequent Proceedings risk sinking into *désuétude*. This prolonged inactivity reinforces the argument made by some that 'Crimes Against Humanity,' as this category of international crimes emerged from the post-World War II experience, were of an exceptional nature, representing no more than 'victors' vengeance' A specialized convention on 'Crimes Against Humanity' is clearly needed – one which cures the defects of earlier formulations and takes into account the many tragic experiences of the last fifty years – before the passage of time validates such arguments.[178]

The lack of a specialised convention on crimes against humanity was perceived as a glaring gap in the 'international normative proscriptive scheme' which allowed perpetrators of such atrocities to escape justice and enjoy immunity.[179]

In 2013, the ILC's Working Group on the Obligation to Extradite or Prosecute (*aut dedere aut judicare*) expressed a similar view by highlighting the existence of 'important [voids] in the present conventional regime governing the obligation to extradite or prosecute which may need to be closed', notably in the area concerning crimes against humanity.[180]

In an attempt to fill this normative gap, on 18 July 2014, the ILC took the decision to include the topic of 'Crimes Against Humanity' in its long-term programme of work to develop an international convention on the subject matter.[181] The ILC's work resulted in the adoption, in 2019, of 20 *Draft Articles on the Prevention and Punishment of Crimes Against Humanity* which are currently being considered by the UN General Assembly.[182]

The document produced by the ILC covers several key points such as the definition of crimes against humanity,[183] States' obligations concerning the prevention and punishment of such crimes,[184] and inter-State cooperation and mutual assistance.[185] Draft Article 6, in particular, sets forth States' obligations

178 M C Bassiouni, 'Crimes Against Humanity: The Need for a Specialized Convention' (1994) 31 Columbia
Journal of Transnational Law 457, 458.

179 Ibid 457 and 493.

180 A/CN.4/L.829, para 20.

181 A/CN.4/680, para 1.

182 Draft articles on Prevention and Punishment of Crimes Against Humanity in International Law Commission, Report of the International Law Commission, 71st session (29 April–7 June and 8 July–9 August 2019), A/74/10, para 44.

183 Ibid Article 2.

184 Ibid Articles 3-4.

185 Ibid Article 14.

concerning the national criminalisation of crimes against humanity and the introduction of 'appropriate penalties commensurate with the grave nature of such crimes'.[186] Among the obligations defined by draft Article 6, of great interest is draft paragraph 8 which specifically addresses the question of the liability of legal persons. Draft Article 6(8) establishes that, subject to the provisions of their domestic law, States 'shall take measures to establish the liability of legal persons for the offences' defined within the Draft Articles.[187] These measures shall be adopted 'where appropriate' and 'may be criminal, civil or administrative' depending on the 'legal principles' of each State.[188]

Though the wording of the draft paragraph 8 may appear less than satisfying to those who advocate for the recognition of corporate criminal liability at the international level, its inclusion within the framework of the Draft Articles should be seen as a 'welcome addition'.[189] Indeed, while the flexible language of the text allows States to provide for the criminal liability of corporations only where it does not conflict with their domestic legal principles, the addition of a provision that contemplates such a form of liability is in itself a development that makes the Draft Articles more innovative than most of the other existing instruments in the field of international criminal law.[190]

The following sections look at the drafting history of draft Article 6(8) and consider the opinions expressed by the various members of the Commission, and States, on the advisability of dealing with the liability of legal persons within the framework of the Draft Articles on Crimes against Humanity. The analysis evidences the great attention given by the Commission to the issue under consideration and highlights that, notwithstanding the ambiguous formulation of draft paragraph 8, most of the debate on legal persons focused on the question of corporate criminal liability.

4.4.1 The 2016 Debate on the Liability of Legal Persons

The decision to provide for the liability of legal persons in the Draft Articles proved to be controversial for the Commission. The question was first contemplated by the Special Rapporteur, Sean D. Murphy, in his Second Report, presented to the Commission in May 2016.[191] The Special Rapporteur appeared to be ambivalent about the possibility of including corporate criminal liability

186 Ibid para 44, Commentary to Article 6.

187 Ibid Article 6(8).

188 Ibid Article 6(8).

189 Elies van Sliedregt, 'Criminalization of Crimes Against Humanity under National Law' (2018) 16 Journal of International Criminal Justice 729, 745. See also Clapham, 'Human Rights Obligations for Non-State Actors. Where Are We Now?' (n 92) 30.

190 Leila Nadya Sadat, 'A Contextual and Historical Analysis of the International Law Commission's 2017 Draft Articles for a New Global Treaty on Crimes Against Humanity' (2018) 16 Journal of International Criminal Justice 683, 688.

191 A/CN.4/690, para. 41 et ss.

in a draft convention on crimes against humanity. Even though he acknowledged that the recent developments provided by the decision of the STL on legal entities and the 2014 Malabo Protocol evidence a shift in the perspective on corporate criminal liability at the international level, the Rapporteur still viewed these developments as mere exceptions to the general rule that sees corporations located outside the scope of the international criminal justice system. As a consequence, he opted to exclude such liability from the text of (then) draft Article 5 on the criminalisation of crimes against humanity under national law.[192] He nonetheless invited the members of the Commission to 'express their standpoint on that matter' to prompt further discussion. [193]

During the debate that followed the presentation of the Special Rapporteur's Second Report, the members of the Commission expressed opposite views on the question under consideration. The focus of the 2016 debate centred entirely on the question of corporate criminal liability, with minimal consideration of the issue of alternative forms of liability such as civil or administrative.[194] Therefore, the arguments discussed by the various members of the Commission appear of particular interest for understanding the current status of the debate on the position of corporations within the scope of international criminal law.

The main arguments raised against the recognition of corporate criminal liability within the body of a specialised convention riveted on the issues of States' discretion and ratification. Regarding State's discretion, Sir Michael Wood argued that, given the different approaches adopted by domestic legal systems on the issue of corporate criminal liability, it was advisable not to include a specific obligation on the matter in an international convention but to leave up to each State the decision of whether or not to impose such a form of liability to address corporate involvement in crimes against humanity.[195] This would have ensured the respect of each State's constitutional principles concerning the definition and scope of domestic criminal law.

Strictly linked to the issue of States' discretion is the one concerning ratification. This argument was formulated, specifically, by Ernest Petric who observed that:

> In order to avoid delays in ratification or refusals to ratify, the provisions should be clear and should avoid dealing with matters that remained controversial and would best be regulated under national law. Corporate responsibility for crimes against humanity seemed to be one such matter.

192 Ibid para 84.

193 Ibid.

194 The sole mention to the advisability of focusing only on civil and administrative liability was made by Hmoud. A/CN.4/SR.3297, pp. 5-6.

195 A/CN.4/SR.3298 p. 16 (Sir Michael Wood). See also A/CN.4/SR.3298, p. 12 (Mr Kolodkin) and A/CN.4/SR.3299, p. 7 (Mr Wisnumurti).

> In trying to regulate it in the draft articles, the Commission might be venturing into extremely controversial territory, at least at the current stage.[196]

Again, the statement suggested that the decision on whether or not to criminalise corporations in the context of the prevention and punishment of crimes against humanity should have not been a concern of the Commission but of each national jurisdiction.

Both arguments lay on similar pragmatic considerations. While the first looks at the difficulties of finding a compromise to reconcile the different approaches adopted at the domestic level on the question of corporate liability, the second considers the importance of producing a draft convention that can swiftly find the support of a high number of States – support that may be hindered by the inclusion of a complex issue such as the liability of legal persons. None of these concerns, however, seems to imply the impossibility of constructing corporate criminal liability for crimes against humanity but solely considers such a form of liability difficult to be transposed at the international level within a reasonable amount of time. As stated during the debate, 'the main objections to the inclusion of a provision [on corporate criminal liability] which had been put forward during the debates had not been legal ... rather they had been of a political nature, or had centred on advisability'.[197]

A different argument against the inclusion of the criminal liability of corporations in the Draft Articles was advanced by Pavel Šturma. In his comment to the Second Report, Šturma stated that, in his view, 'there was no need for a draft article on the responsibility of legal persons', and supported the Special Rapporteur's decision not to include such a provision in draft Article 5.[198] In particular, he observed that '[m]ost international conventions that made reference to such responsibility dealt with organised crime, financial crime or corruption, in other words fields in which it played an important role, *which was not the case in the context of crimes against humanity*'.[199] Even considering such a form of liability as relevant in relation to the offences covered in the Draft Articles, he considered that the absence of a treaty obligation on the matter would not prevent States 'from introducing provisions on corporate criminal responsibility in their national law more generally'.[200]

The comment seems to negate the role played by corporate entities in the commission of international crimes such as crimes against humanity. It implies that corporate involvement in economic crimes is a form of deviance that is considered more significant and common – due to the economic

196 A/CN.4/SR.3300, p. 12.
197 A/CN.4/SR.3301, p. 9.
198 A/CN.4/SR.3300, p. 4.
199 Ibid (emphasis added).
200 Ibid.

interest pursued by corporations – than corporate involvement in core crimes, which remains marginal at best. This view entirely ignores the many instances in which corporations have contributed to the commission of international crimes such as slave labour, murder, torture, and other inhuman treatments.[201]

Already at Nuremberg, the prosecution of corporate officials of German corporations such as I.G. Farben, Krupp, and Flick evidenced the level of complicity of the business sector in the perpetration of heinous crimes.[202] Furthermore, as recalled by van Sliedregt, recent studies on the activity of multinational corporations – especially in the African continent – have repeatedly evidenced that 'corporations involved in the private security industry, oil industry, mining business, diamond and timber trade commit or are complicit in war crimes and crimes against humanity'.[203] Recalling *inter alia* the case of the Apartheid regime in South Africa and the economic support it received from corporations such as IBM and Ford, the author observed that, '[b]y continuing to do business with dictatorial regimes, business entities [can contribute] to the political legitimisation and economic viability of regimes engaged in [crimes against humanity].'[204]

Thus, it is evident that corporate complicity in core international crimes cannot be ignored. While it may be true – as suggested by Šturma – that the cases of corporate involvement in economic crimes are statistically more common than those concerning crimes against humanity, this cannot justify a decision to turn a blind eye to the role played by corporations in the commission and/or facilitation of serious human rights violations.

Opposite views to those discussed so far were expressed by several members of the Commission who shared favourable opinions on the possibility of including corporate criminal liability within the framework of the Draft Articles. Those commissioners recognised the significance of the issue of corporate involvement in international crimes and called for further examination of the matter.[205] Detailed arguments in favour of corporate criminal liability were presented, in particular, by Marie G. Jacobsson, Marcelo Vázquez-Bermúdez, and Maurice Kamto.

In speaking against the decision to leave the issue of corporate liability to the discretion of each State, Jacobsson stated that:

201 Wolfgang Kaleck and Miriam Saage-Maaβ, 'Corporate Accountability for Human Rights Violations Amounting to International Crimes. The Status Quo and its Challenges' (2010) 8 Journal of International Criminal Justice 699, 700 et ss.

202 Ibid 701-702.

203 van Sliedregt, 'Criminalization of Crimes Against Humanity under National Law' (n 189) 747-748.

204 Ibid.

205 A/CN.4/SR.3296, p. 13 (Mr Murase); A/CN.4/SR.3296, p. 16 (Mr Tladi); A/CN.4/SR.3296; p. 17 (Mr Park); A/CN.4/SR.3298, p. 5 (Mr Niehaus); A/CN.4/SR.3298, p. 13 (Mr McRea); A/CN.4/SR.3301, p. 10 (Mr Saboia).

> [A] modern draft convention on one of the most heinous crimes must also reflect the ambitions of the international community to combat such crimes at all levels. It might be difficult to establish clear criminal intent on the part of an executive director while, at the same time, it could be very clear that actions taken by a company could aid or abet the commission of crimes against humanity. [...] The Commission could perhaps take inspiration from the Protocol on Amendments to the Protocol on the Statute of the African Court of Justice and Human Rights, although it was not yet in force. Even if it was not possible to establish the existence of a rule of customary international law on the matter, it would be overly cautious not to at least attempt to put pressure on States to hold corporations responsible for their part in crimes against humanity, as the role of corporations in the commission of such crimes had already been recognized after the Second World War. The Special Rapporteur had mentioned I.G. Farben, but Krupp was another example.[206]

In her intervention, Jacobsson encouraged the Commission to take a brave stand on the issue of corporate criminal liability and to learn from past and recent examples to take a step forward in the development of international criminal law. This view is particularly welcomed as it recognises the opportunity offered by the drafting of a convention on crimes against humanity to adopt a more progressive approach to international criminal law, acknowledging that the system modelled on the Nuremberg experience – deeply rooted in the principle of individual criminal liability – may no longer be able to respond effectively to the issues faced by the international community, especially in relation to corporate wrongdoing.

The view expressed by Vázquez-Bermúdez relied on similar premises. Indeed, he also considered the 2014 Malabo Protocol as an interesting development that could be used by the Commission as evidence of the importance of providing for the criminal liability of corporations for international crimes.[207] Additionally, he noted that, in recent years, corporate criminal liability has become a feature of many domestic jurisdictions – including in his country, Ecuador – and of various international instruments.[208] Looking at the latter, Vázquez-Bermúdez observed that the approach adopted in many of these instruments 'gave States leeway to establish corporate criminal responsibility in their legislation in accordance with their domestic legal principles'.[209] This flexible approach can be found, *inter alia*, in the *International Convention*

206 A/CN.4/SR.3300, p. 7.
207 Ibid pp. 13-14.
208 Ibid p. 14.
209 Ibid.

for the Suppression of the Financing of Terrorism,[210] the *UN Convention against Transnational Organized Crime*,[211] and the *UN Convention against Corruption*.[212]

Arguing against those who claimed that the inclusion of corporate criminal liability may hinder ratification of the proposed convention, the Ecuadorian member of the Commission stated that there is no evidence that the establishment of such a form of liability in the aforementioned international instruments had deterred States from becoming parties to them.[213] Thus, '[i]n the light of the development of international law in that area, he was of the view that the draft articles should include a provision on that matter'.[214] As there is evidence of corporate involvement in the commission of crimes against humanity, 'the establishment of their criminal responsibility [within the framework of the Draft Articles] could help to prevent such crimes, punish the perpetrators and make reparations to the victims'.[215]

In concluding his observation, Vázquez-Bermúdez also suggested how such a form of liability should have been incorporate in the Draft Articles.[216] He proposed to replicate the approach adopted under Article 26 of the (widely ratified) UN Convention against Corruption. The provision of Article 26 requires State Parties to establish forms of liability both for individual and legal persons to deter them from the commission of the offences covered in the instrument.[217] In particular, the provision compels States 'to take the necessary steps, in accordance with their fundamental legal principles, to provide for corporate liability' leaving to each State the decision of whether such a liability should be 'criminal, civil or administrative'.[218] This way, the Convention accommodates the various legal systems and domestic approaches to the issue under consideration. However, Article 26(4) clarifies that, irrespective of the nature of the liability imposed to legal persons, 'the monetary or other sanctions that will be introduced must be effective, proportionate and dissuasive'.[219] In the view of the Ecuadorian commissioner, this approach would have been appropriate also in the context of a convention on crimes against humanity as it will allow balancing the respect of States' domestic legal

210 *International Convention for the Suppression of the Financing of Terrorism* (adopted 9 December 1999, entered into force 10 April 2002), 2178 U.N.T.S. 197.

211 *Convention against Transnational Organized Crime* (adopted 15 November 2000, entered into force 29 September 2003), 2225 U.N.T.S 209.

212 *Convention against Corruption* (adopted 31 October 2003, entered into force 14 December 2005), 2349 U.N.T.S. 41.

213 A/CN.4/SR.3300, p. 14.

214 Ibid.

215 Ibid.

216 Ibid.

217 *Convention against Corruption* (adopted 31 October 2003, entered into force 14 December 2005), 2349 UNTS 41, Article 26.

218 Ibid.

219 Ibid.

principles, on one side, with the need to ensure effective protection to victims of such heinous crimes, on the other.[220]

Lastly, detailed arguments in favour of corporate criminal liability were also presented by Kamto. He observed that the inclusion of a provision on corporate criminal liability within the scope of the Draft Articles on Crimes Against Humanity was fundamental '[i]n the interest of producing an effective convention'.[221] His support for such a provision stemmed from the understanding of the prohibition of crimes against humanity as a rule of *jus cogens* that applied to all. In light of that, Kamto considered that:

> It [is] difficult to see why the Commission would hesitate to admit that that rule of *jus cogens* also applied to corporations. By excluding them, the Commission would be making a political rather than a legal choice, or, more specifically, would be expressing a political preference without any legal justification. Moreover, such a choice would not only ignore the contemporary reality of corporate participation in the commission of certain serious international crimes, but would also run counter to the current evolution of international law.[222]

In particular, he recalled that, at the Rome Conference, 'the States members of the Southern African Development Community had already called for the jurisdiction of the ICC to be extended *ratione personae* to corporations and other legal persons'.[223] Furthermore, he mentioned the decision of the African Union to amend the statute of the (proposed) African Court of Justice and Human Rights to expand the Court's jurisdiction to corporations as an additional example in support of the inclusion of the liability of legal persons in the Draft Articles.[224]

In his observation on the subject matter, the commissioner also referred to the numerous initiatives adopted since the end of the Second World War to address the involvement of corporate actors, and their representatives, in international crimes. Specifically, Kamto directed the Commission's attention to the Nuremberg trials against representatives of I.G. Farben, Krupp, and Flick, the work of John Ruggie as Special Representative of the Secretary-General on human rights and transnational corporations and other business enterprises (from 2005 to 2011), the three-volume study produced in 2008 by the International Commission of Jurists on the subject of Corporate Complicity and Legal Accountability, and the extensive use of the US Alien

220 A/CN.4/SR.3300, p. 14.

221 A/CN.4/SR.3299, p 8. The position was also endorsed by the Commission's Chairman, Pedro Comissario Afonso, see A/CN.4/SR.3299, p. 8.

222 A/CN.4/SR.3300, p. 17.

223 Ibid.

224 Ibid.

Tort Claims Act to establish the (civil) liability of corporations for human rights violations.[225]

In light of that, and for the reasons 'lucidly explained' by Jacobsson and Vázquez-Bermúdez during the debate, Kamto concluded that 'a set of draft articles whose scope did not extend to corporations would seem sclerotic and would contribute almost nothing new in relation to existing treaty regimes on the most serious international crimes'.[226]

The Chairman of the Commission – Pedro Comissario Afonso – also spoke in favour of the inclusion of corporate criminal liability in the body of the Draft Articles, sharing the view of Kamto.[227] On the matter under consideration, he concluded that:

> The Commission must be guided by the object and purpose of the future convention and ensure that all impunity gaps were completely closed. He saw no reason why a corporation that had engaged in the acts defined in draft article 3 should escape liability under that convention; no corporate veil or indirect immunity should be allowed to cover any company that benefited from conflicts around the world.[228]

While the Special Rapporteur remained of the view that there was no need to incorporate the criminal responsibility of corporations in the Draft Articles, he conceded that, in light of opinions discussed in the plenary, the issue warranted further consideration and proposed to refer the question to the Drafting Committee.[229] Consequently, on 19 May 2016, the Commission tasked the Drafting Committee to produce a draft provision on the subject matter to be presented to the plenary on 21 July 2016.[230]

4.4.2 The Drafting Committee's Draft Paragraph on the Liability of Legal Persons

As instructed, the Drafting Committee elaborated an additional paragraph (namely paragraph 7) to draft Article 5 which regulated States' obligations regarding the liability of corporations for the offences covered in the Draft Articles.[231] It is worth noticing that, contrary to other provisions of the Draft Articles, the version of draft paragraph 7 maintained its original formulation during the 4 years in which it continued to be under the consideration of the

225 Ibid pp. 17-18.
226 A/CN.4/SR.3300, pp. 17-18.
227 A/CN.4/SR.3301, p. 3.
228 Ibid.
229 Ibid p. 10.
230 A/71/10, para 81.
231 A/CN.4/L.873/Add.1.

Commission and was incorporated, unaltered, in the final text of the Draft Articles on Crimes against Humanity under the provision of draft Article 6(8).

The text presented by the Drafting Committee in 2016 reads as follows:

> 7. Subject to the provisions of its national law, each State shall take measures, where appropriate, to establish the liability of legal persons for the offences referred to in this draft article. Subject to the legal principles of the State, such liability of legal persons may be criminal, civil or administrative.

Formulated in a way that allowed maximum flexibility, the draft paragraph is modelled on the wording of Article 3(4) of the *Optional Protocol to the Convention on the Rights of the Child on the Sale of Children, Child Prostitution and Child Pornography* and incorporates the 'core aspects' of Article 26 of the Convention against Corruption.[232] The decision to follow the example provided by the aforementioned conventions was based on an evaluation of the number of ratifications received by both instruments: 177 (173 in 2016) for the Optional Protocol,[233] 187 (181 in 2016) for the Convention against Corruption.[234] Furthermore, so far no reservation or declarations regarding the provision on the liability of legal entities has been made by any of the State Parties to the Optional Protocol, 'not even by those states that say they cannot accommodate legal person liability since their law does not allow for it'.[235] As declared by the Chairman of the Drafting Committee, a key concern of the Committee in the drafting of paragraph 7 was to word such a provision in a language that 'could have been accepted by a large part of the international community of States'.[236]

The provision imposes an obligation on States to 'take measures' to establish the liability of legal entities for crimes against humanity but leaves it to the discretion of each State to decide which kind of measures to adopt in accordance with its national law. As explained in the commentary to the provision, the opening clause – 'subject to the provisions of its national law' – is intended to provide States with a considerable margin of appreciation in relation to the measures they wish to adopt to fulfil their obligation on the matter.[237] As such,

232 A/CN.4/SR.3325, p. 3.

233 *Optional Protocol to the Convention on the Rights of the Child on the Sale of Children, Child Prostitution and Child Pornography* (adopted 25 May 2000, entered into force 18 January 2002), 2171 U.N.T.S 227.

234 *Convention against Corruption* (adopted 31 October 2003, entered into force 14 December 2005), 2349 UNTS 41.

235 van Sliedregt, 'Criminalization of Crimes Against Humanity under National Law' (n 189) 745.

236 A/CN.4/SR.3325, pp. 3-4.

237 Ibid.

'the obligation is "subject to" the State's existing approach to liability of legal persons for criminal offences under its national law'.[238]

The inclusion of such a clause is an explicit acknowledgement of the concerns that emerged about the existing differences in the domestic response to corporate wrongdoing. By leaving it to the State the final decision on which model of liability to impose to legal persons in relation to crimes against humanity, the Commission avoided the lengthy process of attempting to develop a uniform model that could have satisfied all parties involved.

The provision further watered-down States' obligations regarding legal persons by stating that States should take action only 'where appropriate', leaving them the freedom to decide not to take any measures against legal persons where they deem it inappropriate in the specific context of crimes against humanity. Lastly, where liability is imposed, it is once again left to the State the determination of whether it would be criminal, civil, or administrative, depending on the legal principles embraced in each State's domestic system. As explained by the Chairman of the Drafting Committee, this formulation 'was designed to allow maximum flexibility with a view to accommodating different legal traditions' and domestic doctrinal approaches.[239] Under the provision, thus, 'there is no obligation to establish criminal liability if doing so is inconsistent with a State's national legal principles'; forms of civil or administrative liability are deemed suitable alternatives to ensure accountability for crimes against humanity.[240]

The last observation on the wording of (then) draft paragraph 7 concerns the additional margin of discretion allowed concerning the definition of which legal persons to subject to criminal, civil, or administrative liability *as per* the Draft Articles. While the provision most certainly does not intend to cover States as a *sui generis* legal persons, it remains to the discretion of each State to determine whether liability should be imposed solely on private persons (mainly corporations) or whether public entities could also be held liable for activities falling outside the public sphere.

The draft text elaborated by the Drafting Committee, with its flexible language, ended up finding the support of the Commission that approved the text with no objection.[241] The provision was thus included among the Draft Articles provisionally adopted by the Commission in its 2016 session and transmitted to the UN General Assembly for further discussion within its Sixth Committee.

238 Ibid.
239 Ibid.
240 A/71/10, paras 36-46.
241 A/CN.4/SR.3325, p. 4.

4.4.3 States' Comments on the Draft Provision on the Liability of Legal Persons

In late 2016, the Sixth Committee of the UN General Assembly reviewed the Report of the ILC, including the chapter relating to the topic of crimes against humanity. On this occasion, various States expressed their view on the inclusion of a provision on the liability of legal persons in the context of draft Article 5. States' responses were mostly positive even though some opposition remained to the addition of such a provision in the Draft Articles.

Representatives for the Republic of Argentina,[242] Austria,[243] and France[244] voiced their interest in the text of draft Article 5, paragraph 7, and welcomed the flexible formulation adopted by the Commission. Chile and Slovakia also viewed the merit in the decision to address the question of the liability of legal persons in a specialised convention and declared their openness to discuss the issue further.[245] Support was received also from Spain that considered it particularly relevant that draft Article 5 included a specific provision on the liability of legal persons (paragraph 7).[246] On this point, the Spanish representative shared the opinion that, 'even though we find it appropriate to foresee that States must adopt measures to establish the liability of legal persons, we believe that the wording of paragraph 7 could go further than existing national practice'.[247]

Positive comments were also expressed by Czech Republic and Slovenia. In particular, Petr Válek, speaking for the Permanent Mission of the Czech Republic to the United Nations, stated their appreciation for 'the wording of [draft paragraph 7 which] provides States with a considerable flexibility in deciding whether to adopt such a measure and to shape these measures in accordance with their national law'. He also declared that his country '[i]n principle, ... support[ed] the idea that legal persons should be liable for commission of crimes against humanity' and, due to the complexity of the issue, invited the Commission to study it more in the detail, 'taking into account the specific context of crimes against humanity, including the organizational policy element contained in the definition of these crimes and different interpretations given to it.'[248]

The statement for Slovenia focused more on the contribution that a provision on the liability of legal persons could have offered to the ongoing

242 A/C.6/71/SR.29, para 85.
243 A/C.6/71/SR.25, para 81.
244 A/C.6/71/SR.20, para 74.
245 A/C.6/71/SR.25, para 99 and A/C.6/71/SR.26, para. 140.
246 A/C.6/71/SR.26, para 6.
247 Ibid.
248 A/C.6/71/SR.24, para 69. Quote from the full speech. See Permanent Mission of the Czech Republic to the United Nations, Statement by Mr Petr Válek, Director of International Law Department, Ministry of Foreign Affairs at https://www.un.org/en/ga/sixth/71/pdfs/statements/ilc/czech_rep_2.pdf Accessed 26 March 2023.

debate on corporate accountability for international crimes. In particular, the Slovenian representative observed that:

> Slovenia welcomed the progressive approach taken by the Commission in including liability of legal persons for the commission of crimes against humanity in article 5, paragraph 7. As rightly noted by the Special Rapporteur, the criminal liability of legal persons had become a feature of several national jurisdictions. Legal persons could have significant involvement in the suffering of victims of crimes against humanity. While recognizing the need to address that aspect, his delegation supported the inclusion of paragraph 7, which was ***progressive in nature*** but allowed States considerable flexibility in its implementation. That paragraph could constitute a ***notable novelty and an important contribution*** to the ongoing work.[249]

Representatives from countries such as Mexico and Portugal, instead, adopted a more cautious view on the topic, emphasising the existing divergences among national responses to corporate liability as an important element to be considered when discussing the provision of draft Article 5, paragraph 7.[250]

Relatively minimal resistance to the inclusion of a provision on the liability of legal persons was expressed by those countries that do not embrace corporate criminal liability within their domestic laws. Both Greece and Russia highlighted the lack of recognition of such a legal construct within their legal systems but seemed to consider the text of draft paragraph 7 flexible enough to accommodate their domestic approach to the question of the liability of legal persons.[251] While accepting the merit of draft Article 5, paragraph 7, the Hungarian representative raised some concerns regarding the practical impact of such a provision. In particular, the statement submitted by Hungary observed that:

> Regarding the probably most thoroughly discussed part of the draft articles, namely paragraph 7 of article 5 on the responsibility of legal persons, my delegation fully accepts the fact that in order to achieve the object and purpose of the future convention, it is important to deal with the question of the responsibility of legal persons. However, I have to highlight that Hungary, like many other states, does not recognize criminal liability of legal persons. Even though civil or administrative liability of legal persons is also foreseen by the draft articles, subject to national legislation, it remains to be discussed whether the existence of a paragraph on liability of legal persons that, in most national legislation,

249 A/C.6/71/SR.26, para 107 (emphasis added).
250 Ibid para 18 and A/C.6/71/SR.25, para 93.
251 A/C.6/71/SR.25, para 28, and A/C.6/71/SR.25, para 65.

> is not understood as criminal liability, has any effect on the general aim of preventing and punishing crimes against humanity.[252]

The comment from the Hungarian delegation seems to imply the existence of a difference in the effectiveness of civil and administrative forms of liability, on the one side, in comparison with criminal liability, on the other. Since the provision of draft Article 5, paragraph 7 leaves to the discretion of States any decision concerning the liability regime applicable to legal persons, it is plausible to assume that States will mostly opt for an administrative or civil approach – especially where corporate criminal liability is not recognised at the domestic level, like in Hungary. As observed in the statement, this less coercive solution may not produce 'any effect on the general aim of preventing and punishing crimes against humanity',[253] making the provision entirely superfluous.

While welcoming the formulation of draft Article 5, paragraph 7, Hungary's statement highlights a clear limitation of the provision – its excessive flexibility – which may end up reducing its impact in the long term.

The comments discussed so far are not dissimilar to those submitted to the ILC, two years later, during the final debate on the Draft Articles on Crimes against Humanity. In 2017, the question of the liability of legal persons was temporarily set aside with the Commission worked on other issues to be incorporated in the Articles, including 'victims, witnesses and other affected persons',[254] 'relationship to competent international criminal tribunals',[255] and 'monitoring mechanisms and dispute settlement'.[256] Following the adoption, in first reading, of a full set of Draft Articles at the end of its 69th session, the Commission invited Governments to express their views ahead of its 71st session, which took place between 29 April–7 June and 8 July–9 August 2019.[257] 38 States sent their written comments upon the topic of the Draft Articles.[258]

In summarising the States' opinions on the provision on the liability of legal persons – now incorporated under draft Article 6, paragraph 8 after 2017 – the Special Rapporteur observed that 'several States expressed their support for the liability of legal persons, especially given the flexibility provided for in the draft article'[259] while some considered that the question should be left to

252 A/C.6/71/SR.24, para 81. Quote from the full speech. See Hungary, Intervention by Dr. Réka Varga Head of International Law Department Ministry of Foreign Affairs and Trade Hungary at https://www.un.org/en/ga/sixth/71/pdfs/statements/ilc/hungary_23.pdf Accessed on 26 March 23.

253 Ibid.

254 A/CN.4/704, para 159-196 and A/72/10, pp. 92 et ss.

255 A/CN.4/704, para 198-207.

256 A/CN.4/704, para 212-263 and A/72/10, pp. 116 et ss.

257 A/72/10, para 35–46.

258 A/CN.4/725, para 5-6. A/CN.4/726; A/CN.4/726/Add.1; A/CN.4/726/Add.2

259 A/CN.4/725, para 151. In favour of the liability of legal persons see, *inter alia*, Czech Republic, A/CN.4/726, p. 66; France, A/CN.4/726, p. 68; Sierra Leone, A/CN.4/726, p. 76' Swiss, A/CN.4/726, p. 77.

the discretion of each State.[260] The complexity of the issue led some States to reiterate the limited scope of the provision on legal persons, maintaining that it should be interpreted as 'obligating States to approach criminal liability for legal persons only in accordance with their existing national laws'.[261]

Notwithstanding the mixed reactions received, the Special Rapporteur decided not to propose any amendment to the provision under consideration and the text was thus deferred to the plenary for a final round of observations. During the debate, the question of the liability of legal persons was only sporadically addressed and the few comments were in general in favour of the Special Rapporteur's decision to maintain the text of draft Article 6, paragraph 8 unchanged.[262] Ultimately, the provision was adopted in second reading and, together with the other Draft Articles developed by the Commission, it was submitted to the General Assembly with the recommendation to elaborate a convention on the prevention and punishment of crimes against humanity based on such Articles.

***

In the context of the international developments that occurred after the adoption of the Rome Statute, the Draft Articles on Crimes Against Humanity are the most recent attempt to incorporate legal entities – and *in primis* corporations – within international criminal law. Differently from the examples provided by the decisions of the STL and the Malabo Protocol, the Draft Articles have the potential to effectively innovate the legal framework concerning the prevention and punishment of core international crimes by recognising the role played by corporations in violating international law and the need to ensure accountability.

Furthermore, the positive opinions and declarations of interest expressed by several States on the opportunity to hold legal persons accountable in the context of crimes against humanity can also be seen as further evidence of a new understanding of the issue under consideration; understanding that it may contribute to creating the conditions to open up a new debate on the feasibility of including corporations within the scope of international criminal law.

At the same time, certain limitations of draft Article 6, paragraph 8 cannot be ignored. As discussed above, the provision on the liability of legal persons is worded rather mildly, reducing the role of corporate criminal liability to one of the options available to States to address corporate wrongdoing in the context

260 A/CN.4/725, para 155. Against the liability of legal persons see, *inter alia*, China, A/C.6/72/SR.18, para. 120; The Islamic Republic of Iran, A/C.6/72/SR.20, para. 41' and the United Kingdom, A/CN.4/726, p. 78.

261 A/CN.4/725, para 152.

262 Mr Murase, A/CN.4/SR.3453, p. 12; Mr Park, A/CN.4/SR.3454, p. 7; Mr Hassouna, A/CN.4/SR.3454, p. 11; Contrary: Mr Zagaynov, A/CN.4/SR.3457, p. 17.

of crimes against humanity. On this point, the comment made by the United Kingdom is not entirely without merit:

> In the UK's view, it is unclear what draft Article 6(8) adds to the legal position. Those States that have liability for legal persons as a matter of course will likely allow such liability for crimes against humanity. Those States that do not have such liability are unlikely to change their position because of draft Article 6(8).[263]

However, in response to this scepticism on the practical impacts of draft Article 6, paragraph 8, it is enough to observe how the inclusion of similar provisions within numerous instruments adopted by the European Union, the Council of Europe and the OECD has indeed generated significant changes in States' responses to corporate misbehaviour, prompting several national jurisdictions to introduce corporate criminal liability within their domestic laws.[264]

Documents such as the *Second Protocol of the Convention on the protection of the European Communities' financial interests*,[265] the Council of Europe *Convention on Action against Trafficking in Human Beings*,[266] and the OECD *Convention on Combating Bribery of Foreign Public Officials in International Business*[267] – to mention a few – have played an important role in encouraging States to depart from the traditional principle of *societas delinquere non potest*. This, even though all of these instruments adopted an 'open approach concerning the kind of responsibility a member state or party to the treaty should introduce for companies in the national system'.[268]

If incorporated in an international convention, the provision of draft Article 6, paragraph 8 may as well play a similar role, encouraging States not only to extend the scope of corporate criminal liability to crimes against humanity – where such a legal construct already exists – but also to consider the value of criminal liability to address the issue of corporate wrongdoing, where such a form of liability still lacks proper recognition. As such, the adoption of draft

263 A/CN.4/726, p. 78.

264 Marc Engelhart, 'Corporate Criminal Liability from a Comparative Perspective' in Dominik Brodowski et al., (eds), *Regulating Corporate Criminal Liability* (Springer, 2014) 54 et ss.

265 European Union, *Second Protocol, drawn up on the basis of Article K.3 of the treaty on European Union, to the Convention on the protection of the European Communities' financial interests* - Joint Declaration on Article 13 (2) - Commission Declaration on Article 7, OJ C 221, 19.7.1997, p. 12–22, Article 3.

266 Council of Europe, *Council of Europe Convention on Action Against Trafficking in Human Beings*, 16 May 2005, CETS 197, Article 22.

267 OECD, *Convention on Combating Bribery of Foreign Public Officials in International Business Transactions: and related documents*, 17 December 1997, S. Treaty Doc. No. 105-43, Article 2.

268 Engelhart (n 264) 55.

Article 6, paragraph 8 by the ILC should be seen as a positive development in the field of corporate criminal liability for international crimes.[269]

4.5 Conclusion

This chapter focused on the post-1998 developments that occurred at the international level in the field of corporate criminal liability. The investigation started with a discussion of the STL's decisions in the *New TV S.A.L.*. contempt case. The chapter began by looking at the views expressed by the two Contempt Judges, Judge Baragwanath and Judge Lettieri, on the question of corporate liability under the Tribunal's Rules of Procedure and Evidence. The Contempt Judges offered conflicting interpretations of the Tribunal's inherent power to hold persons in contempt. While Judge Baragwanath saw no obstacle to including corporations in the scope of the STL's contempt jurisdiction in light of the growing recognition of corporate criminal liability at the domestic level, Judge Lettieri considered such an interpretation as contrary to the spirit of the Tribunal's Statute. The conflict between the two interpretations was ultimately resolved by the Appeals Panel which embraced and expanded on Judge Baragwanath's argument recognising the STL's (contempt) jurisdiction over legal persons. The analysis of the Panel's decision offered relevant insight into the evolution of the debate on corporate criminal liability and allowed the identification of interesting developments in the arguments proposed to support the idea of an international corporate criminal liability. At the same time, the investigation highlighted several gaps in the Panel's reasoning and cast doubt on the overall impact of the 2014 decision on the development of a norm on corporate liability under international criminal law.

The chapter then looked at the 2014 Malabo Protocol and its attempt to include a provision on corporate criminal liability for international crimes (Article 46C) in the Statute of the (proposed) African Court of Justice and Human Rights. The discussion centred on the model of corporate criminal liability adopted under Article 46C and considered the innovative solution proposed by the Protocol. Departing from the traditional approach discussed in Rome, Article 46C proposes a more progressive model of corporate criminal liability largely based on the concept of organisational fault. The chapter

269 At the time of writing, the UNGA has mandated the Sixth Committee to resume its consideration of the Draft Articles in its upcoming sessions in April 2023 and 2024, 'in order to exchange substantive views, including in an interactive format, on all aspects of the draft articles, and to consider further the recommendation of the Commission [...] for the elaboration of a convention by the General Assembly or by an international conference of plenipotentiaries on the basis of the draft articles'. The UNGA has also 'invited States to submit by the end of 2023 written comments and observations on the draft articles [...] and requested the Secretary-General to prepare and circulate a compilation of those comments and observations well in advance of the session of the Sixth Committee to be held in 2024'. UNGA Res 77/249 (30 December 2022).

considered the strengths and weaknesses of such a model and highlighted its value in the context of the debate on the international criminal liability of corporations. At the same time, it is recognised that, at the time of writing, the Malabo Protocol has yet to be ratified by any of the Member States of the African Union and this limits the impact it may have on the development of international criminal law and corporate accountability for international crimes.

Lastly, the analysis focused on the ILC's work on the Draft Articles on Crimes against Humanity and on the Commission's decision to include a provision on the liability of legal persons in the Articles. The wording of the provision leaves significant room for States to define which form of liability – criminal, civil, or administrative – to apply to legal persons. Indeed, the flexibility of the language allows States to provide for the criminal liability of corporations only where it does not conflict with their domestic legal system. Notwithstanding the ambiguous formulation of the proposal, the analysis conducted in the chapter showed how most of the debate on the liability of legal persons focused on the question of corporate criminal liability. This further evidenced the attention paid to the idea of imposing criminal liability to companies involved in international crimes. The chapter ultimately acknowledged the provision's intrinsic limitations; at the same time, it argued that the value of the provision on corporate liability should not be underestimated. If incorporated in the final text of a convention on crimes against humanity, such provision will represent the first recognition of corporate liability in the context of an international instrument in the field of international criminal law.

Considered together, all these developments give a sense of the significance of the topic of corporate criminal liability in today's debate on the scope of international criminal law. At the same time, the chapter argued that each of these developments should be evaluated by taking into account the specific context in which they have emerged. Taken in isolation, these developments may have a limited impact on the establishment of an international corporate criminal liability. Nonetheless, when examined together, the 2014 decision of the STL's Appeal Panel, the 2014 Malabo Protocol, and the Draft Articles on Crimes against Humanity, all provide evidence of the evolving nature of the debate on the role of corporations under international criminal law. Overall, the examination of these three developments further demonstrated that, even after Rome, the liability of corporate entities has continually been raised to the attention of those tasked with promoting the development of international criminal law.

References

Primary Sources

Conventions and Treaties

Convention against Corruption (adopted 31 October 2003, entered into force 14 December 2005), 2349 UNTS 41

Convention against Transnational Organized Crime (adopted 15 November 2000, entered into force 29 September 2003), 2225 UNTS 209

Council of Europe, *Council of Europe Convention on Action Against Trafficking in Human Beings*, 16 May 2005, CETS 197

European Union, *Second Protocol, drawn up on the basis of Article K.3 of the treaty on European Union, to the Convention on the protection of the European Communities' financial interests* - Joint Declaration on Article 13 (2) - Commission Declaration on Article 7, OJ C 221, 19 July 1997

International Convention for the Suppression of the Financing of Terrorism (adopted 9 December 1999, entered into force 10 April 2002), 2178 UNTS 197

OECD, *Convention on Combating Bribery of Foreign Public Officials in International Business Transactions: and related documents*, 17 December 1997, S. Treaty Doc. No. 105-43

Optional Protocol to the Convention on the Rights of the Child on the Sale of Children, Child Prostitution and Child Pornography (adopted 25 May 2000, entered into force 18 January 2002), 2171 UNTS 227

United Nations, *Agreement by the Government of the United Kingdom of Great Britain and Northern Ireland, the Government of the United States of America, the Provisional Government of the French Republic and the Government of the Union of Soviet Socialist Republics for the prosecution and punishment of the major war criminals of the European Axis ('London Agreement')*, 8 August 1945, 82 U.N.T.S. 279

Vienna Convention on the Law of Treaties, 23 May 1969, 1155 U.N.T.S. 331

UN Documents

Crimes against humanity: Addendum / Text of draft article 5, paragraph 7, provisionally adopted by the Drafting Committee on 7 July 2016, A/CN.4/L.873/Add.1, 7 July 2016

Crimes against humanity: additional comments and observations received from Governments, international organizations and others: addendum, A/CN.4/726/Add.1, 28 March 2019

Crimes against humanity: additional comments and observations received from Governments, international organizations and others: addendum, A/CN.4/726/Add.2, 2 May 2019

Crimes against humanity: comments and observations received from Governments, international organizations and others, A/CN.4/726, 21 January 2019

Hungary, Intervention by Dr. Réka Varga Head of International Law Department Ministry of Foreign Affairs and Trade Hungary, available at https://www.un.org/en/ga/sixth/71/pdfs/statements/ilc/hungary_23.pdf Accessed 26 March 2023

International Law Commission, First report on crimes against humanity / by Sean D. Murphy, Special Rapporteur, A/CN.4/680, 17 February 2015

International Law Commission, Fourth report on crimes against humanity / by Sean D. Murphy, Special Rapporteur, A/CN.4/725, 18 February 2019

International Law Commission, Provisional summary record of the 3296th meeting, held on Wednesday, 11 May 2016, A/CN.4/SR.3296

International Law Commission, Provisional summary record of the 3297th meeting, held on Thursday, 12 May 2016, A/CN.4/SR.3297

International Law Commission, Provisional summary record of the 3298th meeting, held on Friday, 13 May 2016, A/CN.4/SR.3298
International Law Commission, Provisional summary record of the 3299th meeting, held on Tuesday, 17 May 2016, A/CN.4/SR.3299
International Law Commission, Provisional summary record of the 3300th meeting, held on Wednesday, 18 May 2016, A/CN.4/SR.3300
International Law Commission, Provisional summary record of the 3301st meeting, held on Thursday, 19 May 2016, A/CN.4/SR.3301
International Law Commission, Provisional summary record of the 3325th meeting, held on Thursday, 21 July 2016, A/CN.4/SR.3325
International Law Commission, Provisional summary record of the 3453rd meeting, held on Monday, 29 April 2019, A/CN.4/SR.3453
International Law Commission, Provisional summary record of the 3454th meeting, held on Tuesday, 30 April 2019, A/CN.4/SR.3454
International Law Commission, Provisional summary record of the 3457th meeting, held on Friday, 3 May 2019, A/CN.4/SR.3457
International Law Commission, Provisional summary record of the 3296th meeting, held on Wednesday, 11 May 2016, A/CN.4/SR.3296
International Law Commission, Report of the Working Group on the Obligation to Extradite or Prosecute (*aut dedere aut judicare*), A/CN.4/L.829, 22 July 2013
International Law Commission, Second report on crimes against humanity / by Sean D. Murphy, Special Rapporteur, A/CN.4/690, 21 January 2016
International Law Commission, Third report on crimes against humanity / by Sean D. Murphy, Special Rapporteur, A/CN.4/704, 23 January 2017
Permanent Mission of the Czech Republic to the United Nations, Statement by Mr. Petr Válek, Director of International Law Department, Ministry of Foreign Affairs, available at https://www.un.org/en/ga/sixth/71/pdfs/statements/ilc/czech_rep_2.pdf Accessed 26 March 2023
Report of the International Law Commission, 53rd session, 23 April-1 June and 2 July-10 August 2001, A/56/10, 2001
Report of the International Law Commission, 68th session, 2 May-10 June and 4 July-12 August 2016, A/71/10, 2016
Report of the International Law Commission, 69th session, 1 May-2 June and 3 July-4 August 2017, A/72/10, 2017
Report of the International Law Commission, 71st session, 29 April-7 June and 8 July-9 August 2019, A/74/10, 2019
UNGA Res 77/249, Crimes against Humanity, A/RES/77/249, 30 December 2022
UNGA, 6th Committee, Summary record of the 18th meeting, held on Monday, 23 October 2017, General Assembly, 72nd session, A/C.6/72/SR.18
UNGA, 6th Committee, Summary record of the 20th meeting, held on Monday, 24 October 2016, A/C.6/71/SR.20
UNGA, 6th Committee, Summary record of the 20th meeting, held on Wednesday, 25 October 2017, General Assembly, 72nd session, A/C.6/72/SR.20
UNGA, 6th Committee, Summary record of the 24th meeting, held on Thursday, 27 October 2016, A/C.6/71/SR.24
UNGA, 6th Committee, Summary record of the 25th meeting, held on Friday, 28 October 2016, A/C.6/71/SR.25
UNGA, 6th Committee, Summary record of the 26th meeting, held on Friday, 28 October 2016, A/C.6/71/SR.26

UNGA, 6th Committee, Summary record of the 29th meeting, held on Wednesday, 2 November 2016, A/C.6/71/SR.29

United Nations Diplomatic Conference of Plenipotentiaries on the Establishment of an International Criminal Court, Report of the Preparatory Committee on the Establishment of an International Criminal Court: Addendum, A/CONF.183/2/Add.1, 14 April 1998

United Nations Diplomatic Conference of Plenipotentiaries on the Establishment of an International Criminal Court, Working Paper on Article 23, Paragraphs 5 and 6: [Draft Statute of an International Criminal Court], A/CONF.183/C.1/WGGP/L.5/Rev.2, 4 July 1998

African Union

African Union, List of Countries Which Have Signed, Ratified/Acceded to the Protocol on Amendments to the Protocol on the Statute of the African Court of Justice and Human Rights (last updated on 20 May 2019)

African Union, Meeting of Government Experts and Ministers of Justice/Attorneys General on Legal Matters 7 to 11 and 14 to 15 May 2012, Addis Ababa, Ethiopia, Draft Protocol on Amendments to the Protocol on the Statute of the African Court of Justice and Human Rights, Exp/Min/IV/Rev.7

African Union, Protocol on Amendments to the Protocol on the Statute of the African Court of Justice and Human Rights, 27 June 2014

International Cases

Akhbar Beirut S.A.L. and Mr Al-Amin, Public Redacted Version of the Judgment, STL-14-06/T/CJ, Contempt Judge, 15 July 2016

Akhbar Beirut S.A.L. and Mr Al-Amin, Redacted Version of Decision in Proceedings for Contempt with Orders in Lieu of an Indictment, STL-14-06/1/CJ, Contempt Judge, 31 January 2014

Ayyash et al., Public Redacted Version of Decision on Allegations of Contempt, STL-11-01//PT/CJ/R60bis.1, Contempt Judge, 29 April 2013

In the matter of El Sayed, Decision on Appeal of Pre-Trial Judge's Order Regarding Jurisdiction and Standing, CH/AC/201 0/02, Appeals Chamber, 10 November 2010

New TV S.A.L. and AI Khayat, Decision on Interlocutory Appeal Concerning Personal Jurisdiction in Contempt Proceedings, STL-14-05/PT/AP/ARI26.1, Appeals Panel, 2 October 2014

New TV S.A.L. and Khayat, Decision on Motion Challenging Jurisdiction and on Request for Leave to Amend Order in Lieu of an Indictment, STL-14-05/PT/CJ, Contempt Judge, 24 July 2014

New TV S.A.L. and Khayat, Defence Preliminary Motion Challenging Jurisdiction, STL-14-05/PT/CJ, 16 June 2014

New TV S.A.L. and Khayat, Public Redacted Version of Judgment on Appeal, STL-14-05/A/AP, Appeals Panel, 8 March 2016

New TV S.A.L. and Ms Khayat, Decision on Interlocutory Appeal Concerning Personal Jurisdiction in Contempt Proceedings, STL-14-05/PT/AP/ARI26.1, Appeals Panel, 2 October 2014

New TV S.A.L. and Ms Khayat, Redacted Version of Decision in Proceedings for Contempt with Orders in Lieu of an Indictment, STL-14-05/1/CJ, Contempt Judge, 31 January 2014

Prosecutor v. Jean-Pierre Bemba Gombo, Decision Pursuant to Article 61(7)(a) and (b) of the Rome Statute on the Charges of the Prosecutor Against Jean-Pierre Bemba Gombo, ICC-01/05-01/08-424, Pre-Trial Chamber II, 15 June 2009

Prosecutor v. Simić et al., Judgment in the Matter of Contempt Allegations Against an Accused and his Counsel, IT-95-9-R77, 30 June 2000

Prosecutor v. Tadić, Judgment on Allegations of Contempt Against Prior Counsel, Milan Vujin, IT-94-1-A-R77, 31 January 2000

United States et al. v Goering et al., Judgment, 30 September-1 October 1946 (1948) 1 IMT 171

Domestic Cases

Jesner v. Arab Bank, PLC, 138 S. Ct. 1386 (2018)

Kiobel v. Royal Dutch Petroleum Co., 621 F.3d 111 (2d Cir. 2010)

Nordik Industries v Regional Controller of Inland Revenue [1976] 1 NZLR 194 (SC)

Statute of International and Internationalised Criminal Courts and Tribunals & Rules of Procedure and Evidence

International Criminal Court, Elements of Crimes (last amended 2011)

Rome Statute of the International Criminal Court (opened for signature 17 July 1998, entered into force 1 July 2002) 2187 UNTS 90

Special Tribunal for Lebanon, Rules of Procedure and Evidence

Special Tribunal for Lebanon, Statute

UN Security Council, Statute of the International Criminal Tribunal for the Former Yugoslavia (25 May 1993)

UN Security Council, Statute of the International Criminal Tribunal for Rwanda (8 November 1994)

UN Security Council, Statute of the Special Court for Sierra Leone (16 January 2002)

Domestic law

Australian Criminal Code Act 1995

Italian Legislative Decree No. 231 of 8 June 2001

Lebanese Criminal Code

Republic of Italy, Constitution

United States Sentencing Commission, Guidelines Manual, §8B2.1. (Nov. 2021).

Secondary sources

Book

Adam J, *Die Strafbarkeit juristischer Personem im Volkerstrafrecht* (Nomos 2015)

Alamuddin A, Jurdi N N, and Tolbert D (eds), *The Special Tribunal for Lebanon: Law and Practice* (OUP 2014)

Cassese A, *International Criminal Law* (2nd edn, OUP 2008)
Meloni C, *Command Responsibility in International Criminal Law* (T.M.C. Asser Press 2010)
Pavanello E, *La Responsabilitá Penale delle Persone Giuridiche di Diritto Pubblico. Societas publica delinquere potest* (Padova University Press 2011)
Wheeler C H, *The Right to be Present at Trial in International Criminal Law* (Brill|Nijhoff 2019)

Contributions in edited books

Ambos K, 'Superior Responsibility' in Antonio Cassese et al. (eds), *The Rome Statute of the International Criminal Court: A Commentary*, Volume 1 (OUP 2002)
Clapham A, 'Human Rights Obligations for Non-State Actors. Where Are We Now?' in Fannie Lafontaine and François Larocque (eds), *Doing Peace the Rights Way: Essays in International Law and Relations in Honour of Louise Arbour* (Intersentia 2019)
Clapham A, 'The Question of Jurisdiction under International Criminal Law over Legal Persons: Lessons from the Rome Conference on an International Criminal Court' in Menno T Kamminga and Saman Zia-Zarifi (eds), *Liability of Multinational Corporations under International Law* (Kluwer Law International 2000)
de Maglie C, 'Country report: Italy' in James Gobert and Ana-Maria Pascal (eds), *European Developments in Corporate Criminal Liability* (Routledge 2011)
Engelhart M, 'Corporate Criminal Liability from a Comparative Perspective' in Dominik Brodowski et al. (eds), *Regulating Corporate Criminal Liability* (Springer 2014)
Foffani L, 'Responsabilitá degli Enti da Reato in Italia' in Antonio Fiorella and A M Stile (eds), *Corporate Criminal Liability and Compliance Programs, First Colloquium* (Jovene Editore 2012)
Gaeta P, 'Trial *in Absentia* Before the Special Tribunal for Lebanon' in Amal Alamuddin, Nidal Nabil Jurdi, and David Tolbert (eds), *The Special Tribunal for Lebanon: Law and Practice* (OUP 2014)
Jurdi N N, 'The Crime of Terrorism in Lebanese and International Law' in Amal Alamuddin, Nidal Nabil Jurdi, and David Tolbert (eds), *The Special Tribunal for Lebanon: Law and Practice* (OUP 2014)
Kyriakakis J, 'Article 46C: Corporate Criminal Liability at the African Criminal Court' in C Jalloh, K Clarke, and V Nmehielle (eds), *African Court of Justice and Human and People's Rights in Context* (Cambridge University Press 2019)
Meloni C, 'Modes of Responsibility (Article 28N), Individual Criminal Responsibility (Artcile 46B) and Corporate Criminal Liability (Article 46C)' in Gerhald Werle and Morits Vornbaum (eds), *The African Criminal Court, A Commentary on the Malabo Protocol* (Springer 2017)
Militello V, 'The Basis for Criminal Responsibility of Collective Entities in Italy' in Albin Eser, Günter Heine, and Barbara Huber (eds), *Criminal Responsibility of Legal and Collective Entities* (Freiburg im Breisgau, edition iuscrim 1999)
van Sliedregt E, 'Regional Criminal Justice, Corporate Criminal Liability and the Need for Non-Doctrinal Research' in Marina Aksenova, Elies van Sliedregt, and Stephan Parmentier (eds), *Breaking the Cycle of Mass Atrocities: Criminological and Socio-Legal Approaches in International Criminal Law* (Hart Publishing 2019)

Werle G and Vornbaum M, 'Creating an African Criminal Court' in Gerhald Werle and Morits Vornbaum (eds), *The African Criminal Court, A Commentary on the Malabo Protocol* (Springer 2017)

Journal Articles

Alkhawaja O, 'In Defense of the Special Tribunal for Lebanon and the Case for International Corporate Accountability' (2020) 20 Chicago Journal of International Law 450

Badar M, 'The Mental Element in the Rome Statute of the International Criminal Court: A Commentary from a Comparative Criminal Law Perspective' (2008) 19 Criminal Law Forum 473

Bassiouni M C, 'Crimes Against Humanity: The Need for a Specialized Convention' (1994) 31 Columbia Journal of Transnational Law 457

Bernaz N, 'Corporate Criminal Liability under International Law. The New TV S.A.L. and Akhbar Beirut S.A.L. Cases at the Special Tribunal for Lebanon' (2015) 13 Journal of International Criminal Justice 313

Cavanagh N, 'Corporate Criminal Liability: An Assessment of the Models of Fault' (2011) 75 The Journal of Criminal Law 414

Colvin E, 'Corporate Personality and Criminal Liability' (1995) 6 Criminal Law Forum 1

Hendin S E, 'Command Responsibility and Superior Orders in the Twentieth Century – A Century of Evolution' (2003) 10 Murdoch University Electronic Journal of Law

Kaeb C, 'The Shifting Sands of Corporate Liability Under International Criminal Law' (2016) 49 George Washington International Law Review 351

Kaleck W and Saage-Maaβ M, 'Corporate Accountability for Human Rights Violations Amounting to International Crimes. The Status Quo and its Challenges' (2010) 8 Journal of International Criminal Justice 699

Kyriakakis J, 'Corporate Criminal Liability and the Comparative Law Challenge' (2009) 56 Netherland International Law Review 333

Lederman E, 'Models for Imposing Corporate Criminal Liability: From Adaptation and Imitation Toward Aggregation and the Search for Self-Identity' (2001) 4 Buffalo Criminal Law Review 641

Manirabona A M, 'The Jurisdiction of the Proposed African Criminal Court over Corporations: Proposals to Strengthen a Novel Mechanism' (2017) 55 Canadian Yearbook of International Law 293

Meernik J et al., 'Judicial Decision Making and International Tribunals: Assessing the Impact of Individual, National, and International Factors' (2005) 86 Social Science Quarterly 683

Michalakea T, 'Article 46C of the Malabo Protocol: A Contextually Tailored Approach to Corporate Criminal Liability and Its Contours' (2018) 7 International Human Rights Law Review 225

Rose A, 'Developments in Criminal Law and Criminal Justice, 1995 Australian Criminal Code Act: Corporate Criminal Provisions' (1995) 6 Criminal Law Forum 129

Rose R, 'Corporate Criminal Liability: A Paradox of Hope' (2006) 14 Waikato Law Review 52

Sadat L N, 'A Contextual and Historical Analysis of the International Law Commission's 2017 Draft Articles for a New Global Treaty on Crimes Against Humanity' (2018) 16 Journal of International Criminal Justice 683

Scheffer D, 'Corporate Liability under the Rome Statute' (2016) 57 Harvard International Law Journal 35

Stern S, 'Constructive Knowledge, Probable Cause, and Administrative Decisionmaking' (2007) 82 Notre Dame Law Review 1085

van Sliedregt E, 'Criminalization of Crimes Against Humanity under National Law' (2018) 16 Journal of International Criminal Justice 729

Online sources

de Jonge F, 'International Corporate Criminal Liability at the Special Tribunal for Lebanon: Prosecutor v. Karma Al Khayat and Al Jadeed' (Peace Palace Library, 8 May 2015) https://peacepalacelibrary.nl/blog/2015/international-corporate-criminal-liability-special-tribunal-lebanon-prosecutor-v-karma-al Accessed 26 March 2023

Hopkins R, 'Forth, Back and Forth on Corporate Criminal Liability at the Special Tribunal for Lebanon' (Corporate War Crimes 2015) https://corporatewarcrimes.com/author/corporatewarcrimes/page/27/ Accessed 26 March 2023

Jacobs D, 'A Molotov Cocktail on the Principle of Legality: STL Confirms Contempt Proceedings against Legal Persons' (Blog at Spread the Jam 6 October 2014) https://dovjacobs.com/2014/10/06/a-molotov-cocktail-on-the-principle-of-legality-stl-confirms-contempt-proceedings-against-legal-persons/ Accessed 26 March 2023

McDermott Rees Y, 'Criminal Liability for Legal Persons for Contempt Returns to the STL' (PhD studies in human rights 8 October 2014) http://humanrightsdoctorate.blogspot.com/2014/10/corporate-liability-for-legal-persons.html Accessed 26 March 2023

Verwiel A and van der Voort K, 'Some Further Thoughts on the STL Appeals Chamber Decision on Criminal Liability for Legal Entities' (Special Tribunal for Lebanon Blog 16 October 2014) http://lebanontribunal.blogspot.com/2014/10/some-further-thoughts-on-stl-appeals.html Accessed 26 March 2023

5 National Developments and the Comparative Law Argument in the Debate on Corporate Criminal Liability

5.1 Introduction

Chapter 4 discussed key international developments in the area of corporate criminal liability that occurred after the adoption of the Rome Statute. The analysis offered a counterargument against the idea that the debate on an international corporate criminal liability lost cogency after the exclusion of corporations from the jurisdiction of the ICC. The chapter explored the 2014 decision of the STL to establish (contempt) jurisdiction over legal persons and the attempt made by the African Union to incorporate a provision on corporate criminal liability in the Statute of the (proposed) African Court of Justice and Human and Peoples' Rights. The analysis of these developments sheds light on the evolution of the arguments used to discuss the feasibility of imposing criminal liability on corporate entities at the international level. It also showed a change in the approach to constructing corporate criminal liability for international crimes. The investigation also touched upon the decision of the ILC to include a provision on the liability of legal persons in the *Draft Articles on Crimes against Humanity*. Of all the developments discussed in Chapter 4, the Draft Articles represent the most recent attempt to expand the scope of international criminal law beyond natural persons. At the time of writing, the discussion on the Draft Articles is still ongoing and may offer a significant contribution to the debate on corporate accountability.

The discussion conducted in the previous chapter thus demonstrated that the question of the criminal liability of legal persons for international crimes has remained a relevant issue in the debate on the scope of international criminal law. At the same time, it offered interesting insights into the way in which domestic advancements in the area of corporate criminal liability were used to support the decision to also consider such a form of liability in the context of international crimes. The STL's reliance on domestic developments to justify its decision to assert its (contempt) jurisdiction over corporations, alongside the numerous references to the growing recognition of corporate criminal liability by national legal systems made during the discussion of the Draft Articles on Crimes against Humanity, are evidence of the significant role currently played by the comparative law argument in the debate on the international

DOI: 10.4324/9781003390534-6

criminal liability of corporations. While the argument still attracts criticism from those who contest the applicability of criminal liability to legal persons,[1] it has nonetheless become a recurring feature in the literature on the international criminal liability of corporations.

This chapter, therefore, considers the strengths and weaknesses of this specific argument and how it has been developed to support the idea of corporate criminal liability as a general principle of law. The discussion starts with a review of the way in which the comparative argument has been addressed in the existing literature on the international criminal liability of corporations. The review allows for a contextualisation of the comparative law argument and to demonstrate a change in the role played by this argument in the debate on corporate criminal liability: from arguments against, to arguments in support of the international criminal liability of companies. Lastly, the chapter evaluates whether the growing recognition of corporate criminal liability at the domestic level can be used as evidence of the emergence of a general principle of law on corporate liability and the relevance (or lack thereof) of such a suggestion.

5.2 The Comparative Law Argument

In the literature on the criminal liability of corporations, the development of a trend towards the recognition of corporate criminal liability at the domestic level is often used to support the adoption of such a model of liability internationally.[2] The decision of a growing number of legal systems to move away from the strict application of the principle *societas delinquere non potest* has been seen as evidence of a 'shift' in states' attitudes towards the criminal liability of corporations.[3] As observed by the International Commission of Jurists Expert Legal Panel on Corporate Complicity in International Crimes, 'as national criminal laws develop to include this type of liability, so do the arguments for an expansion of international courts' jurisdiction over company entities'.[4]

1 Thomas Weigend, 'Societas delinquere non potest? A German Perspective' (2008) 6 Journal of International Criminal Justice 927. See also Judge Lettieri's interpretation in *New TV S.A.L. and Khayat,* Decision on Motion Challenging Jurisdiction and on Request for Leave to Amend Order in Lieu of an Indictment, STL-14-05/PT/CJ, Contempt Judge, 24 July 2014, para 74.

2 Jendrik Adam, *Die Strafbarkeit juristischer Personem im Volkerstrafrecht* (Nomos 2015), 95 et ss.; Caroline Kaeb, 'The Shifting Sands of Corporate Liability Under International Criminal Law' (2016) George Washington International Law Review 351; Joanna Kyriakakis, 'Corporate Criminal Liability and the ICC Statute: the Comparative Law Challenge' (2009) Netherland International Law Review 333; Robert Thompson, Anita Ramasastry and Mark Taylor, 'Translating Unocal: The Expanding Web of Liability for Business Entities Implicated in International Crimes' (2009) 40 George Washington International Law Review 841.

3 The term 'shifting sand' has been used by Kaeb (n 2).

4 International Commission of Jurists, 'Corporate Complicity and Legal Accountability, Vol. II, Report of the International Commission of Jurists Expert Legal Panel on Corporate Complic-

The argument has become central in the debate on the international criminal liability of corporations due to the role played by the 'complementarity objection' in the decision to exclude legal entities from the jurisdiction of the ICC. As discussed in Chapter 4, during the Rome Conference, the lack of a general recognition of corporate criminal liability across states was seen as an insurmountable obstacle to the proper operation of the complementarity scheme adopted in the Statute of the ICC, ultimately leading to the withdrawal of the French proposal. As observed by Kyriakakis:

> The concern was that those States Parties that do not provide for corporate criminal liability within their domestic laws might be viewed as unable or unwilling to prosecute corporate defendants in the context of ICC admissibility determinations if corporations were included within the jurisdiction of the ICC.[5]

Nowadays, the obstacle posed by the limited acceptance of the criminal liability of corporations at the national level seems to be progressively losing its relevance.

Already in 2006, a study conducted by Anita Ramasastry and Robert C. Thompson showed how national jurisdictions were progressively including provisions on corporate criminal liability in their legal system.[6] In particular, the study surveyed the legislation of 16 selected countries and found that 11 jurisdictions – specifically Australia, Belgium, Canada, France, India, Japan, the Netherlands, Norway, South Africa, the United Kingdom, and the United States – already made it 'a general practice to recognize no distinction between natural and legal persons' in the area of criminal law.[7] More importantly, the study highlighted that eight of these countries (State Parties to the International Criminal Court) also 'fully incorporate[d]' – or were in the process of incorporating – the Rome Statute's provisions on genocide, crimes against humanity, and war crimes into their criminal laws, thus making it possible (potentially) to prosecute legal persons for those international crimes.[8] Even though partially outdated,[9] the study still provides evidence of the rapidity with which the domestic framework on corporate criminal liability has evolved in the years following 1998.

ity in International Crimes' (ICJ, 2008) https://icj2.wpenginepowered.com/wp-content/uploads/2012/06/Vol.2-Corporate-legal-accountability-thematic-report-2008.pdf Accessed 26 March 2023, 57.

5 Kyriakakis (n 2) 334.

6 Anita Ramasastry and Robert C Thompson, 'Commerce, Crime and Conflict: Legal Remedies for Private Sector Liability for Grave Breaches of International Law' (FAFO 2006) https://www.biicl.org/files/4364_536.pdf Accessed 26 March 2023.

7 Ramasastry and Thompson (n 6) 13; Thompson, Ramasastry and Taylor (n 2) 871.

8 Ramasastry and Thompson (n 6) 15.

9 The legislation of Spain had changed since the publication of the study.

A year later, the Special Representative of the Secretary-General (SRSG) on the issue of human rights and transnational corporations and other business enterprises, John Ruggie, reached a similar conclusion in his 2007 report *Business and Human Rights: Mapping International Standards of Responsibility and Accountability for Corporate Acts* where he stated that:

> This report has identified areas of fluidity in the business and human rights constellation, which in some respects may be seen as hopeful signs. By far the most consequential legal development is the *gradual extension of liability to companies for international crimes, under domestic jurisdiction but reflecting international standards.* But this trend is largely an unanticipated by-product of states' strengthening the legal regime for individuals [...].[10]

Similarly, in 2014, a study commissioned by the Office of the UN High Commissioner of Human Rights also highlighted the progressive expansion of corporate criminal liability at the domestic level. In the study (known as the Zerk Report), Jennifer Zerk discussed the existing framework on business and human rights at the domestic level observing that, based on the evidence collected, 'most jurisdictions appear[ed] to recognise the possibility of corporate criminal responsibility (if not as a general concept then at least in relation to specific offences or types of offences)'.[11] The Zerk Report also observed that most of the developments concerning corporate criminal liability occurred only recently, 'over the past twenty years', when numerous countries of civil law tradition began to introduce such a form of liability into their criminal laws.[12]

A comparative analysis of corporate criminal liability legislations was also conducted by Engelhart who observed that, since the 1990s, the number of domestic jurisdictions that allow for corporations to be held criminally accountable has significantly increased.[13] In his study, he identified several European countries that, between 1991 and 2011, introduced provisions on the criminal liability of legal entities either by amending their Penal Code or through the adoption of specific laws.[14] Engelhart reported that 'in 2013, only

10 A/HRC/4/035, para 84 (emphasis added).

11 Jennifer Zerk, 'Corporate liability for gross human rights abuses. Towards a fairer and more effective system of domestic law remedies' (OHCHR, 2012) https://www.ohchr.org/sites/default/files/Documents/Issues/Business/DomesticLawRemedies/StudyDomesticeLawRemedies.pdf Accessed 26 March 2023.

12 Ibid 32.

13 Marc Engelhart, 'Corporate Criminal Liability from a Comparative Perspective' in Dominik Brodowski et al., (eds), *Regulating Corporate Criminal Liability* (Springer 2014) 56-57.

14 Ibid.

Germany, Latvia and Greece [had] not yet introduced some kind of corporate criminal liability in Europe'.[15]

Scholars such as Kaeb and Kyriakakis share the view that this progressive adoption of corporate criminal liability by many civil law countries across Europe, alongside other legal systems worldwide, has given 'new dimensions' to the debate on the international criminal liability of corporate entities[16] and 'will likely function as a catalyst for courts to construe international criminal law so as to apply to corporations as non-state actors'.[17] Studies have also explored developments relating to the domestic implementation of the ICC Statute in countries where corporate criminal liability is recognised under criminal law. Domestic criminal laws of countries such as Norway and Australia, in particular, have offered interesting food for thought on the role played by domestic legislations in 'expanding the effective scope of international criminal law',[18] especially in the area of corporate criminal liability.[19]

More recently, the comparative law argument was presented by David Scheffer in the *Jesner v Arab Bank* case.[20] In his submission to the US Supreme Court, Scheffer refers to the developments that occurred at the domestic level to evidence the existence of a trend towards a growing recognition of corporate criminal liability.[21] In particular, the author observes that, since July 1998, 'a number of additional countries have adopted laws providing or expanding corporate liability for a range of international crimes, including atrocity crimes'.[22] Focusing on those states that took part in the Rome Conference, Scheffer proposes a list of 29 States' Parties to the Rome Statute which 'provide for corporate criminal liability … for varying types of crimes, often including atrocity crimes'.[23] Even though positively received by the dissenting judges,[24] the argument ultimately fell on deaf ears and, in the judgment, the majority

15 Ibid 57.

16 Kyriakakis (n 2) 334.

17 Kaeb (n 2) 354.

18 Joanna Kyriakakis, 'Australian Prosecution of Corporations for International Crimes. The Potential of the Commonwealth Criminal Code' (2007) 5 Journal of International Criminal Justice 809, 811.

19 Simon O'Connor, 'Corporations, International Crimes and National Courts: A Norwegian View (2012) 94 International Review of the Red Cross 1007; Kyriakakis, 'Australian Prosecution of Corporations for International Crimes. The Potential of the Commonwealth Criminal Code' (n 18).

20 *Jesner v. Arab Bank, PLC*, 138 S. Ct. 1386 (2018), Brief of Ambassador David J Scheffer, Northwestern University Pritzker School of Law, as Amicus Curiae in Support of the Petitioners, 26 June 2017.

21 Ibid p. 18 et ss. The argument was ignored by the majority but found the acknowledgement of the dissenting judges. See *Jesner v. Arab Bank, PLC*, 138 S. Ct. 1386, at 1425 (2018).

22 Ibid p. 19-20.

23 Ibid p. 21.

24 *Jesner v. Arab Bank, PLC*, 138 S. Ct. 1386, at 1424-25 (2018).

failed to even consider it in its discussion on the status of corporate liability for human rights abuses.[25]

5.2.1 Limitations of the Comparative Law Argument

The review conducted so far demonstrates the central role played by the comparative law argument in the literature on corporate criminal liability and international law. As previously mentioned, this attention to the developments that occurred at the domestic level can be seen as a response to the complementarity objection raised during the negotiation of the Rome Statute and aims to prove that the significant changes that have occurred since the creation of the ICC may deprive such objection of its validity.

As such, the argument has the merit of acknowledging the ever-evolving nature of domestic and international legal systems according to which states' responses to a certain legal phenomenon are not static and can therefore develop under the influences of a variety of factors, including social and economic factors. This is particularly true in the area of corporate accountability where the evolution of the role of corporations within modern society has imposed a re-evaluation of the legal response to corporate misbehaviour.

On this point, the emphasis put on the advancements that occurred in Europe over the past 20 years is particularly relevant. Indeed, if in 1998 only a few countries embraced the concept of corporate criminal liability, over the last two decades the number of countries where corporations can be held criminally accountable has grown exponentially. The comparative law argument has thus the merit of evidencing how the gap between common law and civil law countries in the area of corporate criminal liability has slowly but surely narrowed down to a point where the similarities in the domestic approaches may have become more relevant than the lingering differences.

At the same time, however, the argument raises certain quandaries. Firstly, the existence of certain inaccuracies in the analysis of domestic responses to corporate misbehaviour may undermine the validity of the comparative analysis conducted by scholars. The main example in this regard is provided by the case of Italy. In the literature on corporate criminal liability, Italy is at times presented as yet another example of a country that, in the early 2000s, moved to embrace the concept of corporate criminal liability in its domestic system.[26]

25 The majority only briefly mentioned the STL decision, and other domestic cases on corporate liability, stating that 'even assuming that these cases are relevant examples, at most they demonstrate that corporate liability might be permissible under international law in some circumstances. That falls far short of establishing a specific, universal, and obligatory norm of corporate liability'. *Jesner v. Arab Bank, PLC*, 138 S. Ct. 1386, at 1401 (2018).

26 *Jesner v. Arab Bank, PLC*, 138 S. Ct. 1386 (2018); Brief of Ambassador David J Scheffer, Northwestern University Pritzker School of Law, as Amicus Curiae in Support of the Petitioners, 26 June 2017, p. 19-20; Chip Pitts, 'Corporate Criminal Liability' (2014) The Encyclopedia of Criminology and Criminal Justice 3; Cristina de Maglie, 'Country report: Italy'

While it is correct to say that legal entities are no longer estranged from the Italian criminal justice system, it would be nonetheless incorrect to equate the model of liability adopted by the Italian legislator to those embraced by the countries discussed so far. Indeed, the current legislation on the liability of legal persons for criminal offences (*Decreto Legislativo n. 231/2001 – Responsabilità Amministrativa da Reato*) proposes a model of 'administrative liability *ex crimine*' ('*responsabilitá amministrativa da reato*') that still complies with the principle of '*societas delinquere non potest*' recognised under Article 27 of the Italian Constitution.[27] Such provision establishes the personal nature of criminal liability ('*la responsabilità penale è personale*') and excludes the possibility of imposing criminal responsibility on abstract entities devoid of human consciousness.[28]

As observed in the Explanatory note (*Relazione Ministeriale*) to the Decreto Legislativo n. 231/2001, the mode of liability introduced by the legislator creates a '*tertium genus*' which combines the essential features of the criminal and administrative systems in an attempt to reconcile the reasons for preventive effectiveness with a high standard of procedural guarantees for the accused.[29] To further differentiate the system of corporate liability introduced by the Decreto Legislativo n. 231/2001 from the ordinary system criminal liability, the legislator has opted for an *extra codice* approach, separating the provisions on corporate liability for criminal offences from the Criminal Code.[30]

However, the reference to the 'administrative nature' of corporate liability provided in the title of the law has not quashed the doubts concerning the 'real legal nature' of the system introduced in 2001.[31] Those in support of the 'criminal nature' of corporate liability under the Decreto Legislativo n. 231/2001 draw their arguments from a variety of elements such as (i) the commission of a crime as a prerequisite of the entity's liability; (ii) the criminal jurisdiction; (iii) the applicability of criminal sanctions; (iv) the relevance of inchoate offences; and (v) the possibility of waiving amnesty.[32] In 2007,

in James Gobert and Ana-Maria Pascal (eds), *European Developments in Corporate Criminal Liability* (Routledge, 2011) 253-254; Edward B Diskant, 'Comparative Corporate Criminal Liability: Exploring the Uniquely American Doctrine through Comparative Criminal Procedure' (2008) 118 Yale Law Journal 126, 133; Cristina Chiomenti, 'Corporations and the International Criminal Court' in Olivier De Schutter (ed) *Transnational Corporations and Human Rights* (Bloomsbury Publishing, 2006) 295.

27 Constitution of the Republic of Italy, Article 27.

28 Ibid.

29 Relazione ministeriale al Decreto Legislativo n. 231/2001, p. 2.

30 Luigi Foffani, 'Responsabilitá degli Enti da Reato in Italia' in A Fiorella and A M Stile (eds) *Corporate Criminal Liability and Compliance Programs, First Colloquium* (Jovene Editore 2012) 97.

31 de Maglie (n 26) 253.

32 Ibid 253-254. See also Italian Supreme Court of Cassation, Criminal Division, SS.UU. Judgement 18 September 2014, n. 38343.

this position found the support of the Italian Supreme Court of Cassation (Criminal Division, Section II) which observed that:

> It is known that the Legislative Decree n. 231 of 2001 … differs from the pre-existing [sanctioning system] applicable to legal entities and, as such, it signalled the death of the dogma of '*societas delinquere non potest*'. And this is because, in spite of the '*nomen iuris*', the new responsibility, nominally administrative, conceals its substantially criminal nature; perhaps omitted in order not to open delicate conflicts with the personalistic dogma of criminal liability enshrined in Article 27 of the Constitution.[33]

This interpretation, however, was subsequently reversed by the Court of Cassation itself in its 'Grand Chamber' decision in the *ThyssenKrupp* case.[34] In the Judgment, the Court referred back to the Explanatory note (*Relazione Ministeriale*) to the Decreto Legislativo n. 231 of 2001 to reaffirm the '*tertium genus*' quasi-criminal nature of the corporate liability adopted by the Italian legislator. This approach, therefore, differentiates the Italian model from those adopted by other countries where the liability of corporations is substantially criminal in nature. As observed in Chapter 4 (see Section 4.2.2.), it is in light of this doctrinal interpretation that Judge Lettieri proposed Italy, alongside Germany, as a relevant example of countries that reject the concept of corporate criminal liability.[35] The Italian example, therefore, needs to be considered more carefully to avoid misinterpretation of the law on corporate liability.

However, the main criticism that can be made against the comparative law argument relates to the premise upon which such an argument seems to be based. Specifically, the argument seems to move from the assumption that a growing acceptance towards corporate criminal liability at the domestic level will create – almost certainly – the conditions for the recognition of such a concept within the international legal system, and in particular within the international criminal justice system. Yet, the recognition of a legal concept or principle *in foro domestico* may not be in itself sufficient to demonstrate a state's willingness to support the transposition of the same concept or principle at the international level. Indeed, the decision of a state to champion or not the adoption of a legal construct under international law is influenced by a variety of factors that concur with the determination of its foreign policy.

33 Italian Supreme Court of Cassation, Criminal Division, Sez. II, Judgement 30 January 2006 n. 3615.

34 Italian Supreme Court of Cassation, Criminal Division, SS.UU. Judgement 18 September 2014, n. 38343.

35 *New TV S.A.L. and Khayat*, Decision on Motion Challenging Jurisdiction and on Request for Leave to Amend Order in Lieu of an Indictment, STL-14-05/PT/CJ, Contempt Judge, 24 July 2014, footnote 116.

In this context, domestic legislation may have only a relative impact on the determination of a position of a state at the international level.

An example in this regard is provided by the position adopted by states such as Australia, Canada, the United States, and the United Kingdom during the debate on the feasibility of including legal persons within the scope of the Rome Statute. Historically, these common law countries were among the first to move away from the principle of *societas delinquere non potest* and to accept the applicability of criminal law to corporations in their domestic legal order.[36]

As observed in Chapter 4, the United States recognised corporate criminal liability already in 1909 when the US Supreme Court found 'no valid objection in law and every reason in public policy' to the imposition of criminal liability on a corporation for an act committed by its agents.[37] In the United Kingdom, the recognition of corporate criminal liability also occurred in the first half of the twentieth century when '[t]he industrial revolution and improved transportation resulted in changes in corporations and in the function they played in society'.[38] This change led to a shift in the legal response to corporate wrongdoing and to the development of a model of corporate criminal liability based on the principle that a corporation can be held criminally liable for an offence committed by a person who can be considered its personification (identification principle).[39]

In Canada, a first attempt to recognise the criminal liability of corporations was made in 1909 when an amendment to the Canadian Criminal Code allowed for the applicability of a fine to a corporation found guilty of a criminal offence.[40] Later on, the corporate criminal liability was incorporated into the 1985 Criminal Code, where Section 2 establishes that the terms 'everyone' and 'person' used in the Code must be interpreted to include organisations such as public bodies, bodies corporate, companies, firms, partnerships, trade unions, or municipalities.[41] At the judicial level, the Canadian Supreme Court defined the test for corporate criminal liability in its landmark decision in *Canadian Dredge and Duck Co v The Queen* where it embraced the identification principle developed in the United Kingdom, albeit with some adjustments.[42]

Australia also has a long history of recognising corporate criminal liability in its domestic system. Influenced by the United Kingdom's model, Australia

36 Guy Stessens, 'Criminal Liability: A Comparative Perspective' (1994) 43 The International and Comparative Law Quarterly 493, 495.

37 *New York Central & Hudson River R.R. v. United States*, 212 U.S. 481 (1909) 495.

38 Celia Wells, *Corporations and Criminal Responsibility*, (2nd edn, OUP 2005) 87.

39 Kyriakakis (n 2) 'Corporate Criminal Liability and the ICC Statute: The Comparative Law Challenge' 337.

40 Stessens (n 36) 498.

41 Canadian Criminal Code, Section 2, 'organisation'.

42 *Canadian Dredge & Dock Co. v. The Queen* [1985] 1 S.C.R. 662; Kyriakakis, 'Corporate Criminal Liability and the ICC Statute: The Comparative Law Challenge' (n 2) 338.

initially relied on the identification doctrine proposed by the UK House of Lords in the landmark decision *Tesco Supermarket Ltd. v Nattrass.*[43] Then, in 1995, the Australian legislator adopted the Australian Criminal Code Act and introduced one of the most progressive approaches to corporate criminal liability. As mentioned in Chapter 4, the new model embraced by Australia combines elements from the traditional identification theory and *respondeat superior* doctrine with the novel concept of 'corporate culture' as one of the criteria for ascribing criminal liability to the corporation.[44]

Therefore, in 1998, these common law countries already had a long history of dealing with criminal prosecution of corporate entities. Nonetheless, this 'familiarity' with corporate criminal liability was not enough to influence positively their views on the possibility of adopting the same concept (adequately adjusted) at the international level. Indeed, as observed in Chapter 4, when the opportunity came to support the inclusion of legal entities within the jurisdiction of the ICC, the position of these countries remained mostly ambiguous. In his account of the final discussion on draft Article 23(5) and (6), Clapham observed that while the United Kingdom took an interest in the proposal and 'made serious attempts to find a workable solution', countries such as the United States and Australia were more sceptical, with the former ultimately joining those delegations which considered the issue too complex to be resolved in a three-week time.[45] Also Canada, which otherwise adopted a proactive role during the negotiation of the Rome Statute,[46] refrained from openly supporting the inclusion of legal entities within the jurisdiction of the ICC.[47]

A similar example is provided by two Nordic countries: Norway and Denmark. Norwegian criminal law firstly recognised the criminal liability of corporations (Straffansvar for foretak) in 1991 when the Act on Amendments to the Penal Code introduced Chapter 3a – 'Criminal liability of enterprises' – within the 1902 Norwegian Penal Code.[48] In particular, Section 48a of Chapter 3a established that '[w]hen a criminal provision is contravened by a

43 *Tesco Supermarkets v Nattrass* [1972] A.C. 153, 170; Kyriakakis, 'Corporate Criminal Liability and the ICC Statute: The Comparative Law Challenge' (n 2) 338.

44 Kyriakakis, 'Corporate Criminal Liability and the ICC Statute: The Comparative Law Challenge' (n 2) 339; Kyriakakis, 'Australian Prosecution of Corporations for International Crimes. The Potential of the Commonwealth Criminal Code' (n 18).

45 Andrew Clapham, 'The Question of Jurisdiction under International Criminal Law over Legal Persons: Lessons from the Rome Conference on an International Criminal Court' in Menno Kamminga and Saman Zia-Zarifi (eds), *Liability of Multinational Corporations Under International Law* (Martinus Nijhoff 2000), 158.

46 Valerie Oosterveld, Canada and the Development of International Criminal Law: What Role for the Future? Canada in International Law at 150 and Beyond 16 March 2018 https://www.cigionline.org/publications/canada-and-development-international-criminal-law-what-role-future/ Accessed 26 March 2023.

47 Clapham (n 45) 158.

48 O'Connor (n 19) 1012.

person who has acted on behalf of an enterprise, the enterprise may be liable to a penalty'.[49] The liability of the enterprise was recognised irrespective of whether a natural person can be punished for the specific offence.[50] The criminal liability of corporations was later reaffirmed within the 2005 Norwegian Penal Code under Section 27 which recognises the possibility of imposing criminal liability and criminal penalties to a company in instances where an offence has been committed by a natural person acting on behalf of the company itself.[51] In 1998, thus, the concept of corporate criminal liability was already ingrained in the criminal law of Norway – even though its application at the time remained almost non-existent.[52] Nonetheless, the Norwegian delegation opposed the inclusion of the provision of draft Articles 23(5) and 23(6) into the Statute of the International Criminal Code.[53]

Likewise, Denmark introduced a corporate criminal liability within its domestic legal system already during the 20th century through the adoption of a multitude of special statutes that criminalised legal persons for specific offences.[54] In 1996, the Danish legislator amended the Criminal Code to include a general provision of corporate criminal liability to define a uniform model for this specific form of liability.[55] In particular, Sections 25 and 27(1) of Chapter 5 of the Danish Criminal Code state as follows:

> § 25.
>
> A legal person may be punished by a fine, if such punishment is authorized by law or by rules pursuant thereto.[56]
>
> § 27
>
> (1) Criminal liability of a legal person is conditional upon a transgression having been committed within the establishment of this person at the fault of one or more persons connected to this legal person or at the fault of the legal person himself.[57]

Notwithstanding the inclusion of such provisions within the domestic Criminal Code, the Danish delegation expressed scepticism towards the possibility of including the legal persons within the jurisdiction *ratione personae* of the ICC.

49 Norwegian Criminal Code, Chapter 3a, Section 48a (1902).
50 Ibid.
51 Norwegian Criminal Code, Chapter 4, Section 27 (2005).
52 O'Connor (n 19) 1025.
53 Clapham (n 45) 157.
54 Thomas Elhom, 'Criminal Liability of Legal Persons in Denmark' in Antonio Fiorella and A M Stile (eds) *Corporate Criminal Liability and Compliance Programs, First Colloquium* (Jovene Editore 2012), 317.
55 Ibid.
56 Danish Criminal Code, Chapter 5, Section 25.
57 Ibid Section 27(1).

Specifically, during the initial discussion on the French proposal on criminal organisations – in the formulation of 2 April 1998 (see Chapter 4, Section 4.2 and 4.5 above) – the delegate from Denmark stated that:

> [Denmark] shared Sweden's scepticism about the inclusion in the Statute of the criminal responsibility of legal persons. Denmark's view in principle was that the emphasis in the Statute should be on individual responsibility and that the extension of such responsibility to legal persons would *complicate matters unduly*, especially with regard to national implementation.[58]

Once again, domestic recognition of the criminal liability of corporations did not prevent a delegation from adopting a more sceptical approach when a proposal to translate such a concept at the international level was advanced.

In the case of Denmark, however, an additional observation must be made. The Danish delegation expressed its initial opposition to the inclusion of legal persons within the Statute of the ICC when the model under consideration was still heavily based on the concept of criminal organisations *á la* Nuremberg.[59] This may have played a role in Denmark's decision not to side with the French proposal at the beginning of the Rome Conference. Evidence of that may be provided by the account presented by Clapham on the final stage of the negotiation of draft Articles 23(5) and 23(6) where the author did not include Denmark in the list of countries that ultimately spoke against the proposal.[60]

The observations proposed so far demonstrate that the question of countries' willingness to transpose a domestic concept to the international legal system cannot be ignored when evaluating the relevance of the comparative law argument in the debate on corporate criminal liability. In the case at hand, a possible explanation of the ambiguous positions adopted by the aforementioned States regarding the transposition of corporate criminal liability at the international level may be found in the peculiar context in which the negotiation of the Rome Statute took place. The limited time that was allocated to the delegations to reach an agreement on the Statute of the ICC surely had a strong impact on their agenda. As supported by Clapham and Scheffer, when it became clear that the adoption of a model of corporate criminal liability at the international level would have required extensive discussion, the delegations considered it more pragmatic to set aside too controversial a proposal to increase the chances of developing a final draft adoptable by the highest number of States.[61] Had the circumstances been different, it is possible to speculate

58 A/CONF.183/C.1/SR.1, para 55 (emphasis added).

59 A/AC.249/1998/DP.14.

60 Clapham (n 45) 157.

61 *Jesner v. Arab Bank, PLC*, 138 S. Ct. 1386 (2018); Brief of Ambassador David J Scheffer, Northwestern University Pritzker School of Law, as Amicus Curiae in Support of the Petitioners, 26 June 2017, pp. 22-23; Clapham (n 45) 158.

that these countries would have been more open to the idea of including corporate criminal liability in the Statute of the ICC.

5.3 A Step Further: Corporate Criminal Liability as a General Principle of Law

Recently, the comparative law argument has also been used to support the idea that corporate criminal liability has attained (or is in the process of attaining) the status of a general principle of law. As observed in the previous chapter, in its *Decision on Interlocutory Appeal Concerning Personal Jurisdiction in Contempt Proceedings*,[62] the Appeals Panel of the STL observed that 'corporate liability for serious harms is a feature of most of the world's legal systems and therefore qualifies as a general principle of law'.[63] While the Panel recognised the existence of some differences in the model adopted at the domestic level, it still considered that 'corporate criminal liability is on the verge of attaining, at the very least, the status of a general principle of law applicable under international law'.[64]

This approach has been further developed by Jendrik Adam, who argues in favour of the inclusion of corporate criminal liability within the international criminal justice system by observing, *inter alia*, that recent developments at the domestic level are evidence of the existence of a general principle of law on the criminal liability of corporations. In doing so, Adam refers to Article 38(1)(c) of the Statute of the International Court of Justice (ICJ) which listed 'general principles of law recognized by civilized nations' as one of the sources of international law that the Court shall apply to solve disputes falling under its jurisdiction.[65]

Looking at the role of general principles of law in the context of international criminal law, Adam points out how a reference to such a source of law can also be found in Article 21(1)(c) of the ICC Statute, albeit in a slightly different formulation.[66] Embracing the interpretation proposed *inter alia* by Antonio Cassese,[67] Adam views Article 21(1)(c) of the Rome Statute as equivalent to Article 38(1)(c) of the Statute of the ICJ, to evidence the 'enormous

62 *New TV S.A.L. and Ms Khayat*, Decision on Interlocutory Appeal Concerning Personal Jurisdiction in Contempt Proceedings, STL-14-05/PT/AP/ARI26.1, 2 October 2014.

63 Ibid para 67.

64 Ibid 67.

65 Adam (n 2) 85 et ss.

66 Rome Statute of the International Criminal Court (opened for signature 17 July 1998, entered into force 1 July 2002) 2187 UNTS 90, Article 21(1)(c).

67 Antonio Cassese, 'The Contribution of the International Criminal Tribunal for the Former Yugoslavia to the Ascertainment of General Principles of Law Recognized by the Community of Nations' in Wang Tieya and Sienho Yee (eds) *International Law in the Post-Cold War World. Essays in Memory of Li Haopei* (Routledge 2001) 43, 47-49. The interpretation was also embraced by the ILC Special rapporteur, Marcelo Vázquez-Bermúdez, in its First Report on General Principles of Law, A/CN.4/732, 5 April 2019, para 120. *Contra* William

importance of general principles of law in a rudimentary legal system, such as international criminal law'.[68]

To support his conclusion on the status of corporate criminal liability as a general principle of law, Adam examines 47 national legal systems from all around the world, 40 of which recognise the applicability of criminal law to legal entities within their domestic legislation.[69] Despite the existing differences between states' approaches, the author considers that the findings demonstrate that the principles of corporate criminal liability, in its abstract form, have attained general recognition at the domestic level.[70] In particular, according to the author:

> The differences between individual legal systems are irrelevant for a general principle of law. Differences are due to the legal dogmatic of each national legal system and also exist in relation to other general principles of law ... The individual criminal liability of natural persons also differs from one legal system to the other. The basic principle behind the different models, however, is crucial for the question of the existence of a general principle of law: A legal person can be accused of engaging in behaviour disapproved by the state and, as a consequence, it can be subject to sanctions.[71]

The use of the comparative law argument in both Adam's study and in the decision of the STL is particularly interesting as it draws attention to the growing recognition of corporate criminal liability at the domestic level not solely as proof of a progressive change in states' attitudes towards this peculiar form of liability but as evidence of a development of a norm on corporate criminal liability applicable at the international level. As such, the argument deserves to be considered more in detail to evaluate its accuracy and to assess the impact that the recognition of the existence of a general principle of law on corporate criminal liability may have on the international criminal justice system.

5.3.1 General Principles of Law: Practical Implications

General principles of law are recognised as essential to the growth of international law as they lay the foundation for the development of 'new norms

---

A Schabas, *The International Criminal Court: A Commentary on the Rome Statute*, (2nd edn, OUP, 2016) 525.

68 Adam (n 2) 109. Original in German: '... da gerade in einem rudimentaren Rechtsystem, wie es das Volkerstrafrecht immer noch ist, allgemeine Rechtsprinzipien eine enorme Bedeuntung haben'. Translation provided by the author.

69 Ibid 142-152.

70 Ibid 155. Translation provided by the author.

71 Ibid 155. Translation provided by the author.

of conventional and customary international law'.[72] As observed *inter alia* by Jain, general principles of law are better understood as a mechanism for filling existing legal gaps in 'areas where the law is insufficient, obscure, or imperfect'.[73] This interpretation follows the position adopted in the late 1950s by Lauterpacht who considered general principles of law as an essential tool for international judges to ensure the 'completeness' of international law.[74]

Understanding general principles of law as a 'subsidiary' source of international law, however, does not imply their subordinate nature. As observed by Bassiouni, such a conclusion would contrast with the general interpretation of Article 38 of the Statute of the ICJ according to which no hierarchical order exists among the different sources listed in the article.[75] Therefore, the 'subsidiary nature' of general principles of law does not affect the relationship between the sources of international law *ex* Article 38 but solely defines the main functions of general principles of law which are identified by Raimondo in the following: '(i) to fill legal gaps, (ii) to interpret legal rules, and (iii) to confirm decisions based on other legal rules, as to reinforce the legal reasoning'.[76]

General principles of law originating *in foro domestico* are defined as substantial or procedural legal principles which are the expression of a sufficiently large number of domestic legal systems and are determined by legal comparison.[77] It is widely accepted that the process of extraction of principles from domestic jurisdictions should follow a two-step approach.[78] The first step requires a comparative assessment of domestic laws to determine the existence of a legal principle common to the community of nations, whilst the second involves an evaluation of whether such a legal principle can be transposed to the international legal system.[79]

The first stage of the analysis can be further divided into two sub-steps involving (i) the comparative analysis of national jurisdictions to investigate the commonality of a legal principle among a variety of states, and (ii) the identification of a common denominator through a process of abstraction

72 M C Bassiouni, 'A Functional Approach to "General Principles of International Law"' (1990) 11 Michigan Journal of International Law 768, 775-776.

73 Neha Jain, 'Judicial Lawmaking and General Principles of Law in International Criminal Law' (2016) 57 Harvard International Law Journal 111, 113.

74 Hersch Lauterpacht, *The Development of International Law by the International Court* (Stevens & Sons Limited, London, 1958) 166.

75 Bassiouni (n 72) 781-3.

76 Fabián Raimondo, *General Principles of Law in the Decisions of International Criminal Courts and Tribunals* (BRILL, 2008) 48. See also Alain Pellet and Daniel Müller, 'Article 38' in Andreas Zimmermann et al., (eds), *The Statute of the International Court of Justice: A Commentary*. (3rd edn, OUP 2019), 921-931. For a critique of the use of general principles of law as a gap-filling mechanism in international criminal law see Jain (n 73) 113.

77 Bassiouni (n 72) 768. Adam (n 2) 109. A/CN.4/732, para 167.

78 A/CN.4/741, paras 19-22.

79 Ibid para 19.

or 'distillation'.[80] Looking at the first sub-step, Special Rapporteur Marcelo Vázquez-Bermúdez observed that 'this first step ... translates into a requirement to cover as many national legal systems as possible to ensure that a principle has effectively been recognised by the community of nations'.[81] It is generally accepted that a comprehensive evaluation of all legal systems of the world is beyond the capacity of any international judge or scholar.[82] As a result, international courts and tribunals – alongside scholars – have opted to focus their attention on a limited number of domestic systems deemed representative of the community of nations.[83]

In his contribution on the role of general principles in the jurisprudence of international criminal tribunals, Raimondo suggested a new comparative test based on more equitable geographic distribution.[84] According to the author, this approach would allow scholars and judges to identify general principles representative of 'the community of nations rather than of an oligarchic international society' thus enhancing the legitimacy of this source of law.[85] Indeed, while such an approach may pose some practical difficulties linked to information accessibility and language barriers, it undeniably allows for a higher degree of accuracy than a test solely based on the study of Western legal traditions. A similar view was expressed as well by Special Rapporteur Vázquez-Bermúdez who observed that 'the comparative analysis for purpose of determining the existence of a general principle of law must be wide and representative, covering different legal families and various regions of the world'.[86]

Applying this first step to the concept of corporate criminal liability, it is evident that, over the past 20 years, this specific legal construct has gained recognition in a relevant number of jurisdictions around the world. As evidenced in the academic studies reviewed in Section 5.2, and in the analysis conducted by the STL's Appeals Panel and by Adam, countries in Europe, Africa, Asia, and South America have progressively moved away from the principle of *societas delinquere non potest* to accept the possibility of imposing criminal liability to corporate entities. This demonstrates the increasing level of recognition that the concept of corporate criminal liability has recently received worldwide. While exceptions still exist – e.g., the case of Italy (discussed above), Germany, and Russia – they are not in themselves sufficient to invalidate the conclusion that corporate criminal liability has become 'common' to the majority of the countries of the world.

80 Jaye Ellis, 'General Principles and Comparative Law' (2011) 22 European Journal of International Law 949, 954.
81 A/CN.4/741, para 26.
82 Ellis (n 80) 957.
83 Ibid. A/CN.4/741, paras 27 et ss.
84 Raimondo (n 76) 59.
85 Ibid.
86 A/CN.4/741, para 50.

A further step in the identification of a general principle common to the community of nations requires scholars and judges to undergo a process of 'distillation of the municipal principle to its essential elements'.[87] As observed by the judges of the International Criminal Tribunal for the former Yugoslavia in the *Kunarac* case:

> In considering [a broad spectrum of] national legal systems the Trial Chamber does not conduct a survey of the major legal systems of the world in order to identify a specific legal provision which is adopted by a majority of legal systems but to consider, from an examination of national systems generally, whether it is possible to identify certain basic principles ... in those legal systems which embody the principles which must be adopted in the international context.[88]

This process of abstraction aims at reconciling the existing differences among states' responses to a legal phenomenon to identify a 'common denominator'[89] to be then translated at the international level. For leading comparatists Konrad Zweigert and Hein Kötz, in conducting such processes of abstraction, scholars and judges should 'follow the principle of functionality' according to which 'solutions [found] in the different jurisdictions must be cut loose from their conceptual context and stripped of their national doctrinal overtones so that they may be seen purely in the light of their function, as an attempt to satisfy a particular legal need'.[90] According to Kolb, as a result of this process of abstraction, general principles of law derived from domestic legal systems 'have that just degree of abstraction and concreteness, to be able to be dynamic and filled with some specific legal meaning at once'.[91]

In this regard, both Adam and the Appeals Panel have recognised the necessity to look beyond the existing differences among states' approaches to corporate criminal liability to identify the core elements underlining this form of liability. Adam, in particular, observed that divergences 'are due to the legal dogmatic of each national legal system and also exist in relation to other general principles of law'.[92] In his study, the author used the example of individual criminal liability to demonstrate that differences in the domestic approach to

87 Ellis (n 80) 958.

88 *Prosecutor v. Dragoljub Kunarac, Radomir Kunac and Zoran Vuković*, Judgment, Case No. IT-96-23-T & IT-96-23/1-T, 22 February 2001, para 439.

89 *Prosecutor v. Anto Furundžija*, Judgment, Case No. IT-95-17/1-T, 10 December 1998, para 178.

90 Konrad Zweigert and Hein Kötz, *An Introduction to Comparative Law*, (3rd edn, OUP 1998) 34.

91 Robert Kolb, 'Principles as Sources of International Law (With Special Reference to Good Faith)' (2006) 53 Netherlands International Law Review 1 9.

92 Adam (n 2) 155. Translation provided by the author.

a legal construct do not invalidate the possibility to recognise its status as a general principle of law under international law.[93]

This view on the limited relevance of existing divergences among the domestic models of corporate criminal liability is meritorious. Indeed, it is possible to argue that, despite certain dissimilarities, the core elements of corporate criminal liability remain unchanged in every domestic system which embraces such a form of liability. These core elements can be identified in (a) the idea that a legal person – either through the actions of its employees and/or managers or through its own policies – can violate norms dictated by the state under criminal law; (b) that, as a consequence of such violation, criminal liability can be imposed to the legal person itself and, ultimately, (c) it can be subject to criminal sanctions.

These elements represent the 'common denominator' among the different models of corporate criminal liability and, as such, may be viewed as the core content of an emerging general principle of law on the criminal liability of legal persons.

As mentioned above, the process of identification of a general principle of law originating *in foro domestico* is not exclusively based on a comparative assessment of domestic legal systems. An additional step is required to evaluate the possibility of transposing such a principle to the international legal system. The need for this further step is due to the 'uniqueness' of the international legal system which does not allow for the automatic transposition of domestic principles into its legal framework.[94] As observed by Judge Sir Gerald Fitzmaurice in his Separate Opinion in the *Barcelona Traction* case, the 'conditions in the international field are sometimes very different from what they are in the domestic [field], and … rules which this latter's conditions fully justify may be less capable of vindication if strictly applied when transposed onto the international level'.[95]

Thus, the test to ascertain the possibility of transposing a domestic principle into the international system requires the assessment of whether the principle can be deemed 'compatible with the fundamental principles of international law' and that conditions must exist to allow 'the adequate application of the principle in the international legal system'.[96]

In Adam's work and in the decision of the STL Appeals Panel no attention has been paid to the question of whether corporate criminal liability, as an alleged general principle of law, could adequately be transposed into the international criminal justice system. Indeed, it is at this stage of the analysis that the argument loses its practical significance. While there is scope to

93 Ibid. Translation provided by the author.

94 A/CN.4/741, para 73.

95 *Barcelona Traction Case* (Belgium v. Spain) (Judgment, Sep. Op. Fitzmaurice) [1970] ICJ Rep 64, 67, para 5.

96 A/CN.4/741, para 74.

support the idea that corporate criminal liability can fit within the international criminal justice system, the transposition of such a concept necessarily requires certain adjustments that demand a positive intervention from States.

Looking first at the possibility to transpose corporate criminal liability under international criminal law, the analysis of the Nuremberg trials against groups and organisations (see Chapter 2) indicates that specific procedures can be put in place to allow for the prosecution of legal entities without altering the structure of an international trial. Indeed, the rudimentary procedural measures adopted by the International Military Tribunal recognised the groups or organisations' right to be represented by a counsel, to submit evidence in support of their defence, and to present arguments on legal issues of their concern.[97] As observed above, notwithstanding the significant challenges posed by the case against criminal groups and organisations – especially in relation to the submission of evidence – the Tribunal was still able to deal with them in an effective way. Additional support to the idea that trials against corporate defendants can be carried out at the international criminal level is provided by the two contempt cases at the STL where proceedings were successfully conducted to ascertain the liability of the two corporations accused of interfering with the administration of justice. The prosecution of legal entities, therefore, is not incompatible with the structure of international criminal law.

However, it is essential to clarify that this compatibility does not allow for an automatic transposition as the recognition of corporations as subjects of international criminal law call for an amendment of the current legal framework of international criminal law. Currently, the statutes of international criminal courts and tribunals expressively limit their personal jurisdiction to individuals with the exclusion of other non-human beings.[98] Consequently, there is no gap in the provisions that may justify the inclusion of corporate criminal liability on the grounds that such a form of liability may or may not have reached the status of general principle of law.

In the case of the STL, the Appeals Panel was able to justify its expansive interpretation of the Tribunal's jurisdiction by relying on the gender-neutral language used specifically in Rule 60bis of the Tribunal's Rules of Procedure

97 *Trial of the Major War Criminals before the International Military Tribunal*, Vol. I – Official Documents (14 November 1945–1 October 1946), Library of Congress, 19-23.

98 Rome Statute of the International Criminal Court (adopted 17 July 1998, entered into force 1 July 2002), 2187 U.N.T.S. 90, Article 23; UN Security Council, Statute of the International Criminal Tribunal for the Former Yugoslavia (as amended on 17 May 2002), 25 May 1993, Articles 6 and 7; UN Security Council, Statute of the International Criminal Tribunal for Rwanda (as last amended on 13 October 2006), 8 November 1994, Articles 5 and 6; UN Security Council, Statute of the Special Court for Sierra Leone, 16 January 2002, Article 6; Law on the Establishment of the Extraordinary Chambers, with inclusion of amendments as promulgated on 27 October 2004 (NS/RKM/1004/006), Article 29.

and Evidence.[99] However, this gender-neutral approach is not common to all provisions under the founding documents of the Tribunal. Article 3 of the STL Statute, for example, provides for the ***individual*** criminal responsibility of those 'individually responsible for crimes within the jurisdiction of the Special Tribunal'.[100] In this case, the language does not leave any room for an expansive interpretation as that proposed for Rule 60bis. A similar conclusion can be reached in relation to the interpretation of the founding documents of other international criminal jurisdictions. Article 23(1) of the Rome Statute specifically states that '[t]he Court shall have jurisdiction over ***natural*** persons pursuant to this Statute'.[101] Likewise, the Statutes of the International Criminal Tribunals for the former Yugoslavia and Rwanda include specific provisions that limit the Tribunal's personal jurisdiction to natural persons only.[102]

Therefore, the legal framework provided by the Statutes of all international criminal tribunals and courts leaves no room for the operation of a general principle of law on corporate criminal liability. Only an intervention by States by means of an amendment to the statute of one or all these tribunals and courts may create the conditions to transpose corporate criminal liability at the international criminal level. Without such an intervention, the international legal system cannot be bent to incorporate corporate defendants within its scope of applications.

Whether States may be willing to take a step in that direction is still a matter of contention. As discussed in Section 5.2.1. above, while the growing recognition of corporate criminal liability at the domestic level may work in favour of a decision to amend the current framework on international criminal liability, additional factors may play a role in states' decisions to support a project to enhance corporate criminal liability at the international level. In conclusion, therefore, the argument proposed by Adams and by the Appeal Panel of the STL is devoid of any practical value at the present moment.

5.4 Conclusion

This chapter considered the use of domestic developments in the field of corporate criminal liability as an argument to support the transposition of such a

99 *New TV S.A.L. and Al Khayat,* Decision on Interlocutory Appeal Concerning Personal Jurisdiction in Contempt Proceedings, STL-14-05/PT/AP/ARI26.1, Appeals Panel, 2 October 2014, para 37.

100 Statute of the Special Tribunal for Lebanon, 10 June 2007 (UN Doc S/Res/1757(2007), Annex), Article 3.

101 Rome Statute of the International Criminal Court (adopted 17 July 1998, entered into force 1 July 2002), 2187 U.N.T.S. 90, Article 23(1).

102 UN Security Council, Statute of the International Criminal Tribunal for the Former Yugoslavia (as amended on 17 May 2002), 25 May 1993, Article 6; UN Security Council, Statute of the International Criminal Tribunal for Rwanda (as last amended on 13 October 2006), 8 November 1994, Article 5.

concept at the international level. Over the last two decades, more and more countries have adopted national provisions to hold corporations criminally accountable at the domestic level. Countries of civil law tradition have progressively moved away from the principle of *societas delinquere non potest* and recognised the importance of establishing a more robust system of corporate accountability through criminal law. The literature on corporate criminal liability and international criminal law has seen in these developments evidence of a change in the attitude of the State towards the possibility of imposing criminal liability on non-human entities. The chapter considered the significance of such an argument while highlighting potential limitations and inaccuracies in the discussion on domestic approaches to corporate criminal liability.

Indeed, a change in the domestic response to corporate wrongdoing may not be sufficient to demonstrate states' willingness to also embrace such a form of liability at the international level. Nonetheless this growing acceptance of corporate criminal liability at the domestic level may have a positive impact on the debate on the possibility of holding corporations criminally accountable at the international level. Specifically, it may offer a valid counterargument to the complementarity objection raised during the negotiation of the Rome Statute. As more and more States have now adopted models of corporate criminal liability, the inclusion of such forms of liability may pose fewer challenges than in the past.

The chapter also examined whether the argument based on domestic developments can be used to support the idea that corporate criminal liability is on the verge of becoming a general principle of law within the meaning of Article 38(1)(c) of the Statute of the ICJ. On this point, the analysis demonstrated that, even though there may be grounds to support such a conclusion, the recognition of corporate criminal liability as a general principle of law would have no practical implication. Indeed, there is currently no gap in international criminal law that may justify the application of such a principle. Only an amendment to the legal framework will allow for the establishment of an international criminal liability of corporations. It is therefore necessary to proceed with an evaluation of the way in which such an amendment can be drafted to accommodate corporate criminal liability at the international level. The last chapter of this book addresses this question and offers insight into the practical issues arising from the designing of a model of international corporate criminal liability.

References

Primary sources

UN Documents

Human Rights Council, Business and Human Rights: Mapping International Standards of Responsibility and Accountability for Corporate Acts, Report of the Special Representative of the Secretary-General (SRSG) on the Issue of Human Rights and Transnational Corporations and Other Business Enterprises, A/HRC/4/035, 9 February 2007

International Law Commission, Second report on general principles of law / by Marcelo Vázquez-Bermúdez, Special Rapporteur, A/CN.4/741, 9 April 2020

UN Preparatory Committee on the Establishment of an International Criminal Court, *Article 17, Individual criminal responsibility: proposal / submitted by France*, A/AC.249/1998/DP.14, 2 April 1998

United Nations Diplomatic Conference of Plenipotentiaries on the Establishment of an International Criminal Court, Committee of the Whole, Summary Record of the 1st Meeting Held at the Headquarters of the Food and Agriculture Organization of the United Nations on Tuesday, 16 June 1998, A/CONF.183/C.1/SR.1

Statutes of International and Internationalised Criminal Courts and Tribunals

Law on the Establishment of the Extraordinary Chambers, with inclusion of amendments as promulgated on 27 October 2004 (NS/RKM/1004/006)

Rome Statute of the International Criminal Court (adopted 17 July 1998, entered into force 1 July 2002), 2187 U.N.T.S. 90

Statute of the Special Tribunal for Lebanon, 10 June 2007 (UN Doc S/Res/1757(2007), Annex)

UN Security Council, Statute of the International Criminal Tribunal for the Former Yugoslavia (as amended on 17 May 2002), 25 May 1993

UN Security Council, Statute of the International Criminal Tribunal for Rwanda (as last amended on 13 October 2006), 8 November 1994

UN Security Council, Statute of the Special Court for Sierra Leone, 16 January 2002

Domestic laws

Constitution of the Republic of Italy (27 December 1947)

Criminal Code, Canada (1985)

Criminal Code, Denmark (2005)

Criminal Code, Norway (as amended 2021)

Norwegian Criminal Code (2005)

Relazione ministeriale al Decreto Legislativo n. 231/2001

Case Law

International cases

Barcelona Traction Case (Belgium v. Spain) (Judgment, Sep. Op. Fitzmaurice) [1970] ICJ Rep 64

Prosecutor v. Dragoljub Kunarac, Radomir Kunac and Zoran Vuković, Judgment, Case No. IT-96-23-T & IT-96-23/1-T, 22 February 2001

New TV S.A.L. and Al Khayat, Decision on Interlocutory Appeal Concerning Personal Jurisdiction in Contempt Proceedings, STL-14-05/PT/AP/ARI26.1, Appeals Panel, 2 October 2014

New TV S.A.L. and Khayat, Decision on Motion Challenging Jurisdiction and on Request for Leave to Amend Order in Lieu of an Indictment, STL-14-05/PT/CJ, Contempt Judge, 24 July 2014

New TV S.A.L. and Khayat, Decision on Motion Challenging Jurisdiction and on Request for Leave to Amend Order in Lieu of an Indictment, STL-14-05/PT/CJ, Contempt Judge, 24 July 2014

New TV S.A.L. and Ms Khayat, Decision on Interlocutory Appeal concerning personal jurisdiction in contempt proceedings, STL-14-05/PT/AP/ARI26.1, 2 October 2014

Prosecutor v. Anto Furundžija, Judgment, Case No. IT-95-17/1-T, 10 December 1998

Domestic cases

Canadian Dredge & Dock Co. v. The Queen [1985] 1 S.C.R. 662

Italian Supreme Court of Cassation, Criminal Division, Sez. II, Judgement 30 January 2006 n. 3615

Italian Supreme Court of Cassation, Criminal Division, SS.UU. Judgement 18 September 2014, n. 38343

Jesner v. Arab Bank, PLC, 138 S. Ct. 1386 (2018)

Jesner v. Arab Bank, PLC, 138 S. Ct. 1386 (2018), Brief of Ambassador David J. Scheffer, Northwestern University Pritzker School of Law, as Amicus Curiae in Support of the Petitioners, 26 June 2017

Jesner v. Arab Bank, PLC, 138 S. Ct. 1386 (2018), Brief of Ambassador David J. Scheffer, Northwestern University Pritzker School of Law, as Amicus Curiae in Support of the Petitioners, 26 June 2017

Jesner v. Arab Bank, PLC, 138 S. Ct. 1386 (2018), Brief of Ambassador David J. Scheffer, Northwestern University Pritzker School of Law, as Amicus Curiae in Support of the Petitioners, 26 June 2017

New York Central & Hudson River R.R. v. United States, 212 U.S. 481 (1909)

Tesco Supermarkets v Nattrass [1972] A.C. 153

Secondary sources

Books

Adam J, *Die Strafbarkeit juristischer Personem im Volkerstrafrecht* (Nomos 2015)

Lauterpacht H, *The Development of International Law by the International Court* (Stevens & Sons Limited 1958)

Raimondo F, *General Principles of Law in the Decisions of International Criminal Courts and Tribunals* (Brill 2008)

Schabas W A, *The International Criminal Court: A Commentary on the Rome Statute* (2nd edn, OUP 2016)

Wells C, *Corporations and Criminal Responsibility* (2nd edn, OUP 2005) 87

Zweigert K and Kötz H, *An Introduction to Comparative Law* (3rd edn, OUP 1998)

Contributions to edited books

Cassese A, 'The Contribution of the International Criminal Tribunal for the Former Yugoslavia to the Ascertainment of General Principles of Law Recognized by the Community of Nations' in Wang Tieya and Sienho Yee (eds), *International Law in the Post-Cold War World. Essays in Memory of Li Haopei* (Routledge 2001)

Chiomenti C, 'Corporations and the International Criminal Court' in Olivier De Schutter (ed), *Transnational Corporations and Human Rights* (Bloomsbury Publishing 2006)
Clapham A, 'The Question of Jurisdiction under International Criminal Law over Legal Persons: Lessons from the Rome Conference on an International Criminal Court' in Menno Kamminga and Saman Zia-Zarifi (eds), *Liability of Multinational Corporations Under International Law* (Martinus Nijhoff 2000)
de Maglie C, 'Country report: Italy' in James Gobert and Ana-Maria Pascal (eds), *European Developments in Corporate Criminal Liability* (Routledge 2011)
Elhom T, 'Criminal Liability of Legal Persons in Denmark' in Antonio Fiorella and A M Stile (eds), *Corporate Criminal Liability and Compliance Programs, First Colloquium* (Jovene Editore 2012)
Engelhart M, 'Corporate Criminal Liability from a Comparative Perspective' in Dominik Brodowski et al. (eds), *Regulating Corporate Criminal Liability* (Springer 2014)
Foffani L, 'Responsabilitá degli Enti da Reato in Italia' in Antonio Fiorella and A M Stile (eds), *Corporate Criminal Liability and Compliance Programs, First Colloquium* (Jovene Editore 2012)
Pellet A and Müller D, 'Article 38' in Andreas Zimmermann et al. (eds), *The Statute of the International Court of Justice: A Commentary* (3rd edn, OUP 2019)

Journal Articles

Bassiouni M C, 'A Functional Approach to "General Principles of International Law"' (1990) 11 Michigan Journal of International Law 768
Diskant E B, 'Comparative Corporate Criminal Liability: Exploring the Uniquely American Doctrine through Comparative Criminal Procedure' (2008) 118 Yale Law Journal 126
Ellis J, 'General Principles and Comparative Law' (2011) 22 European Journal of International Law 949
Jain N, 'Judicial Lawmaking and General Principles of Law in International Criminal Law' (2016) 57 Harvard International Law Journal 111
Kaeb C, 'The Shifting Sands of Corporate Liability Under International Criminal Law' (2016) 49 George Washington International Law Review 351
Kolb R, 'Principles as Sources of International Law (With Special Reference to Good Faith)' (2006) 53 Netherlands International Law Review 1
Kyriakakis J, 'Australian Prosecution of Corporations for International Crimes. The Potential of the Commonwealth Criminal Code' (2007) 5 Journal of International Criminal Justice 809
Kyriakakis J, 'Corporate Criminal Liability and the ICC Statute: The Comparative Law Challenge' (2009) 56 Netherland International Law Review 333
O'Connor S, 'Corporations, International Crimes and National Courts: A Norwegian View' (2012) 94 International Review of the Red Cross 1007
Pitts C, 'Corporate Criminal Liability' (2014) The Encyclopedia of Criminology and Criminal Justice 3
Stessens G, 'Criminal Liability: A Comparative Perspective' (1994) 43 The International and Comparative Law Quarterly 493
Thompson R, Ramasastry A, and Taylor M, 'Translating Unocal: The Expanding Web of Liability for Business Entities Implicated in International Crimes' (2009) 40 George Washington International Law Review 841

Vázquez-Bermúdez M, in its First Report on General Principles of Law, A/CN.4/732, 5 April 2019

Weigend T, 'Societas delinquere non potest? A German Perspective' (2008) 6 Journal of International Criminal Justice 927

Official Publications

Trial of the Major War Criminals Before the International Military Tribunal, Vol. I – Official Documents (14 November 1945 – 1 October 1946), Library of Congress

Online sources

International Commission of Jurists, Corporate Complicity and Legal Accountability, Vol. II, Report of the International Commission of Jurists Expert Legal Panel on Corporate Complicity in International Crimes (International Commission of Jurists 2008) https://icj2.wpenginepowered.com/wp-content/uploads/2012/06/Vol.2-Corporate-legal-accountability-thematic-report-2008.pdf Accessed 26 March 2023

Oosterveld V, Canada and the Development of International Criminal Law: What Role for the Future? Canada in International Law at 150 and Beyond | Paper No. 16 – March 2018 https://www.cigionline.org/publications/canada-and-development-international-criminal-law-what-role-future/ Accessed 26 March 2023

Ramasastry A and Thompson R C, 'Commerce Crime and Conflict: Legal Remedies for Private Sector Liability for Grave Breaches of International Law' (FAFO 2006) https://www.biicl.org/files/4364_536.pdf Accessed 26 March 2023

Zerk J, 'Corporate Liability for Gross Human Rights Abuses. Towards a Fairer and More Effective System of Domestic Law Remedies' (OHCHR 2012) https://www.ohchr.org/sites/default/files/Documents/Issues/Business/DomesticLawRemedies/StudyDomesticeLawRemedies.pdf Accessed 26 March 2023

6 Translating Corporate Criminal Liability into the International Criminal Justice System

Amending the ICC Statute

6.1 Introduction

The analysis conducted in the previous chapters highlighted how the international criminal liability of corporations has been a recurring feature of the broader debate on the scope of international criminal law since the 1940s. Even though the concept has yet to be formally adopted, the numerous attempts made to incorporate corporate criminal liability within the international criminal justice system demonstrate the significance of the issue under consideration. Far from being a 'settled matter', the criminal liability of corporations for international crimes remains a topic open to debate. Building on the considerations expressed so far in this book, this final chapter offers some food for thought regarding potential issues arising from the transposition of corporate criminal liability into the international criminal justice system. As corporate involvement in international crimes is becoming more and more relevant globally, the time has come for the international criminal justice system to evolve to address such a phenomenon.

The ICC Statute is adopted as the relevant frame for the discussion on the assumption that, as the key institution within the international criminal justice system, the Court could be the most appropriate forum to establish the international criminal liability of corporations. In the following sections, particular attention is paid to the issues arising from the definition of a model of attribution of criminal liability to legal persons, to the applicability of fundamental procedural rights such as the presumption of innocence and the right to be present at trial to the case of corporate defendants, and to the question of corporate sanctioning.

Relying on the analysis conducted in previous chapters on the models of corporate criminal liability proposed in Rome and in the Malabo Protocol, and on the precedents offered by the Nuremberg trials against groups and organisations, and the STL's contempt cases, this final chapter highlights some issues that negotiators of an amendment to the Rome Statute should consider in developing an effective framework to hold corporations accountable under international criminal law.

DOI: 10.4324/9781003390534-7

6.2 The Applicability of the Rome Statute to Corporations: Some Considerations on the Mode of Attribution

From a substantive law perspective, the transposition of corporate criminal liability within the domain of international criminal law requires a determination of a suitable model of attribution to impute criminal liability to the corporate entity. Over the years, two potential models of attribution have been proposed to establish the liability of legal persons for international crimes, one developed in the context of the negotiation of the Rome Statute and the other adopted in the Malabo Protocol.

As seen in Chapter 3, the model proposed during the negotiation of the ICC Statute embraced a narrow approach to corporate criminal liability. The final working paper on the liability of legal persons of 3 July 1998 adopted a strict derivative approach to the criminal liability of corporations by subordinating it to the conviction of the individual(s) who physically perpetrated the offence (draft Article 23(5)(d)).[1] The theoretical underpinning of the final text relied primarily on the identification theory developed under English law according to which the liability of the corporation derives solely from the acts of those individuals who are in a position of control within the entity. Indeed, draft Article 23(5)(b) provided that 'charges may be filed by the Prosecutor against a juridical person' only where the natural person charged with the same crime was 'in a position of control within the juridical person under the national law of the State where the person was registered at the time the crime was committed'.[2] Additionally, draft Article 23(5)(c) required that, in committing the crime, the individual was 'acting on behalf of and with the explicit consent of that juridical person and in the course of its activities'.[3] This further requirement ensured that, at the time the crime was committed, the individual perpetrator(s) had actual authority to act on behalf of the entity and that such an act was authorised by the entity itself.

Conversely, the model adopted in the Malabo Protocol finds its theoretical underpinning in a combination of the 'organisational theory' of attribution of corporate criminal intent, on one side, and the aggregation model of corporate knowledge, on the other. Specifically, Article 46C of the Malabo Protocol provides that '[c]orporate intention to commit an offence may be established by proof that it was the *policy of the corporation* to do the act which constituted the offence' and that such policy 'may be attributed to a corporation where it provides the most reasonable explanation of the conduct' of the entity.[4] As seen in Chapter 4, Article 46C does not derive the corporate intent from the act (and state of mind) of one or more individuals but infers it from

1 A/CONF.183/C.1/WGGP/L.5/Rev.2.

2 Ibid.

3 Ibid.

4 African Union, Protocol on Amendments to the Protocol on the Statute of the African Court of Justice and Human Rights, 27 June 2014, Annex, Article 46C (emphasis added).

those company policies that, evaluated in relation to the committed crime, are deemed to have enabled the perpetration of such crime. Furthermore, the Malabo Protocol relies on the doctrine of collective corporate knowledge (or aggregation model) by attributing knowledge to the corporation through the aggregation of individual states of mind that, singularly considered, may not cover all the aspects of the mental element of the alleged crime (Article 46C, paragraphs 4 and 5).[5]

Both approaches present several advantages and limitations that should be taken into consideration when assessing the feasibility of either of these models to provide an effective tool to address corporate involvement in international crimes.

The 'Rome model' has the practical advantage of having been the result of a lengthy drafting process which involved several delegations from countries all around the world. Consequently, the model already incorporates several compromises reached during the negotiation of the Statute of the ICC. As such, the text may appear an appealing working document to the negotiators of a potential amendment to the Court's Statute. Additionally, the traditional and narrow approach embraced by the 'Rome model' may also be seen as a strength as it set stringent requirements for the attribution of criminal liability to corporations. Indeed, the adoption of the identification theory can ensure that the ICC's jurisdiction over legal persons may be triggered solely in those cases where a crime is committed by the company's management, with the exclusion of all those situations where an offence is committed by corporate personnel sitting at the bottom of the entity's hierarchy. Such a limitation will allow the Court to focus solely on these crimes where corporate culpability is most significant as they require the involvement of the corporation's 'brain'.

Furthermore, the wording of the 'Rome model' presents a high degree of accuracy in relation to the definition of which legal persons can fall under the scope of the Court's jurisdiction, i.e. corporations 'whose concrete, real or dominant objective is seeking private profit or benefit'.[6] The 'Rome model' explicitly excluded from the Court's jurisdiction the State and other public entities 'in the exercise of State authority, a public international body or organisation registered, and acting under the national law of a State as a non-profit organisation'.[7] Once again, the narrow stance embraced in the 'Rome model' may be deemed as more appropriate to set clear boundaries for the establishment of corporate criminal liability for international crimes.

The fact that other international instruments on economic crimes also direct states to adopt forms of corporate liability based on the identification

5 Ibid.
6 A/CONF.183/C.1/WGGP/L.5/Rev.2.
7 Ibid.

theory may add additional value to the Rome model.[8] A significant example is provided by Article 3(1) of the *Second Protocol to the Convention on the Protection of the European Communities' Financial Interests.*[9] According to the provision, Member States of the European Union shall adopt all 'necessary measures' to hold legal persons liable for crimes affecting the financial interests of the Union – i.e., fraud, active corruption, and money laundering – where such crimes have been committed for the benefit of the legal person by any individual in a '*leading position*' within the organisation.[10] In 2017, the Convention and the Protocols thereto were replaced by the *Directive (EU) 2017/1371 of the European Parliament and of the Council of 5 July 2017 on the fight against fraud to the Union's financial interests by means of criminal law* which further emphasises the importance of employing criminal law to address economic crimes of transnational nature.[11] The provision of Article 3(1) of the Second Protocol was transposed, almost verbatim, into Article 6 which once again reinforces the idea that liability should be attributed to the corporation when the crime has been committed by a leading member of the organisation – e.g., a manager or a director.[12]

The impact that provisions such as Article 3 of the Second Protocol and Article 6 of the Directive on the Fight Against Fraud have had on the domestic legislations of EU Member States plays in favour of the adoption of the Rome model as a working document for a future amendment to the Rome Statute. As observed by Mark Pieth and Radha Ivory, countries such as 'Austria, Hungary, Italy, Luxembourg, Poland, and Switzerland were motivated by these [instruments] to enact new corporate liability statutes' which 'closely reflect' the content of the EU rules.[13] Thus, European countries – historically more reluctant to accept the applicability of criminal law to abstract entities – may look with favour on a model of international corporate criminal liability based on a principle of attribution already familiar to their domestic laws.

8 Council Framework Decision 2003/568/JHA of 22 July 2003 on Combating Corruption in the Private Sector [2003] OJ L 192/54, Article 5(1); Council of Europe, *Criminal Law Convention on Corruption*. Council of Europe Treaty Series 173 (adopted on 27 January 1999, entered into force on 1 July 2002), Article 18; Council Act of 19 June 1997 drawing up the Second Protocol of the Convention on the protection of the European Communities' financial interests [1997] OJ C 221/ 0011, Article 3.

9 Council Act of 19 June 1997 drawing up the Second Protocol of the Convention on the protection of the European Communities' financial interests [1997] OJ C 221/ 0011, Article 3.

10 Ibid (emphasis added).

11 European Parliament and of the Council Directive (EU) 2017/1371 of 5 July 2017 on the fight against fraud to the Union's financial interests by means of criminal law EU [2017] OJ L 198/29.

12 Ibid Article 6(1).

13 Mark Pieth and Radha Ivory, 'Emergence and Convergence: Corporate Criminal Liability Principles in Overview' in Mark Pieth and Radha Ivory (eds), *Corporate Criminal Liability, Emergence, Convergence, and Risk* (Springer 2011), 11 and 30 et ss.

However, criticisms of the effectiveness of the identification theory may cast a shadow on the validity of the 'Rome model'. Over the years, several scholars have highlighted significant deficiencies in the identification theory.[14] At a theoretical level, the model developed under English law has been seen as 'constructed upon a highly anthropomorphic and outmoded model of the corporation' and as such is inadequate to address the complex structure of modern corporations.[15] This consideration has relevant practical implications. Indeed, it has been observed how the identification theory is 'ill-fitted to diffuse operations', where day-to-day functions are delegated to middle and low management levels.[16] Indeed, in situations where the responsibility for an operation is distributed among several layers of the company's hierarchy – from the director formally in charge of the operation, to the middle-level managers tasked to oversee the implementation of relevant corporate policies, to the low-level employees who physically perform each task – the identification theory is perceived as inadequate to 'capture the complexity of the modem company'.[17]

As observed by James Gobert, '[p]olicies may be misconceived, supervision may be lax, and execution may be faulty' to the point that '[b]lame cannot be neatly tied to a single individual'.[18] This is particularly true in cases involving large corporations. Large (national or multinational) corporations employ complex organisational structures which include several hierarchical levels. In this context, the identification of individuals who 'impersonate' the entity, as required by the identification theory, becomes almost impossible. The theory, thus, creates a significant imbalance between the position of small businesses, which adopt a simple organisational structure, and large corporations. As stated by Gobert, '[o]ne of the prime ironies' of the identification theory developed under English law 'is that it propounds a theory of corporate criminal liability which works best in cases where it is needed least and works least in cases where it is needed most'.[19]

For years, scholars have advocated a 'fundamental reconceptualisation of the nature of corporate criminality', moving away from the derivative approach to corporate criminal liability in favour of an organisational approach where

14 James Gobert, 'Corporate Criminal Liability: Four Models of Fault' (1994) 14 Legal Studies 393; Stewart Field and Nico Jorg, 'Corporate Liability and Manslaughter: Should We Be Going Dutch?' (1991) Criminal Law Review 156, 159; Neil Cavanagh, 'Corporate Criminal Liability: An Assessment of the Models of Fault' (2011) 75 Journal of Criminal Law 414, 417 et ss.

15 Jennifer G. Hill, 'Corporate Criminal Liability in Australia: An Evolving Corporate Governance Technique?' (2003) Journal of Business Law 1, 12.

16 Ibid 11-12.

17 Gobert (n 14) 395.

18 Ibid.

19 Gobert (n 14) 401 See also Mark W H Hsiao, 'Abandonment of the Doctrine of Attribution for Gross Negligent Test on the Corporate Manslaughter and Corporate Homicide Act 2007' (2009) 30(4) Company Lawyer 110, 111.

the company's liability is based 'on its own blameworthiness'.[20] Thus, the proposal discussed during the negotiation of the Rome Statute may be perceived as outdated and unable to address in an effective way the phenomenon of corporate crime.

In this regard, the Malabo Protocol may offer a more progressive alternative to the Rome model. Indeed, the approach adopted in Article 46C of the Malabo Protocol acknowledges the limitation of locating corporate fault solely in the mind and conduct of a specific individual within the company's structure by shifting the focus from individual behaviour to the company's ethos and policies. In doing so, the model reflects the position expressed by scholars such as Peter A. French, who recognised corporations as moral agents whose intention can be found in their internal decision-making process.[21]

Moving away from the more traditional forms of corporate criminal liability, the Malabo Protocol incorporates a more modern approach to impose criminal liability on legal entities which seems to better address the compartmentalised structure of large corporations and allow the tackling of issues arising from diffuse operations.[22] If adopted within the Statute of the ICC, this model may provide the Court with a more effective tool to deal with corporate involvement in international crimes. It may also present a significant evidentiary advantage as it partially avoids the problem of tracing the elements of criminal liability to a single individual which, in cases involving large corporations and diffuse operations, presents relevant obstacles.

Lastly, as it shifts the blame from the individual to the corporate entity itself, the model adopted in the Malabo Protocol can significantly reduce the risk of corporate scapegoating. By focusing the attention on dysfunctional internal decision-making mechanisms, the Malabo Protocol recognises the limitation of identifying the root of corporate misbehaviour in those individuals in a managerial position which are often exchangeable. As observed by Eli Lederman, 'if the legal body, including its tradition and organizational culture, is the fixed and stable element, while people are the changing, dependent, and replaceable element', a model of corporate criminal liability that focuses on managerial figures 'will seldom lead to real changes in the organisation's behaviour and work processes'.[23]

However, the model adopted in the Malabo Protocol also presents certain limitations. As previously observed (Chapter 4), Article 46C leaves many issues open to interpretation, including the definition of 'legal person' and 'corporate policy', and the scope of application of the aggregation model of

20 James Gobert and Maurice Punch, *Rethinking Corporate Crime* (Butterworths 2003) 81.

21 Peter A French, 'The Corporation as a Moral Person' (1979) 16 American Philosophical Quarterly 207.

22 See, e.g., Eli Lederman, 'Models for Imposing Corporate Criminal Liability: From Adaptation and Imitation Toward Aggregation and the Search for Self-Identity' (2000) 4 Buffalo Criminal Law Review 641.

23 Ibid 688.

corporate knowledge. Lack of precision on these points affects the quality of the provision on corporate criminal liability and is to be avoided.

Therefore, the adoption of Article 46C as a working paper will require negotiators to address the gaps in the provision of the Malabo Protocol in order to properly construct a model of corporate accountability based on the organisational theory and on the aggregation model. Regarding the former, the drafters of an amendment should be guided by the legal scholarship on corporate culpability which has identified a range of factors to assess corporate liability.[24] In particular, de Maglie suggests that:

> The best approach would find corporate culpability in any of the following circumstances: by having a policy that expressly or implicitly compelled, encouraged, authorized, or in any way tolerated the commission of the offense; by having a culture that directed, encouraged or tolerated the commission of the offense; by failing to implement a compliance program or exercise due diligence preventing the commission of the offense; or by failing to take preventive measures in response to the commission of an offense.[25]

Those factors should be incorporated into a provision on corporate criminal liability or, at least, in a specific Rule of the Rules of Procedure and Evidence.

Regarding corporate knowledge, the need for legal certainty is linked to the risk of over-criminalisation of the corporation. As pointed out by Lederman:

> claiming that all the information possessed by the various corporate organs is collected and concentrated in the 'company's brain' entails, according to this approach, an artificial form of over-personification. The result is that criminal liability is imposed on the corporation for a clear offense of criminal intent when, in fact, no one has the knowledge required by the definition of this offense. In practice, this is equivalent to renouncing the demand of criminal intent in the circumstances of the case and turning the offense in question into one of strict or even absolute liability.[26]

Thus, if a decision is taken to rely on the aggregation model as developed in the Malabo Protocol, the drafters of an amendment to the Rome Statute should provide more detailed guidelines on whose knowledge could be aggregated and whether such a process of aggregation should focus solely on those

24 See, e.g., Cristina de Maglie, 'Models of Corporate Criminal Liability in Comparative Law' (2005) 4 Washington University Global Studies Law Review 547; Eric Colvin, 'Corporate Personality and Criminal Liability' (1995) 6 Criminal Law Forum 1.

25 Ibid 560.

26 Lederman (n 23) 674.

individuals in a position of control (often seen as the 'brain' of the entity) or whether it should consider all employees and agents of the company, irrespectively of their status. Lack of clarity on this point may infringe upon the principle of legality and legal certainty. On this point, the jurisprudence of the European Court of Human Rights is indicative of the importance of ensuring precision and clarity in the wording of criminal provisions.[27] While absolute legal certainty is considered unattainable and ultimately detrimental as it may lead to 'excessive rigidity',[28] the Strasbourg Court still observed that:

> a norm cannot be regarded as a 'law' unless it is formulated with sufficient precision to enable the citizen to regulate his conduct: he must be able – if need be, with appropriate advice – to foresee, to a degree that is reasonable in the circumstances, the consequences which a given action may entail.[29]

Again, a decision to integrate an aggregation model within a provision on corporate criminal liability should be carefully considered and supported by specific guidelines for the Court to ensure proper interpretation of the law.

Finally, the progressive model of corporate criminal liability adopted in the Malabo Protocol may face opposition due to its scant recognition at the domestic level. While the organisational theory has been widely supported in legal literature for decades now,[30] it has yet to achieve a prominent position at the legislative and judicial levels. As such, it may still be perceived as a novel model by those jurisdictions that currently rely on a more traditional approach to corporate criminal liability. This can ultimately hinder the chances of an amendment based on this approach to receive enough support to be adopted in accordance with Article 121 of the Rome Statute.[31]

Notwithstanding the potential opposition that a model based on the organisational theory may receive, it is undeniable that it ultimately offers a progressive framework to address the criminal liability of corporate entities. Sharing the view expressed by Neil Cavanagh, a model of corporate criminal

27 Damien Scalia, 'A Few Thoughts on Guaranties Inherent to the Rule of Law as Applied to Sanctions and the Prosecution and Punishment of War Crimes' (2008) 90 International Review of the Red Cross Volume 343.

28 ECTHR, *Sunday Times v. United Kingdom*, Application No. 6538/74, 26 April 1979, para 49.

29 Ibid.

30 See, e.g., Neil Cavanagh, 'Corporate Criminal Liability: An Assessment of the Models of Fault' (2011) 75 Journal of Criminal Law 414; Meaghan Wilkinson, 'Corporate Criminal Liability. The Move Towards Recognising Genuine Corporate Fault' (2003) Canterbury Law Review 142; Richard Mays, 'Towards Corporate Fault as the Basis of Criminal Liability of Corporations' (1998) 2 Mountbatten Journal of Legal Studies 31; Eric Colvin, 'Corporate Personality and Criminal Liability' (1995) 6 Criminal Law Forum 1.

31 Rome Statute of the International Criminal Court (adopted 17 July 1998, entered into force 1 July 2002), 2187 U.N.T.S. 90, Article 121.

liability based on organisational fault (or corporate culture) can offer an effective tool to capture the reality of modern corporate decision-making and represents 'the most suitable model for imposing liability upon a large complex corporation'.[32] Indeed, by shifting the attention from the individual culprit to the policies and ethos of the company itself, the model allows for a proper evaluation of the internal organisation and management of the legal entity and acknowledges the existence of a distinctive corporate culture which may 'transcend individuals and even generations'.[33]

As rightfully observed by authors such as Pamela H. Bucy and Wally Olins, organisations greatly differ from each other as they develop a unique personality and ethos 'which is so ingrained, so much a part of them, that the corporate identity expresses itself in their every action'.[34] By addressing this distinctive dimension of the corporation, a model of corporate criminal liability based on organisational fault allows for the tackling of potential deficiencies in the corporate management which may have encouraged the commission of the crime. In doing so, it can prompt the legal entity to amend its internal policies. As such, future negotiators of an amendment to the Rome Statute should not dismiss the advantages offered by this model of attribution of corporate criminal liability.

Considering the strengths and weaknesses of the two models, a sensible solution may be to combine them to design a more effective system to attribute criminal liability to corporate entities. In this regard, the Australian Criminal Code Act 1995 offers a remarkable example.

Sections 12.2 and 12.3 of the Australian Criminal Code Act define the mode of attribution of *actus reus* and *mens rea* in the context of corporate crimes. Under section 12.2, the physical elements of a crime can be imputed to the corporation when an offence is committed 'by an employee, agent or officer ... acting within the actual or apparent scope of his or her employment, or within his or her actual or apparent authority'.[35] As for the *mens rea*, section 12.3 recognises that the mental element of a crime can be attributed to a corporation when the company has 'expressly, tacitly or impliedly authorised or permitted the commission of the offence'.[36] The provision then clarifies the 'means by which such an authorisation or permission may be established'.[37] These include:

32 Cavanagh (n 31) 432-433.

33 Pamela H Bucy, 'Corporate Ethos: A Standard for Imposing Corporate Criminal Liability' (1991) Minnesota Law Review 1095, 1123.

34 Wally Olins, *The Corporate Personality*, (1st edn, Mayflower Books 1978) 82, and ibid p. 1123.

35 Australian Criminal Code Act 1995, § 12.2.

36 Ibid § 12.3(1).

37 Ibid § 12.3(2).

a) proving that the body corporate's board of directors intentionally, knowingly or recklessly carried out the relevant conduct, or expressly, tacitly or impliedly authorised or permitted the commission of the offence; or
b) proving that a high managerial agent of the body corporate intentionally, knowingly or recklessly engaged in the relevant conduct, or expressly, tacitly or impliedly authorised or permitted the commission of the offence; or
c) proving that a corporate culture existed within the body corporate that directed, encouraged, tolerated or led to non-compliance with the relevant provision; or
d) proving that the body corporate failed to create and maintain a corporate culture that required compliance with the relevant provision.[38]

On one side, the Australian model embraces a vicarious approach in relation to the *actus reus* attributable to a corporation; on the other, it combines elements of the identification theory (letters a) and b)) and of the organisational theory (letters c) and d)) to define a comprehensive approach to the determination of corporate fault.

If adopted as a working document, the Australian model allows for a joined evaluation of the two main models discussed above – the Rome model and the Malabo Protocol – demonstrating the possibility of merging elements from different theories of corporate criminal liability to elaborate a multi-layered approach to tackle corporate wrongdoing. This may be particularly useful when attempting to create a model of accountability able to address corporate involvement in international crimes.

6.3 Corporate Criminal Liability Arising from a Lack of Due Supervision

In developing an effective model of international corporate criminal liability, a question that requires in-depth consideration relates to whether the lack of due supervision or control within a company (also referred to as organisational or structural fault) may be considered as a ground to establish corporate criminal liability.

The question of the criminal relevance of the lack of due supervision or control within a corporation finds its justification in the unique structure of corporate entities. Indeed, corporate bodies operate through complex organisational structures where the power is diffused through the various levels of the company's hierarchy. To ensure the proper functioning of this structure, corporations implement several control systems to monitor the level of performance within the organisation and to identify significant areas of concern and to assess the risk related to corporate operations. A failure of this system of control is seen as an indicator of a dysfunctional corporate organisation.

38 Ibid.

At the European level, the relevance of due supervision and control has been established in *Directive (EU) 2017/1371 of the European Parliament and of the Council of 5 July 2017 on the Fight Against Fraud to the Union's Financial Interests by Means of Criminal Law*.[39] Article 6(2) states that 'Member States shall also take the necessary measures to ensure that legal persons can be held liable where the lack of supervision or control by a person [in a position of control] has made possible the commission' of an offence listed in the Directive.[40] Article 6(2) introduces a form of recklessness or negligence as a standard to impose corporate criminal liability. In the model proposed by the Directive, the liability of the entity can be established only when the commission of a crime has been made possible by the lack of proper supervision or control by a person high up in the company hierarchy, meaning a person authorised to act on behalf of the company or bestowed with the power to exercise control within the entity.[41] This limitation derives from the theoretical approach adopted in the Directive which relies on the identification theory of corporate criminal liability (as observed in Section 6.2).

At the domestic level, Italy provides a prime example of a model of corporate liability based on the lack of due diligence and control within the corporate entity. The Italian Decreto Legislativo n. 231 of 2001 introduced the concept of structural negligence to impute a quasi-criminal liability to corporations for offences committed by their senior managers and directors (Article 6) or by personnel subjected to direction and control of those senior managers or directors (Article 7).[42] In particular, Article 6 provides that, where an offence is committed by individuals in a position of control, the corporation is liable unless it is able to prove that:

a) the senior executive organ adopted and efficiently enacted, prior to commission of the act, organisational and management models which are capable of preventing offences of the type occurring,
b) the task of overseeing such operations, compliance with the models and seeing to updating of same has been delegated to an organisation within the body vested with powers to act on its own initiative and conduct monitoring,
c) the persons committed the offence by fraudulently circumventing the organisational and management models,

39 European Parliament and of the Council Directive (EU) 2017/1371 of 5 July 2017 on the fight against fraud to the Union's financial interests by means of criminal law [2017] OJ L 198/29.

40 Ibid Article 6(2).

41 Ibid Article 6(1).

42 Italian Legislative Decree No. 231 of 8 June 2001 *(Decreto Legislativo* 'Disciplina della responsabilità amministrativa delle persone giuridiche, delle società e delle associazioni anche prive di personalità giuridiche').

d) there has been no omission or insufficient oversight on the part of the organisation referred to in subparagraph b).[43]

Similarly, Article 7 ruled out the liability of the entities for offences perpetrated by its personnel when, 'prior to commission of the offence, [the corporation has] adopted and efficiently implemented an organisational, management and control model which is capable of preventing offences of the type occurring'.[44]

The provisions of the Decreto Legislativo n. 231 of 2001, thus, impose upon the corporation two positive obligations: first, to adopt specific organisational and management models ('*modelli di organizzazione e gestione aziendale*'), and second, to oversee that such models are properly followed within the organisation. Even though the model still partially relies on a derivative approach to impose corporate liability and qualifies the nature of such liability as 'administrative' or quasi-criminal, it has the merit of acknowledging the complex reality of corporate decision-making and of adopting an organisational approach to corporate fault.[45] As such, it has been praised for its ability to provide a 'conceptually sound model' for imposing (criminal) liability upon a corporate entity.[46]

The failure to supervise or implement compliance programmes is an element of establishing corporate criminal liability also in countries such as Switzerland and Australia. Article 102(1) of the Swiss Criminal Code establishes that companies are criminally liable for an offence committed in the 'exercise of commercial activities … and if it is not possible to attribute this act to any specific natural person' when the offence was committed 'due to the *inadequate organisation* of the undertaking'.[47] Additionally, Article 102(2) provides that, for a limited list of specific crimes, a corporation 'is penalised irrespective of the criminal liability of any natural persons, provided the [it] has *failed to take all the reasonable organisational measures* that are required in order to prevent such an offence'.[48] Both provisions put great emphasis on the lack of adequate organisational measures as a condition to impose criminal liability on the legal entity. Therefore, compliance programmes and control and prevention mechanisms are at the core of the model of corporate criminal liability embraced by the Swiss legal system.

Similarly, in the Australian Criminal Code Act, the lack of proper supervision becomes relevant both in the context of negligence offences and in that of offences which require intent, knowledge, or recklessness. When negligence is

43 Ibid Article 6(1).
44 Ibid Article 7(1).
45 Cavanagh (n 31) 437-438.
46 Gobert and Punch (n 20) 108-114.
47 Swiss Criminal Code, Article 102(1).
48 Ibid Article 102(2) (emphasis added).

the fault element of an offence, Section 12.4 of the Australian Criminal Code Act provides that corporate negligence:

> [...] may be evidenced by the fact that the prohibited conduct was substantially attributable to:
>
> (a) inadequate corporate management, control or supervision of the conduct of one or more of its employees, agents or officers; or
> (b) failure to provide adequate systems for conveying relevant information to relevant persons in the body corporate.[49]

In the context of offences that require intent, knowledge, or recklessness, the Australian Criminal Code Act provides that corporate criminal liability can be established where a 'body corporate failed to create and maintain a corporate culture that required compliance with the relevant provision'.[50] This provision can be read to include all those situations where a corporation fails to create and enforce proper control systems or mechanisms to ensure due diligence in corporate operations.

Under international criminal law, the question of whether legal persons should be held criminally accountable for their failure to exercise supervision or control over their employees and agents, or for their failure to create specific mechanisms to ensure due diligence, has never been properly addressed, either during the negotiation of the Rome Statute or in Article 46C of the Malabo Protocol. This, however, should not prevent the negotiators of an amendment to the Rome Statute from considering the issue.

Consideration of this matter, however, requires careful evaluation of how a provision linking corporate criminal liability to a failure to supervise can fit within the international criminal justice system. In particular, attention should be paid to the legal framework related to the mental element of international crimes as a provision on lack of supervision carries with it concerns relating to the possibility of introducing an element of negligence-based liability.

Under international criminal law, it is generally accepted that individual criminal liability requires intent and knowledge. This principle is established in the Rome Statute by Article 30(1) which provides that '[u]nless otherwise provided, a person shall be criminally responsible and liable for punishment for a crime ... only if the material elements are committed with intent and knowledge'.[51] Nonetheless, negligence – and specifically gross negligence (or *culpa gravis*) – has been admitted as a mental element for international

49 Australian Criminal Code Act 1995, § 12.4.

50 Ibid § 12.3.

51 Rome Statute of the International Criminal Court (adopted 17 July 1998, entered into force 1 July 2002); 2187 U.N.T.S. 90, Article 30(1) 17 July 1998, in force on 1 July 2002, United Nations, Treaty Series, vol. 2187, No. 38544.

crimes, in particular in the context of command responsibility.[52] Article 28 of the Rome Statute recognises the possibility of imposing criminal liability to military commanders who 'either knew or ... should have known' that forces under their 'effective command and control' were committing or about to commit crimes under the jurisdiction of the Court and they 'failed to take all necessary and reasonable measures' to prevent or repress the perpetration of such crimes.[53]

Article 28 also covers the criminal liability of civilian commanders who 'failed to take all necessary and reasonable measures' within their power 'to prevent or repress' the commission of a crime by their subordinates or failed 'to submit the matter to a competent authority for investigation and prosecution'.[54] However, in the Rome Statute, the *mens rea* standard applicable to civilian commanders slightly differs from that required in the context of military commanders. Indeed, Article 28(b)(i) establishes that the liability of civilian commanders can arise in situations where they 'either knew, or consciously disregarded information which clearly indicated, that the subordinates were committing or about to commit' a crime.[55]

Thus, in the case of civilian commanders, the Rome Statute requires a more demanding standard than that applicable to military commanders. As observed by Schabas, the standard of 'consciously disregarding information' is better read as a form of recklessness that still falls under the umbrella of the provision of Article 30 – '[u]nless otherwise provided' – even though it does not depart too much from the general requirements concerning the mental elements of international crimes (intent and knowledge).[56]

52 Antonio Cassese (ed), *The Oxford Companion to International Criminal Justice* (OUP 2009), 433 et ss; Alejandro Kiss, 'Command Responsibility under Article 28 of the Rome Statute' in Carsten Stahn (ed), *The Law and Practice of the International Criminal Court* (OUP 2015) 641-647; Elies van Sliedregt, 'Article 28 of the ICC Statute: Mode of Liability and/or Separate Offense?' (2009) 12(3) New Criminal Law Review: An International and Interdisciplinary Journal 420. See also *The Prosecutor v. Jean-Pierre Bemba Gombo*, Decision Pursuant to Article 61(7)(a) and (b) of the Rome Statute on the Charges of the Prosecutor Against Jean-Pierre Bemba Gombo, ICC-01/05-01/08-424; Pre-Trial Chamber II, 15 June 2009, 429; *The Prosecutor v. Germain Katanga and Mathieu Ngudjolo Chui*, Decision on the Confirmation of Charges, ICC-01/04-01/07-717; Pre-Trial Chamber I, 30 September 2008, 251-252; *The Prosecutor v. Thomas Lubanga Dyilo*, Decision on the Confirmation of Charges, ICC-01/04-01/06-803-TEN, 29 January 2007, 358-359. Against the recognition of negligence in the context of command responsibility see *Prosecutor v Bagilishema*, Judgment, Case No. ICTR-95-1A-A, 3 July 2002, para 35, *Prosecutor v Blaškić*, Judgment, Case No. IT-95-14-A, 29 July 2004, para 63.

53 Rome Statute of the International Criminal Court (adopted 17 July 1998, entered into force 1 July 2002), 2187 U.N.T.S. 90, Article 28(a).

54 Ibid Article 28(b).

55 Ibid Article 28(b)(i).

56 William A Schabas, *The International Criminal Court: A Commentary on the Rome Statute*, (2nd edn, OUP 2016), 617.

In drafting a provision on lack of supervision and proper due diligence, therefore, specific attention should be paid to the *mens rea* standard upon which such provision will be based. As discussed above, in the corporate context, the lack of supervision as a ground for corporate criminal liability is often constructed as a form of negligence where the corporation (or its directors and managers) fails to enact effective compliance programmes to oversee and control the conduct of its employees. If transposed at the international criminal level, a provision on negligence may create a parallel between the position of corporations, on one side, and that of military commanders, on the other.

This however may raise some controversy as corporations are *private* entities, established under national laws, and as such are more akin to civilian commanders than to military commanders. While the introduction of a negligence standard as part of a model of corporate criminal liability may be justified by the peculiar characteristics of corporations, consistency within the international criminal justice system should be ensured. Consequently, it may be advisable to apply a recklessness standard in line with that defined under Article 28(b) of the Rome Statute to assimilate the position of corporations to that of civilian commanders.

By linking the company's liability to its 'conscious disregard' of its duty to adopt and implement due diligence programmes and control measures, the provision on corporate criminal liability would still be able to capture the complexity of corporate decision-making and day-to-day operations. In doing so, it would provide the Court with an effective tool to promote corporate accountability for international crimes.

6.4 Reverse Onus, the Presumption of Innocence and Corporate Defendants

The adoption of a provision on organisational fault raises an additional question regarding the relevance of a defence of due diligence and the impact it may have on the burden of proof and the presumption of innocence. Where liability is based on an organisational failure on the side of the corporation, the entity should be able to raise the defence that it operated with due diligence.[57] As due diligence is the antithesis of fault, a corporation that had adopted all reasonable measures to prevent and avoid the commission of a crime should be able to avoid criminal liability.[58] This, however, poses the practical question of who should carry the burden of proving that the corporation had indeed conducted its business activities with due diligence.

In criminal law, it is generally recognised that the burden of proof falls on the prosecutor who must prove the defendant's guilt beyond reasonable doubt. Consequently, where a defence is raised, the defendant will only bear

57 Gobert and Punch (n 20) 100.
58 Ibid.

the evidential burden of proof – i.e., the burden of producing sufficient evidence to raise the issue to the attention of the court – while it will remain for the prosecutor to disprove beyond reasonable doubt that the defence applies to the case. At the domestic level, however, derogations to this rule are considered admissible in relation to affirmative defences which switch the legal burden of proof to the defendant. In the area of corporate criminal liability, the defence of due diligence is often constructed as an affirmative defence.[59] It is therefore essential to consider whether such a defence can be introduced within the legal framework of the Statute of the ICC.

Article 67(1)(i) of the Rome Statute lists, among the fundamental rights of the accused, the right 'not to have imposed on him or her any reversal of the burden of proof or any onus of rebuttal'.[60] The prohibition of any shift of the burden of proof on the defendant is a necessary corollary to the presumption of innocence that represents one of the cardinal principles of criminal law.[61]

The presumption of innocence allows for a redistribution of the risk within criminal trials 'by helping redress the imbalance of power between the government and the accused'.[62] As a fundamental human right, the presumption of innocence is enshrined in the text of core international human rights documents such as the *Universal Declaration of Human Rights*,[63] the *International Covenant on Civil and Political Rights*,[64] the *European Convention on Human Rights*,[65] and the *American Convention on Human Rights*.[66] In the jurisprudence of the European Court of Human Rights, the presumption of innocence has been deemed to require, *inter alia*, that 'when carrying out their duties, the members of a court should not start with the preconceived idea that the accused has committed the offence charged; the burden of proof is on the prosecution, and any doubt should benefit the accused'.[67]

59 Ibid 100-102 and 204-213. See also, Jordi Gimeno Beviá, 'Compliance Programs as Evidence in Criminal Cases' in Dominik Brodowski et al., (eds), *Regulating Corporate Criminal Liability* (Springer 2014) 227.

60 Rome Statute of the International Criminal Court (adopted 17 July 1998, entered into force 1 July 2002), 2187 U.N.T.S. 90, Article 67(1)(i).

61 Michelle Coleman, *The Presumption of Innocence in International Human Rights and Criminal Law* (Routledge 2021) 29.

62 Ibid 29.

63 Universal Declaration of Human Rights (adopted 10 December 1948 UNGA Res 217 A(III) (UDHR), Article 11.

64 International Covenant on Civil and Political Rights (adopted 16 December 1966, entered into force 23 March 1976) 999 U.N.T.S. 171 (ICCPR), Article 14(2).

65 Convention for the Protection of Human Rights and Fundamental Freedoms (European Convention on Human Rights, as amended) (ECHR), Article 6.

66 Organization of American States (OAS), American Convention on Human Rights, 'Pact of San Jose', Costa Rica, 22 November 1969, Article 8(2).

67 ECtHR, *Barbera, Messegue and Jabardo v Spain*, Application no. 10588/83; 10589/83; 10590/83, 13 June 1994, para 77.

Within the Rome Statute, the presumption of innocence is recognised under Article 66 which provides that:

> 1. Everyone shall be presumed innocent until proved guilty before the Court in accordance with the applicable law.
> 2. The onus is on the Prosecutor to prove the guilt of the accused.[68]

The Court noted that Article 66 entails that all 'elements of the crime and the mode of liability alleged against the accused, as well as the facts which are 'indispensable for entering a conviction' must be established beyond reasonable doubt by the Prosecution'.[69] When asked to consider the burden and standard of proof applicable to Article 31 of the Rome Statute (Grounds for Excluding Criminal Responsibility), Trial Chamber IX noted that a reading of Article 66 in conjunction with Article 67(1)(i) of the Statute justifies the conclusion that 'an accused must never be required to affirmatively disprove the elements of a charged crime or a mode of liability, as it is the Prosecution's burden to establish the guilt of the accused'. The defendant should only bear an 'evidential obligation to raise the grounds for excluding criminal responsibility under Articles 31 of the Statute'.[70]

Therefore, the Rome Statute forecloses the possibility of constructing a defence as an affirmative defence in the application of the presumption of innocence and the corollary duty of the prosecutor to prove the guilt of the accused beyond reasonable doubt. While such a strict interpretation of the presumption of innocence is fully justified in the context of individual defendants, it remains open to debate whether the presumption of innocence and its procedural corollary should apply in the same way to corporate defendants.

The position of the European Union on the matter is particularly illustrative. On 9 March 2016, the European Parliament and the Council of the European Union jointly adopted the *Directive on the Strengthening of Certain Aspects of the Presumption of Innocence and of the Right to Be Present at the Trial in Criminal Proceedings* (commonly known as the Presumption of Innocence Directive).[71] Adopted as part of the 'Roadmap' designed by the Council in 2009 to enhance the protection of procedural rights in criminal proceedings

68 Rome Statute of the International Criminal Court (adopted 17 July 1998, entered into force 1 July 2002), 2187 U.N.T.S. 90, Article 66.

69 *The Prosecutor v. Dominic Ongwen*, Decision on Defence Request for the Chamber to Issue an Immediate Ruling Confirming the Burden and Standard of Proof Applicable to Articles 31(1)(a) and (d) of the Rome Statute, ICC-02/04-01/15-1494, Trial Chamber IX, 5 April 2019, para 14.

70 Ibid para 15.

71 European Parliament and of the Council Directive (EU) 2016/343 of 9 March 2016 on the strengthening of certain aspects of the presumption of innocence and of the right to be present at the trial in criminal proceedings [2016] OJ L 65/1.

across the Union,[72] the Presumption of Innocence Directive aims to reinforce the 'right to a fair trial through the adoption of common minimum rules on certain points of the presumption of innocence and the right to be present at trial'.[73] Together with the Translation and Interpretation Directive, the Right to Information Directive, and the Access to a Lawyer Directive, the Presumption of Innocence Directive seeks to increase 'trust between the Member States in the field of criminal justice' and, in doing so, facilitate the judicial cooperation in criminal matters.[74]

The provision of Article 2 of the Presumption of Innocence Directive defines its (narrow) scope of application. Indeed, conversely to the three Directives that preceded its adoption, Article 2 of the Directive explicitly states that the provisions enshrined in the document apply 'to *natural persons* who are suspects or accused persons in criminal proceedings',[75] with the consequent exclusion of legal persons.

In the Explanatory Memorandum presented by European Commission in 2013 on the (then) proposed Directive on the Presumption of Innocence, the Commission specifically suggested to limit the scope of application of the proposed legislative act to natural persons.[76] In particular, the Commission observed that the presumption of innocence 'encompasses different needs and degrees of protection regarding natural persons and legal persons'.[77] As such, a Directive on this specific subject matter should 'only appl[y] to natural persons'.[78]

Even though during the discussion of the text of the proposed Directive a number of amendments were proposed to extend the applicability of its provisions to legal persons,[79] the Commission's proposal to limit the scope of the Directive to individuals prevailed. The justification for this approach is

72 Council Resolution on a Roadmap for strengthening the procedural rights of suspected or accused persons in criminal proceedings [2009] OJ C 295/1.

73 Anita Nagy, 'The Presumption of Innocence and of the Right to Be Present at Trial in Criminal Proceedings in Directive (EU) 2016/343' (2016) 12 European Integration Studies 5, 5.

74 Ibid.

75 European Parliament and of the Council Directive (EU) 2016/343 of 9 March 2016 on the strengthening of certain aspects of the presumption of innocence and of the right to be present at the trial in criminal proceedings [2016] OJ L 65/1, Article 2.

76 European Commission, Proposal for a Directive of the European Parliament and of the Council on the Strengthening of Certain Aspects of the Presumption of Innocence and of the Right to Be Present at Trial in Criminal Proceedings, Explanatory Memorandum, COM(2013) 821, 27 November 2013.

77 Ibid para 26.

78 Ibid.

79 Report on the proposal for a directive of the European Parliament and of the Council on the strengthening of certain aspects of the presumption of innocence and of the right to be present at trial in criminal proceedings (COM(2013)0821–C7-0427/2013–2013/0407(COD)) Committee on Civil Liberties, Justice and Home Affairs Rapporteur: Nathalie Griesbeck.

included in the final text of the Presumption of Innocence Directive, under points 13 to 15 and reads as follows:

> (13) This Directive acknowledges the different needs and levels of protection of certain aspects of the presumption of innocence as regards natural and legal persons. As regards natural persons, such protection is reflected in well-established case-law of the European Court of Human Rights. The Court of Justice has, however, recognised that the rights flowing from the presumption of innocence do not accrue to legal persons in the same way as they do to natural persons.
>
> (14) At the current stage of development of national law and of case-law at national and Union level, it is premature to legislate at Union level on the presumption of innocence with regard to legal persons. [...]
>
> (15) The presumption of innocence with regard to legal persons should be ensured by the existing legislative safeguards and case-law, the evolution of which is to determine whether there is a need for Union action.[80]

Thus, the Directive positions natural persons and legal persons on two different levels on the assumption that the presumption of innocence operates differently in relation to these two categories of defendants.

This idea that the presumption of innocence may be constructed in a narrower way when applied to legal persons has also been supported by Roger A. Shiner.[81] According to the author, 'when it comes to criminal defence protections for corporations, there is something morally unintuitive about treating corporate legal persons exactly the same way as natural persons'.[82] In Shiner's view, the presumption of innocence has its roots in a 'form of deontological morality' which is based on principles such as the respect of human dignity, a person's autonomy and liberty and the fundamental right not to be subject to coercive measures unless strictly required under the law.[83] However, the moral justifications which require a strict applicability of the presumption of innocence to the case of individuals may not apply in the case of corporations. In this regard, Shiner observed that:

80 European Parliament and of the Council Directive (EU) 2016/343 of 9 March 2016 on the strengthening of certain aspects of the presumption of innocence and of the right to be present at the trial in criminal proceedings [2016] OJ L 65/1, points 13-15.

81 Roger A Shiner, 'Corporations and the Presumption of Innocence' (2014) 8(2) Criminal Law and Philosophy 485.

82 Ibid 490.

83 Ibid 487-8.

> [corporations] have no original autonomy rights, rights rooted in the ethical primacy of autonomy that belong to them *natura sua* .... On the face of it, therefore, the standard reasons why it would be unacceptable from the point of view of criminal justice to treat natural persons merely as means to social welfare do not apply to treating corporations merely as means to social welfare. In fact, ... frankly it looks like a good idea to do that.[84]

The peculiar nature of corporations as non-human beings and the consideration that, in the context of criminal trials, corporate entities are in a 'significantly less disadvantageous position' than individuals as they do not face a potential deprivation of their liberty (imprisonment), may justify the introduction of a different standard in the application of the presumption of innocence.[85] While the onus of proving the elements of the crime must remain on the prosecutor, it may be possible to introduce a derogation to the provision of Article 67(1)(a) in the case of a defence of due diligence. Another practical consideration weighs in favour of the admissibility of an affirmative defence of due diligence for corporate defendants. As observed by Gobert and Punch:

> It will generally be easier for a company to show what it has done to avert illegality than for the prosecutor to prove what it has not done. The relevant documents and memoranda will lie within the company's file, and its directors, executive officers and senior managers will be able to testify as to what steps the company has taken to prevent the commission of the crime.[86]

While the relative easiness in proving a defence cannot be considered sufficient to justify a shift in the burden of proof, it may be seen as a relevant factor in the evaluation of whether the inclusion of an affirmative defence of due diligence severely affects the position of a corporate defendant.

At the domestic level, the possibility of shifting the burden of proof on the corporate defendant in a case of organisational fault is accepted in several countries such as Australia, the United Kingdom, Italy, and the United States.[87] In Australia, section 12.3(3) of the Criminal Code provides that, when 'a high managerial agent of the body corporate intentionally, knowingly or recklessly engaged in the relevant conduct, or expressly, tacitly or impliedly authorised or permitted the commission of the offence', the liability of the corporation is excluded 'if the body corporate *proves* that it exercised

84 Ibid 488.
85 Gobert and Punch (n 20) 203.
86 Ibid 100.
87 Ibid 204 et ss., Allens Arthur Robinson, '"Corporate Culture" as a Basis for the Criminal Liability of Corporations' (*Business & Human Rights Resource Centre*, 1 February 2008).

due diligence to prevent the conduct, or the authorisation or permission'.[88] Similarly, the Italian Decreto Legislativo n. 231 of 2001 allows a shift in the burden of proof in relation to corporate due diligence. Under Article 6 of the Decreto, when an offence is committed by a senior officer, corporate liability will be excluded if the corporation is able to demonstrate that it has efficiently implemented 'organisational and management models capable of preventing offences of the type occurring'.[89]

The possibility of reversing the burden of proof in the case of corporate criminal liability was considered reasonable by the OECD examiners in their *Phase 2 Report on Application of the Convention on Combating Bribery of Foreign Public Officials in International Business Transactions* in Switzerland. In evaluating the position of the Swiss authorities on the defence of due diligence, the OECD examiners observed that:

> in the Examiners' opinion it seems inappropriate to place the burden of proof on the prosecutor (or magistrate). The enterprise is much more familiar than the judiciary with the nature of its own internal organisation, its qualities and its defects. The justice system will probably find it difficult to prove defective organisation, especially when an enterprise is part of a complex group, and this could deter prosecutions.[90]

As suggested by Allens Arthur Robinson, 'it is arguable that considerations such as those articulated by the OECD Examiners could justify a reverse burden of proof' in the case of corporate prosecutions without infringing upon the presumption of innocence as stated under Article 6 of the European Convention on Human Rights.[91]

Considering the above, the introduction of a derogation to the provisions of Articles 66 and 67 of the Rome Statute may not affect the overall perception of fairness of international criminal proceedings as the application of a less stringent standard of protection to corporate defendants may be seen as proportionate and reasonable.

Even if a reverse onus is not introduced, the relevance of due diligence programmes and control measures can still be emphasised as part of the sentencing system applicable to corporate defendants. According to Rule 145(1)

88 Australian Criminal Code Act 1995, § 12.3 (emphasis added).

89 Italian Legislative Decree No. 231 of 8 June 2001 (*Decreto Legislativo* 'Disciplina della responsabilità amministrativa delle persone giuridiche, delle società e delle associazioni anche prive di personalità giuridiche'), Article 6.

90 OECD, 'Switzerland: Phase 2 Report on Application of the Convention on Combating Bribery of Foreign Public Officials in International Business Transactions and the 1997 Recommendations on Combating Bribery in International Business Transactions' (*OECD* 2004) https://www.oecd.org/corruption/switzerland-oecdanti-briberyconvention.htm Accessed 26 March 2023, para 112.

91 Robinson (n 86).

(b) of the Rules of Procedure and Evidence, in determining the appropriate sentence applicable postconviction, 'the Court shall … [b]alance all the relevant factors, including any mitigating and aggravating factors and consider the circumstances both of the convicted person and of the crime'.[92] The rule offers limited guidance regarding what may constitute a mitigating circumstance for the determination of the sentence. It solely refers to those 'circumstances falling short of constituting grounds for exclusion of criminal responsibility' (Rule 145(2)(a)(i)) and to the conduct of the convicted person 'after the act, including any efforts by the person to compensate the victims and any cooperation with the Court' (Rule 145(2)(a)(ii)).[93]

In drafting an amendment on corporate criminal liability, an alternative option to the inclusion of a provision on a defence of due diligence could be to list the adoption of appropriate due diligence measures as one of the factors to evaluate for the determination of the appropriate penalty to impose upon the corporation. This approach is not dissimilar to that adopted by the United States in the US Sentencing Commission's Guidelines Manual which provides that the 'two factors that mitigate the ultimate punishment of an organisation are: (i) the existence of an effective compliance and ethics program; and (ii) self-reporting, cooperation, or acceptance of responsibility'.[94] The Manual also offers a detailed overview of the factors to consider in evaluating the effectiveness of corporate compliance and ethics programmes.[95]

An amendment of the Rules of Procedure and Evidence may provide a more practical solution to the issue under consideration as it does not require a re-interpretation of the scope of the presumption of innocence within the Rome Statute to make room for corporate defendants. At the same time, relegating the relevance of due diligence programmes to the postconviction stage may render the provision of corporate criminal liability for organisational failure mostly ineffective as the prosecution will face relevant obstacles in proving that a company did not fulfil its due diligence obligations. Aside from those cases where a corporation neglects to adopt any control measure or compliance programme – the absence of which may be used by the prosecutor as evidence of systemic failure – where such measures and programmes are in place only the company will have access to the relevant documentation concerning their implementation and may not be compelled to submit them to the prosecution. In these cases, the corporate defendant may justify a refusal to provide incriminating evidence by relying on Article 67(1)(g) of the Rome Statute which recognises the defendant's right against self-incrimination and the right

92 International Criminal Court, Rules of Procedure and Evidence, U.N. Doc. PCNICC/2000/1/Add.1 (2000), Rule 145.

93 Ibid.

94 United States Sentencing Commission, Guidelines Manual, §3E1.1 (Nov. 2021), 509.

95 Ibid 517 et ss.

to silence.[96] As a consequence, the prosecution may be unable to discharge its burden of proof in the case of corporate prosecutions, rendering the provision of corporate criminal liability void of any practical value.

6.5 Corporations and Procedural Guarantees

The discussion on whether the presumption of innocence should apply to legal persons in the same way in which it applies to natural persons is part of a broader debate on whether non-human beings such as corporations enjoy fundamental human rights and procedural guarantees to the same extent as human beings.

Several scholars have investigated whether corporations enjoy the fundamental rights and freedoms enshrined in international human rights documents that are often viewed as 'intrinsically human in nature'.[97] Referring in particular to the position of corporations under the European Convention on Human Rights, Amanda Pinto and Martin Evans observed that 'it is beyond doubt that [legal persons] do enjoy Convention rights'.[98]

This interpretation is supported by the wording of Article 1 of the Convention which requires each Contracting Party to 'secure to *everyone* within their jurisdiction the rights and freedoms defined in Section 1 of this Convention'.[99] The use of the term 'everyone' allows a broader interpretation of the scope of the Convention *ratione personae* that can include legal persons alongside individuals. Similar language is used in Article 34 of the Convention, recognising the right to submit an application to the Court to 'any person, nongovernmental organisation or group of individuals claiming to be the victim of a violation by one of the High Contracting Parties of the rights set forth in the Convention or the Protocols thereto'.[100]

As per the Convention's jurisdiction *ratione materiae*, only Article 1 of Protocol 1 on the protection of property mentions legal persons alongside natural persons among the subjects entitled to protection under the Convention.[101]

96 Rome Statute of the International Criminal Court (adopted 17 July 1998, entered into force 1 July 2002), 2187 U.N.T.S. 90, Article 67(1)(g).

97 Amanda Pinto, QC, and Martin Evans, QC, *Corporate Criminal Liability*, (3rd edn, Sweet &Maxwell, 2013) 179.

98 Ibid.

99 Council of Europe, *European Convention for the Protection of Human Rights and Fundamental Freedoms, as amended by Protocols Nos. 11 and 14*, 4 November 1950, ETS 5, Article 1 (emphasis added).

100 Ibid Article 34. For an analysis on the protection of corporations under the European Convention on Human Rights see Marius Emberland, *The Human Rights of Companies: Exploring the Structure of ECHR Protection* (OUP 2006).

101 Council of Europe, *European Convention for the Protection of Human Rights and Fundamental Freedoms, as amended by Protocols Nos. 11 and 14*, 4 November 1950, ETS 5, Protocol 1, Article 1.

This, however, does not imply the inapplicability of other provisions of the Convention to legal persons.

The jurisprudence of the European Court of Human Rights has often recognised the possibility of extending the protection provided by the Convention to corporations even in the absence of a specific reference to 'legal persons' in the text of the provisions. Regarding in particular the rights enshrined in Article 6 of the Convention – Right to a Fair Trial – the jurisprudence of the European Court of Human Rights has recognised its applicability to legal persons, at least in relation to civil cases. Indeed, in *Comingersoll S.A. v. Portugal*, the Court confirmed the possibility for a company to receive just compensation, under Article 41 of the Convention, for non-pecuniary losses sustained due to the violation of the right to trial within reasonable time enshrined under Article 6(1).[102]

Unlike civil proceedings, the applicability of Article 6 to legal persons in the context of criminal trials has yet to be addressed by the Court. However, the development of the Court's jurisprudence on the conventional rights of legal persons may suggest the applicability of the procedural rights under Article 6 to corporate defendants in criminal trials.[103]

However, according to Piet Hein Van Kempen, the fact that corporations 'do have standing under the European Convention' does not automatically mean that 'corporations ... enjoy exactly the same protection under the rights as are applicable to them as individuals'.[104] Examples of this are provided by the provisions of the Convention on the 'prohibitions of torture and of slavery, the right to marry and to equality between spouses'.[105]

Even though corporations may not enjoy the same level of protection as natural persons, procedural guarantees still need to be applied to ensure the fairness of criminal proceedings against corporate defendants. Otherwise, the legitimacy of the criminal justice system may inevitably be affected. As remarkably stated by Antonio Cassese:

> the rights of the accused are central to the concept of justice. For [an international criminal tribunal or court], its moral authority – as opposed to its legal authority – to try accused persons derives in large part from the fact that the accused is guaranteed a fair trial ... and all that that entails.[106]

102 ECtHR, *Comingersoll S.A. v. Portugal*, Judgment of 6 April 2000, para 35.

103 Zlata Đurđević, 'Pravna osoba kao okrivljenik: temeljna prava i predstavljanje' (2005) 12 Croatian Annual of Criminal Law and Practice 739, 744.

104 Piet Hein Van Kampen, 'Human Rights and Criminal Justice Applied to Legal Persons. Protection and Liability of Private and Public Juristic Entities under the ICCPR, ECHR, ACHR and AFCHHPR' (2010) 14(3) Electronic Journal of Comparative Law, 3.

105 Ibid 13.

106 Antonio Cassese, Lecture at the British Institute of Human Rights, 1 May 1997. Quote cited in *Amnesty International, The International Criminal Court: Drafting effective Rules of Procedure and Evidence for the Trial, Appeal and Revision*, 1999.

Similarly, Paul Roberts observed that, while '[a] court that enforces an unjust law might still be regarded as a properly constituted criminal tribunal', a court – whether international or domestic – 'which fails to secure fair trials with due process is a self-parody'.[107]

Therefore, even if a lower standard of protection for corporate defendants may be considered admissible, it is still essential to ensure that certain guarantees apply to legal persons as well. A key example of a procedural right that should apply to corporate defendants at the international level is the right to be present at trial. The application of such right to corporate defendants is discussed in the following section.

6.5.1 Representation and the Right to Be Present at Trial: Article 63 ICC St.

A key issue related to the introduction of corporate defendants within the scope of the international criminal justice system pertains to the participation of legal entities in criminal trials. Specific procedural arrangements need to be made to ensure that corporations can effectively take part in the proceedings.

It is generally accepted that an individual defendant has the right to be present at trial under international criminal law. Indeed, such a right represents '[o]ne of the defining components of the right to a fair trial'.[108] Article 63(1) of the Rome Statute establishes the right of the accused to be present at trial. While trials *in absentia* are not entirely inadmissible under international criminal law, the approach adopted by the negotiators of the Statute of the ICC explicitly ruled out the possibility of conducting a trial in the absence of the accused. The provision of Article 63 is reinforced by Article 67 which provides, under section (d), that the accused has the right:

> To be present at the trial, to conduct the defence in person or through legal assistance of the accused's choosing, to be informed, if the accused does not have legal assistance, of this right and to have legal assistance assigned by the Court in any case where the interests of justice so require, and without payment if the accused lacks sufficient means to pay for it.[109]

Article 63(2) recognises certain limitations to the right to be present at trial in circumstances where the accused 'continues to disrupt the trial', allowing the Court to remove the person from the courtroom and to make provision for them 'to observe the trial and instruct counsel from outside the courtroom,

107 Paul Roberts, 'The Priority of Procedure and the Neglect of Evidence and Proof: Facing Facts in International Criminal Law' (2015) 13 Journal of International Criminal Justice 479, 488.

108 Caleb H Wheeler, *The Right to Be Present at Trial in International Criminal Law* (Brill | Nijhoff 2019), 9.

109 Rome Statute of the International Criminal Court (adopted 17 July 1998, entered into force 1 July 2002), 2187 U.N.T.S. 90, Article 67.

through the use of communications technology, if required'.[110] These measures can be adopted only exceptionally and only for the time they are strictly required.

Corporations, as abstract entities with 'no body to be kicked',[111] cannot physically be present at trial in the same way as individuals, but require the mediation of a natural person who can represent them and act on their behalf. The legal framework concerning the protection of the defendant's right to be present at trial does not explicitly consider the position of corporate defendants. No jurisprudence has yet emerged on the applicability of Article 6 of the European Convention on Human Rights on whether the right to be present at trial applies to corporate entities and, if so, to what extent.

Nonetheless, domestic laws generally recognised the rights of corporate defendants to be present at trial in the form of the person of their legal representative or of any individual to whom the corporation has granted a power of attorney for this purpose by the law, company's statute, or articles of association.[112] The approach is not dissimilar to that adopted in civil and administrative cases where the legal person is represented in court by an individual who has been granted decision-making and management power by the corporation and who has the right to represent and act on behalf of the entity.

Due to the lack of proper recognition of corporate criminal liability, there are limited examples of legal entities' representation in international criminal proceedings. One of these is provided by the trial of criminal organisations and groups at the International Military Tribunal of Nuremberg. As observed in Chapter 2, even though the model of criminal organisation embraced in the London Charter cannot be equated to the modern concept of corporate criminal liability, the Nuremberg trial still offers significant insight into the possibility of prosecuting legal entities.

Regarding the specific issue of representation, the approach adopted by the International Military Tribunal is quite peculiar. The Tribunal's Rules of Procedure did not expressly address the right to be present at trial in relation to the accused legal entities. Rule 2 of the Rules of Procedure, which recognised the right of the accused groups or organisations to be represented by a defence counsel, made no mention of the right of each group or organisation

110 Ibid Article 63(2).

111 Quote from Edward, First Baron Thurlow (1731-1806) as cited in John C Coffee Jr., 'No Soul to Damn: No Body to Kick: An Unscandalized Inquiry into the Problem of Corporate Punishment' 79 (1981) Michigan Law Review 386, 386.

112 See, e.g. French Code of Criminal Procedure, Article 706-43; Italian Legislative Decree No. 231 of 8 June 2001 (*Decreto Legislativo* 'Disciplina della responsabilità amministrativa delle persone giuridiche, delle società e delle associazioni anche prive di personalità giuridiche'), Article 39(1); Spanish Code of Criminal Procedure, Article 786 a; Republic of Slovenia, Liability of Legal Entities for Criminal Offenses Act, 59/1999, 12/2000, Article 31(1) and (4); Swiss Criminal Code, Article. 100quinquies, para 1., Criminal Justice Act 1925, section 33(6).

to be present at trial in the form of a legal representative. This, however, may be justified by the fact that all legal entities that stood trial before the International Military Tribunal were political organisations which had already been disbanded by the time the proceeding began and not business corporations still in operation.

It may be arguable that a form of representation was still allowed under Article 9(1) of the London Charter.[113] The provision linked the possibility for the Tribunal to declare the criminal nature of a group or organization to the trial and conviction of any of the individual members who stood trial before the Tribunal. Indeed, the declaration could have only been made '[a]t the trial of any individual member of any group or organization' and 'in connection with any act of which the individual may be convicted'.[114] Those individuals who stood trial before the International Military Tribunal operated at the highest level of each entity, shaping their policies and managing their operations, and – to a certain extent – may be seen as 'representatives' of the groups and organisations.

However, while this approach may have been justified by the peculiar nature of the trial of criminal organisations and groups at Nuremberg, it is unlikely to be applicable in the context of modern corporate prosecutions as it is generally recognised that the role of the legal representative of the accused corporation is incompatible with that of co-accused. The French Code of Criminal Procedure, for example, provides that, where the legal representative of a legal person is subject to criminal prosecution for the same actions allegedly imputed to the company, or for connected offences, a request may be submitted to the president of the competent tribunal for the purposes of appointing a judicial proxy ('*un mandataire de justice*') to represent the legal person.[115] A similar approach is adopted in the Italian systems where Article 39 of the Decreto Legislativo n. 231/2001 established that the legal person participates in the criminal proceedings by its legal representative, 'unless the representative is charged with the crime upon which the administrative offense depends'.[116]

In this regard, the trial of Al Jadeed/New TV S.A.L. before the STL offers a more pertinent example regarding the presence of a corporate defendant at

113 United Nations, *Agreement by the Government of the United Kingdom of Great Britain and Northern Ireland, the Government of the United States of America, the Provisional Government of the French Republic and the Government of the Union of Soviet Socialist Republics for the prosecution and punishment of the major war criminals of the European Axis ('London Agreement')*, 8 August 1945, 82 U.N.T.S. 279, Annex, Article 9.

114 Ibid.

115 French Code of Criminal Procedure, Articles 706-43.

116 Italian Legislative Decree No. 231 of 8 June 2001 (*Decreto Legislativo* 'Disciplina della responsabilità amministrativa delle persone giuridiche, delle società e delle associazioni anche prive di personalità giuridiche'), Article 39(1). See also Italian Court of Cassation, III Sez. Criminal, *Judgment n. 56427 of 19 December 2017.*

trial. Even in the absence of a specific provision on the matter, the Tribunal recognised the importance of ensuring the presence of a trial of the legal person through the figure of the legal representative who can put a human face on the corporation. Indeed, the legal representative was invited to attend the first hearing against the corporation and was informed that the initial appearance may have been made by video-conference pursuant to Rule 105 of the Tribunal's Rules of Procedure and Evidence.[117]

Consequently, on 13 May 2014, the corporate defendant firstly appeared in front of the Contempt Judge in the person of its general manager, Mr Dimitri Khodr, who was given power of attorney by Al Jadeed/New TV S.A.L.[118] While Ms Karma Khayat, co-defendant in the trial, could have reasonably acted as the legal representative of the corporation, the Tribunal distinguished between her position and that of the corporation, tacitly acknowledging the incompatibility of the role of co-accused with that of legal representative.

This approach is more in line with the modern construct of corporate criminal liability and can be used as an example for future trials against corporate defendants at the international criminal level. It also allows the application of a similar standard to individual defendants and corporate defendants, preventing the arising of questions concerning the existence of a double standard in relation to the protection of the right to be present at trial.

The drafters of an amendment to the Rome Statute to incorporate corporate criminal liability should thus consider either adding a new paragraph under Article 63 or including a new Article 63bis in the Statute to provide specific guidelines regarding the appointment of legal representatives and the identification of situations of incompatibility. In this regard, the provision of *Model Codes of Criminal Procedure for Post-Conflict Criminal Justice* (MCCP) may offer a suitable starting point for a discussion on the matter.[119]

Designed to provide model provisions to national and international actors involved in peacebuilding operations in post-conflict societies, the MCCP was the result of the combined effort of the United States Institute of Peace and the Irish Centre for Human Rights, in cooperation with the United Nations Office of the High Commissioner for Human Rights and the United Nations Office on Drugs and Crime. The Model Code was drafted to serve several practical goals. Among those, it was envisaged as a valuable tool for any post-conflict state that may decide to become party to the Statute of the ICC as it provides guidelines on how to incorporate elements from the Rome Statute, Elements of Crimes and Rules of Procedure and Evidence into domestic

117 *New TV S.A.L. and Khayat,* Summons to Appear (Ms Karma Khayat), STL-14-05/PT/CJ, Contempt Judge, 18 March 2014, p. 2.

118 *New TV S.A.L. and Khayat,* Public Transcript of the first hearing held on 13 May 2014 in the Case against New TV S.A.L. & Karma Khayat, STL-14-05/PT/CJ), Contempt Judge, 13 May 2014.

119 Vivienne O'Connor et al., (eds), *Model Codes for Post-Conflict Criminal Justice. Vol. 2* (Washington: United States Institute of Peace Press 2008).

legislation.[120] In addition to that, it also offers suggestions on matters not yet addressed under international criminal law, including the criminal liability of legal persons.[121] As such, the document could form the basis of a working paper on the procedural measures required to prosecute corporate defendants.

Regarding the issue under consideration, Article 81 of the MCCP – Representative for a Legal Person in Criminal Proceedings – provides that:

1. Where a legal person is being prosecuted for a criminal offence or offences, one representative of the legal person must be present at all proceedings.
2. A representative of a legal person is a person who is authorised to represent the legal person under the applicable law.
3. A person may not act as a representative of the legal person where:
    a. The person is a witness at the trial of the legal person; or
    b. The person has been prosecuted for the same criminal offence, unless he or she is the only representative of the legal person.

    4.Where a person is not eligible to be a representative of the legal person under paragraph 3, the competent trial court must request the competent body of the legal person to appoint another representative within a specific period and notify the court of the appointment in writing. If this is not done within the specified period, the court may appoint a representative of the legal person.
5. The registry of the competent trial court must notify the [insert name of body responsible for registering legal persons in the state] that the legal person is subject to legal proceedings and cannot be dissolved during proceeding against the legal person.[122]

The use of this provision as a working paper will give the drafters the opportunity to define the way in which the right to be present at trial can be applied to corporate defendants. It will also provide for a solution to those situations where the position of the legal representative as co-defendant in the trial against the corporation may lead to a conflict of interest.

Another point that deserves specific attention relates to the question of how the Court should deal with the decision of the legal person not to send a legal representative to attend the trial. If such a decision is communicated to the Court alongside the request to be represented solely by counsel, the provision of Rule 134-*ter* of the Court's Rules of Procedure and Evidence should apply provided that the conditions of paragraph 2 of such provision are met.

120 Vivienne O'Connor et al., (eds), *Model Codes for Post-Conflict Criminal Justice. Vol. 1* (Washington: United States Institute of Peace Press 2007), 14 and 17-18.

121 Ibid 72 et ss; Vivienne O'Connor et al., (eds), *Model Codes for Post-Conflict Criminal Justice. Vol. 2* (Washington: United States Institute of Peace Press 2008), 138 et ss.

122 Vivienne O'Connor et al., (eds), *Model Codes for Post-Conflict Criminal Justice. Vol. 2* (Washington: United States Institute of Peace Press 2008), 139-140.

Specifically, a request to be excused from attending the trial can be granted only if the Court is satisfied that:

(a) exceptional circumstances exist to justify such an absence;
(b) alternative measures, including changes to the trial schedule or a short adjournment of the trial, would be inadequate;
(c) the accused has explicitly waived his or her right to be present at the trial; and
(d) the rights of the accused will be fully ensured in his or her absence.[123]

However, if such a declaration is not submitted and the corporation refuses to cooperate by not sending a legal representative, the trial may not proceed as it would otherwise breach the prohibition of conducting a trial *in absentia*.

In addressing this issue in the context of the Malabo Protocol, Kyriakakis suggested the possibility of introducing a derogation to the right to be tried in person in the case of a corporation. According to the author:

> Proceeding against an accused in absentia, even for serious crimes, is allowed in some jurisdictions in such circumstances, although the challenge of enforcing the verdict against the person and their assets beyond the territory of state parties remains. To further protect defence rights, protections may be built into any such trial in absentia scheme, for example allowing for retrial should a corporate representative be subsequently appointed.[124]

While this option may be explored as part of the negotiation of an amendment to the Rome Statute, it may still raise relevant concerns in relation to the fairness of *in absentia* trials. Alternatively, it may be possible to bestow the Court with the power of appointing an *ad hoc* legal representative to represent the corporation during the trial. This solution has been adopted in the French system where Article 706–43, paragraph 5, establishes that:

> In the absence of any person authorised to represent the legal person under the conditions provided for in this article, the president of the tribunal appoints, at the request of the public prosecutor, the investigating judge or the civil party, a legal representative to represent it.[125]

123 International Criminal Court, Rules of Procedure and Evidence, U.N. Doc. PCNICC/2000/1/Add.1 (2000), Rule 134-*ter*.

124 Joanna Kyriakakis, 'Article 46C: Corporate Criminal Liability at the African Criminal Court' in Charles C Jalloh et al., (eds), *African Court of Justice and Human and People's Rights in Context* (Cambridge University Press 2019), 834.

125 French Code of Criminal Procedure, Article 706-43. Translation provided by the author.

The adoption of a similar solution within the Rome Statute may not be enough to mitigate all the concerns relating to protection of the defendant's right to a fair trial. The drafters of an amendment, therefore, should still consider the possibility of allowing for retrial should the corporation decide, at a later stage, to cooperate with the Court by appointing a representative for the trial.

The issues addressed in this section give a sense of the peculiar procedural challenges posed by the inclusion of corporate defendants within the international criminal justice system. While these challenges may slow the process for the adoption of a provision on corporate criminal liability, they are not without solution. As demonstrated in this section, there are several alternatives that may be explored to ensure that the inclusion of corporations as a new category of defendant will not adversely impact on the legitimacy of the whole international justice system.

6.6 A Sentencing System for Corporate Defendants

A final point that requires attention in drafting a model of corporate criminal liability at the international level concerns the determination of a sentencing system applicable to corporate defendants. This section considers, in particular, three issues relating to corporate sentencing: (a) pecuniary sanctions, (b) non-pecuniary sanctions, and (c) the corporate death penalty.

The legal framework on sentencing at the ICC is provided by Articles 76 to 78 of the Rome Statute, complemented by the provisions of Rules 145 to 148 of the Rules of Procedure and Evidence.[126] Article 76 of the Statute states that, in case of a conviction, the Court 'shall consider the appropriate sentence to be imposed' taking into account all 'evidence presented, and submissions made during the trial that are relevant to the sentence'.[127] Additional evidence can also be heard by the Court in a separate hearing whenever relevant to determine the most appropriate sentence.[128] Article 77 then defines the range of penalties available to the Court by establishing that:

1. [...] the Court may impose one of the following penalties on a person convicted of a crime referred to in article 5 of this Statute:
   (a) Imprisonment for a specified number of years, which may not exceed a maximum of 30 years; or

126 For an analysis of sentencing in international criminal law see Alice Riccardi, *Sentencing at the International Criminal Court. From Nuremberg to the Hague* (Giappichelli Editore and Eleven International Publishing 2016). See also Michelle Coleman, 'Culture and Sentencing at the ICC' in Julie Fraser and Brianne McGonigle Leyh (eds) *Intersections of Law and Culture at the International Criminal Court* (Edward Elgar 2020) 268-287.

127 Rome Statute of the International Criminal Court (adopted 17 July 1998, entered into force 1 July 2002), 2187 U.N.T.S. 90, Article 76(1).

128 Ibid Article 76(2).

(b) A term of life imprisonment when justified by the extreme gravity of the crime and the individual circumstances of the convicted person.

2. In addition to imprisonment, the Court may order:
   (a) A fine under the criteria provided for in the Rules of Procedure and Evidence;
   (b) A forfeiture of proceeds, property and assets derived directly or indirectly from that crime, without prejudice to the rights of bona fide third parties.[129]

As per Article 78, in determining the most appropriate sentence to be imposed in each case, the Court is required to take into consideration 'such factors as the gravity of the crime and the individual circumstances of the convicted person'.[130] Rule 145 of the Rules of Procedure and Evidence directs the Court to consider additional factors such as the extent of the harm caused to the victims, the nature of the crime and the means employed to execute it, the degree of participation and of intent, the circumstances, time and location of the crime, and the personal characteristics of the convicted person.[131] The rule also provides that 'the totality of any sentence of imprisonment and fine' imposed by the Court 'must reflect the culpability of the convicted person'.[132]

When considering the range of penalties applicable to corporate defendants, a central role is played by pecuniary sanctions. As artificial actors – devoid of a physical body – corporations cannot be subjected to imprisonment. Consequently, fines are generally deemed the primary form of punishment applicable in the context of corporate proceedings. An overview of the proposal submitted in Rome and of the approach adopted in the Malabo Protocol indicates a convergence on the feasibility of imposing monetary sanctions on corporations under international criminal law. During the negotiation of the Rome Statute, the French delegation submitted a draft provision (draft Article 69) on the penalties applicable to legal entities which included fines, forfeiture of instrumentalities of crime and proceeds, property and assets obtained by criminal conduct, and appropriate forms of reparation.[133] As discussed in Chapter 3, the decision to limit the discussion on penalties applicable to legal persons to monetary sanctions was justified by the attempt to 'build a bridge between the countries that accept criminal responsibility for organisations or groups and those that did not'.[134] A similar approach was adopted also in the Malabo Protocol where pecuniary fines are the only penalties applicable to

129 Ibid Article 77.
130 Ibid Article 78.
131 International Criminal Court, Rules of Procedure and Evidence, U.N. Doc. PCNICC/2000/1/Add.1 (2000), Rule 145(1)(c).
132 Ibid Rule 145(1)(a).
133 A/AC.249/1998/DP.14, pp. 2-3.
134 A/CONF.183/C.1/SR.1, para 33.

corporations alongside the 'forfeiture of any property, proceeds or any asset acquired unlawfully or by criminal conduct'.[135]

As for pecuniary sanctions, the introduction of a regime of corporate criminal liability within the Statute of the ICC does not raise significant issues. Indeed, Article 77(2) can be deemed applicable to the case of corporate defendants without any specific adjustments. Likewise, the criteria listed under Rule 146 for the determination of a fine under Article 77 remains applicable, especially those referring to the financial capacity of the convicted person and to the motive of 'personal' financial gain.[136]

It remains questionable, however, whether the sanctioning system applicable to corporate defendants should provide for non-monetary penalties, such as injunction measures and reputation-oriented sanctions.

A proposal to include injunction measures in the list of penalties potentially applicable to legal persons was presented in the early stage of the drafting of the ICC Statute. Submitted in 1996 as part of a draft Statute proposed by the French delegation, draft Article 95 listed under letters (c) and (d) the following penalties applicable to legal persons:

> (c) Prohibition, in perpetuity or for a period freely determined by the Court, of the direct or indirect exercise of one or more professional or social activities;
> (d) Closure, in perpetuity or for a period freely determined by the Court, of the establishments used in the commission of the crimes.[137]

The decision to exclude such penalties from the final proposal on the criminal liability of legal persons was motivated by the necessity to present a working document that could have won the approval of the highest number of delegations.[138] Concerns related to differences in states' approaches to corporate punishment, while still relevant, may not be as pressing as they were in 1998. As discussed at length in Chapter 5, national developments that occurred over the past 20 years demonstrate that more and more legal jurisdictions recognise the applicability of criminal sanctions on corporations – including prohibitory (or negative) injunctions.[139] Thus, objections to the inclusion of injunctions measures within the Rome Statute based on the assumption that they would

135 African Union, Protocol on Amendments to the Protocol on the Statute of the African Court of Justice and Human Rights, 27 June 2014, Annex, Article 43A.

136 International Criminal Court, Rules of Procedure and Evidence, U.N. Doc. PCNICC/2000/1/Add.1 (2000), Rule 146(1).

137 A/AC.249/L.3, p. 64.

138 A/CONF.183/C.1/SR.1, para 33.

139 See, e.g., French Criminal Code, Article 131-39; Spanish Criminal Code, Article 33(7); United States Sentencing Commission, Federal Sentencing Guidelines, Chapter 8; Italian Legislative Decree no. 231 of 8 June 2001, Article 9 et ss. See also Clifford Chance, Corporate Criminal Liability (*Clifford Chance*, 26 April 2016) < https://www.cliffordchance

hinder states' cooperation in the enforcement of a judgment against corporate defendants may have now lost their cogency. Consequently, nothing is preventing the negotiators of an amendment on corporate criminal liability to take a more progressive view on the subject matter.

As for reputation-oriented sanctions, such as the publication of the sentence, there is merit in suggesting the inclusion of such penalties within the Rome Statute. Indeed, like individuals, corporations can suffer the stigma and damage to their reputation that derive from a criminal conviction. As observed by Gobert and Punch, 'reputation may be an even *more* valuable commodity to a company than it is to an individual'.[140] As such, the possibility for the ICC to impose reputation-oriented sanctions can enhance the deterrent and retributive effect of an international judgment against a corporation.

The suggestion to adopt a more inclusive package of penalties for corporations is in line with the position adopted by the Council of Europe in its Recommendation No. R (88) 18 on the *Liability of Enterprises for Offences* of 20 October 1988.[141] In the Recommendation, the Council suggested that, in providing an appropriate sanctioning system for corporate entities, States should consider the following range of penalties, which may be imposed alone or in combination:

- warning, reprimand, recognisance;
- a decision declaratory of responsibility, but no sanction;
- fine or other pecuniary sanction;
- confiscation of property which was used in the commission of the offence or represents the gains derived from the illegal activity;
- prohibition of certain activities, in particular exclusion from doing business with public authorities;
- exclusion from fiscal advantages and subsidies;
- prohibition upon advertising goods or services;
- annulment of licences;
- removal of managers;
- appointment of a provisional caretaker management by the judicial authority;
- closure of the enterprise;
- winding-up of the enterprise;
- compensation and/or restitution to the victim;
- restoration of the former state;
- publication of the decision imposing a sanction or measure.[142]

.com/content/dam/cliffordchance/briefings/2016/04/corporate-criminal-liability.pdf> Accessed on 1 November 2021.

140 Gobert and Punch (n 20) 203 (emphasis added).

141 Council of Europe, Committee of Ministers, Recommendation No. R (88) 18 on the Liability of Enterprises for Offences, 20 October 1988, Appendix, para. 6 et ss.

142 Ibid para 7.

The list includes several non-pecuniary measures that qualify as injunctions or reputation-oriented sanctions. According to the Council of Europe, the adoption of a wide range of penalties would allow States to pursue 'objectives other than punishment such as the prevention of further offences and the reparation of damage suffered by victims of the offence'.[143] As prevention (or deterrence) and victims' reparations are fundamental goals at the international criminal justice level, there are grounds to support the idea that the ICC should be able to rely on a more inclusive package of sanctions for corporate defendants. Considering that one of the main criticisms of the Malabo Protocol specifically refers to its narrow approach to corporate sanctioning,[144] the adoption of a more comprehensive system of corporate punishment may be seen as a step forward on the path of corporate accountability.

A final point concerns the issue of judicial dissolution of the corporation or corporate death penalty. In 2001, Diane Marie Amann raised the following point on the question of corporate punishment for international crimes:

> What, short of closing the business, would give a corporation its just deserts? Today, human defendants convicted of war crimes, crimes against humanity and genocide routinely receive sentences ranging from twenty years to life in prison. Can a money-based penalty, such as a fine or disgorgement of assets, approximate prolonged incarceration?[145]

A corporate death penalty is not a foreign concept at the international level. The *I.G. Farben* case provides a significant precedent in relation to the possibility of dissolving a business entity as a punishment for its involvement in gross violations of international law.

As discussed in previous chapters, the German company was the largest industrial supporter of the Hitlerian regime, and it actively cooperated with the regime by supplying Zyklon B gas – used for the systematic extermination of millions in the Nazi concentration camps – and by profiting from the slave labour of inmates in its rubber factory built on the edge of Auschwitz III–Monowitz. The scale of I.G. Farben's involvement with the German regime led the Allied Powers to enact Control Council Law No. 9 which provided for the seizure of property owned by the company and its dissolution.[146]

143 Ibid para 6.

144 Taygeti Michalakea, 'Article 46C of the Malabo Protocol: A Contextually Tailored Approach to Corporate Criminal Liability and Its Contours' (2018) 7 International Human Rights Law Review 225, 244.

145 Diane Marie Amann, 'Capital Punishment: Corporate Criminal Liability for Gross Violations of Human Rights' (2001) 24 Hastings International and Comparative Law Review 327, 335.

146 Control Council Law No. 9, 'Providing for the Seizure of Property Owned by I.G. Farbenindustrie and the Control Thereof' (30 November 1945), reprinted in Enactments and Approved Papers of the Control Council and Coordinating Committee, 225.

The dissolution of I.G. Farben was not the consequence of a judgment of an international criminal court or tribunal, but the result of a decision adopted by an international body – the Allied Control Council – which represented the four Allied Powers and was tasked to govern occupied Germany in the aftermath of the Second World War. The special treatment reserved for I.G. Farben was mostly a political decision which the Allied Powers were able to carry out due to the peculiar circumstances of the case. Indeed, they did not require any collaboration from the state to enforce the extra-judicial sanction against I.G. Farben as Germany was under the control of the Allied Control Council. Thus, the *I.G. Farben* case falls short of offering a relevant precedent to justify the possibility of imposing the *judicial* dissolution of a corporation through criminal proceedings.

At a conceptual level, there is no compelling moral reason to exclude the corporate death penalty from the range of sanctions for corporate defendants. The judicial dissolution of a corporate entity does not carry with it the same moral quandaries related to the death penalty for individuals which is excluded under the Rome Statute. As observed by Van Kempen, while corporations do enjoy certain fundamental human rights, their position cannot be equated to that of natural persons.[147] This is particularly true in relation to the right to life.[148] While the dissolution of a corporation may be compared to a death penalty for the legal person, in no way it is arguable that such a measure is an infringement of a company's rights.[149]

The corporate death penalty, therefore, is perceived as morally neutral and is recognised – at the domestic level – as one of the penalties applicable to corporations as the result of a judicial determination of corporate criminal liability.[150] Judicial dissolution is also listed in the Council of Europe's Recommendation No. R (88) 18 which includes the closure or the winding-up of the enterprise among the potential penalties applicable to corporations.[151]

Nonetheless, the inclusion of such a measure within the Rome Statute may carry with it a range of practical issues related to state cooperation and enforcement of judicial decisions. Indeed, it is undeniable that the imposition of a corporate death penalty can adversely affect many individuals, *in primis* the company's employees, to the point that it can generate opposition from not only the corporate world but also from labour unions and by communities.[152]

147 Van Kampen (n 104) 3.

148 Council of Europe, *European Convention for the Protection of Human Rights and Fundamental Freedoms, as amended by Protocols Nos. 11 and 14*, 4 November 1950, ETS 5, Article 2.

149 Van Kampen (n 104) 13.

150 See, e.g., French Criminal Code, Article 131-39; Spanish Criminal Code, Article 33(7).

151 Council of Europe, Committee of Ministers, Recommendation No. R (88) 18 on the Liability of Enterprises for Offences, 20 October 1988, Appendix, para 7.

152 John F Hulpke, 'If All Else Fails, A Corporate Death Penalty?' (2017) Journal of Management Inquiry 1, 3.

More generally, the dissolution of a corporation can send unwanted shockwaves through a whole country's economy (if not a whole geographical area). While the dissolution of a corporation may be deemed as the only appropriate response in case of involvement in mass atrocities, such sanctions may have devastating consequences on the financial situation of a country that may ultimately hinder its economic development with vast repercussions on the whole society. Therefore, states may be less open to supporting a model of corporate criminal liability which allows for the judicial dissolution of a company, or they may end up refusing to cooperate with the Court in the enforcement of a judgment in all cases in which the corporate death penalty is imposed.

A final consideration that may weigh against the corporate death penalty concerns its incompatibility with the aim of rehabilitation. While rehabilitation plays a peripheral role in the sentencing system of the ICC,[153] it is still relevant to observe that the corporate death penalty entirely negates the possibility to rehabilitate the corporate offender and to promote compliance in future business operations. In the context of corporate involvement in international crimes, the goal of rehabilitation should be kept in great consideration due to the impact that companies can have on the economic development of a country or region. Adopting a sanctioning system that reprimands deviant behaviours without permanently banning the corporate offender from society can provide a fundamental tool to enhance corporate compliance with human rights standards as it will provide the company with the opportunity to change its internal mechanisms to continue to operate within a community more sustainably. Furthermore, even though the corporate death penalty appears to rest on less ambiguous moral grounds, its exclusion from the Rome Statute may also be seen as consistent with the decision to reject capital punishment for individual defendants.[154]

Overall, the creation of an effective sanctioning system applicable to corporate defendants is instrumental to the development of an effective model of corporate criminal liability. The attribution of international criminal liability can only promote greater accountability if followed by the imposition of appropriate and proportionate sanctions to reprimand the corporations, promote organisational changes, and deter future violations of international criminal law. Therefore, the drafters of an amendment to the Rome Statute need to approach the question of sentencing with an open mind to develop an inclusive package of penalties for corporate entities.

153 *The Prosecutor v Jean-Pierre Bemba Gombo*, Decision on Sentence pursuant to Article 76 of the Statute, ICC-01/05-01/08, Trial Chamber III, (21 June 2016) para 11. See also Coleman, 'Culture and Sentencing at the ICC' (n 126); Edith Riegler, 'Rehabilitating Enemies of Mankind: An Exploration of the Concept of Rehabilitation as a Sentencing Aim at the ICTY and the ICC' (2020) 20(4) International Criminal Law Review 701. In support of a more central role of rehabilitation at the ICC see Riccardi (n 126).

154 William A Schabas, 'Life, Death and the Crime of Crimes: Supreme Penalties and the ICC Statute' (2000) 2(3) Punishment and Society 263.

6.7 Conclusion

This chapter outlined the main substantive and procedural issues arising from drafting an amendment to the Rome Statute to include corporate entities within the jurisdiction of the ICC. The discussion began with a consideration of the mode of attribution of international criminal liability to corporations. The investigation compared the two modes of attribution proposed in Rome and in the Malabo Protocol to highlight the strengths and weaknesses of both approaches. The chapter suggested that a combination of both models may represent the most sensible solution to design an effective system to attribute international criminal liability to corporations. In this sense, it has been argued that the Australian approach to corporate criminal liability may offer a remarkable starting point for future discussion on the mode of attribution of international criminal liability to corporate entities.

The chapter further investigated the question of whether a model of international corporate criminal liability should consider lack of supervision as a ground to establish liability. Lack of supervision or control plays a fundamental role in establishing corporate liability at the domestic level and is recognised as a key indicator of a dysfunctional corporate organisation. The analysis showed the relevance of this issue and highlighted potential concerns relating to the introduction of an element of negligence-based liability at the international level and its impact on the burden of proof and presumption of innocence.

Attention was also paid to the procedural guarantees applicable to corporate defendants in an international trial. The chapter engaged with the question of whether corporations as non-human beings enjoy fundamental human rights and fair trial guarantees to the same extent as natural persons. In particular, the analysis focused on the company's right to be present at trial. The discussion considered potential options to ensure representation in court and explore challenges linked to a company's decision not to send a legal representative to attend the trial. The investigation has been conducted considering the principle of fair trial and the risks linked to proceeding against an accused in absentia.

Lastly, the chapter addressed the question of sentencing for corporate defendants. The analysis took into account the sentencing systems proposed in Rome and in the Malabo Protocol to evaluate options for a future amendment to the Rome Statute. Pecuniary and non-pecuniary sanctions were investigated to determine an appropriate range of penalties applicable to corporations. Judicial dissolution was also considered in light of the precedent set by the *I.G. Farben* case. On this final point, the chapter acknowledged the potential shockwaves that the dissolution of a corporation can send through a country's economy and the challenges that it may pose in relation to state enforcement of such a penalty.

Overall, the analysis conducted in this chapter sheds some light on the complexity of designing a suitable model of international corporate criminal liability. The determination of an appropriate model of international corporate criminal liability poses several challenges in relation to both substantive and procedural law. It requires states to reconcile different views on the scope and limit of corporate criminal liability in the development of a model capable of effectively capturing the multifaceted reality of modern companies. While a conservative approach may facilitate the diplomatic discussion of the subject under consideration, it presents the risk of devoiding the model of any practical value. A too narrow model, even if adopted, may remain a dead letter in the Rome Statute and ultimately hinder the prospect of promoting a stronger system of corporate accountability. Conversely, a too-progressive and innovative approach may be ostracised by states who may see it as incompatible with domestic legal principles.

Negotiators of an amendment, therefore, should attempt to strike a careful balance that allows for the creation of an effective mechanism of corporate criminal liability. The task will not be simple, but this should not deter countries from embarking on such a project. The implementation of a strong system of corporate accountability could only take the international community a step further in its fight against impunity.

References

Primary sources

Conventions and Treaties

Council of Europe, *Convention for the Protection of Human Rights and Fundamental Freedoms* (ECHR) (adopted 4 November 1950, entered into force 3 September 1953) CETS 5 (European Convention on Human Rights, as amended) (ECHR)

Council of Europe, *Criminal Law Convention on Corruption* (adopted on 27 January 1999, entered into force on 1 July 2002) CETS 173

International Covenant on Civil and Political Rights (ICCPR) (adopted 16 December 1966, entered into force 23 March 1976) 999 UNTS 171

Organization of American States (OAS), *American Convention on Human Rights*, "Pact of San Jose", Costa Rica, 22 November 1969

Rome Statute of the International Criminal Court (adopted 17 July 1998, entered into force 1 July 2002), 2187 U.N.T.S. 90

United Nations, *Agreement by the Government of the United Kingdom of Great Britain and Northern Ireland, the Government of the United States of America, the Provisional Government of the French Republic and the Government of the Union of Soviet Socialist Republics for the prosecution and punishment of the major war criminals of the European Axis ('London Agreement')*, 8 August 1945, 82 U.N.T.S. 279

International Rules of Procedure and Evidence

International Criminal Court, Rules of Procedure and Evidence, U.N. Doc. PCNICC/2000/1/Add.1 (2000)

UN Documents

UN Preparatory Committee on the Establishment of an International Criminal Court, *Article 17, Individual criminal responsibility: proposal / submitted by France*, A/AC.249/1998/DP.14, 2 April 1998

UN Preparatory Committee on the Establishment of an International Criminal Court, *Draft statute of the International Criminal Court: working paper / submitted by France*, A/AC.249/L.3, 6 August 1996

United Nations Diplomatic Conference of Plenipotentiaries on the Establishment of an International Criminal Court, Committee of the Whole, Summary Record of the 1st Meeting Held at the Headquarters of the Food and Agriculture Organization of the United Nations on Tuesday, 16 June 1998, A/CONF.183/C.1/SR.1

United Nations Diplomatic Conference of Plenipotentiaries on the Establishment of an International Criminal Court, Working Paper on Article 23, Paragraphs 5 and 6: [Draft Statute of an International Criminal Court], A/CONF.183/C.1/WGGP/L.5/Rev.2, 4 July 1998

Universal Declaration of Human Rights (adopted 10 December 1948 UNGA Res 217 A(III) (UDHR)

African Union

African Union, Protocol on Amendments to the Protocol on the Statute of the African Court of Justice and Human Rights, 27 June 2014

European Union

Council Act of 19 June 1997 drawing up the Second Protocol of the Convention on the protection of the European Communities' financial interests [1997] OJ C 221/0011

Council Framework Decision 2003/568/JHA of 22 July 2003 on Combating Corruption in the Private Sector [2003] OJ L 192/54

Council Resolution on a Roadmap for strengthening the procedural rights of suspected or accused persons in criminal proceedings [2009] OJ C 295/1

European Commission, Proposal for a Directive of the European Parliament and of the Council on the Strengthening of Certain Aspects of the Presumption of Innocence and of the Right to Be Present at Trial in Criminal Proceedings, Explanatory Memorandum, COM(2013) 821, 27 November 2013

European Parliament and of the Council Directive (EU) 2016/343 of 9 March 2016 on the strengthening of certain aspects of the presumption of innocence and of the right to be present at the trial in criminal proceedings [2016] OJ L 65/1

European Parliament and of the Council Directive (EU) 2017/1371 of 5 July 2017 on the fight against fraud to the Union's financial interests by means of criminal law EU [2017] OJ L 198/29

Report on the proposal for a directive of the European Parliament and of the Council on the strengthening of certain aspects of the presumption of innocence and of the right to be present at trial in criminal proceedings (COM(2013)0821 – C7-0427/2013 – 2013/0407(COD)) Committee on Civil Liberties, Justice and Home Affairs Rapporteur: Nathalie Griesbeck

Council of Europe

Council of Europe, Committee of Ministers, Recommendation No. R (88) 18 on the Liability of Enterprises for Offences, 20 October 1988

Domestic laws

Code of Criminal Procedure, France (as amended 2020)
Code of Criminal Procedure, Spain (1995)
Criminal Code Act 1995, Australia
Criminal Code, France (as amended 2016)
Criminal Code, Spain (1995)
Criminal Code, Switzerland (as of 2021)
Criminal Justice Act 1925 (England and Wales)
Italian Legislative Decree No. 231 of 8 June 2001 (Decreto Legislativo n. 231/2001 'Disciplina della responsabilità amministrativa delle persone giuridiche, delle società e delle associazioni anche prive di personalità giuridiche')
Republic of Slovenia, Liability of Legal Entities for Criminal Offenses Act, 59/1999, 12/2000
United States Sentencing Commission, Guidelines Manual (Nov. 2021)

Case law

International and Regional cases

ECtHR, *Barbera, Messegue and Jabardo v Spain*, Application no. 10588/83; 10589/83; 10590/83, 13 June 1994
ECtHR, *Comingersoll S.A. v. Portugal*, Judgment of 6 April 2000
ECtHR, *Sunday Times v. United Kingdom*, Application No. 6538/74, 26 April 1979
New TV S.A.L. and Khayat, Public Transcript of the first hearing held on 13 May 2014 in the Case against NEW TV S.A.L. & Karma Khayat, STL-14-05/PT/CJ), Contempt Judge, 13 May 2014
New TV S.A.L. and Khayat, Summons to Appear (Ms Karma Khayat), STL-14-05/PT/CJ, Contempt Judge, 18 March 2014
Prosecutor v Bagilishema, Judgment, Case No. ICTR-95-1A-A, 3 July 2002
Prosecutor v Blaškić, Judgment, Case No. IT-95-14-A, 29 July 2004
The Prosecutor v Jean-Pierre Bemba Gombo, Decision on Sentence pursuant to Article 76 of the Statute, ICC-01/05-01/08, Trial Chamber III, (21 June 2016)
The Prosecutor v. Dominic Ongwen, Decision on Defence Request for the Chamber to Issue an Immediate Ruling Confirming the Burden and Standard of Proof Applicable to Articles 31(1)(a) and (d) of the Rome Statute, ICC-02/04-01/15-1494, Trial Chamber IX, 5 April 2019
The Prosecutor v. Germain Katanga and Mathieu Ngudjolo Chui, Decision on the Confirmation of Charges, ICC 01/04-01/07-717, Pre-Trial Chamber I, 30 September 2008
The Prosecutor v. Jean-Pierre Bemba Gombo, Decision Pursuant to Article 61(7)(a) and (b) of the Rome Statute on the Charges of the Prosecutor Against Jean-Pierre Bemba Gombo, ICC-01/05-01/08-424, Pre-Trial Chamber II, 15 June 2009
The Prosecutor v. Thomas Lubanga Dyilo, Decision on the Confirmation of Charges, ICC-01/04-01/06-803-tEN, 29 January 2007

Domestic cases

Italian Court of Cassation, III Sez. Criminal, *Judgment n. 56427 of 19 December 2017.*

Secondary sources

Books

Cassese A (ed), *The Oxford Companion to International Criminal Justice* (OUP 2009)

Coleman M, *The Presumption of Innocence in International Human Rights and Criminal Law* (Routledge 2021)

Emberland M, *The Human Rights of Companies: Exploring the Structure of ECHR Protection* (OUP 2006)

Gobert J and Punch M, *Rethinking Corporate Crime* (Butterworths 2003)

O'Connor V et al. (eds), *Model Codes for Post-Conflict Criminal Justice.* Vol. 1 (United States Institute of Peace Press 2007)

O'Connor V et al. (eds), *Model Codes for Post-Conflict Criminal Justice.* Vol. 2 (United States Institute of Peace Press 2008)

Olins W, *The Corporate Personality* (1st edn, Mayflower Books 1978)

Pinto A and Evans M, *Corporate Criminal Liability* (3rd edn, Sweet & Maxwell 2013)

Riccardi A, *Sentencing at the International Criminal Court. From Nuremberg to the Hague* (Giappichelli Editore and Eleven International Publishing 2016)

Schabas W A, *The International Criminal Court: A Commentary on the Rome Statute* (2nd edn, OUP 2016)

Wheeler C H, *The Right to Be Present at Trial in International Criminal Law* (Brill | Nijhoff 2019)

Contributions to edited books

Beviá J G, 'Compliance Programs as Evidence in Criminal Cases' in Dominik Brodowski et al. (eds), *Regulating Corporate Criminal Liability* (Springer 2014)

Coleman M, 'Culture and Sentencing at the ICC' in Julie Fraser and Brianne McGonigle Leyh (eds), *Intersections of Law and Culture at the International Criminal Court* (Edward Elgar 2020)

Kiss A, 'Command Responsibility under Article 28 of the Rome Statute' in Carsten Stahn (ed), *The Law and Practice of the International Criminal Court* (OUP 2015)

Kyriakakis J, 'Article 46C: Corporate Criminal Liability at the African Criminal Court' in Charles C Jalloh et al. (eds), *African Court of Justice and Human and People's Rights in Context* (Cambridge University Press 2019)

Pieth M and Ivory R, 'Emergence and Convergence: Corporate Criminal Liability Principles in Overview' in Mark Pieth and Radha Ivory (eds), *Corporate Criminal Liability, Emergence, Convergence, and Risk* (Springer 2011)

Journal Articles

Amann D M, 'Capital Punishment: Corporate Criminal Liability for Gross Violations of Human Rights' (2001) 24 Hastings International and Comparative Law Review 327

Bucy P H, 'Corporate Ethos: A Standard for Imposing Corporate Criminal Liability' (1991) 75 Minnesota Law Review 1095

Cavanagh N, 'Corporate Criminal Liability: An Assessment of the Models of Fault' (2011) 75 Journal of Criminal Law 414

Coffee Jr. J C, 'No Soul to Damn: No Body to Kick: An Unscandalized Inquiry into the Problem of Corporate Punishment' 79 (1981) Michigan Law Review 386
Colvin E, 'Corporate Personality and Criminal Liability' (1995) 6 Criminal Law Forum 1
de Maglie C, 'Models of Corporate Criminal Liability in Comparative Law' (2005) 4 Washington University Global Studies Law Review 547
Đurđević Z, 'Pravna osoba kao okrivljenik: temeljna prava i predstavljanje' (2005) 12 Croatian Annual of Criminal Law and Practice 739
Field S and Jorg N, 'Corporate Liability and Manslaughter: Should We Be Going Dutch?' (1991) Criminal Law Review 156
French P A, 'The Corporation as a Moral Person' (1979) 16 American Philosophical Quarterly 207
Gobert J, 'Corporate Criminal Liability: Four Models of Fault' (1994) 14 Legal Studies 393
Hill J G, 'Corporate Criminal Liability in Australia: An Evolving Corporate Governance Technique?' (2003) Journal of Business Law 1
Hsiao M W H, 'Abandonment of the Doctrine of Attribution for Gross Negligent Test on the Corporate Manslaughter and Corporate Homicide Act 2007' (2009) 30(4) Company Lawyer 110
Hulpke J F, 'If All Else Fails, A Corporate Death Penalty?' (2017) 26(4) Journal of Management Inquiry 1
Lederman E, 'Models for Imposing Corporate Criminal Liability: From Adaptation and Imitation Toward Aggregation and the Search for Self-Identity' (2000) 4 Buffalo Criminal Law Review 641
Mays R, 'Towards Corporate Fault as the Basis of Criminal Liability of Corporations' (1998) 2 Mountbatten Journal of Legal Studies 31
Michalakea T, 'Article 46C of the Malabo Protocol: A Contextually Tailored Approach to Corporate Criminal Liability and Its Contours' (2018) 7 International Human Rights Law Review 225
Nagy A, 'The Presumption of Innocence and of the Right to Be Present at Trial in Criminal Proceedings in Directive (EU) 2016/343' (2016) 12 European Integration Studies 5
Riegler E, 'Rehabilitating Enemies of Mankind: An Exploration of the Concept of Rehabilitation as a Sentencing Aim at the ICTY and the ICC' (2020) 20(4) International Criminal Law Review 701
Roberts P, 'The Priority of Procedure and the Neglect of Evidence and Proof: Facing Facts in International Criminal Law' (2015) 13 Journal of International Criminal Justice 479
Scalia D, 'A Few Thoughts on Guaranties Inherent to the Rule of Law as Applied to Sanctions and the Prosecution and Punishment of War Crimes' (2008) 90 International Review of the Red Cross Volume 343
Schabas W A, 'Life, Death and the Crime of Crimes: Supreme Penalties and the ICC Statute' (2000) 2(3) Punishment and Society 263
Shiner R A, 'Corporations and the Presumption of Innocence' (2014) 8(2) Criminal Law and Philosophy 485
Van Kampen P H, 'Human Rights and Criminal Justice Applied to Legal Persons. Protection and Liability of Private and Public Juristic Entities under the ICCPR, ECHR, ACHR and AfChHPR' (2010) 14(3) Electronic Journal of Comparative Law

van Sliedregt E, 'Article 28 of the ICC Statute: Mode of Liability and/or Separate Offense?' (2009) 12(3) New Criminal Law Review: An International and Interdisciplinary Journal 420

Wilkinson M, 'Corporate Criminal Liability. The Move Towards Recognising Genuine Corporate Fault' (2003) 9 Canterbury Law Review 142

Online sources

Clifford Chance, Corporate Criminal Liability (Clifford Chance, 26 April 2016) https://www.cliffordchance.com/content/dam/cliffordchance/briefings/2016/04/corporate-criminal-liability.pdf Accessed 24 March 2023

OECD, 'Switzerland: Phase 2 Report on Application of the Convention on Combating Bribery of Foreign Public Officials in International Business Transactions and the 1997 Recommendations on Combating Bribery in International Business Transactions' (OECD 2004) https://www.oecd.org/corruption/switzerland-oecdanti-briberyconvention.htm Accessed 24 March 2023

Robinson A A, '"Corporate Culture" as a Basis for the Criminal Liability of Corporations' (Business & Human Rights Resource Centre, 1 February 2008) https://media.business-humanrights.org/media/documents/f72634fd87adfd3d31a22f5f4b93150267b8a764.pdf Accessed 24 March 2023

Miscellaneous Secondary Sources

Cassese A, Lecture at the British Institute of Human Rights, 1 May 1997. Quote cited in Amnesty International, The International Criminal Court: Drafting effective Rules of Procedure and Evidence for the Trial, Appeal and Revision, 1999

Control Council Law No. 9, Providing for the Seizure of Property Owned by I.G. Farbenindustrie and the Control Thereof, 30 November 1945, in *Enactments and Approved Papers of the Control Council and Coordinating Committee*, Library of Congress

Conclusions

This book examined the international criminal liability of corporations with the purpose of providing a comprehensive analysis of the way in which the concept has been discussed at the international level. It offered unique insight into the history of international criminal law and on the role played by corporations. Since the 1940s, the issue of corporate involvement in international crimes has posed significant challenges to those involved in the development of an effective international criminal justice system. As highlighted in the analysis, several attempts have been made to incorporate corporate criminal liability under international criminal law to strengthen the framework of international accountability. The failure of these attempts has not been due to the rejection of the concept as incompatible with the principles of international criminal law. Conversely, the obstacles that so far have prevented the recognition of corporate criminal liability appear to rest on practical and political grounds. As such, they are not without solution.

Chapter 1 began with an examination of the Nuremberg experience to assess its precedential value in today's debate on corporate liability for international crimes. It first considered the case against groups and organisations to compare the legal basis for prosecution under Articles 9 and 10 of the London Charter with the rationale underlying the modern concept of corporate criminal liability. While the former had the purpose of facilitating the prosecution of the individual members of each group or organisation, the latter concerned the criminal liability of the entity as separate to that of its agents and employees. Therefore, it is argued that the use of the Nuremberg trial against groups and organisations as a legal precedent to support corporate criminal liability can be misleading.

Nonetheless, the chapter did not negate the relevance of Nuremberg in the context of the debate on the feasibility of prosecuting legal entities at the international level. Indeed, the analysis showed that, from a procedural standpoint, the Nuremberg trial demonstrates that entities can fit in the context of an international criminal trial. Although the case against criminal groups and organisations presented several procedural challenges, the IMT was still able to deal with them in an effective way. The analysis therefore calls for a

DOI: 10.4324/9781003390534-8

re-evaluation of the way in which the Nuremberg Trial can be used as an argument in favour of the inclusion of corporations within international criminal law.

The chapter also evaluated the relevance of the industrialist cases conducted by the United States under CCL10. The analysis of the preparatory phase of these trials has demonstrated that it is at this stage that the first significant attempt was made to indict corporate entities for their involvement in the perpetration of international crimes.[1] Even though the attempt ultimately failed, it still demonstrated the attention paid to the question of corporate criminal liability in the aftermath of the Second World War. Furthermore, the lack of recognition of corporate criminal liability in the industrialist cases did not prevent the judges from considering at length the position of the corporation in the context of the proceedings. In the *I.G. Farben* case, specifically, the liability of the entity was a central part of the trial to the point that I.G. Farben became the 'invisible defendant in the case'.[2] Overall, the chapter aspired to offer an objective narrative of the Nuremberg experience, shedding light on its precedential value. In doing so, it endeavoured to provide a more nuanced reading of its impact on the debate on the international criminal liability of corporations.

Chapter 2 investigated to what extent the question of corporate criminal liability for international crimes was addressed in the late 1940s to early 1950s. This analysis offered unique insights into the ongoing nature of the debate on the possibility of including corporations within the scope of international criminal law. Indeed, the chapter showed that proposals on corporate criminal liability emerged both in the context of the drafting of a Code of Offences against Peace and Security of Mankind and during the work of the 1951 and 1953 Committees on International Criminal Jurisdiction. These proposals specifically focused on the criminal liability of private corporations and demonstrated the attention paid to the issue of corporate accountability. As emerged from the investigation conducted in the chapter, the rejection of these proposals was never based on theoretical considerations. Indeed, the international criminal liability of corporations was set aside either because of a failure to distinguish between private corporations and the State or due to the novelty of the concept itself. This demonstrates that the obstacles to the recognition of corporate criminal liability can be overcome.

Continuing with the historical analysis, Chapter 3 scrutinised the negotiation of the Rome Statute of the ICC as a fundamental moment in the history of international criminal law and corporate criminal liability. In the years

1 Memorandum of 27 August 1946, reprinted as an annex in Jonathan A Bush, 'The Prehistory of Corporations and Conspiracy in International Criminal Law: What Nuremberg Really Said' (2009) 109(5) Columbia Law Review 1094, 1247-8.

2 *United States of America vs. Carl Krauch et al.* (Case 6), Transcript of Proceedings, National Archives Microfilm Publication M895, Roll 15, Vol. 42, June 7-9, 1948, 15400.

preceding the adoption of the Rome Statute, the question of whether corporations should have been included among the subjects of international criminal liability was discussed at length. The preparatory works of the Rome Statute indicate that a detailed model of corporate criminal liability was first proposed by France in 1996.[3] In the following two years, the proposal was frequently amended to win the approval of other delegations. It regressed to a model of criminal organisation *à la* Nuremberg,[4] and subsequently developed into a model based on the identification doctrine.[5] The analysis of the evolution of the proposal demonstrated the complexity of the task of defining a provision on corporate criminal liability. It also evidenced a willingness on the side of several States to test the boundaries of international criminal law and to offer a solution to the issue of corporate impunity.

Even though the proposal was ultimately withdrawn, the attempt made in Rome gives a sense of the importance of the issue under consideration. Additionally, the examination of the preparatory works of the Statute of the ICC once again confirmed the conclusion that the exclusion of corporate criminal liability from the Statute did not rest on theoretical grounds or on an incompatibility between the concept and international criminal law. Conversely, the withdrawal of the proposal was due to practical considerations such as the lack of sufficient time to properly discuss the issue and to solve the challenges posed by the (then) limited recognition of corporate criminal liability at the domestic level. Accordingly, it is submitted that the failure of the French proposal should be interpreted in this context without overestimating its impact on future discussions on the subject matter.

In recent times, the exclusion of corporations from the scope of the Rome Statute has been read as the swan song of corporate criminal liability.[6] Far from being the case, the analysis conducted in Chapter 4 illustrated how the debate on international corporate criminal liability has continued to evolve in the years following the adoption and entry into force of the Statute of the International Criminal Court. The examination aspired to contextualise the developments discussed in the chapter – the decision of the Appeal Panel of the STL, the 2014 Malabo Protocol, and the draft Articles on Crimes against Humanity – to offer insights into the contribution provided by each of them to the debate on international corporate criminal liability. Indeed, while these developments give a sense of the centrality of the issue of corporate accountability, they also highlight relevant limitations. A discussion of their impact on the development of the international criminal liability of corporations must

3 A/AC.249/L.3, p. 64.

4 A/AC.249/1998/DP.14.

5 A/CONF.183/C.1/WGGP/L.5/Rev.2.

6 *Kiobel v. Royal Dutch Petroleum Co.*, 621 F.3d 111, at 120 (2d Cir. 2010), *Jesner v. Arab Bank, PLC*, 138 S. Ct. 1386, at 1400-1 (2018).

acknowledge such limitations and use them to propose new solutions in the fight against corporate impunity.

Chapter 5 shifted the focus from the international domain to the domestic domain. It looked at the way in which domestic developments in the field of corporate criminal liability have been used as an argument in support of the recognition of such a concept at the international level. The emphasis put on domestic developments should be interpreted in light of the main argument historically used to dismiss the idea of an international criminal liability of corporate entities, meaning the limited recognition of such a form of liability at the national level. Indeed, the relative novelty of the concept under consideration has posed significant challenges to the establishment of an international model of corporate criminal liability. It is therefore significant to observe that several national jurisdictions have now moved away from the principle of *societas delinquere non potest* to recognise corporations as subjects of criminal liability. Understood in this sense, the comparative law argument has merit and demonstrates the evolving nature of the legal framework on corporate criminal liability. At the same time, its value cannot be overinflated. The analysis conducted in Chapter 5, indeed, illustrated that a change in States' domestic approaches to corporate criminal liability may not be sufficient to demonstrate States' willingness to transpose such a concept at the international level. The review of the positions of several States during the negotiation of the Rome Statute has shown an apparent lack of correlation between domestic recognition of corporate criminal liability and State's decisions to support the French proposal. Therefore, the practical implications of the comparative law argument must be carefully considered.

Even more speculative is the argument that sees in the domestic recognition of corporate criminal liability evidence that such a concept is on the verge of becoming a general principle of law within the meaning of Article 38(1)(c) of the Statute of the International Court of Justice. The argument has been notoriously used by the Special Tribunal for Lebanon to justify the decision to extend the Tribunal's contempt jurisdiction to corporate actors. Even recognising the possibility of considering corporate criminal liability as a general principle of law, this interpretation would have no practical relevance in the context of the international criminal justice system. As observed, general principles of law operate as mechanisms to fill existing gaps in 'areas where the law is insufficient, obscure, or imperfect'.[7] While it may be open to debate whether the international criminal law framework could be considered 'imperfect', it is undeniable that, at the present stage, it leaves no gap for the operation of a general principle of law on corporate criminal liability. As the statutes of all the main international or internationalised criminal courts and tribunals explicitly refer to individual criminal liability, only an amendment to their

7 Neha Jain, 'Judicial Lawmaking and General Principles of Law in International Criminal Law' (2016) 57 Harvard International Law Journal 111, 113.

texts may allow for the incorporation of the international criminal liability of corporations.

As an amendment to the ICC Statute seems to be the only viable path forward on corporate criminal liability, the final chapter of this book offered some suggestions for the development of an effective mechanism to hold corporations accountable under international criminal law. The debate on corporate criminal liability under international criminal law can no longer approach the question solely from a theoretical perspective but must offer practical solutions to the challenges posed by the incorporation of corporate defendants within the scope of the international criminal justice system. In light of that, Chapter 6 offered unique insights that would be relevant to the drafters of a future amendment to the Rome Statute in defining a framework for the incorporation of legal persons in international criminal law. The analysis focused, in particular, on the model of attribution of corporate criminal liability, on the procedural guarantees applicable to corporate defendants and on the issue of corporate sanctioning. All these aspects have been examined taking into account the complex structure of modern corporations and their ability to operate on a large scale.

Overall, the analysis conducted in the book contributes to a more open debate on the potential role that international criminal law can play in the fight against corporate impunity. In today's globalised world, multinational corporations pose significant regulatory challenges that have so far prevented the creation of a system of accountability. As the number of allegations of corporate involvement in gross violation of human rights continues to grow, the international community is slowly starting to explore different paths to reduce the negative impact of corporate operations.

Outside the scope of international criminal law, initiatives to hold corporations accountable for their adverse impact on human rights are gaining traction. The most recent example is the ongoing attempt to draft a binding international treaty on business and human rights.[8] Under negotiation since 2014, the project has yet to reach a sufficient level of maturity to allow for a proper assessment of its relevance and impact on the development of a framework of corporate accountability. With specific regard to its ability to influence the development of international corporate criminal liability, at the current stage it seems unlikely that the proposed treaty will add significantly to the debate on corporations under international criminal law. The scope of

8 A/HRC/RES/26/9. See *inter alia* Surya Deva and David Bilchitz (eds), *Building a Treaty on Business and Human Rights: Context and Contours* (Cambridge University Press 2017), Nadia Bernaz, 'Conceptualizing Corporate Accountability in International Law: Models for a Business and Human Rights Treaty' (2021) 22 Human Rights Review 45.

the treaty is still too vague, and the proposed model of legal accountability is still too undefined.[9]

Nonetheless, the inclusion of a specific provision that compels State Parties to provide for 'the criminal or functionally equivalent liability of legal persons for human rights abuses that amount to criminal offenses under international human rights law ... or customary international law' bodes well.[10] If such a provision will emerge unscathed from the negotiation, it may encourage States to re-evaluate their position on the applicability of criminal liability to corporations for serious human rights abuses and international crimes.

Tentative developments are also starting to emerge at the domestic level. The recent indictment of the French cement company LaFarge Holcim for its activities in Syria may indicate a change in the domestic approach toward corporate criminal liability for international crimes.[11] The French company is accused of making financial arrangements with ISIS and other jihadist groups to secure and maintain the production of its cement plant in Syria.[12] In an unprecedented decision, the company has been additionally charged with complicity in crimes against humanity committed in Syria by ISIS.[13] Despite an attempt by the Paris Court of Appeals to revoke the complicity charge against LaFarge, in 2021 the French Court of Cassation reinstalled the charge, clearing the way for the first domestic criminal trial against the company for crimes against humanity.[14]

While it is too early to evaluate whether the LaFarge case will signal a shift in domestic prosecutorial strategies to address corporate involvement in mass atrocities, the case still represents a welcome development. It evidences the

9 David Birchall, 'Between Apology and Utopia: The Indeterminacies of the Zero Draft Treaty on Business and Human Rights' (2019) 42 Suffolk Transnational Law Review 289, 290.

10 Open-Ended Intergovernmental Working Group on Transnational Corporations and Other Business Enterprises with Respect to Human Rights (OEIGWG), Third Revised Draft Legally Binding Instrument to Regulate, in International Human Rights Law, the Activities of Transnational Corporations and Other Business Enterprises, A/HRC/49/65/Add.1, 17 August 2021, Draft Article 8(8).

11 Madeline Young, 'LaFarge's Case Cemented: Holding Corporations Liable for Crimes Against Humanity' (2021) 36 Emory International Law Review Recent Developments 1, 5. Nina H B Jørgensen (ed), *The International Criminal Responsibility of War's Funders and Profiteers* (Cambridge University Press 2020), 7.

12 Madeline Young, 'LaFarge's Case Cemented: Holding Corporations Liable for Crimes Against Humanity' (2021) 36 Emory International Law Review Recent Developments 1, 3.

13 ECCHR, Lafarge in Syria: Accusations of complicity in grave human rights violations (ECCHR, 2022) https://www.ecchr.eu/en/case/lafarge-in-syria-accusations-of-complicity-in-grave-human-rights-violations/#case_case Accessed 26 March 2023.

14 French Court of Cassation [Crim], Appeal No. 19-87.367, (7 September 2021) ECLI:FR:CCASS:2021:CR00868. In May 2022, the decision was confirmed by the Paris Court of Appeal. See Amal Clooney, 'Paris Court of Appeal confirms charges against French multinational Lafarge for complicity in crimes against humanity committed by ISIS' (Doughty Street Chambers, 23 May 22) https://www.doughtystreet.co.uk/news/paris-court-appeal-confirms-charges-against-french-multinational-lafarge-complicity-crimes Accessed 26 March 2023.

ongoing relevance of the question of corporate criminal liability for international crimes and the necessity of exploring innovative solutions to put an end to the culture of impunity connected with crimes committed by businesses. Domestic prosecution can prove to be a useful tool in this sense, but it cannot represent the only pathway available to pursue corporate liability.

As the framework on corporate accountability is slowly evolving, it is argued that the time is now ripe to rethink the role that the international criminal justice system can play to promote a more effective system to address corporate involvement in international crimes. The book demonstrates that the international criminal justice system can be amended to incorporate corporate criminal liability in its legal framework. Corporations can – and should – be subjects of international criminal law.

As observed by William Schabas, even though 'commercial corporations present a special challenge to international regulation, … the technical issues involved in efforts to control their operations are all capable of solution'.[15] This book confirms this conclusion and offers practical suggestions on how to overcome the challenges arising from the creation of a feasible model of international corporate criminal liability.

References

Primary Sources

UN Documents

UN Preparatory Committee on the Establishment of an International Criminal Court, *Article 17, Individual criminal responsibility: proposal / submitted by France*, A/AC.249/1998/DP.14, 2 April 1998

UN Preparatory Committee on the Establishment of an International Criminal Court, *Draft statute of the International Criminal Court: working paper / submitted by France*, A/AC.249/L.3, 6 August 1996

United Nations Diplomatic Conference of Plenipotentiaries on the Establishment of an International Criminal Court, Working Paper on Article 23, Paragraphs 5 and 6: [Draft Statute of an International Criminal Court], A/CONF.183/C.1/WGGP/L.5/Rev.2, 4 July 1998

HRC Res 26/9, Elaboration of an international legally binding instrument on transnational corporations and other business enterprises with respect to human rights, A/HRC/RES/26/9, 14 July 2014

Open-Ended Intergovernmental Working Group on Transnational Corporations and Other Business Enterprises with Respect to Human Rights (OEIGWG), Third Revised Draft Legally Binding Instrument to Regulate, in International Human Rights Law, the Activities of Transnational Corporations and Other Business Enterprises, A/HRC/49/65/Add.1, 17 August 2021

15 William A Schabas, 'War Economies, Economic Actors, and International Criminal Law' in Karen Ballentine and Heiko Nitzschke (eds), *Profiting from Peace. Managing the Resource Dimensions of Civil War* (Lynne Reinner Publishers 2005) 438.

Cases

French Court of Cassation [Crim], Appeal No. 19-87.367, (7 September 2021) ECLI:FR:CCASS:2021:CR00868.

Jesner v. Arab Bank, PLC, 138 S. Ct. 1386 (2018)

Kiobel v. Royal Dutch Petroleum Co., 621 F.3d 111 (2d Cir. 2010)

United States Military Tribunal at Nuremberg, *United States of America vs. Carl Krauch et al.* (Case 6), Transcript of Proceedings, National Archives Microfilm Publication M895, Roll 15, Vol. 42, June 7-9, 1948

Secondary sources

Books

Deva S and Bilchitz D (eds), *Building a Treaty on Business and Human Rights: Context and Contours* (Cambridge University Press 2017)

Jørgensen N H B (ed), *The International Criminal Responsibility of War's Funders and Profiteers* (Cambridge University Press 2020)

Contributions to edited books

Schabas W A, 'War Economies, Economic Actors, and International Criminal Law' in Karen Ballentine and Heiko Nitzschke (eds), *Profiting from Peace. Managing the Resource Dimensions of Civil War* (Lynne Reinner Publishers 2005)

Journal Articles

Bernaz N, 'Conceptualizing Corporate Accountability in International Law: Models for a Business and Human Rights Treaty' (2021) 22 Human Rights Review 45

Birchall D, 'Between Apology and Utopia: The Indeterminacies of the Zero Draft Treaty on Business and Human Rights' (2019) 42 Suffolk Transnational Law Review 289

Bush J A, 'The Prehistory of Corporations and Conspiracy in International Criminal Law: What Nuremberg Really Said' (2009) 109(5) Columbia Law Review 1094

Jain N, 'Judicial Lawmaking and General Principles of Law in International Criminal Law' (2016) 57 Harvard International Law Journal 111

Young M, 'LaFarge's Case Cemented: Holding Corporations Liable for Crimes Against Humanity' (2021) 36 Emory International Law Review Recent Developments 1

Online sources

Clooney A, 'Paris Court of Appeal Confirms Charges against French Multinational Lafarge for Complicity in Crimes against Humanity Committed by ISIS' (Doughty Street Chambers, 23 May 2022) https://www.doughtystreet.co.uk/news/paris-court-appeal-confirms-charges-against-french-multinational-lafarge-complicity-crimes accessed 26 March 2023

ECCHR, 'Lafarge in Syria: Accusations of Complicity in Grave Human Rights Violations' (ECCHR, 2022) https://www.ecchr.eu/en/case/lafarge-in-syria-accusations-of-complicity-in-grave-human-rights-violations/#case_case accessed 26 March 2023

Index

1951 Committee on International Criminal Jurisdiction 59–62; corporate criminal liability 62; legal persons 61–62; liability of states 62; model of attribution 61–62
1953 Committee on International Criminal Jurisdiction 59, 63–67; criminal liability of corporations 63, 65; private corporations 65–66
1995 *ad hoc* Committee 78, 82
1996 Preparatory Committee 78, 82–83, 86

accountability 9, 48, 63, 135, 148, 151, 155, 169, 200, 227, 235–237; *see also* corporate accountability
act of State xi, 10
Adam, Jendrik 178–179, 181–182
Afonso, Pedro Comissario 149
African Court of Justice and Human Rights 108, 128, 146, 148, 157; *see also* Malabo Protocol
aggregation model 134–135, 192–193, 196–198
aggressive war 25, 32–34, 38, 56
Al-Baharna, Husain M. 76
Alien Tort Statute 8, 42; *Jesner v. Arab Bank* 9; *Kiobel v. Royal Dutch Petroleum Co.* 9
Alkhawaja, Osama 120, 127
Amann, Diane Marie 225
Angola 1
Apartheid xi, 145
Argentina 64–65, 92, 152
attribution, model of 62, 85–86, 131, 191–192, 199, 239; *á la* Nuremberg 88, 92, 100, 177, 237; identification 62, 86, 96, 100, 131, 140, 174–175, 192–193, 195, 200–201, 237; organisational 131–132, 134, 138, 140, 157, 192, 197–201, 205, 210; *respondeat superior* 86, 100, 140, 175
Australia 61–62, 64, 92, 168, 202, 210; position on corporate criminal liability 170, 174–175; *see also* Australian Criminal Code Act
Australian Criminal Code Act 132–133, 175, 199, 202–203
Austria 152, 194

Bassiouni, M Cherif 82, 141, 180
Belgium xi, 168
Bernaz, Nadia 122–123, 125, 127
British East India Company xi
Bruno Tesch et al. case 26; *see also* subsequent proceedings
Bucy, Pamela H. 199
burden of proof 205–206, 210–211, 213, 228; reverse onus 205, 211
Bush, Jonathan 30, 35
business and human rights 109, 127, 169, 239; Treaty 239

Canada 80, 168, 174–175
Canadian Dredge and Duck Co v The Queen 174
case against groups and organisations 12, 16–17, 41; declaration of criminality 15, 17–19; evidence 16; origin 12–14; *see also* criminal organisation
Cassese, Antonio 178, 214
Cavanagh, Neil 198
China xi, 92
Churchill, Winston x
civil law 169–171, 186; *see also* comparative law argument
Clapham, Andrew 53, 95–98, 126, 175, 177

Colombia 1
Colvin, Eric 131
Comingersoll S.A. v. Portugal 214
command responsibility 136–137
Committee of the Whole 89, 93; *see also* Rome Statute
common law 62, 66, 171, 174–175; *see also* comparative law argument
comparative law argument 114–115, 126, 166–171, 173, 177, 179, 238; inaccuracies 171–172; limitations 171–179; main criticism 173–178; *see also* domestic developments
compliance programmes 134–135, 202, 205
contempt cases 109, 114, 116, 118, 127, 184, 191; *Akhbar Beirut S.A.L.* case 108–110, 116; appeal panel 121–122, 158, 185; inherent jurisdiction 111, 117; *New TV S.A.L.* case 108–110, 116–117, 121, 217–218; *see also* comparative law argument; Special Tribunal for Lebanon
Control Council Law No. 9 (CCL9) 39–40
Control Council Law No. 10 (CCL10) 9–10, 23, 26–27, 29, 33, 37, 39–40, 42, 236; *see also* Subsequent proceedings
Convention on Action against Trafficking in Human Beings 156
Convention on Combating Bribery of Foreign Public Officials in International Business 156
corporate accountability 39–41, 109, 124–125, 132, 140, 153, 158, 166, 171, 197, 205, 225, 237, 241; development of a framework of 239; issue of 123, 236; system of 186, 229
corporate crimes 93, 137, 139, 196, 199; *see also* corporate involvement in human rights violations
corporate culture 132–134, 175, 199–200, 203; *see also* Malabo protocol
corporate death penalty 221, 225–227; adverse effect 226; judicial dissolution 225–228; morally neutral 226; rehabilitation 227; *see also* extra-judicial sanction
corporate identity 199
corporate involvement in human rights violations 239–240; amounting to international crimes 2, 10, 143, 145, 147, 191, 193, 196, 200, 227, 235; in Africa 131, 139
corporate scapegoating 196
corporate wrongdoing 2, 43, 139, 146, 151, 155–156, 174, 186, 200
criminal corporations 29
criminal organisation 8, 10, 12, 14, 16, 18–23, 31–32, 41, 87–88, 90–92, 95, 100, 119, 125, 177, 216–217, 237; *vs.* corporate criminal liability 19–23; *see also* London Charter; membership, crime of
Czech Republic 152

de Maglie, Cristina 197
Decreto Legislativo n. 231/2001 172–173, 201–202, 211, 217
Democratic Republic of the Congo 1
Denmark 92, 175–177
diffuse operations 195–196
Directive on the Fight Against Fraud to the Union's Financial Interests by Means of Criminal Law 201
domestic developments 114–116, 119, 122–126, 166, 185–186, 238; *see also* comparative law argument
domestic prosecution 241
Dominican Republic 53
Draft Articles on Crimes against Humanity 140–142, 148, 150, 154; argument against 143–144; argument in favour 145–149; flexibility 130, 150–155, 158; liability of legal persons 142–151; States' Comments 152–155; State's discretion 143
Draft Articles on State Responsibility 57, 130
Draft Code of Offences against Peace and Security of Mankind 54–58, 67, 73–74, 77–78; responsibility of legal entities 55–56; Vespasian V. Pella 55–57, 67
DuBois Jr, Josiah E. 33
due diligence 134–135, 137, 197, 201, 203, 205–206, 210–212; defence of 205–207, 210–212; lack of 200–201

economic crimes 57, 144–145, 193–194
Egypt 92
El Salvador 92
Engelhart, Marc 169

European Court of Human Rights 198, 206, 209; application to corporations 213–214
European Union 156, 194, 207; European Commission 208
Evans, Martin 213
extra-judicial sanction 39–40, 42, 226; *see also* Control Council Law No. 9; I.G. Farben

fairness 211, 214, 220
France xi, 13, 25, 35, 37, 86, 91, 152, 168, 237; *see also* French Proposal
French proposal 83–100, 137, 168, 177; approach *á la* Nuremberg 88–93; complementarity 98–99, 168, 171, 186; discussion 90–94; draft article 23(6) 98–99; final text (draft article 23(5)) 95–99; French Penal Code 85, 96; juridical person 97; narrow scope 96–97; original formulation 83–85; sanctioning system 84, 91; time constraints 81, 89, 92–93, 99; withdrawal 98–100; *see also* French proposal, complementarity

general principle of law 126–127, 167, 178–186; Article 38 ICJ Statute 178, 180, 186; common denominator 180, 182–183; corporate criminal liability 178–186; Special Rapporteur 181; subsidiary nature 180; transposition 183–184
Genocide Convention 49–53, 58–59; Article IV 49–51; International criminal court 58–59; responsibility of states 51–53, 58
German industry 24, 26, 39; *see also* industrialist cases
Germany x, 8, 39, 40, 226; position on corporate criminal liability 119, 170, 173, 181
Gobert, James 195, 210, 224
Graefrath, Bernhard 75–76
Greece 92, 153, 170
Grotian moment 2

Hague Regulations (1907) 35, 37
Hungary 153–154, 194

I.G. Farben 4, 9–10, 24, 28, 31–42, 47, 145–146, 148, 225–226, 228, 236; *invisible defendant* 36, 42, 236; Judge Paul Macarius Hebert 38; *see also* extra-judicial sanction
impunity 5, 73, 149, 229; corporate impunity 237–239
India xi, 168
individual criminal liability 9, 11, 37–38, 41–42, 65, 135–137, 146, 179, 182, 203, 238
industrialist cases 23–24, 26–28, 30–39; charges 31; defence of necessity 33–34; *Flick* case 30–33, 35; *Krupp* case 28, 31–34, 146, 148; *see also* Krupp, Gustav; outcome 33, 38; slave labour 31, 34–35; *see also* I.G. Farben; plunder; spoliation
International Commission of Jurists 148, 167
International Criminal Court: early debate 58–67; Elements of Crimes 136; Rule 145 211–212, 222; *see also* French proposal; Rome Statute; Rule of Procedure and Evidence (Rule 134-ter) 219
international criminal justice system 3, 5, 89, 108, 143, 173, 178–179, 183–184, 191, 203, 205, 215, 221, 235, 238–241
international criminal liability 9, 47, 185; attribution of 5, 61, 227–228; of corporations 2–4, 10, 40–41, 48, 53–55, 58, 61–68, 72–77, 81–85, 92–93, 98, 100, 107–108, 114, 128, 140, 158, 167–168, 170, 186, 191; subjects of 65; *see also* individual criminal liability
International Criminal Tribunal for Rwanda 78, 81
International Criminal Tribunal for the former Yugoslavia 78–81; *Kunarac* case 182
International Military Tribunal of Nuremberg (IMT) 9–23, 95, 119, 125; *see also* London Charter
Iran 92
Israel 63–64
Italy 99, 119, 171, 173, 181, 194, 201, 210

Jackson, Robert H. 13–14, 17, 26–27, 30
Jacobsson, Marie G. 145–146, 149
Jain, Neha 180
Japan 92, 168

Jordan 92
Jørgensen, Nina H. B. 21
juridical persons 79, 83–88, 94–95, 97, 99; *see also* French Proposal

Kaeb, Caroline 170
Kamto, Maurice 145, 148–149
Kelly, Michael J. 50–51
Kelsen, Hans 11
Kötz, Hein 182
Krupp, Alfred 26, 32
Krupp, Gustav 25–26
Kubuschok, Egon 21
Kyriakakis, Joanna 133–134, 137, 168, 170, 220

LaFarge case 240
Laternser, Hans 21
Lauterpatcht, Hersch 180
Le Fraper du Hellen, Beatrice 89–90; *see also* French proposal
Lebanese Criminal Code 114–115, 120, 127; *see also* contempt cases; Special Tribunal for Lebanon
Lebanon 92; *see also* Special Tribunal for Lebanon
Lederman, Eli 196–197
London Agreement 11, 23, 29; *see also* London Charter
London Charter 8, 10–11, 14, 16, 19, 29–30, 41, 47, 55, 87, 90–91, 119, 125, 216–217, 235; Article 9 8, 10, 14–22, 41, 47, 87, 90–91, 119, 125, 217, 235; Article 10 15, 90
Loomes, Australian representative 64–66; *see also* 1953 Committee on International Criminal Jurisdiction

Mahiou, Ahmed 76
Malabo Protocol 108, 128–129, 138, 140, 143, 146, 155, 191–193, 196–198, 200, 203, 220, 222, 225; Article 46C 128–140, 157, 192–193, 196–197, 202; corporate culture 132–134; corporate intent 129, 132, 134, 192; corporate knowledge 129, 132, 134–135, 137, 192–193, 197; ratification 140
mass atrocities 24, 81, 227, 240
mass criminality 21, 41
Maxwell-Fyfe, David 22
McDermott Rees, Yvonne 124
Meloni, Chantal 129
membership, crime of 19–20, 23, 31; *see also* case against groups and organisations; criminal organisation
Mexico 92, 153
Michalakea, Taygeti 139
Model Codes for Criminal Procedure for Post-Conflict Criminal Justice 218
Morgenthau Jr, Henry 12
Murray C. Bernays 12–13

negligence 133, 136–137, 201–203, 205, 228
Netherlands xi, 64–66, 168
Norway 170, 175–176
Nuremberg trials 2, 10, 41, 67, 77, 92, 148, 184, 191; *see also* industrialist cases; International Military Tribunal of Nuremberg; subsequent proceedings; Trial of the Major War Criminals

OECD 156, 211
Ogiso, Motoo 76
Olins, Wally 199
Optional Protocol on the Sale of Children, Child Prostitution and Child Pornography 150
organisational fault 140, 157, 199, 205, 210
organisational structure 36, 195, 200

penalties 36, 57, 61, 75, 84, 87, 89, 91, 95, 98, 138, 142, 176, 221–228
Petric, Ernest 143
Philippines 65
Pinto, Amanda 213
plunder 31–32, 36–37
political organisations 20, 217
Pomerantz's Memorandum 28–30
Portugal xi, 153
position of control 94, 96, 100, 131, 192, 198, 201
presumption of innocence 191, 205–207, 209–213, 228; directive 207–209
procedural guarantees 23, 172, 213–214, 228, 239; representation at trial 215–221, 228
Punch, Maurice 210, 224

quasi-criminal liability 119, 173, 201–202

Raimondo, Fabián 180–181
Ramasastry, Anita 168
Ratner, Steven R. 35
recklessness 132–133, 201–204
Recommendation No. R (88) 18 on the Liability of Enterprises for Offences 224
Reich Cabinet, case against 19–20; *see also* case against groups and organisations
Report on Cartel and National Security 24
Resolution 44/39 (1990) 74–75
Resolution 808 (1993) 79–80
right to a fair trial 208, 214–215, 221
Robinson, Allens Arthur 211
Roechling case 26; *see also* subsequent proceedings
Rome Conference 89, 94, 126, 148, 168, 170, 177; *see also* French proposal
Rome model 193–196, 200; *see also* French Proposal
Rome Statute: amendment to the 185, 191–194, 197–199, 203, 218, 220, 227–228; Article 23(1) 185; Article 28 136, 204–205; Article 30(1) 203; Article 66 207; Article 67(1) 206–207, 210, 212; Article 77 221, 223; *mens rea* standard 204–205; preparatory works 83–89; *see also* 1951 Committee on International Criminal Jurisdiction; *1953* Committee on International Criminal Jurisdiction; French proposal
Ruggie, John 125, 148, 169
Russia 80, 153, 181
Rwanda, corporate crimes 93

Saland, Per 86
Schabas, William 204, 241
Scheffer, David 99, 126, 170, 177
Second Protocol of the Convention on the protection of the European Communities' financial interests 156, 194, 201
Second World War 41, 55, 73, 146, 148, 226, 236
sentencing system 138, 211, 221, 227–228; fines 21–22, 62, 84, 91, 93, 98, 138–139, 222; injunction measures 223, 225; non-pecuniary sanctions 228, 231; pecuniary sanctions 139, 221–222; publication of the sentence 224; *see also* corporate death penalty
Shi, Jiuyong 76
Shiner, Roger A. 209
Sierra Leone 1
Slovenia 78, 92, 152–153
Smith, Bradley F. 16
Societas delinquere non potest 113, 115, 124, 156, 167, 172–174, 181, 186, 238
Solomon Islands 94
South Sudan 1
Special Rapporteur (ILC), Draft Articles on Crimes against Humanity 142–144, 146, 149, 153–155; Draft Code of Offences 55, 57, 74–77; on General Principles of Law 181
Special Tribunal for Lebanon (STL) 108–112, 119, 127, 143, 155, 166, 178–179, 181, 183–185, 191, 217; Rule 60bis 111–113, 115–118, 121, 123–124, 126–127, 184–185; *see also* contempt cases
spoliation 31–37
state liability 60–62, 67, 72
Statute of the International Criminal Court *see* Rome Statute
Šturma, Pavel 144
subsequent Proceedings 13, 15, 23–28, 141; *see also* industrialist cases
Subsequent Proceedings Division 27–28
Sweden 53, 92
Swiss Criminal Code 202
Syria 1, 92, 240

Tanzania 92
Telford Taylor 27–28, 30
Tesco Supermarket Ltd. v Nattrass 175
Thompson, Robert C. 168
Topf & Söhne 26; *see also* subsequent proceedings
trial *in absentia* 220; *see also* procedural guarantees
Trial of the Major War Criminals 15; *see also* International Military Tribunal of Nuremberg
Trinidad and Tobago 75
Tunisia 92

Ukraine 92
UN Convention against Corruption 147, 150

UN Guiding Principles on Business and Human Rights 123, 125
UN High Commissioner of Human Rights 169
United Kingdom 13, 22, 52–53, 62, 156, 168, 174–175
United Nations 12, 47, 72, 79, 89, 118, 123, 152, 218; General Assembly 54, 59, 73–74, 78, 87, 141, 151–152, 155; Secretary-General xi, 74, 79–80, 89, 148, 169; Security Council 79, 81; UNGA Sixth Committee 51, 59, 77, 151–152; *see also* Genocide Convention
United States 8, 21, 25–27, 53, 80, 97, 168, 174–175, 210, 212, 218, 236
United States v. Cincotta 97
US Senate Subcommittee on War Mobilization 24

Van Kempen, Piet Hein 214, 226
Vázquez-Bermúdez, Marcelo 145–147, 149, 181
Vienna Convention on the Law of Treaty 50, 116, 121–122, 130

Wynes, Australian representative 61–62, 86; *see also* 1951 Committee on International Criminal Jurisdiction

Yemen 92

Zerk Report 169
Zweigert, Konrad 182

Made in the USA
Las Vegas, NV
19 September 2026

17f33fb4-756f-4818-b3ff-993247664b95R01